Cohousing Communities

About the Cover
It only takes two things to get a high-functioning community built—a vision and a clear set of steps.

Cohousing Communities

Designing for High-Functioning Neighborhoods

CHARLES DURRETT, ARCHITECT, AIA

WITH JINGLIN YANG, ALEX LIN, SPENCER NASH,
AND NADTHACHAI KONGKHAJORNKIDSUK

WILEY

This book is printed on acid-free paper. ♾

Published by John Wiley & Sons, Inc., Hoboken, New Jersey

Published simultaneously in Canada

For general information about our other products and services, please contact our Customer Care Department within the United States at (800) 762-2974, outside the United States at (317) 572-3993 or fax (317) 572-4002.

Wiley publishes in a variety of print and electronic formats and by print-on-demand. Some material included with standard print versions of this book may not be included in e-books or in print-on-demand. If this book refers to media such as a CD or DVD that is not included in the version you purchased, you may download this material at http://booksupport.wiley.com. For more information about Wiley products, visit www.wiley.com.

Library of Congress Cataloging-in-Publication Data applied for

ISBN: 9781119897705 (Paperback)
ISBN: 9781119897729 (ePDF)
ISBN: 9781119897712 (ePub)

Cover image: Courtesy of Charles Durrett
Cover design: Wiley

SKY10077057_061024

This book is dedicated to all those who teach us that architecture is more than "sexy" façades. Architecture is about making lives and environments better. Architecture can help facilitate a more viable society, and architecture and its associated social settings can address our most noble intentions in building healthier and just realities.

And this book is to the brave souls—the mothers, the fathers, the grandmothers and the grandfathers—who ventured forth to make these environments real.

This book is to all the children that motivated us and deserve a social life that is vibrant and makes them healthy, nurtured, and wise.

And lastly to the bookstores that facilitate the culture change that we need, and to all of the planners, commissioners, councilors, and administrators who know that smarter land use can start with high-functioning neighborhoods like cohousing.

Contents

Introduction

"For me, architecture is a social act."
David Adjaye

Five years of architecture school in California did not prepare me for designing community-enhanced neighborhoods or cohousing communities. Cohousing was a foreign concept here in the U.S. and even the notion of multi-family with enhanced community facilities, such as a place to break bread together, sharing tools, lawnmowers and cars; private kitchens oriented toward common spaces, and remote parking to keep the center free of cars, is rare. Realizing this, Kathryn McCamant and I went off to Denmark to study cohousing design and community-enhanced developments from the best of the best in the world; from the people who started cohousing in Denmark (Jan Gudmand-Høyer), perfected it (Tegnestuen Vandkunsten), and mastered its programming (Jan Gehl and Hans Skifter Anderson). Once we had convinced our many mentors there that we were serious (and not just another looky-loo), it was obvious to them and us that we were not ready to practice after only six months. So, we stayed for another seven months before we felt like we could design cohousing and community-enhanced housing as well as they had done. It was too important to do otherwise. As an architect, it wouldn't be ethical for me to take a penny from anyone to design their community or even to say that I could if I didn't know exactly what I was doing. A routine knee surgery op might be easy with learned hands, but you wouldn't want it to be the surgeon's first time, not to mention they not having gone to medical school.

EMERYVILLE, CA

The second cohousing community finished in the U.S., completed in two years. Most of the residents were born outside of the U.S. and had experienced true community previously in their lives, so they were excited to embrace it again.

Undoubtedly the most important lesson we learned was that the difference between what works to enhance community and what doesn't can be subtle, but the results are vast and the impact on a community is permanent. For example, in a poorly designed cohousing community, a common house might receive less than 50 people-hours of use per week, whereas in a well-designed cohousing community, the common house might receive more than 450 people-hours per week. And they both cost about $500,000 to build! Whether it's people-hours in the common house or people-hours on the sidewalks, individual smiles per half-hour, or collective smiles per half-hour, design makes all the difference.

My mantra is, "If it doesn't work socially, why bother?" How to make that happen is not always obvious. Subtle design factors affect how people feel about their community and their own homes. For instance, buildings that feature natural light have a major positive impact on these feelings. Likewise, the relationships between spaces and other experiential metrics (how close or far things are from each other, acoustics, and hundreds of other little details) affect how happy people are collectively. The arrangement of spaces across the landscape, the common house location, and the floor plans of the private houses impact how happy people are and affect the experiential progressions of what happens first, second, third, and so on as residents walk through the site. These design decisions all have major implications on the social metrics of a given community, such as the amount of conversation on the sidewalks to the number of times people visit each other's houses. All this is to say that this book is a critical resource for anyone interested in living in, learning about, or designing a high-functioning neighborhood. With it, you will have a much better idea of what really matters and why.

Cohousing Communities: Designing for High-Functioning Neighborhoods is designed to help local architects, both new and experienced, to successfully create these enhanced communities. Very

PLEASANT HILL, CA

The common building, be it in cohousing or in any community-based design, is the heart of the site plan. It is the essential neutral common place that plays a big role in transforming a collection of houses into a high-functioning neighborhood.

few architects have experience in designing cohousing or high-functioning neighborhoods. Even after designing more than 50 cohousing communities and a hundred multi-family buildings and/or neighborhoods, I am still learning. I always feel like my next one will be the best one. I want you, the designer and consumer, to have the best point of departure that you can—informed by what we have learned over the past 40 years. This knowledge must be shared for future generations of architects who hope to create housing that provides people with more than just a place to sleep, eat, and watch TV. When the Danish architects Jan Gudmand-Høyer and Àngels Colom both retired at the same time, the result was noticeable. Upon losing two of the most experienced architects in Denmark, cohousing and neighborhood design there took a dive. Multi-family developments in Denmark started to feel like apartments again, instead of communities. During those years, ironically, seven Danish architects did six-month internships in our office. After returning home to Denmark, they went on to design extremely successful new cohousing communities, and a second wave of success is well underway again there.

I suspect that less than 1 percent of the U.S. population today lives in a high-functioning neighborhood—places where people feel a strong sense of belonging, identity, and accountability; where everyone knows each other's names, cares about each other, and are prepared to support each other in times of need. A client once told me that she lived in an attractive neighborhood cluster for five years, designed by a famous architect. During her time living there, not one person ever came to her front door. Not once. The houses may have been nice, but the neighborhood was not a high-functioning one. In the case of community-enhanced design, it's as much a political act as anything else. Private developers, non-profit developers, and city planners take a lot of convincing to build community-enhanced neighborhoods. But that is changing too. My hope is that this book

COTATI, CA

Best in American Living Award – Best Smart Growth Community 2004 by the National Association of Home Builders. It makes sense, and these moms sitting here had a huge role in planning this project. Too often it's the businessmen, bureaucrats, builders, and bankers who make all the relevant decisions in housing. That's wrong. Everyday residents know how to make a high-functioning neighborhood.

will serve as a tool to guide a much bigger market to community-enhanced design than currently subscribes to it.

This book is also designed to get more people interested in a career in social architecture. If you're interested in sociology and art, you may discover, with one stroke of the pen, the huge difference that you can make in people's lives, emotional well-being, and in their appreciation of the environment. Collectively those strokes add up to a setting, a meaning, and reaching out, as methods for living lighter on the planet while living better and getting along with others at the same time.

Finally, this book was written in collaboration with four millennials: Jinglin Yang, Alex Lin, Spencer Nash, and Nadthachai Kongkhajornkidsuk. If we are going to make headway in the future, millennials need to have a seat at the table.

You will notice that here at The Cohousing Company we approach architecture from an anthropological point of view. We design communities for people. We start the process by asking key questions: Who are these people? What are they seeking? What are their experiences? What are their values? Who are they as a culture, or at least as a subculture? How do relationships and kinships actually work, and how do they wish them to work into the future?

DESIGN FOR STRONG COMMUNITIES

Cohousing Communities is about how to successfully design cohousing and community-enhanced multi-family housing, for-sale condominiums, for-rent apartments, and subsidized affordable projects. Strong communities and positive neighborly relationships are worth it—they are not injured by proximity but enhanced by it. I began this book by looking at condominium and cohousing common facilities exclusively. However, on my first day of writing, I realized that successful common facilities rely on the plans of the site and of the private houses as well. In other words, as the German philosopher G.W. Hegel would say: It's all connected. The data in this book was informed by my visits to over 300 cohousing communities in Europe and studying a hundred of them in great detail, designing over 50 cohousing communities in North America, and consulting on many more around the world; and, just as important, by having lived in three cohousing communities over the past 37 years: Trudeslund in Denmark, Emeryville in the San Francisco Bay Area, and Nevada City in rural California.

There is a lot of conversation in North America about how to scale-up cohousing—how to make more of them faster. McDonaldization is not the solution. At 300 communities in a country of five million, Denmark has more cohousing per capita than any other country and likely will for a long time to come. They use a slower and more thorough organic approach with an eye toward quality and duration. Every project is a model of what we can reach—not a compromise, not an ode to the rearview mirror. Yes, we need to make projects even more affordable, and, yes, we have to make cohousing more accessible and ethnically diverse. But these are not just words; we can accomplish more with deliberate outreach and work than by any other means. When The Cohousing Company won the World Habitat Award, presented by the United Nations in Osaka, Japan, in 2001, for a cohousing community in Atlanta, Georgia, it was a clear sign that the UN recognized that a change to the status quo of a home's environment was necessary. The American middle class needs to find a much smaller footprint. They simply produce too much pollution per capita. The U.S. has an average per capita footprint of 16.2 tons per year, followed by Canada at 15.6 tons. That large-scale metric is perhaps best understood when it's illustrated on a personal scale. The example of Butch, a resident from a nearby cohousing community, comes to mind. Butch told me that he was burning five to six

TRUDESLUND

The carefully considered nooks and crannies of this site are based on the work of the best cohousing programmer in Denmark. Life between these buildings is measurably successful from both a community and privacy point of view. There is a balance: plenty of private outdoor space plus compelling and inviting common space.

VALLEY OAKS. AFFORDABLE HOUSING SONOMA, CA

A 41-unit affordable housing project designed to be as community enhanced as possible. Parking at the periphery allows kids to play, parents to discuss, and old folks to relate to each other face-to-face in the interior. Subsidized projects with community-enhanced architecture are easier to manage because accountability among neighbors kicks in.

tanks of gas per month for the 20 years he lived in his old single-family house. Now that he lives in cohousing, he burns less than one tank per month while living in the same town.

Community-enhanced neighborhoods needn't be more difficult or complicated. It's actually simpler and a lot easier to get right, if you are organized and deliberate. Yes, the methodologies presented in this book drill down and turn over the rocks. And, yes, the Danes have practicing anthropologists and working sociologists who help get cohousing projects off the ground. But architects can learn these disciplines too—although they have to be motivated to do so. Once you've done it a couple of times, it gets easier, but it really helps if you do the first one with a mentor who knows exactly what they are doing. The trick is to see a culture (that is, a group of residents) for who they really are and who they really want to become.

WHAT IS A FUNCTIONAL NEIGHBORHOOD?

What is the definition of a functional neighborhood? Well, imagine that you are the city council and supporting working people and cutting costs are key goals. You would want to invest in, more than anything else, high-functioning neighborhoods. In some neighborhoods people know each other, care about each other, and support each other. In some neighborhoods people know how to share resources, assist each other, and talk to each other about opportunities to cooperate or to mediate disagreements. In some neighborhoods a disabled senior can get dinner from neighbors or a ride to the pharmacy. Someone can pick up groceries routinely if necessary, or a child can safely carpool home with a neighbor if a parent needs to stay at work for another critical half an hour. These neighborhoods and relationships are built on trust and community. Some of these neighborhoods do exist in the United States. They exemplify the sense of strong community and unity that are the building blocks of a functioning society. Conversely, they offer a solution to many ills that result from social isolation and estrangement.

This book started before the COVID-19 pandemic, straddled it, and finished in what seemed to be the pandemic's waning months in the United States. During that time, most people in communities supported each other in meaningful ways and helped each other to stay safe. People often ask us at The Cohousing Company, "How might you alter your designs because of what you learned during the pandemic?" The answer is simple. We would make even more certain that the design facilitates community in the good times (non-pandemic) so that when the bad times come (pandemic or otherwise), people have relationships that they can rely on to help each other to make it through. Cohousing and community-enhanced design allow people to be socially distanced, but not socially isolated. Ultimately, it's community-enhanced designs that help us create a better functioning society.

SAVVAERKET IN HØJBJERG, DENMARK

This is what a high-functioning neighborhood looks like, feels like.

The life between buildings is a direct result of architecture and planning. This book outlines how design can be used to stitch the reality of a high-functioning neighborhood and village together.

NEVADA CITY, CA

Common lunch in a socially separated but not socially isolated community during the COVID-19 pandemic. Relationships must go on. Relationships are built during the good times so that they transcend the bad times.

NEVADA CITY, CA

The houses are different when the design's purpose is to get people connected and to keep them connected. The kitchen sinks face the common walkways. The living rooms are located toward the back. Folks tend not to close their blinds then—they don't mind being seen washing the dishes.

NEVADA CITY, CA

Central but remote parking and central nonvehicular circulation play positive roles in sustaining community. The social community is actually built during the development phase—not brick by brick, but decision by decision. The right architecture and planning are key to maintaining the community once the honeymoon period has worn off after move in.

VALLEY VIEW SENIOR HOMES AMERICAN CANYON, CA

There is so much to learn from high-functioning neighborhoods. Many small changes can be incorporated into low-functioning neighborhoods in order to make them more high-functioning.

NEVADA CITY, CA

Love is where the dog is and where the people are—on the sidewalks, in between the houses in the car-free area.

NEVADA CITY, CA

This isn't Italy, France, Spain, Denmark, or a village in Tanzania where neighbors routinely hang out. This is an American neighborhood where there are opportunities for neighbors to gather spontaneously with no other agenda than to say, "What's up with you?"

OLD NEIGHBORHOOD, NEW COMMON BUILDING

A neighborhood of single-family houses asked us to design a new common building (technically an outbuilding to one of the houses) to meet their needs and desires for facilitating an enhanced community. They wanted not only a place to come together to meditate and dance, but a place to meet, talk, plan, coordinate care for elderly residents, and to break bread. They wanted a space that was right in the middle of the 30 residential houses that everyone could walk to. Still under construction, the barn raising itself played a consequential role in stitching the community together tightly. Whether it was pulling electrical wire or making lunch, everyone contributed and— in collaboration with the contractor—even made trusses. It was all doable.

QUIMPER VILLAGE, WA

Some would argue that the front porch is the most important room in the house.

COTATI, CA

Simple and frequent—having dinner together. It's not a buffet, it's not a wedding reception, we're not in the Navy—we're just sitting down to have dinner with people who we know, care about, and support.

BELLINGHAM, WA

Pedestrian-friendly, car-free environment makes people feel safe without the smell, the sound, and the threat of autos.

PART 1

Intergenerational Cohousing Design

In too many neighborhoods everyone is a stranger. Streets are dominated by cars, empty sidewalks, rows of houses behind fences, and closed garage doors. The residents mostly keep to themselves. Adults watch TV by themselves; kids play video games alone. But in community-enhanced neighborhoods, everyone knows each other, cares about each other, and supports each other. The difference between these two kinds of neighborhoods is palpable, and the lives that are led in them are noticeably different.

BELLINGHAM, WA

Strong relationships are what make neighborhoods work over time, but the design plays a huge role in fostering or detracting from those relationships.

1

Intergenerational Neighborhood Design

Neighborhood Site Design

"Architecture is a social act and the material theater of human activity."
Spiro Kostof

Of course, the design of the home itself is of great importance, but the site design concepts ultimately make the biggest difference to the long-term success of a community-enhanced neighborhood. For example, "two hands clapping" means a high-functioning community, where houses face each other and are about 20 feet apart, in contrast with typical neighborhoods where houses are 100–150 feet from doorknob to doorknob, creating a street of anonymity.

When a site has the space, the one-to-three-story scenario is generally the least expensive way to build and to keep construction costs down, and 10–30 units per acre is usually the least costly density to build at if you include site work. However, if the site is small or expensive (or both), it's common to reach 80 units per acre. This can be even denser if the development is associated with other uses, such as other private houses or commercial use. There are certainly high-functioning one-building neighborhoods around the world. I have met plenty of folks from Chicago who talk about five-story walk-up flats where semi-private rear decks connect each floor. Definitely they have a storied sense of community—I have visited many of them and can testify to it. I could see it, feel it, it's palpable, but it's hard to replicate. Then, there is a cohousing community in Gothenburg, Sweden, which is a ten-story building retrofit of a 40-unit rental project that was in need of major repair. The group bought the building and turned the fourth floor into the common house; converted the bottom floor into a utility common area with mailboxes, childcare, and a workshop; and refurbished the 32 apartments into ownership units. From a design point of view, the common house on

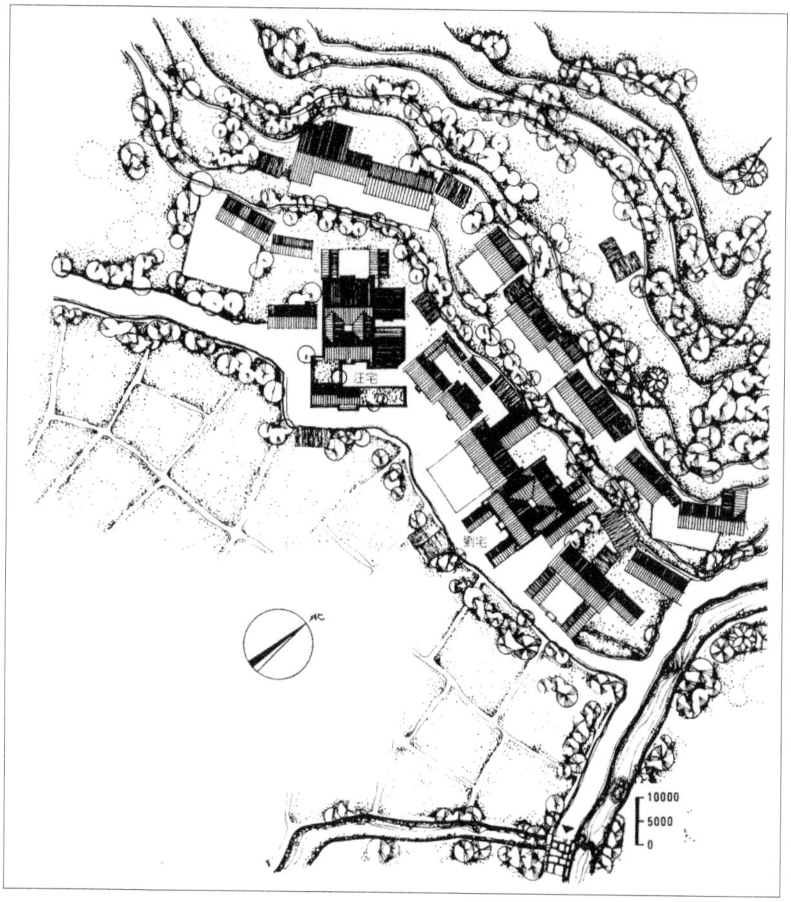

SITE DESIGN

If the site has any land at all (2 acres or more), the site plan often evolves toward the form of an ancient Chinese village when choosing to build a community. It flows along the topographic lines marrying the people, the land, and in this case, the farm.

VEHICLES AFFECT SITE DESIGN

Small, often shared, electric vehicles to get you to the nearest neighborhood center for groceries. This is how you meet the parking requirements without miles and miles of asphalt, as occurs in one American town after another.

Sharing is the new having. In other words, without sharing, you often don't have something. The holistic way of imagining high-functioning neighborhoods is individuals having practical advantages that benefit the entire community. If you can share cars, for example, you can have less asphalt, less consumed land, less concrete, and less costs. The Cohousing Company designed a 31-unit project a couple of years ago that had 31 parking spots and 4 shared cars. It was required to have 2 parking spots per unit, or 62 parking spots in total, but sharing 4 cars dispensed with that requirement for this project.

In the 55 cohousing communities and 100 affordable housing projects that we have designed, no one has ever asked for anything like this. Driving down that road, you could imagine a lonely and forlorn senior every 12th house in front of a TV, and a lonely and unhappy child every 10th house plugged into their Nintendo device. It's car-predominant (and therefore dangerous), atomized, and estranged. Inefficient both environmentally and socially.

the fourth floor had to be designed to be attractive—the same is true of the common area on the first floor and the landscaped area around the building. This type of project is completely plausible and we have designed a number of similar projects, including a four-story 19-unit project on 0.24 acres (80 units per acre density) with a 3,500-square-foot common area and a 30-unit project on 0.9 acres with a 4,000-square-foot common area. This dig-deep programming has everything to do with reaching real goals and nothing to do with rear-view mirror thinking, other than the values and experience that you bring to the table. This dig deep programming has everything to do with finding the target and hitting it, finding the problem and solving it. That's the essence of the book titled, *Problem Seeking: An Architectural Programming Primer*, first written in the 1950s by William Peña, which is still

MUIR COMMONS SITE PLAN

It's easy to see why there is so much child-to-parent activity in Muir Commons from the site plan alone. It feels like a village. Muir Commons—the first cohousing community in the U.S.—started in 1989 and finished in 1991.

one of the best books on the topic.[1] Why try to solve any problem without fully understanding it? Dig deep programming generates hundreds of design criteria (see Chapter 2). That's what moves a culture forward. Many cohousing common houses in North America receive less than 100 people-hours a week. Spending $500,000 for less than 100 people-hours per week is not worth it, yet that sum of money for 450 people-hours a week is well worth it because it also improves how your house works and that's where you save.

And this dig deep programming (cultural change, or at least a cultural pivot) has nothing to do with prejudices, pop magazines, Pinterest, Facebook, or the flavor *du jour*. It has everything to do with the question of "Who do we really want to be?," at least in the context of land-use and neighborhoods.

This is what cohousing groups strive for and why architects design multi-family housing to deliver sustainability to the greatest extent feasible and to promote diversity best. It's all about moving closer to where you want to be, as fast as you can, at least compared to where you used to be.

NOTE

1. William Peña and Steven A. Parshall, *Problem Seeking: An Architectural Programming Primer*, 5th edition (Hoboken, NJ: Wiley, 2012).

MUIR COMMONS, CA

It's easy to make something that works for all the kids—"our gang." And of course, there is a sense of accomplishment when you make a bridge that lets everyone get around. Not all site projects have to be bought and built at move-in. These kids (with the help of a parent) built this project after move-in.

MUIR COMMONS, CA

Fire pits are fun, and they bring the whole neighborhood together. Breaking bread together, sitting around the fire, working together for tasks like a mini barn raising—this is life in a socially and physically well-designed neighborhood.

NEVADA CITY, CA

Working it, then reworking it.

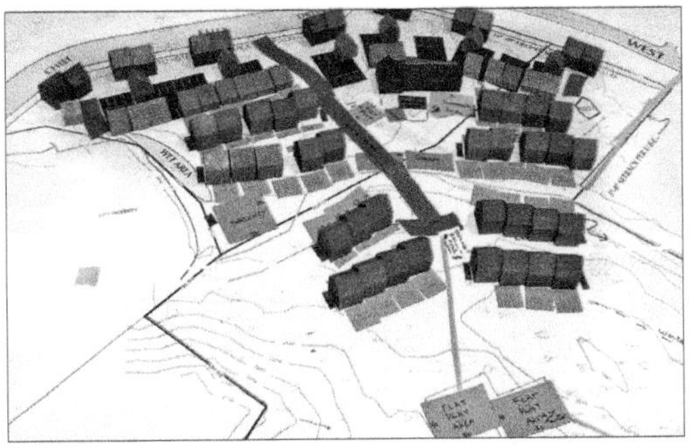

NEVADA CITY, CA

The house blocks laid out after two days of programming and establishing criteria.

NEVADA CITY, CA

When people are outside of their house (but still on their property) in regular suburban neighborhoods, they are in their front yard about 20 percent of the time and in the backyard the other 80 percent of the time. In high-functioning neighborhoods, it's the other way around, 80 percent on the front porch, and 20 percent in the back.

Something happens when you know and care about your neighbor. You want to stay connected and see how they are doing.

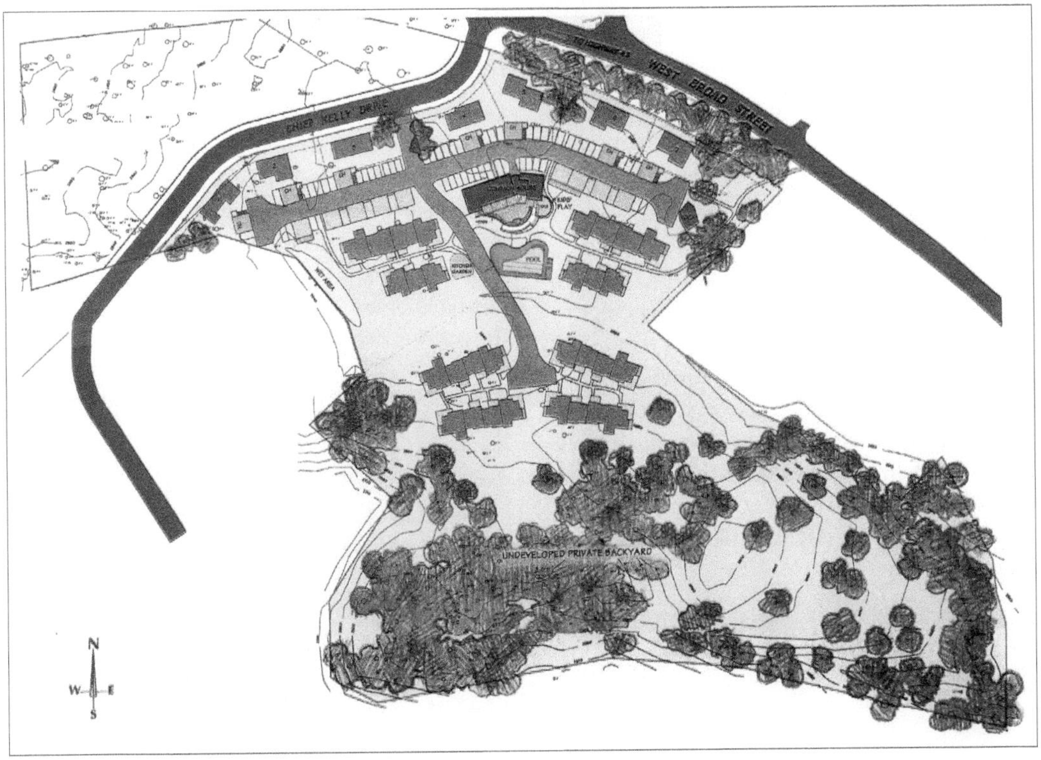

NEVADA CITY, CA

One of the mechanisms to get the new houses to half of the average house price in Nevada City was to sell off seven lots at the north periphery of the interface of the site and the street. Each of the lots had an extra ADU unit, meaning the project sold off a total of 14 other units. This also kept the cohousing from getting too large and therefore too difficult to manage by consensus. In the end, 3.5 acres went to cohousing, 1.5 acres went to the seven lots that were sold, and 6 acres are left as open space. In the final four days of site planning, as the group came to grips with the economics and social performance of less spread-out houses, it was decided to leave 6 acres of open space and to use an acre of that for a vegetable garden.

The private house porches add a friendly interface to the street, which is much better than seeing the rear end of 50 cars, even if some of them are electric.

NEVADA CITY, CA

A spontaneous lifestyle is a commonly stated goal in high-functioning neighborhoods. On the left, Victoria is texting her boyfriend to let him know that she's joining her three neighbors going to the movies this Sunday evening. The movies aren't a big deal, but parents talking about childrearing, elders talking about aging successfully, and people discussing and solving the myriad of issues in life are what makes a high-functioning neighborhood a great neighborhood... and sometimes going to the movie with friends.

NEVADA CITY, CA

Site plans in community-enhanced neighborhoods make this activity easy and natural.

NEVADA CITY, CA

Meg (to the right) was encouraged to move to the closest house to the parking by her kids, after all, she was 89 when she moved in—just a few dozen feet from her home. Then, one day, she moved to the house farthest from the parking, about seven-hundred feet away. I queried her one day—"Meg, why?" She said that she relied on her relationships with her neighbors much more than she did on her automobile. Seven-hundred feet away meant that she saw more of them on her way home every day. Meg passed away three weeks before her 100th birthday.

NEVADA CITY, CA

Community-enhanced design is a 100 percent pedestrian neighborhood. People walk from a central parking area to their housing elsewhere. We have become conditioned to have our vehicles practically enter our bedrooms, but those who can use a pull wagon or a wheelchair live a much richer life. Those who want to live next to the parking can do that.

NEVADA CITY, CA

This is exactly what this neighborhood was designed to do—to create a life and a pulse between the buildings

NEVADA CITY, CA

This is the point of community-enhanced design. The residents are talking about the issues of the day and helping each other out when it makes sense. The people are the picture, the buildings are the picture frame.

NEVADA CITY, CA

Play, play, play. That's the world where kids grow, grow, grow.

NEVADA CITY, CA

Kids just want a place to be and converge with one another. To see, to be seen, and to see who else might come along and join them.

NEVADA CITY, CA

Make a safe place for the kids to hang out. Kids need and want flat grassy playfields, but it works better if they are populated with peers and if you can see it from most houses. Few single-family houses have a big enough lawn, much less kids nearby, not to mention that this flat spot is open to any kid at any time. It's the quintessential activity that attracts activity for any high- functioning neighborhood.

NEVADA CITY, CA

Perches

Places to see what's going on (if done right). The kids really own the place, as they should.

NEVADA CITY, CA

The kids, as usual, make high-functioning neighborhoods worthwhile. Kids play a big role in stitching a neighborhood together. It is important to make sure that they have plenty of car-free space. Make sure that they have each other—recruit young families. Have lots of open space, wild areas, water, slopes, flat hardscapes, and flat green areas if there is enough space.

What does design have to do with the relationship of these kids? Everything. In a safe neighborhood, they can go from house to house without interacting with cars. Parents feel safe, and the kids are safe.

NEVADA CITY, CA

There is not as much TV in a high-functioning neighborhood. Also adventurous free-range kids seem to like sloped sites. Open-ended play opportunities are the beginning and the end to invention. It may seem trivial, but it's not—it's the point. The younger kids trust the bigger kids to not let them crash.

NEVADA CITY, CA

The point of a high-functioning neighborhood—kids figuring out what this whole life deal is all about with others.

NEVADA CITY, CA

Kids like flat spots, too.

NEVADA CITY, CA

Even the simplest of structures has play value when you can see it and the kids playing there from all of the houses.

NEVADA CITY, CA

Rocks, logs, water, trees, and a swale here and there. Natural elements bring the best play value.

NEVADA CITY, CA

Mentoring happens readily when one kid can safely stroll to another kid's house without their parents' supervision.

NEVADA CITY, CA

The Vortex, as the residents refer to the neighborhood pool. A key tenet of community-enhanced design is that activity attracts activity.

NEVADA CITY, CA

The common basketball hoop and two surrounding houses in the neighborhood.

NEVADA CITY, CA

A car-free world does a lot to bring people together and makes them more social and safer.

NEVADA CITY, CA

Exercise and fun is all over the site. That is the nature of a village. There doesn't have to be a special exercise room to get that job done. Relationships fostered during design and management decisions make this possible.

NEVADA CITY, CA

Playing dress up on the walkway.

NEVADA CITY, CA

Nature goes a long way toward "play value" for kids. Have some places for them to hide, like here in the large swale. They need "wild" places.

NEVADA CITY, CA

Vegetable and fruit gardens seem to be a part of just about every new high-functioning neighborhood. Vegetables are planted in both individual and collective plots. There usually is a committee or a club, who plan out the spring plantings as well as the summer and fall harvests. They have special work days where anyone can participate. Usually, individual harvesting is limited to those who have participated, even if only a little, but there is always an abundance and widespread generosity.

SPOKANE, WA

The common building is often prominent in a cohousing community. It's neither a public nor private building—it's common, it's ours to steward and ours to collectively imagine how we can assist the larger community. The light switch to the cupola of the common building is in the sitting room so that people can tell if someone is there from the entire neighborhood.

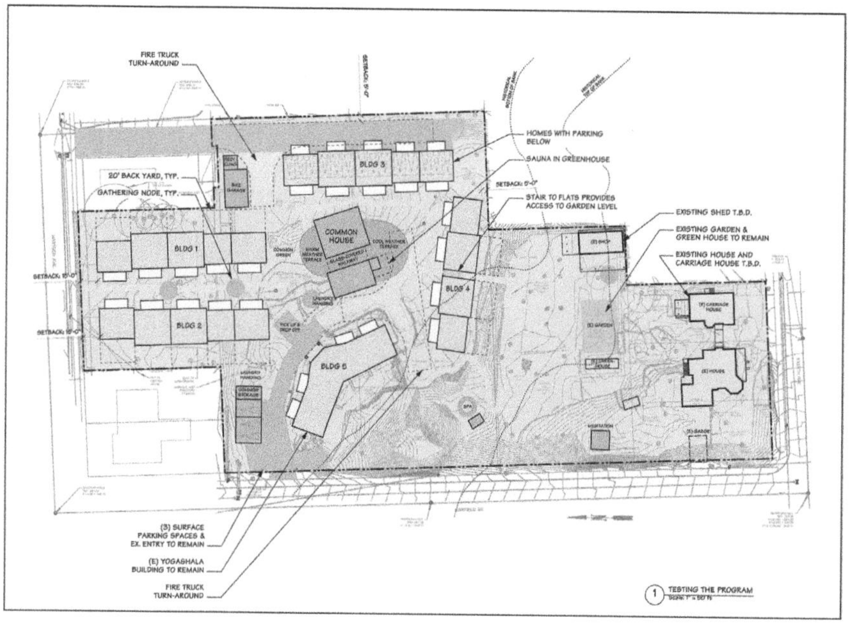

SPOKANE, WA

Site plan.

SPOKANE, WA

After two days of site criteria, then two evenings of site design with the group.

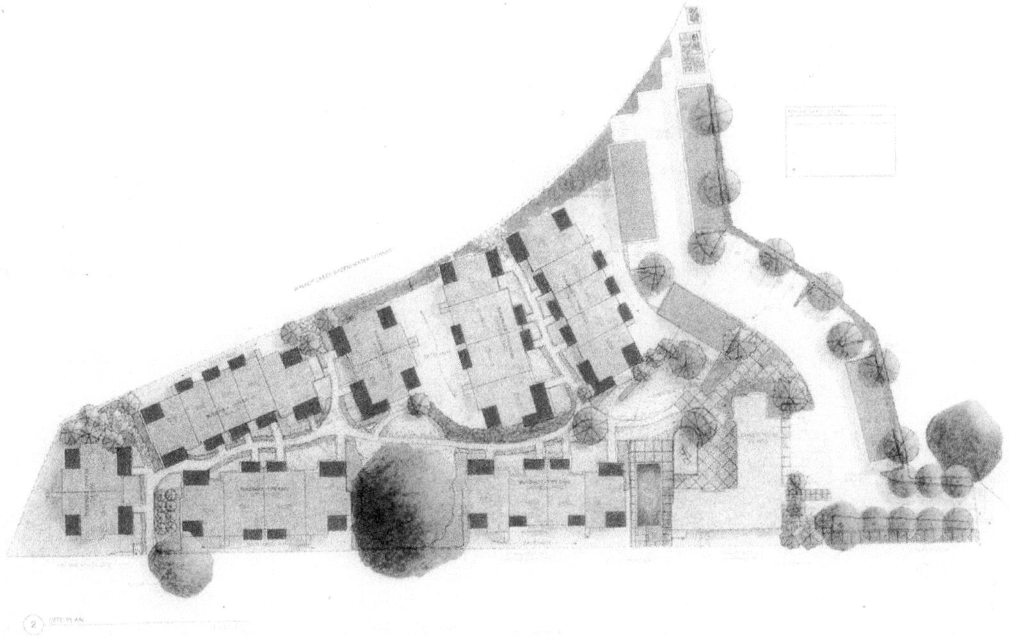

PLEASANT HILL, CA

Site Plan.

Note all of the parking on the south end of the site plan, leaving the neighborhood feeling like a village.

PLEASANT HILL, CA

Condominiums can be anonymous where people keep to themselves and seldom talk to their neighbors—or they can be a vibrant neighborhood.

PLEASANT HILL, CA

Preferably, residents should make it a habit to walk by the common building when walking home from their car.

Pooling the parking like this facilitates the possibility of using much less asphalt per house (between 300–400 square feet per house) compared to typical suburban housing (often higher than 1,500 square feet per house).

Asphalt effectively destroys the soil below it.

PLEASANT HILL, CA

The ability to see the sidewalks and the circulation of people from innumerable vantage points is a great way to stitch a neighborhood together. First there's the eye contact, then there's the smile, then there's the wave, then the "how are you?" and then the "do you have a minute?" All of these relationships and meaningful interactions are built; if you don't have time, just smile and say, "have to keep going." Then there's Damien on the right who is blind, but very interested in the community. So, he sits out front and people stop to talk to him.

FAIR OAKS, CA

Socially distanced, but not socially isolated.

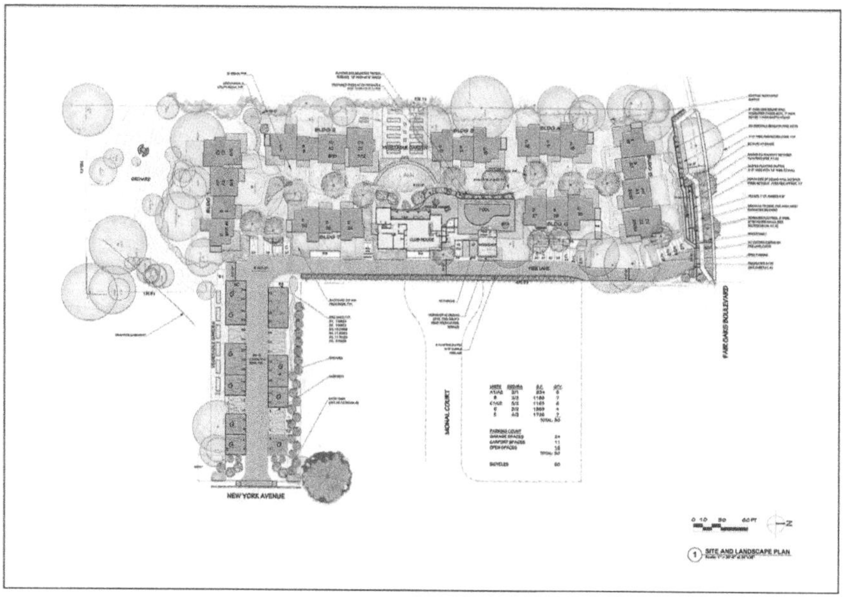

FAIR OAKS, CA

Flag lots and single spine circulation are perfect for community-enhanced design. Everyone is included, everyone is appreciated.

FAIR OAKS, CA

The drawings have to tell the story. Neighbors are always concerned about ticky-tacky new multi-family in their neighborhood. They need to see life between the buildings, real architecture and color. So when I show them our other projects—they see the vibrancy.

BELLINGHAM, WA

This is what leaving the wetland alone looks like. The houses were designed away from the wetlands to preserve their character. It feels like a village. I feel like I can say that after having lived in a village and having moved to and "designed" villages with others in Africa for a year.

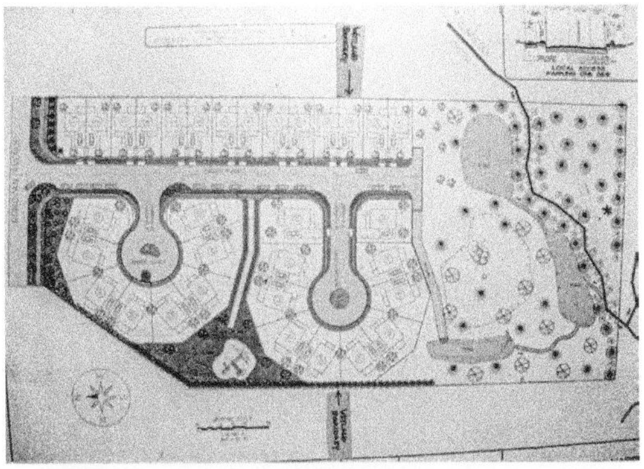

BELLINGHAM, WA

As planned by the previous developer, the site plan had a much larger carbon footprint. Single-family lots were given a pie shape, and the entire front of the houses was a garage door. Among other things this "solution" used four times more concrete and asphalt hardscape (driveways, sidewalks, roads, and walkways) than the 33 socially centripetal houses that were built on the site.

BELLINGHAM, WA

Cozy, two hands clapping.

BELLINGHAM, WA

Inexpensive garages with appeal.

BELLINGHAM, WA

One lane and two courtyards, remote parking, saving the wetlands, all furthered the intentions of the program. We rehabilitated the private house on the 5-acre property into the common house. And since it's all new, it has to be accomplished with each group and site because it changes what inhabiting the neighborhood is like—in other words, it's not just neighborhood-making, it's culture change. It's not the neighborhood that they inhabited before, it's not looking in the rear-view mirror—it's leaning toward their aspirations instead.

TUCSON, AZ

Singular circulation or courtyards along the central spine both work well.

TUCSON, AZ

Teens often wonder if they are too closely supervised in a village. But in interview after interview, they all say that in the end, "I'm just glad that people care," "it's good to be noticed," "it's good to be seen."

FRESNO, CA

In a neighborhood surrounded by beige, this common house in Fresno raised eyebrows when it was painted. Red, white, and blue went up on a Saturday. The neighbors came over on Sunday and I happened to be there. As they were leaving, one exclaimed, "Well, as long as there's no purple." Well, there wasn't on Sunday, but there was on Monday. Since then, the neighbors and residents have expressed that the colors make their day every day.

TUCSON, AZ

A modern-day village with mountains in the backdrop.

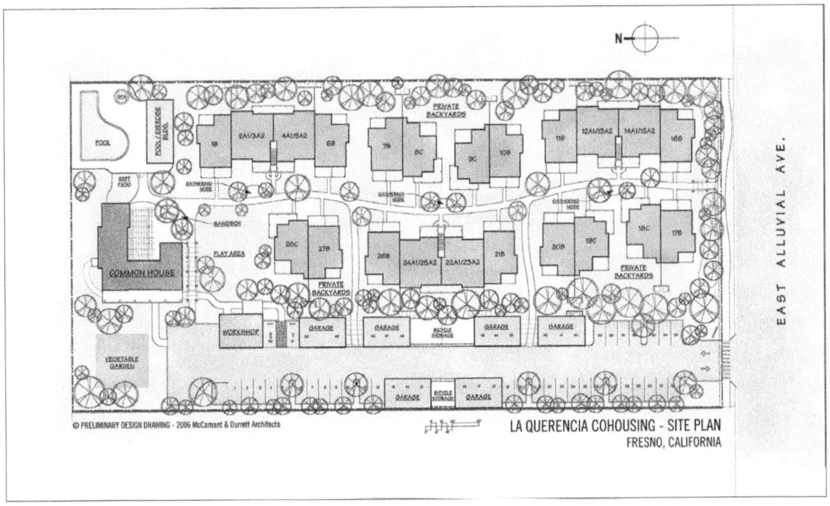

FRESNO, CA

The single circulation is the tried and true—the best way to maintain community over time—and La Querencia Cohousing does it as good as any.

FRESNO, CA

La Querencia is a very successful cohousing site plan because of the singular circulation and remote parking.

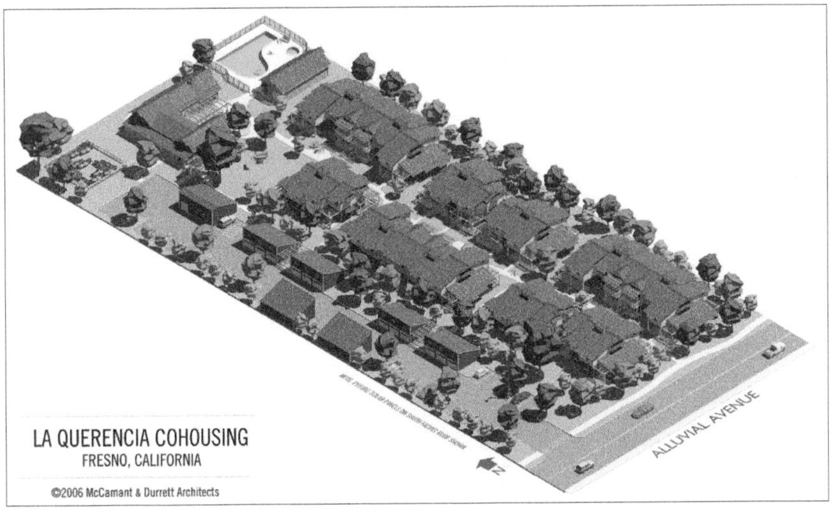

FRESNO, CA

The site plan and the overhanging roofs were designed to keep the building as cool as possible. Shading sombreros, if you will, in the baking central California heat. The summer noon-day sun does not go into the house.

SOUTHSIDE, CA

Since when were setbacks considered a benefit to the street? Who wants setbacks in their lives?

Sacramento City asked that the houses be close (5–7 feet) to the sidewalks because that would help define the street, give the street interest, and make the street more walkable and put eyes closer to the street. The Fifth and T Street neighborhood is not known as safe, but with more eyes on the street, the safer it is. Designers and advocates for better urban design contest setbacks when they do not make sense.

SOUTHSIDE, CA

Site planning with the folks of Southside Cohousing in Sacramento, California. Two days of developing criteria and then two evenings of creating a site plan based on that criteria (two different groups in two separate rooms) until—since they are working on the same criteria—the two site plans merged into one.

WINDSONG, LANGLEY, B.C., CANADA

A common street "living room" make for perfect circulation in a high-functioning neighborhood. Covered streets provide for a lovely "common living room" for neighbors to enjoy for at least three seasons a year.

SOUTHSIDE, CA

The closer the houses are to the street, the more common area there is behind, as seen in this small 1.25 acre for 25 units site.

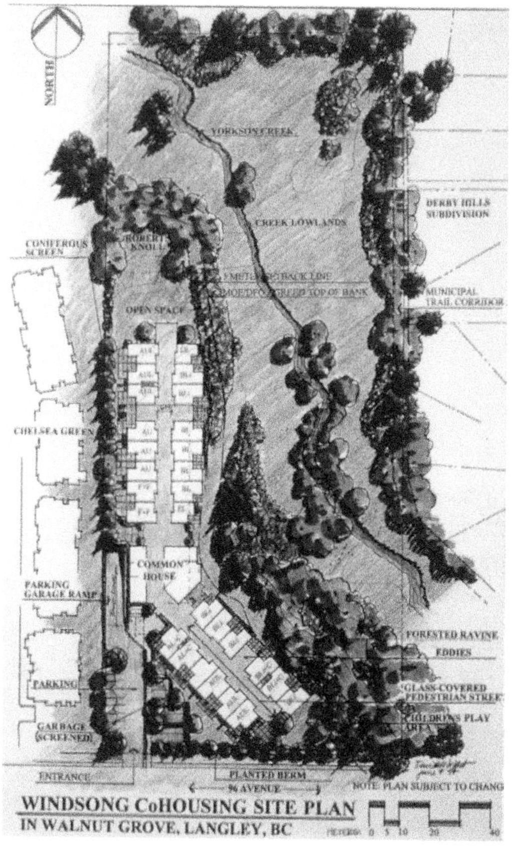

WINDSONG, LANGLEY, B.C., CANADA

EMERYVILLE, CA

A dilapidated factory transformed into warm and cozy cohousing community.

EMERYVILLE, CA

Start with a one-story factory, derelict and abandoned. Learn every beam, every timber, every brick and bolt, overlay a carefully considered cohousing program, and boom. . .

Old buildings can often bring charm, even when not obvious, that you can't buy today.

EMERYVILLE, CA

. . .turn it into a three-story, lively cohousing community right in the heart of a built-up industrial area with a new café across the street. These condominiums started at $130,000, a question that never goes away—how much did it cost?

EMERYVILLE, CA

This project took four major variances to accomplish entitlements, otherwise known as city approvals. Three feet over the 30-foot height limit; zero-foot setback in lieu of the 15-foot setback; half of the required parking; and twice the allowable number of dwelling units.

Even in high-rise solutions, residents' participation shows a new story for how dense downtown housing (80 units to the acre) can be designed. One hundred percent of the time they will be quite different to what a typical Business, Banker, Architect, Bureaucrat, Builder (the BBABB team) would come up with.

SANTA CRUZ, CA

Front Façade

Zero setback on the streets, balconies over the sidewalk (left), common terrace (on the right) over underground parking access.

WALNUT COMMONS IN SANTA CRUZ, CALIFORNIA

Note the floor plans—different than typical. Common space on every floor, gracious corridors, adequate outdoor area. Windows from the kitchens to corridors and houses that really fit the long-term needs of the community, rooftop gardens, gathering areas near the vertical circulation (stairs and elevator), and the oversize mail room and sitting areas in the corridors. That's what makes benign, palatable high-density (80 units to the acre) vertical cohousing work.

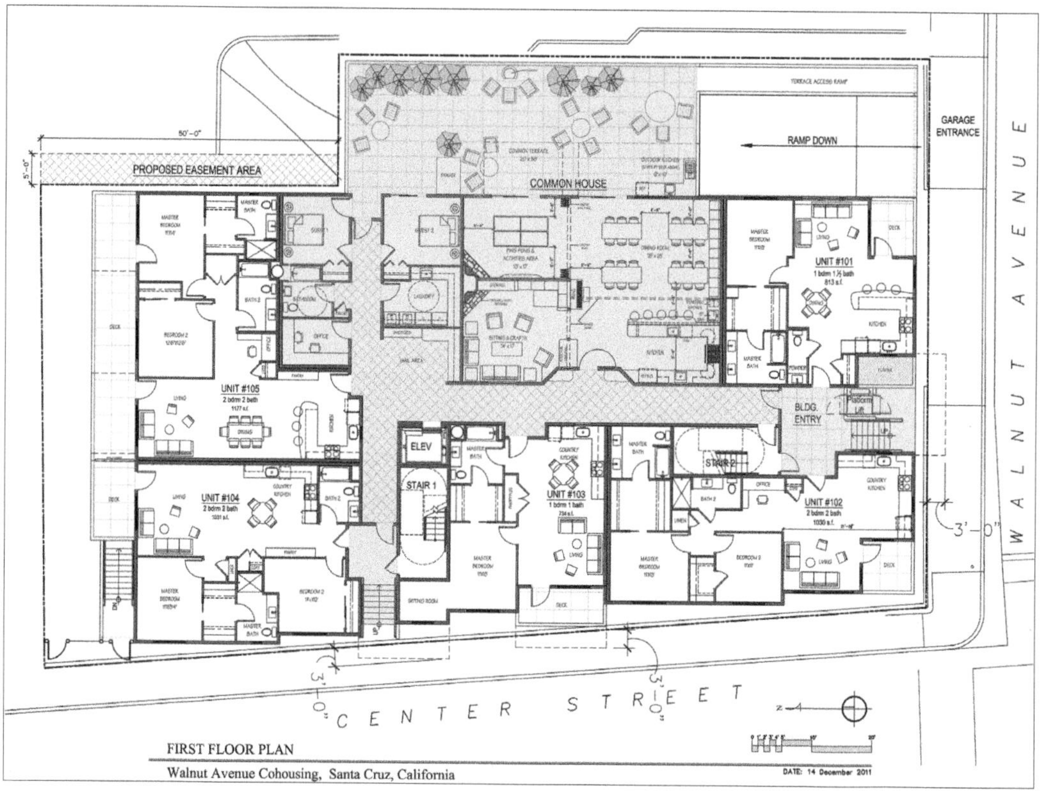

SANTA CRUZ, CA

An upper floor at Walnut Commons. Private condominiums and common spaces at each floor.

SANTA CRUZ, CA

The couple on the right moved from a 20-acre vineyard with a sprawling house in a sprawling neighborhood to a 1,200-square-foot condo in a high-functioning neighborhood in the city. The new community is an amenity that they did not have previously—such as neighbors who make dinner for them several times a week. As they added amenities, their house is far from the least expensive, but we need units like theirs in order to make the other units less expensive.

BERKELEY, CA

Neighborly life between the houses is obvious and frequent.

BERKELEY, CA

This project brought a lot of affordability to the table. First, it had three single moms and two elderly single women who needed houses for $130,000 each.

The average house in Berkeley at the time (1995) was $500,000. They bought a dilapidated rental project with no renters and turned it into ownership housing that was less costly to the new owners than their rental properties were previously. Then we doubled the density and the square footage by raising houses up, putting new houses under them, and built new houses on top of the old ones.

BAKKEN, DENMARK

A good site design is crucial to letting the community develop and sustain itself long after the honeymoon period has worn off.

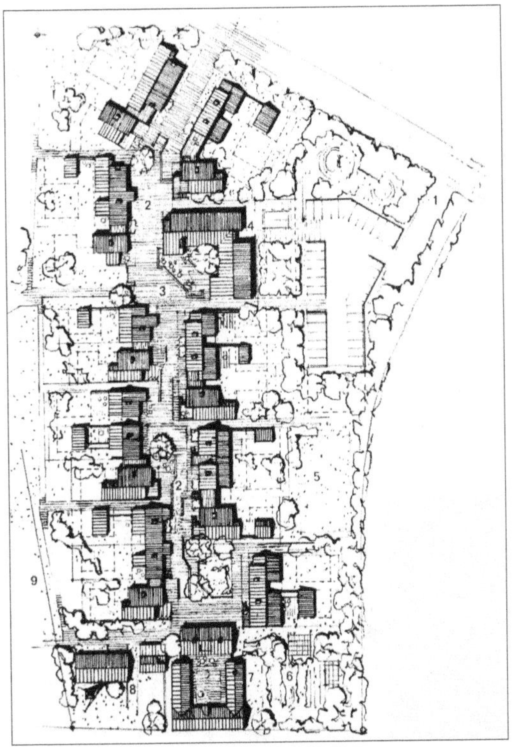

BAKKEN, DENMARK

Bakken is widely considered to have one of the best site plans in Denmark for community making. Why? Because they had the second-most thorough of all of the design programs. It was developed with the help of world-famous architect Jan Gehl who truly understands the potential for healthy human behavior in the built environment. And definitely the best professor I ever had.

SAVVAERKET

Højbjerg, Denmark

This is what a modern-day village can feel like.

TRUDESLUND, DENMARK

I planned to sit on the peak of this community's common building roof from 4:30 p.m. to 5:30 p.m. on a lovely spring day to track site foot traffic. But after just 25 minutes, the page became crowded with demarcated circulation lines. So the circulation you see is that afternoon over 25 minutes. It illustrates just how busy a high-functioning neighborhood is. I did this on the roofs of 15 high-functioning cohousing communities in Denmark and they all looked about the same—chocked full of foot traffic from house to house, to common house, to the common garden, parking to common house, common house to play yard, and so on.

There were so many aspects of the design in combination with the social success that put a lot of lines on the paper.

Someone would announce that we have far too little parking. Then, the next day, someone would announce that we have far too much parking. Only observation would illuminate the facts. The fact is that the very careful 20-minute neighborhood-wide discussion about parking two years earlier was more or less exactly right and that's what they built.

There are many reasons that they have the highest common house use that we know of, right at 750 people-hours per week. One is that the parking is very concentrated, people run into each other in the parking lot and continue their conversation over a cup of tea in the common house. Additionally, most people walk by the common house on their way home. People can tell if there is life there from their own houses. And they moved in with 60 kids so after school there was (and sometimes still is) a popular program.

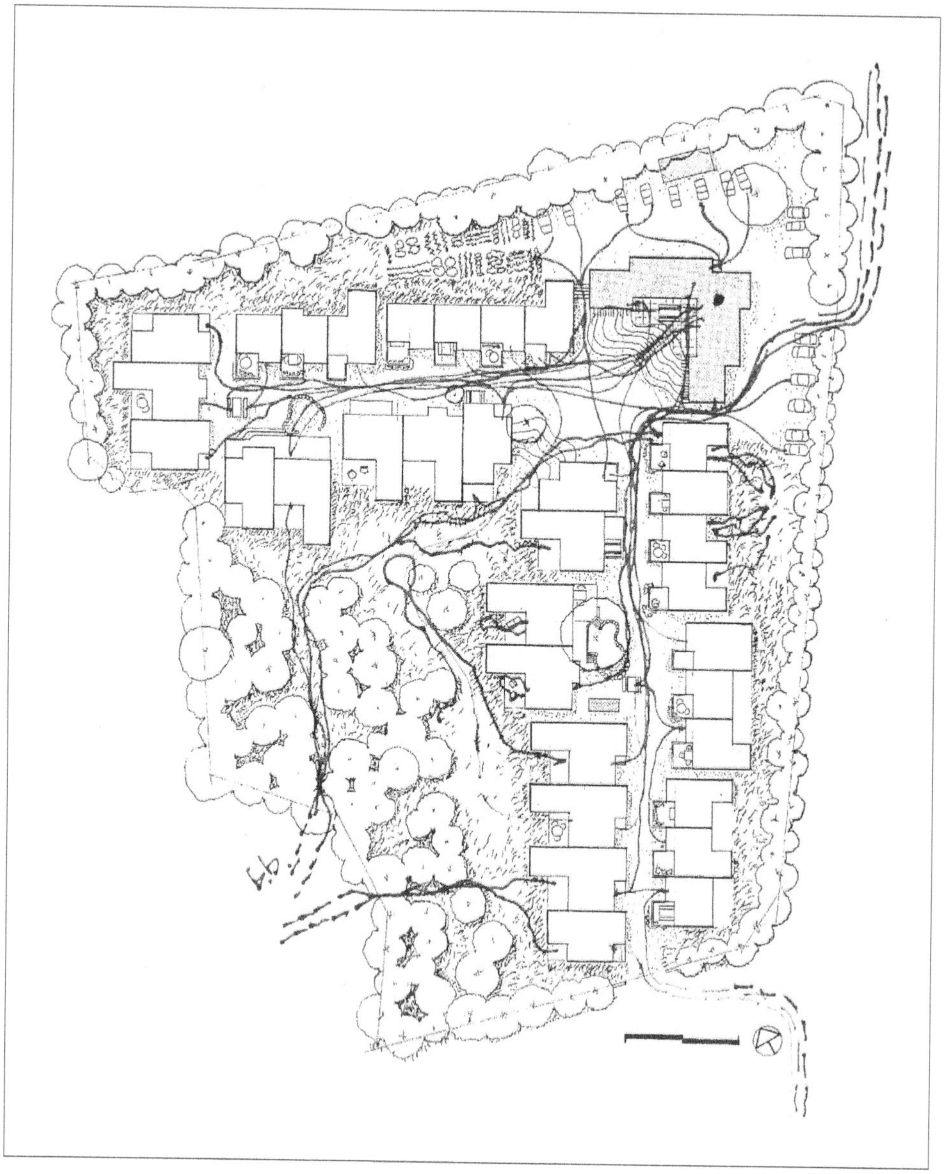

TRUDESLUND, DENMARK

In Trudeslund not only is the common house on the way home from parking, but you can also see it from almost every house. That helps with the 750 people-hours that the cohousing common house garners each week.

Trudeslund, still the gold standard in excellent site design. Programmed (including schematic design) by the best cohousing architect in Denmark (Jan Gudmand-Høyer), the design was then finished by one of the best architectural firms in Denmark (Vandkunsten).

TRUDESLUND, DENMARK

People stopping to chat, to be a neighbor, to catch up—that's the point of a functioning neighborhood.

COTATI, CA

With mixed-use comes an interface with the larger neighborhood.

COTATI, CA

This cohousing community features 30 dwellings on 2.2 acres (8 of which are above the 7,500 square feet of commercial), 4,000 square feet of common house, and 32 dedicated parking spaces. In terms of density, 10–30 units per acre is the sweet spot for keeping the costs down in high-functioning neighborhoods.

COTATI, CA

Surrounded by two other new neighborhoods, Cotati Cohousing took three years to get designed, approved, financed, and built. The surrounding two projects took five and seven years. The magic bullet for innovation and expedition is having future residents on board before the design begins. This is truly the best way to get a project designed, approved, sold out, and financed more quickly and in a higher quality.

COTATI, CA

This cohousing was the first project in 30 years in this town of 5,000 people to be mixed-use with commercial below and residential above. Businessmen and city officials alike did not think mixed-use was a good idea. But future residents can usually push the envelope and make innovations possible and move forward. Sometimes, in development, what's new, what's better, is what's old when things were less vehicle-oriented. Traditional land use patterns like neighborhood centers, residential dwellings above shops, towers at the entry to town, canopies, walkable streets, and storefronts are new again.

COTATI, CA

Living over commercial uses is old world for sure—but revived today as it should be. This pattern brought life back to Cotati, California, after a 30-year hiatus. No developer would do it. However, ever since this project was built, numerous other mixed-use developments have been built in Cotati.

COTATI, CA

"Yes, I'm leading, let's go." Safe for everyone, even the toddler and the 86-year-old grandpa whose house they are toddling over to. Cohousing works well for extended families. You can be with in-laws without living with in-laws.

COTATI, CA

Free range kids grazing on raspberries while they take a nourishment break from playing. An edible fruit element is a popular landscape choice in the community-by-design scenario.

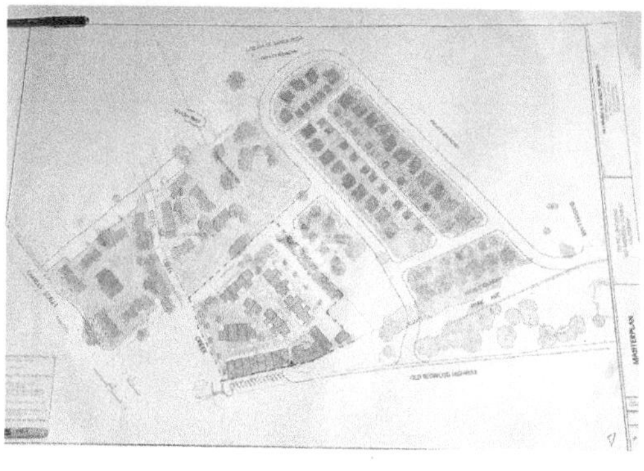

COTATI, CA

The subsidized senior housing (blue) took five years to get approved. The market rate, for sale, single-family houses (pink) took seven years. They both took a long time and are fine neighborhoods with no future residents involvement. The cohousing community (orange)—which engaged future residents in the design process—took less than a year to get approved and residents moved in less than one year later. When real people are involved, everyone gets motivated to get these people moved in. The larger community gets behind community-based design.

BELFAST, ME

Site Plan

As the future residents talked longer and longer about the site plan, the houses (little blocks) came closer and closer together. Many of the residents were moving from extremely remote rural areas, one living miles down a dirt road. But moving the houses closer together was not only driven by costs, it was also driven by environmental concerns and a desire to live a balanced social/private life in a functioning village.

BELFAST, ME

None of these folks had lived in a village before, but somehow they knew what it would look and feel like— when facilitated in a way that turns over all relevant rocks, and all of the right questions were answered.

YARROW ECOVILLAGE, B.C.

An early rendering of the mixed-use portion of the Yarrow Ecovillage. The Yarrow Ecovillage was designed to set the cohousing and the farm up to be the foundation to an ecovillage dedicated to sustainable living and farmland preservation. In addition, it supports a live/work community, a learning center, a farmers' market, a deli, and a mixed-use town center. The cohousing starts on the upper right. Commercial right next to a cohousing makes the commercial, just like in the old world, a serious nexus for community.

The 33-unit Yarrow Ecovillage with their 20-acre farm in the foreground, and a new 17-unit senior cohousing planned behind it, and a 30,000-square-foot commercial planned on the other side of that on the street.

YARROW ECOVILLAGE, B.C.

Commercial space situated on the busy street to the north side of the site promises life and activity, and separates the cohousing from the busy street. Commercial uses populate the street with a café, a recreation store, a deli, a yoga study with dancing classes, a farmers' market, and eventually, enough diverse uses that anything is possible.

This project creates a real ecovillage, a cohousing, a senior cohousing, a farm that employs some of the cohousers, a farmers' market, and 30,000 square feet of commercial space. It is genuinely an ecovillage.

YARROW ECOVILLAGE, B.C.

A mound of dirt can go a long way in creating a great place to play.

YARROW ECOVILLAGE, B.C.

Play accoutrements are usually provided by a parent.

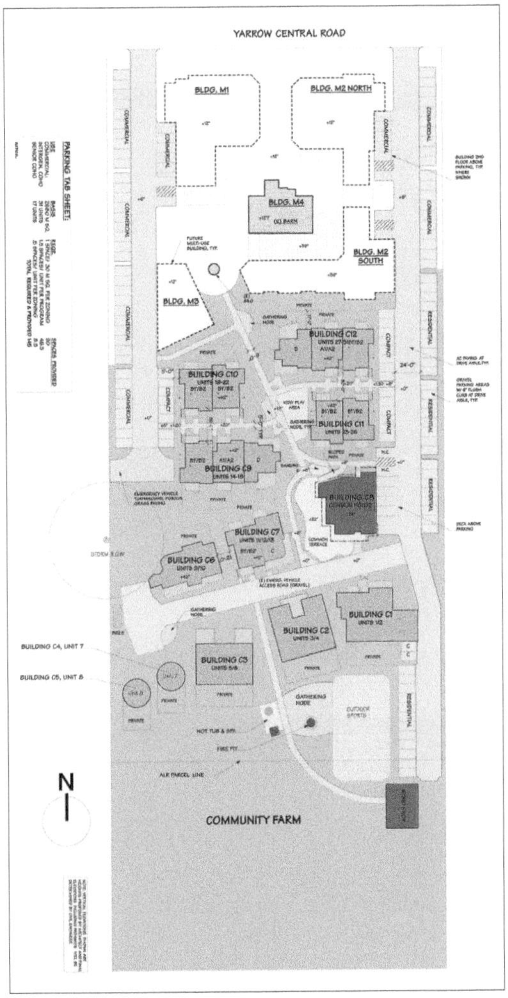

YARROW ECOVILLAGE, B.C.

The Yarrow Ecovillage site plan with the cohousing at the center. The site of this community is a former dairy farm that was left inactive in the 1980s. Quite conveniently, the site is also on a main road that connects the small town of Yarrow to both urban Vancouver and the natural beauty of the Fraser Valley. That road fosters the mixed use, the farmers' market, and the commercial on the street.

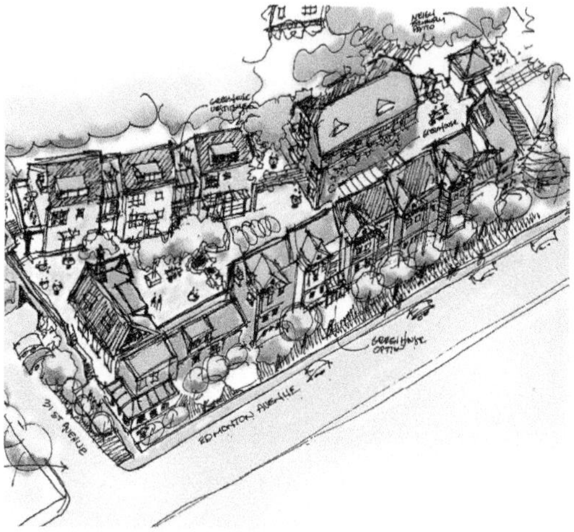

PRAIRIE SKY COHOUSING, CALGARY, AB, CANADA

Seventeen new cohousing units on a busy corridor in Calgary. Parking is underground and tandem. People trust each other to move other people's car. This was the most economical way to get it built.

PRAIRIE SKY COHOUSING, CALGARY, AB, CANADA

Fun on the common terrace over the parking.

PRAIRIE SKY COHOUSING, CALGARY, AB, CANADA

The common house is well used.

LEGACY PROJECT—HARAMBEE HOMES, IL.

LEGACY—HARAMBEE HOMES, IL

Harambee House in Chicago, IL, is a place developed by Perry Bigelow, awarded Builder of the Year in the U.S. Professional Builder in 2005. Not the non-profit builder of the year or for-profit builder of the year, but builder of the year. He didn't exclusively look into the rear-view mirror when planning his next project, which is what too often happens. So at Harambee Homes (Harambee means "life is better when we push together" in Swahili), he looked to cohousing to be inspired. Which means it's a legacy project. It was one of the first projects that we consulted on as a quality housing/neighborhood just after we had designed the first few cohousing communities in the U.S. It was an all African-American resident group with a Caucasian developer and a Caucasian design consultant, and after we started, the group was encouraged to design the community for themselves. So they decided to scale back the common house and as a result (in my view) it's rarely used. Sometimes just making the space 15 percent too small can curtail its use by 90 percent or it could be a cultural choice, we're not sure. They decided to put that money into the houses—their choice. It is still by far an excellent neighborhood, very inspired and informed by cohousing. Harambee is still functioning today, kids have successfully grown up there and gone off successfully to attend college due in part to the very supportive community that they grew up in.

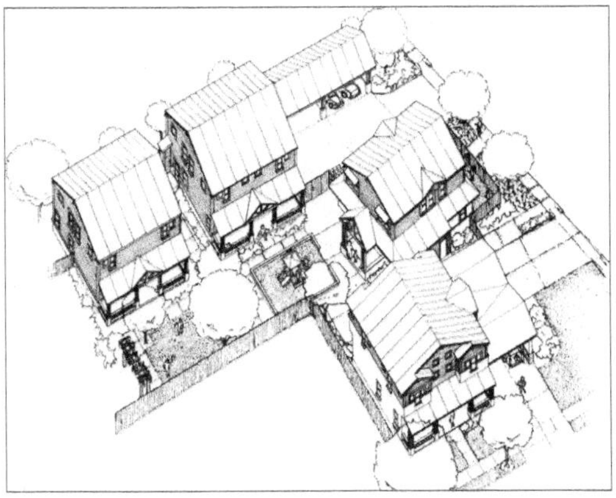

LEGACY—DEPOT COMMONS, CA

I spoke to a housing developer in Washington, D.C., and he said that the D.C. Housing Authority spends $10,000/ year "managing" each unit. "The rent is due." "Yes. I see that the bushes are hitting your windows." "No, I can't do anything about the neighbor making too much noise until after nine." In contrast, at Depot Commons—a low-income subsidized project, management told me that it is the easiest of all of their properties to manage because the residents have dialogue, relationships, community, a sense of belonging, and a sense of accountability. They manage most things themselves—keeping their costs down. The management team is there only half a day per week. Thirteen suites and all of their common facilities were built for total of $650,000 (1997). That, in combination with their management system accomplished mostly by the residents, keeps this project affordable.

LEGACY—DEPOT COMMONS, CA

There are three buildings that each have four private suites. Each suite contains a shared kitchen serving four families and a bedroom/bathroom for a mom and one or two children. There is a common dining room, common kitchen, and a common living room, among plenty of other places to do homework. Each parent (it turns out that they are all moms) has to be enrolled in school. The architects, The Cohousing Company, asked that a mom not be asked to leave when she graduated, and the non-profit developer agreed. Duration facilitates a high-functioning neighborhood.

There is a mom and child who live above the childcare center (upper right) for a total of 13 units. This design is extremely straightforward but comfortable: 12 suites, one full dwelling unit, and a childcare center.

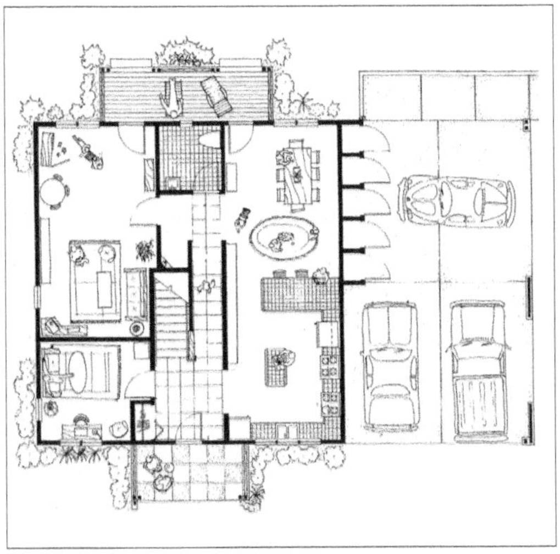

LEGACY—DEPOT COMMONS, CA

Downstairs common living, dining, kitchen, and study. Each mom is in school.

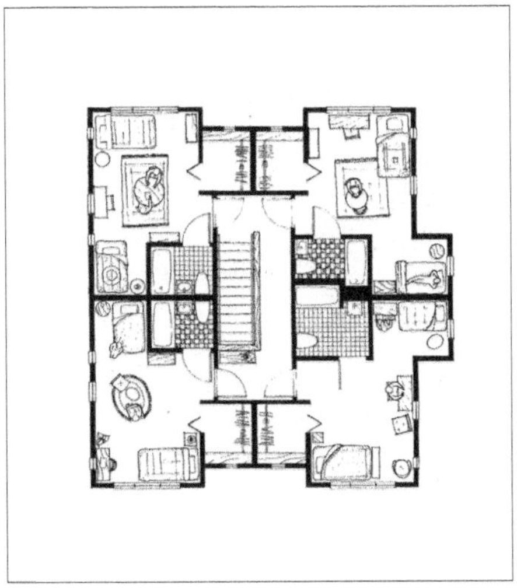

LEGACY—DEPOT COMMONS, CA

Four suites in each building for four families each makes this co-living situation particularly affordable ($650,000 construction for 13 single moms in 1997).

LEGACY—PARK GROVE, CA

A new 400-unit, subsidized development across from the hospital and serving veterans (who would be closer to needed services). Each group of housing was designed to feel like its own neighborhood. It was planned in Fresno, CA, by The Cohousing Company in 2006 and 2007, but was abandoned in the 2008 economic crash. The need for multi-family and non-profit multi-family housing both for rent and for sale requires professionals who are willing to organize the residents to set them up for long-term success.

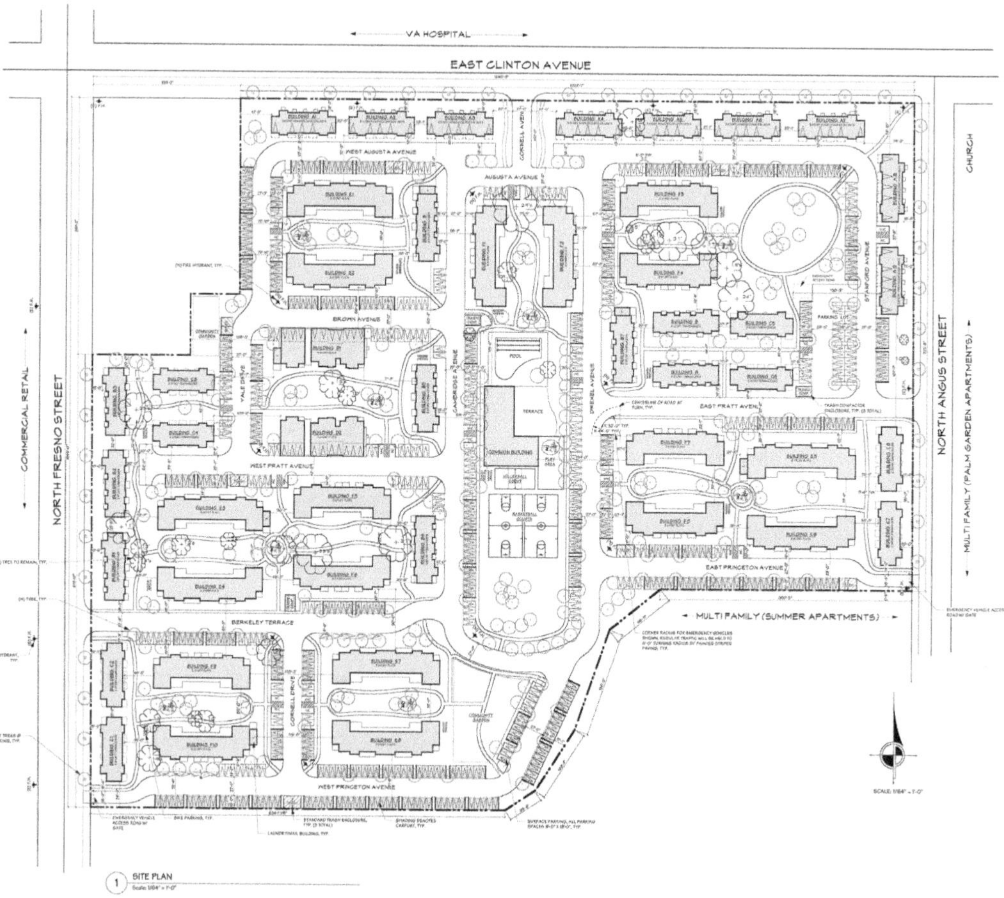

LEGACY—PETALUMA HOMES, CA

While not cohousing, this project was approved by the city, because we agreed to make it as high a functioning neighborhood as possible. A warm and giving common building is an essential component toward fulfilling that intent.

LEGACY—SCHOOL

The legacy of cohousing, just like in Europe, has extended far beyond cohousing and community-enhanced housing to other building typologies like schools. This is a 20,000-square-foot preschool that The Cohousing Company designed at San Francisco State University. Many of the components of this school extended the concept of community much further than a typical neighborhood childcare center.

LEGACY—PETALUMA AVENUE HOMES, CA

Forty-one very affordable units. The planning commission was very clear that they would approve this project if it were cohousing. Therefore, The Cohousing Company were hired. But without being allowed to work with the future residents it was never cohousing. It was designed with remote parking (very child/senior/everybody pedestrian-friendly) generous gardens, generous common house, and generous front porches so people can play Scrabble together instead of just watching TV separately.

LEGACY—SCHOOL

Many of the photos in this book are of housing communities, but not all. But the design world at large can gain a great deal from real, rich neighborhoods like schools that feel like villages. For example, our firm has designed over 50 childcare centers, whose designs were informed from cohousing. Every new center is more community-oriented than the last. From three–four sinks at the entry so that four or five kids can wash their hands at the same time, watching and learning from the others, to places for parents to do homework together before they get their kid and go home with the imagery of "it takes a village."

For example, there are places for parents/students to study for that critical test tomorrow before going home to start their second job—parenting. These spaces serve as an afterschool program of sorts for parents and their children with every nature of community resource. "Who's going to the zoo this weekend? Can we come with you?" And hundreds of other cooperative ventures where it's collectively easy to make the lives of those parents more practical, convenient, economical, and fun.

LEGACY

New multi-family project in Marin County, California, for film director George Lucas, incorporating 120 units with 50,000 square feet of commercial.

By seeing the site plan alone, the design is clearly community-enhanced and village- inspired.

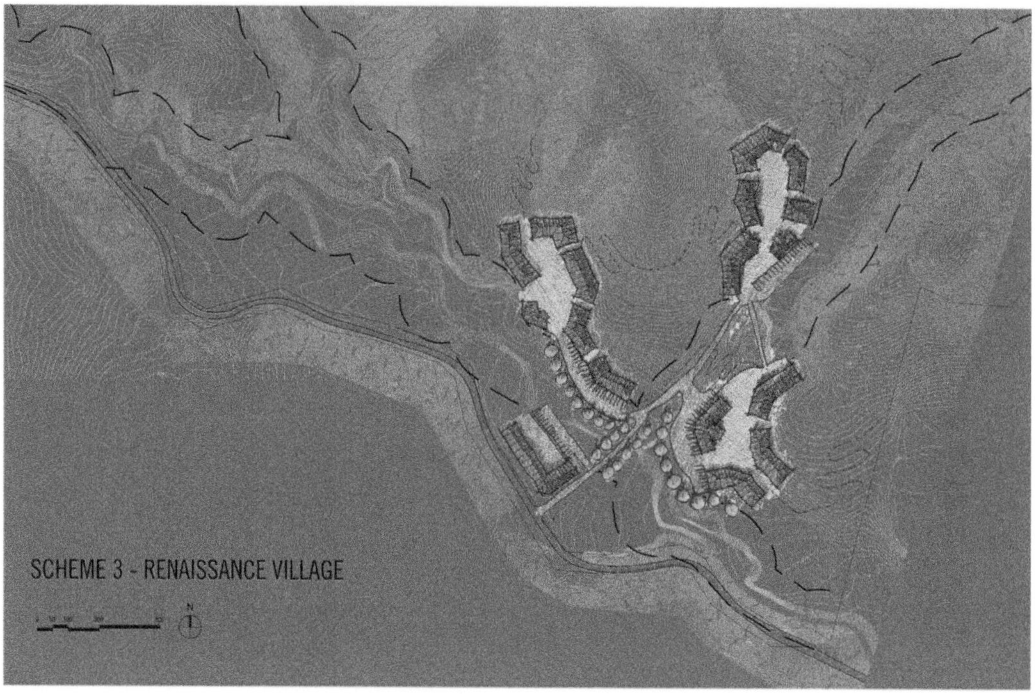

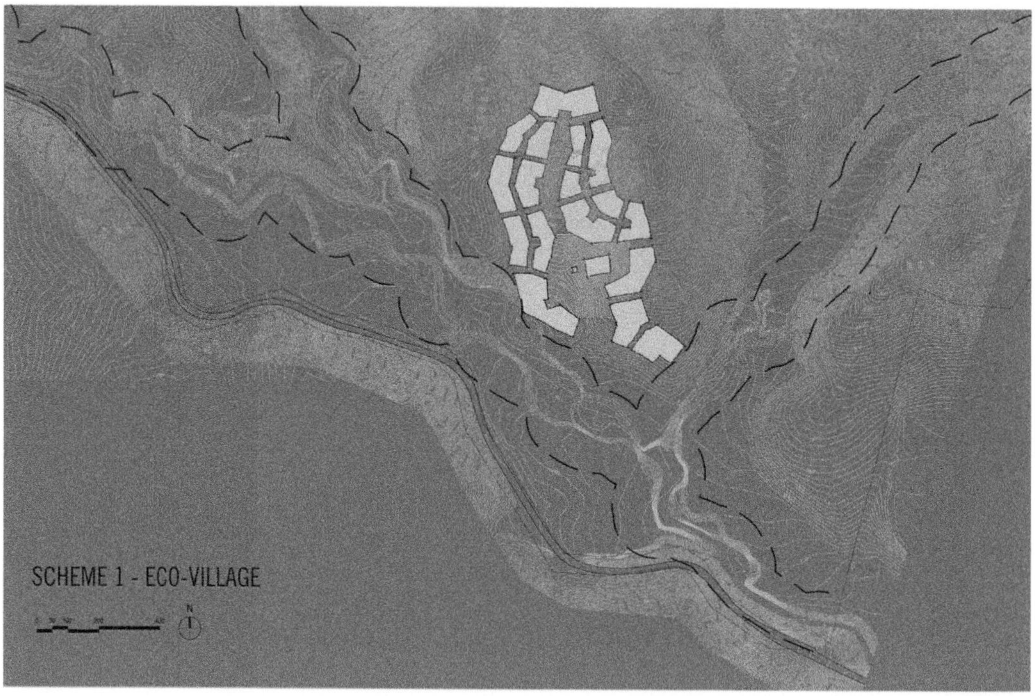

LEGACY

A second scheme of 120 units with 50,000 square feet of commercial for a George Lucas development.

Unfortunately, a couple of neighbors with very large houses on the hill looking down on the site stopped it from being built. Sometimes people with single-family houses are apprehensive of villages in their neighborhood, when in fact they turn out to be an amenity of consequence.

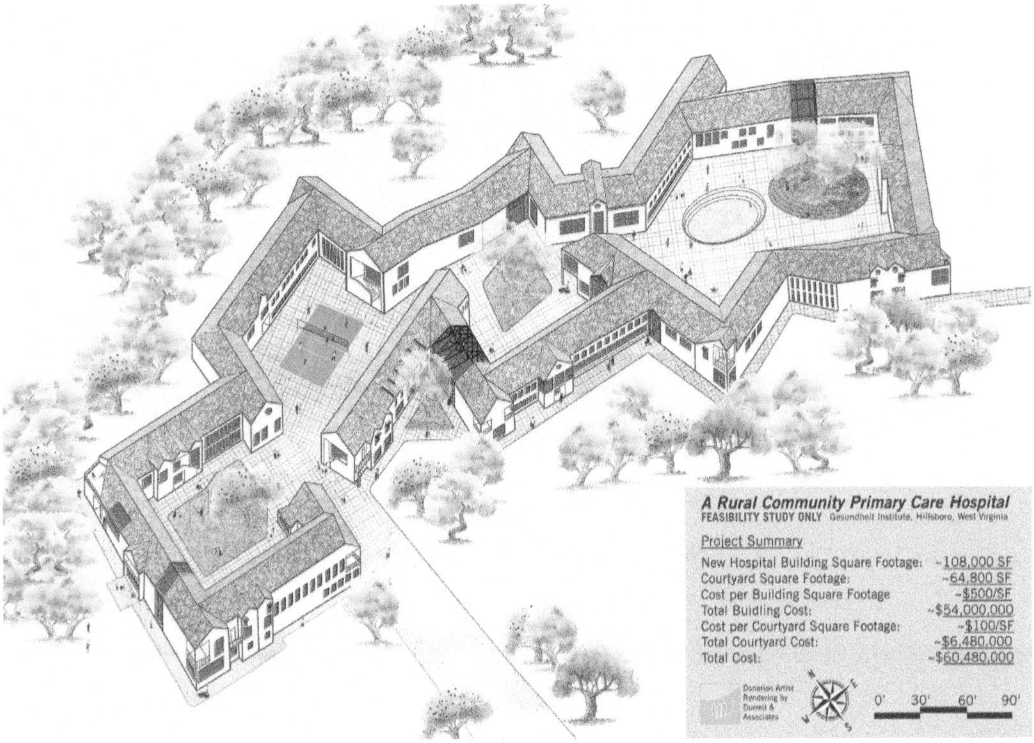

A Rural Community Primary Care Hospital
FEASIBILITY STUDY ONLY Gesundheit Institute, Hillsboro, West Virginia
Project Summary
New Hospital Building Square Footage: ~108,000 SF
Courtyard Square Footage: ~64,800 SF
Cost per Building Square Footage ~$500/SF
Total Buidling Cost: ~$54,000,000
Cost per Courtyard Square Footage: ~$100/SF
Total Courtyard Cost: ~$6,480,000
Total Cost: ~$60,480,000
Donation Artist Rendering by Durrett & Associates
N E S W
0' 30' 60' 90'

LEGACY

Community by design, a schematic design for a new hospital in West Virginia developed by Dr. Patch Adams to feel as village-like as possible—and very much inspired by community-enhanced design. Hospitals have their own criteria, but this one had to be built at $250 per square foot (in 2019, not including equipment), which is half the average for this type of building. That calls of course for wooden frame or maybe steel but nothing fancy, and a simple geometric extrusion with a single-loaded corridor ad nauseam.

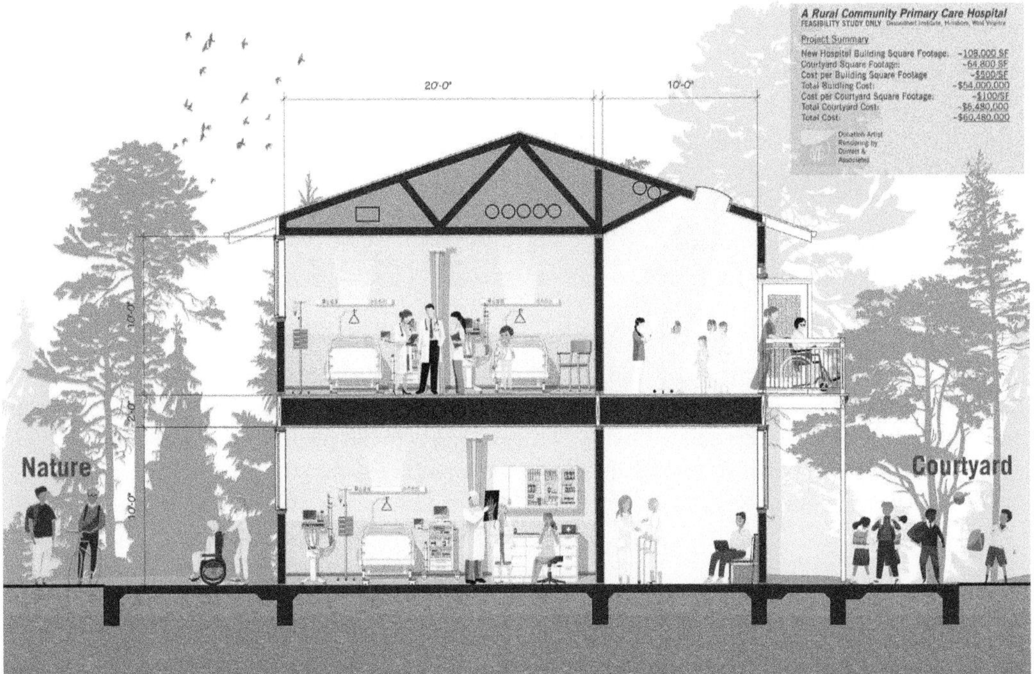

LEGACY

This project is in the woods and really feels like it. Dr. Adams is one of the most eccentric people that you'll ever meet. But he was clear about creating a healthy relationship between patients and nurses, doctors and nurses, and doctors and patients is the main point, and parents with everyone. He personifies, "If it doesn't work socially, why bother?"

LEGACY—STRØGET, DENMARK

The Strøget, Denmark, community-oriented street design. Again, the Danes lead the way. Sales went up 35% overnight (you don't see people driving down shopping malls), and is up a thousand percent today. Quality community-oriented design always starts with a careful analysis, and a building of ownership.

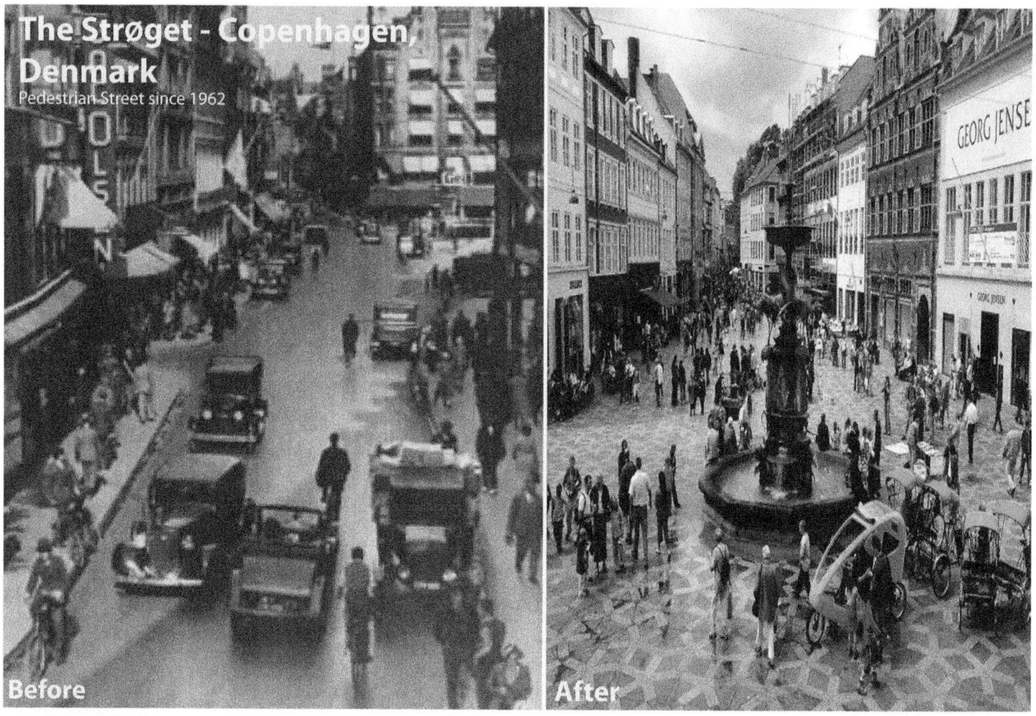

These principles of inclusion can be extrapolated to all forms of public use. Although this genre of inclusion makes sense in order to accomplish smart land use planning decisions, we have a long way to go for it to become popular.

We have a lot of aspirations based on magazine articles about, usually, foreign cities. But for us to evolve, it's easy to appreciate the "product" but nearly impossible to understand the process to get there.

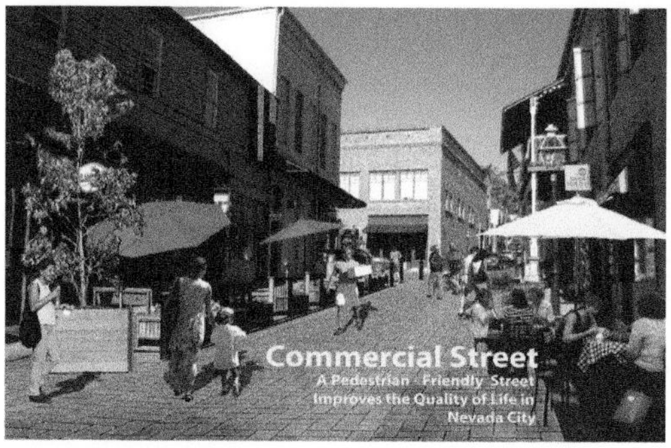

LEGACY—NEVADA CITY, CA

Daytime view. When the street was closed during the COVID-19 pandemic, an entirely new atmosphere of relaxation and conviviality was created—even during a worldwide pandemic—people separated and masked but communicated.

LEGACY—NEVADA CITY, CA

One of our main commercial streets in Nevada City. When I asked a crowd of 20 people, "What's wrong with this poster?" An 8-year-old girl stepped forward to the front of the crowd to point at the white truck, and exclaimed, "There's a car on the road where all of the people want to be." Over and over again, it seems that we have to go to the unlikely sources to understand the point of it all—make places that work for people.

LEGACY—NEVADA CITY, CA

Night view

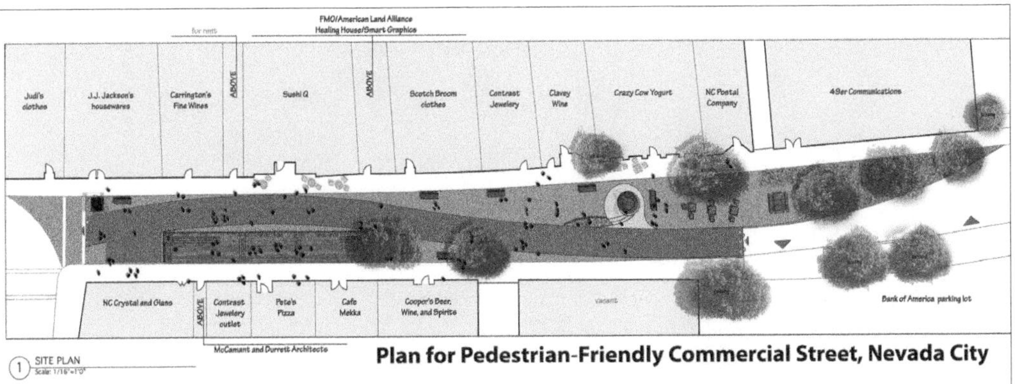

Plan for Pedestrian-Friendly Commercial Street, Nevada City

Pearl Street - Boulder, Colorado

Montreal, Canada

Church Street - Burlington, Vermont

LEGACY—COMMERCIAL STREET, NEVADA CITY

So with a little community work, we came up with a pedestrian-friendly, merchant-acceptable solution reminiscent of villages. The first four meetings were with 17 teenagers and young adults (those who use the street the most) and 10 businesspeople (those who have their livelihood at stake but don't always want to take chances even when it looks like business will bump upward). The analysis has to be holistic. For example, what made Pearl Street so successful in Boulder, CO, was building a new homeless shelter right around the corner. That gave the homeless folk somewhere to shelter other than Pearl Street itself and once the walking street itself was up and running, their presence was diluted by the thousands of shoppers every day. Also at the meetings was the Chief of Police.

LEGACY—CHAPTER 44 STREET, DENMARK

Chapter 44 Street in Denmark—before.

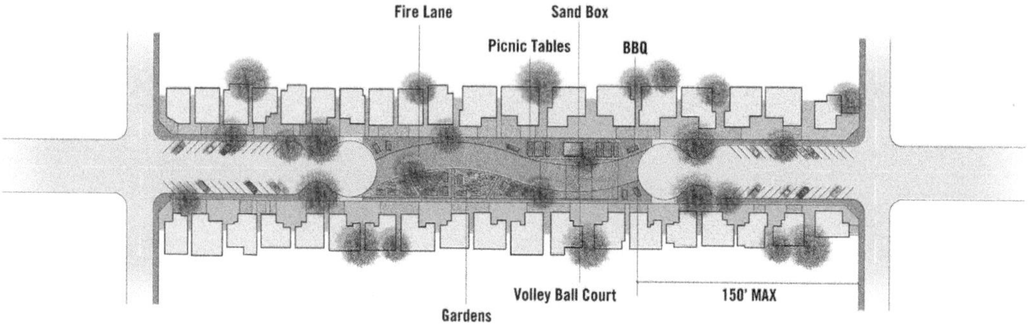

LEGACY—CHAPTER 44 STREET, DENMARK

Under some circumstances the residents of a street can vote to close the street to through traffic in order to make it more people-friendly. Sand boxes, picnic tables, BBQs, volleyball courts, gardens, and much more ensue. Yes, we have to have public safety (fire access, etc.).

But smart public safety starts with smart preventative care like accountability which comes with, first and foremost, community and a high-functioning neighborhood.

LEGACY—CO-LIVING AT HOLLYWOOD, CA

A village in a box. Co-living. When you make a standard apartment building, it's not uncommon to have 15–20% of the floor area be common area (the lobby, hallways, laundry rooms, and mail area). In this project and others like it, we have made the common area 35–40% of the floor area. This building in Hollywood, California, is geared toward millennials. There are large common dining areas, a large makerspace (workshop), laundries, sitting areas, recreation areas, a gym, a media room, and 61 small private rental rooms (SROs) with the bathroom down the hall (about 80 people total). The Cohousing Company was the Design Criteria Programming and Architecture Consultant.

Haystack Heights Cohousing Site Plan Workshop.

Everyone has their fingers in the design, and it's always better as a result.

2

Haystack Heights Cohousing

Site Planning Workshop

"A rich community life may grow from numerous seemingly unimportant, casual meetings with neighbors."

Clare Cooper Marcus & Wendy Sarkissian

This written program is designed to take the mystery out of the process—how do they get these things done anyway? This is how. The biggest mistake in cohousing design is that the program is half this long and consequently the community is less than half as functional. We included all of these programs because in the past we have tried to explain how to do the program. In this book we showed exactly how it has been accomplished in the past.

HAYSTACK HEIGHTS COHOUSING

www.spokanecohousing.com

SITE PROGRAM AND DESIGN CRITERIA

Write-up from Site Planning Workshop

Facilitated by Charles Durrett with Erik Bonnett
The Cohousing Company
Hosted at Eastern Washington University
Urban and Regional Planning Program
Spokane, Washington

October 21–24, 2017

Spokane Cohousing Vision Statement

Spokane Cohousing is an intergenerational village that is close to downtown with clustered townhouses and flats to maximize efficiency, interaction, and green space where we share skills and facilities where it makes sense, and respect privacy and independence where it is needed and desired. We right-size our lives to limit our ecological footprint and our decision making and group process is inclusive, as simple as possible, and flexible.

Table of Contents

Some images were not taken during the workshop. They depict other cohousing communities and do not suggest the building style that will result in Spokane. Each photo shows a desirable situation, activity, or programmed place that was accommodated in a way that was appropriate for that specific community in which it exists. The design of Haystack Heights will be specific and appropriate to the unique needs and desires of this group, while drawing inspiration from the successful design of other communities.

PART 1. CONTEXT

The following summary was prepared to help familiarize ourselves with Spokane. It may be useful to share with future residents who might not be familiar with the area and its many amenities. It also may be interesting for current residents to see a characterization of your community.

Spokane City Facts

County: Spokane
State: Washington
Latitude: 47.7°N
Longitude: 117.4°W
Elevation: about 1800–2400 feet
Land area: 60 square miles
Population in 2016: 216,000 people Population (metro): 557,000 people
Population density: 3,526 people per sq. mi.

Local History, Economy, and Demographics

The area where the City of Spokane now sits was first inhabited by the Spokane Tribe, from whom the modern city gets its name. The first nation lived in the area for about 8000–13000 years until trappers of European descent entered the area in the early 1800s.

Colonization of the area began slowly, primarily driven by trapping. In 1881, the Northern Pacific Railway was completed, opening the area to extensive settlement. The city grew steadily through the 1980s as a regional hub for the agricultural, mining, and forestry economies.

In the last thirty-five years the economy has shifted from industry to service with Fairchild Air Force Base, local school districts, and hospitals now the largest employers. Spokane is the third largest city in the Pacific Northwest. Spokane remains the agriculture, industry, and transportation hub of the Inland Northwest, the basin between the Rocky and Cascade Mountains within Washington and Idaho. This includes an international airport with over 100 flights each day.

Local Culture and Events

Spokane boasts six institutions of higher education, including Washington State, Eastern Washington, and Gonzaga Universities. The presence of these institutions along with dozens of independent arts and culture organizations has led to a strong and diverse arts and culture community. Examples include outdoor summer symphony concerts on a floating Spokane River stage and numerous sculpture installations.

The three primary universities have also co-located in an interconnected campus district spanning the Spokane River. This, along with robust redevelopment in the adjacent downtown district, is driving the development of a vibrant downtown city life.

The 1974 World's Fair ground is also adjacent to downtown and has been converted into Riverfront Park, the crown jewel of the Spokane parks system, which is one of the best funded in the nation. Riverfront Park is currently undergoing a makeover so its waterfalls, islands, and overlooks continue to be a prized resource for residents and tourists alike.

No description of Spokane would be complete without mentioning the outdoors. There are many natural areas and trails within the urban parks system and endless opportunities for recreation nearby. In the summer, swimming and boating are popular on the 76 lakes within 50 miles of town. In winter, there are five ski resorts located within two hours' drive. For longer trips, some of the most remote, pristine, and dramatic landscapes in North America are within a day's drive.

Spokane's motto is "Near Nature, Near Perfect," which aims to capture the cultural vibrancy and celebration of local culture typical throughout the Pacific Northwest, along with a level of access to nature unparalleled within the American Pacific Northwest.

COMMENTS: ***If you're going to approach design from an anthropological point of view, it's critical to understand the culture of the town to the fullest extent possible. All of the group's needs become obvious. This group happens to be very active, and they want to accommodate that in their design. Obviously, the town's culture is a foundational part of the planning.***

Climate and Design

Climatic Synopsis

Spokane is located in the transition between the more arid Columbia Basin and the forested western slope of the Rockies. The National Weather Service characterizes Spokane summers as mild and arid and winters as cold. There are also distinct albeit brief spring and fall seasons separating the varied summer and winter.

Summer in Spokane is characterized by warm days and cooler nights. The mean daily range of temperature is high, similar to desert regions (i.e., how much it cools down at night).

High temperatures are typically comfortable, reaching the 70s and 80s, with highs above 90°F occurring only about 20 days a year. Humidity is relatively low, typically dropping to between 20 and 40 percent. Breezes are common, especially from the southwest and northeast.

Winter in Spokane is more influenced by its regional proximity to the coast. Nearly three-quarters of annual precipitation occurs in the winter with rain or snowfall occurring on about half of winter days. Skies are overcast or partly cloudy about 75 percent of November through January days. With its inland location, temperatures are cold: typical highs only reach the 30s. However, the daily temperature range is small, so lows typically only drop into the 20s. Although the Rockies tend to protect Spokane from frigid air descending from Canada, lows in the single digits and teens are not uncommon. With these cold temperatures, half of all 17 inches of annual precipitation falls as snow.

COMMENTS: ***The architect must understand the climate intimately. Spokane can have up to five freeze/thaw cycles per day. The architect brings a lot of this data together—it's the bedrock to sustainable design.***

By the Numbers

Summer Ave. Low/High Temp.[a]: 55°/84°F

Summer Diurnal Temp. Range[a]: 29°F

Summer Daily Min. Rel. Humidity[b]: ~25 percent

Winter Ave. Low/High Temp.[a]: 20°/31°F

Heating Degree Days[c]: 6687

Cooling Degree Days[c]: 423

October–March Precipitation[a]: 70 percent

Jan. Global Horiz. Radiation[b]: 298 kBtu/sf

Notes:

(a) Data from US NWS Spokane station info.

(b) Data from US DOE TMY3 dataset for Felts Field.

(c) Heating Degree Days are a measure of the need for heating, in this case heating to 65°F (the number is the sum of the differences between the average outdoor temperature and 65°F for each day of the year). Cooling Degree Days are the inverse of Heating Degree Days. Data from ASHRAE 2009.

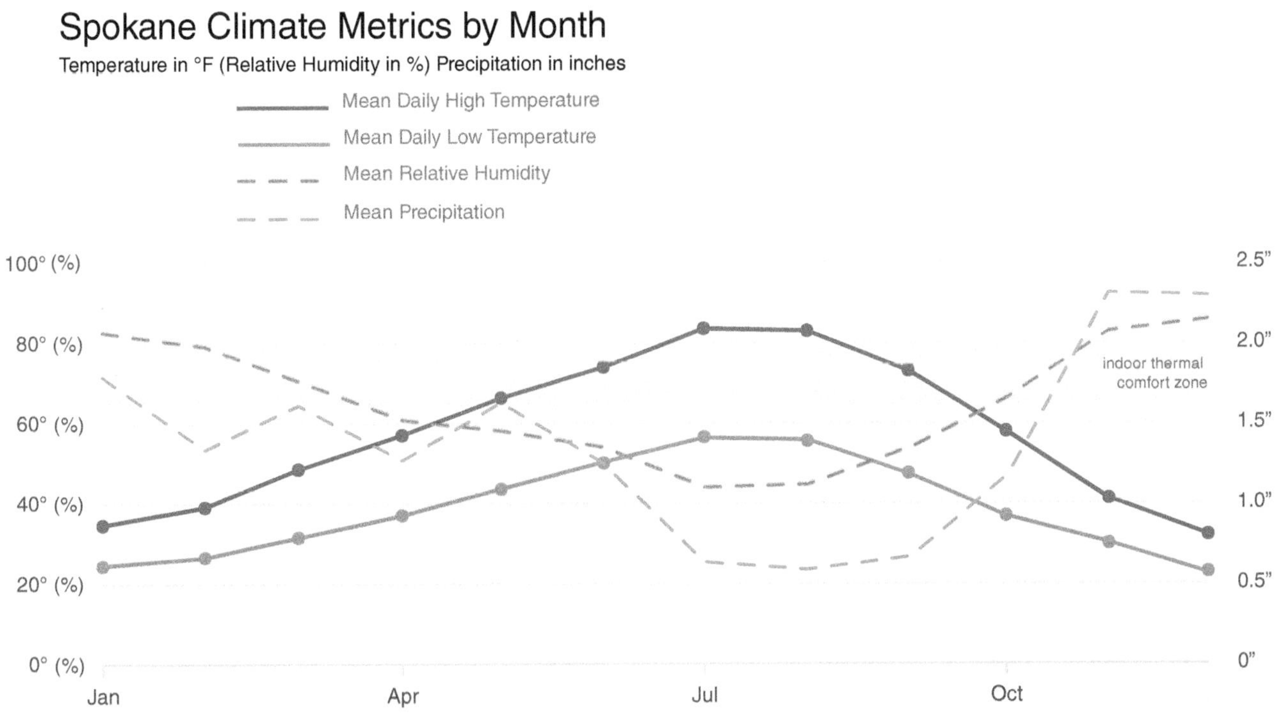

Climate as Form-Giver

Several aspects of the Spokane climate suggest specific design responses. These responses will improve the energy performance of the project, increase thermal comfort, bolster community resilience, and also contextualize the architecture—making it relevant and meaningful in this specific place.

The most immediately obvious and important characteristic of the climate is the pleasant summers. Shade and breeze during hot hours and protection from wind and access to sun in the cooler hours will be key to facilitating the outdoor living that drives community interaction in cohousing.

At the same time, recognizing that eight months of the year outdoor temperatures are typically not warm enough for sedentary outdoor activities, the common house and common facilities must be designed to provide space for robust community interaction indoors.

Based on the Spokane climate, appropriate climate-driven design responses include:

1. Tight floor plans: In cold overcast winters, well-insulated tight buildings perform well. Compact floor plans and attached housing minimize heat loss through exterior walls.
2. Sheltering outdoor spaces from wind: Courtyards work well to extend outdoor hours in cooler shoulder seasons.
3. Solar orientation: Spokane doesn't have a particularly ideal climate for passive solar heating. However, spaces used in the daytime will benefit from southern solar access so winter sunlight can be enjoyed when it is available. Trees should be avoided on the south of buildings within 45° of windows. Outdoor living spaces should be provided with ample access to sunlight, as well as opportunities for shade in the summer.
4. Natural ventilation: with the high summer daily temperature range, night ventilation of gypsum board and wood floors will effectively provide comfortable indoor temperatures.

COMMENTS: ***Knowing the weather is key to designing for the comfort of the residents, and meshing that with the community lifestyle. But it's also important to what information is critical for the residents to know and how to facilitate this information in the right direction. And knowing this intimately is critical to keeping the energy use minimal and to using the correct energy.***

Site Context

The site is located in the South Perry neighborhood, a hillside district sloping down toward the Spokane River, downtown, and the university district. A few blocks away, the South Perry neighborhood center sports several restaurants, coffee shops, a yoga studio, and other shops. Liberty and Grant parks are also only a few blocks from the site, offering open space, ball fields, play structures, and access to the Ben Burr Trail. Grant Elementary School is also located within walking distance, and private and Montessori schools are also nearby. The hospital district lies west of the site. The neighborhood character is surprisingly quiet, given it is less than a mile from downtown. But it is clear it is up and coming as well, due to the proximity to downtown and the resurgence of the South Perry Center.

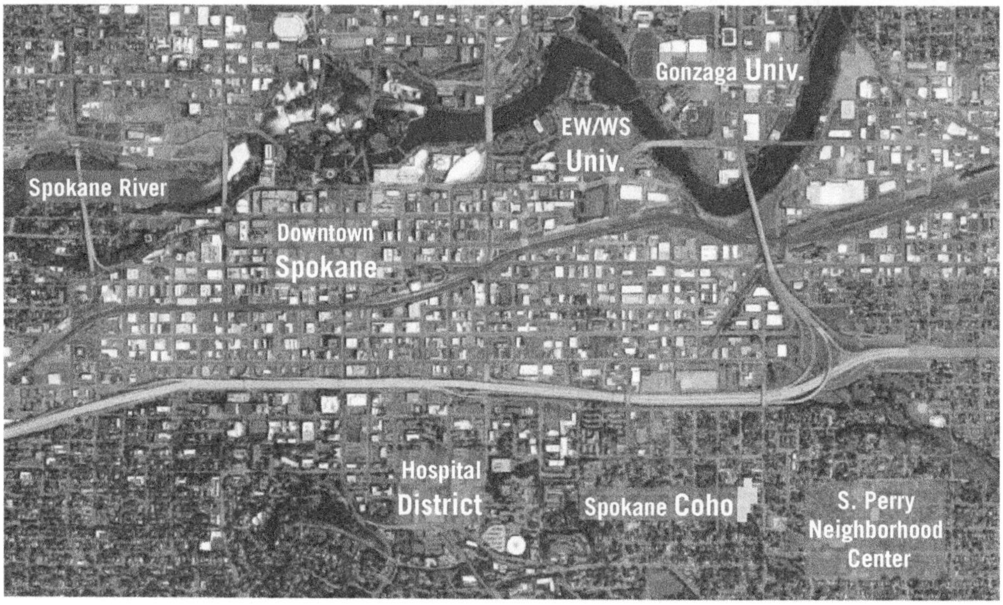

COMMENTS: ***This work helps one to think about and address the bigger issues. What role does this new high-functioning neighborhood play in the larger neighborhood? In particular, how will it affect the success of a fledgling neighborhood center? The common house usually plays a very positive role in neighborhood politics. Where else are the neighbors going to meet when the city decides to cut down all of the local street trees because of one arborist's suggestion? And where can citywide issues be discussed? Statewide? Nationwide? It soon becomes obvious that cohousing is the logical antidote to "divide and conquer."***

Project Description

The cohousing site has a number of valuable assets as well as a great deal of complexity. High on this list is the topography, which varies 59′ from top to bottom and includes sheer cliffs and steep embankments in places. There are also five significant buildings on the site, including Yogashala with its five studio apartments and two yoga studio rooms, a single-family house, carriage house, shop, and a garage. The soils are varied, ranging from iconic basalt haystacks and exposed bedrock, to sandy soils and rubble fill deposited more than a century ago. There are multiple potential access points to the irregularly shaped site. There is also an orchard and garden located on the top level of the site. Many of the above items offer both challenges and benefits to the future development.

COMMENTS: ***This information has to be somewhere. Otherwise, each new consultant that gets on board will be as confused as the last one was when they began, and aspects of the design will fall through the cracks.***

PART 2. DESIGN PROGRAM

Outline of Process

COMMENTS: ***There's a reason that cohousing started in Denmark and has been so successful. The shortest poem in the English language is "Me, We." In the U.S., we often subscribe to the "Me." If I worry about me, I will be better off. The Danes subscribe to the notion that I will never reach my full potential unless We all reach our potential. The actor who has starred in the most American films is John Wayne at 126 movies. That's a lot of pick yourself up by the bootstraps—that's a lot of propaganda. And I can imagine a community picking you up by the bootstraps, but not you by yourself.***

BRAINSTORM

- Generate ideas (as freely as possible)
- Get creative juices flowing
- Ensure the opportunity for everyone to be heard
- Provide a fast and fun way to get started on a new topic
- Avoid discussion and judgment

DISCUSS

- Have goal in mind
- Debate merits of an issue
- Clarify issues
- Put forth proposals

CONSENSUS

- Break question down to lowest common denominator
- Ask for objections and ask for consensus (straw poll)
- State the decision

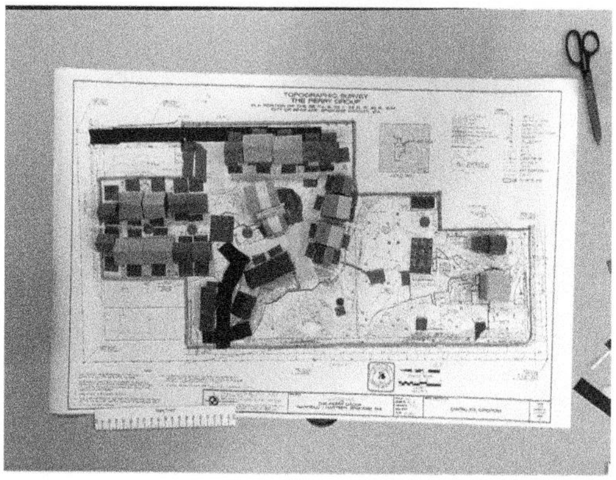

Site Design Goals

Imagine it is a grey morning in 2019 and you're walking from your house up to the common house. You are going to join half a dozen people on the landscape committee; the agenda is to get winter ready (clean out drains or similar). With coffee cup in hand you walk up to the common terrace and think to yourself: Wow! We did it! We optimally satisfied our goals. I didn't get every last thing I wanted as an individual, but as a group we couldn't have done better. And together we achieved so much more than I could have done alone.

What are those goals?

- Presence of beauty
- Somehow can interact with each household
- Welcoming environment
- Easy to navigate physically
- Whole site is accessible to all, including gardens
- All works together, just like we designed
- Ease of use and maintenance
- Feels like a village
- Centers of activity and centers of stillness
- Sustainability
- A pack of kids
- Feels like a green oasis
- Supports friendliness, fun, and companionship
- Effortless and spontaneous community
- Integration of privacy and togetherness
- A sense of spaciousness and intimacy
- An environment rich in art and color
- Pets included (joy and help get unstuck)
- Safe for children et al., physically safe too
- Familiar community
- Permaculture
- Flow inside and onto site
- Dedicated space that feels sacred and invites spiritual exploration on site
- Site enables a close connection with nature
- Edible beauty
- Quiet spaces, car-noise-free as much as possible
- Surrounded by caring friends
- Learning environment
- Environment that contributes to emotional and physical health
- Facilitates sharing
- Benign to indigenous and migrating animals as possible, and accommodates domestic animals
- Also works well in winter and summer
- Feels like Spokane, not foreign. A concentration of the best of Spokane and its potential, rooted in region
- Integrated into the rest of the neighborhood (balanced, by invitation, welcoming boundary)
- Centralized circulation/clear sense of entry
- Varied access to parking
- Affordability
- Diversity
- Demonstration of better urban living

COMMENTS: ***A thorough program is the best antidote to a culture of "me." It is the best way to describe our aspirations, put them down on paper, and ascribe to them. It is the best road for cultural change. When I was studying cohousing in Denmark, there was serious pushback from the Danes. They were certain that we would make it a tool to make more real estate and money, and that's it. They were certain that we would not do the work necessary to make it a cultural act. That's what these programs do. They ask, as best as possible, and there is always room for improvement, "Who are we? And who do we want to become?" How do we make culture change happen? This is how.***

Activities Between Buildings*

- Roasting, grilling, BBQing food, smoking – Y&N
- Joking – N
- Napping – N
- Celebrating – Y
- Music jamming – Y
- Reading/writing – N
- Nurturing – N
- Meditating, contemplating – Y
- Fooling around – N
- Sports baseball, soccer, volleyball, frisbee, openspace – Y
- Playing with your dog – N but revisit if residual space
- Harvesting, foraging, gleaning, planting, pruning – Y
- Composting – Y
- Talking, socializing, pontificating, soap boxing – N
- Camp firing – Y
- Collaborating – N
- Laundry/clothes drying – Y
- Bee keeping – Y
- Keeping chickens – Y
- Giggling – N
- Observing – N
- Child rearing, herding – N
- Sitting quietly – Y
- Hanging around – N
- Snow shoveling – N
- Sunbathing – N
- Swimming (water play for kids) – N

* Activities marked with a "Y" for yes will get specific accommodations. Other activities will be accommodated at other designated places on the site (those marked with a "N" for not a specific space, but to be accommodated elsewhere on and off site). This will depend on site conditions, economics, and group choices. Large cost items will be prioritized at Workshop 6.

- Star gazing – N
- Hot tubbing – N
- Saunaing – Y
- Romanticizing – N
- Tree climbing – N
- Rock climbing – N
- Fort/Tree house – N
- Playing – Y
- Dancing – N
- Canning/solar drying – N
- Project working/construction, crafting
- Bicycling and storing bikes
- Stretching, yoga, Tai chi, exercising – N
- Performing – Y
- Sledding
- Skating
- Car parking – Y
- Tidying
- Swinging and rocking
- Lending library – ?
- Gathering – Y
- Communing with nature – N
- Sharing – N
- Eating and drinking – Y
- Recycling, disposing – Y
- Wood splitting – N
- Whistling – N
- Singing – N

COMMENTS: ***The most bothersome aspect of cohousing is that many people believe that there must be an easier way to do it. There may be, but you will never have the same success if you do it any faster, like so many communities in North America. Two days of site criteria to challenge each other on how we use the landscape—if changing the suburb or changing the cityscape is changing the culture, then two days is nothing. The list of goals really became a constitution for the design process to follow. It isn't something that you can design to, but you can apply it to guide and evaluate this next list, the activities, in a direction that responds to the goals. The neighborhood landscape, the nature of the play that plays out on that stage front, and the nuance of relaxing body language made it clear that this neighborhood could be and should be different. In other words, if we're going to evolve in a deliberate direction, we have to know exactly where we want to go. That's what this document does.***

COMMENTS:
Reaching an agreement to the amount of on-site parking needed among 15 people seems like it would be challenging, but in over 50 projects to date, it has rarely taken more than a 15–20-minute discussion. How many cars do you own now? How many do you want to own after you move in? Assuming shared electric cars and borrowing cars. It usually goes something like 1.5 to 2 per household and sometimes 2 down to 1 in cases like Vancouver. The big game changer is the shared common electrical vehicles in cohousing. This is a clear example of understanding exactly who the group is and then after some conversation—where they want to go and how they can best see themselves contributing to that vision.

PART 3. PROGRAM PLACES

Place	Activities	Character	Relationship	Details
<u>Parking</u> Group's pre-cohousing parking: 78 for 34 households (23/10hh @ wksp) Initial estimate of cohousing parking desire: 54 for 34 households (16/10hh @ wksp) Personal garage straw poll was 19 for 34 households (6/10hh @ wksp). Straw poll for opinion on total garages for community: 10 (8/19ppl), 16 (10/19ppl) 19 (1/19).			• Consensus considered Spokane climate, marketability, varying generational needs, on-site space constraints, high anticipated cost of construction	• Garage parking: 17 consensed • All other parking off-site on the street • 39 total parking spaces programmed (including 22 street parking spaces and w17 garage) • About 12 spaces min. on-site required by city

Place	Activities	Character	Relationship	Details
<u>Bike Storage</u> Group's pre-cohousing bike ownership: 132 for 34 households (39/10hh @ wksp)	• Parking bikes	• Secure • Ease of use, circulation • Natural light • Kids' bike area and adult bikes separate	• Visible from common areas • High traffic • No schlepping upstairs required • Where stairs use runners in stairs	• Programmed bike parking: 102 for 34 hh (32/10hh @ wkshp) • Bikes, trikes, electric bikes, electric scooters • 110 charging (x2), solar powered • Motion sensor light, door w/key pad, self closer, & grate • With interior rack/ lockable, w/ shelving or locker for things, and concrete floor

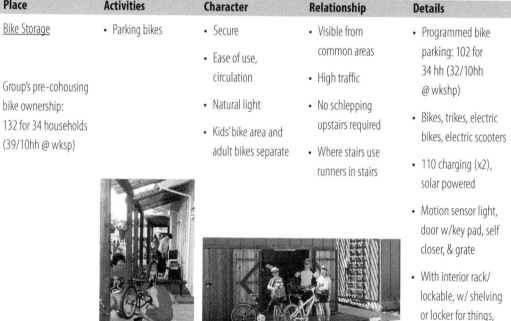

Place	Activities	Character	Relationship	Details
Sauna	• Taking saunas • Informal community management			• Programmed for 5–9 adults

Place	Activities	Character	Relationship	Details
Gathering Nodes	• Gathering • Talking • Eating • Visiting	• Some quiet • Some boisterous	• Each house to have line of sight • Some central • Some remote • Some near kid zone	• 6–8 total nodes • Dark/quiet at night • Sun shaded in summer • Sunny and wind-protected in spring/fall

Place	Activities	Character	Relationship	Details
Meditation Pavilion/ Chapel-like place • Straw poll: 13–14 people interested/ 10hh @ workshop	• Meditating • Sleeping • Reading	• Quiet • Cozy • Like a Japanese tea house • Chapel or sanctuary	• View of beauty	• Programmed for 9–12 people • Meditation at 6am, also in evening, Used ~2 hrs/day • Covered • Could be natural construction • With heat and light

Source: Li Ding / Adobe Stock

Source: Li Ding / Adobe Stock

COMMENTS: ***Again, I want to stress that this design criterion took much less time to establish than with any private developer that I have worked for. Of course, it seems like the latter would be faster. All you have to do is look in the rear-view mirror and ask, "What made a profit last month? Let's do that." Meanwhile, they spend the next six months second-guessing themselves. In cohousing, the site plan takes up two days and two evenings to look at the horizon and design the future in the direction that the neighborhood wants, not based on old, bad habits.***

COMMENTS: ***These days, gardening is the greatest activity since racketball or skiing. Getting your hands in the dirt is all the rage. Happy kids playing is key in intergenerational cohousing. If the kids are happy, the parents are more happy. The biggest criticism that we get from parents these days is, "I wish I had the benefits of what these kids have." Play spaces and car-free environments make for free-range children. Left to their own curiosities, they have fun and it's easy to make friends, to learn a lot about getting along, nature, sports, teamwork, and themselves.***

Place	Activities	Character	Relationship	Details
Garden	• Common gardening	• Sunny, at least partial		• Lots of interest

Place	Activities	Character	Relationship	Details
Kid's Play	• Open-ended play • Natural play • Hopscotch, jump rope • Fort building • Scavenging	• Places of wonder preserved • Some undeveloped, wild areas • Incorporated in landscape • Not too safe • A variety of space	• Some kids play at a gathering node • Need for supervision and limits when they are young, then increasing freedom and range as they grow	• Sand box? • Seating for parents • Area for kids pools • Could be playable sculpture • Big pile of dirt • Could have moving water feature • Some hard spaces • Zip line? • Consider neighboring areas • Open green space

Place	Activities	Character	Relationship	Details
Clothes Lines • Straw poll: 11/19 people @ workshop would use common laundry hanging	• Hanging clothes outside		• Optimally located • Away from dust (away from pile of dirt) • Away from kids	• Line fits king-sized sheet • (5) 10′ clothes line lengths

Place	Activities	Character	Relationship	Details
Chicken Coop • Straw poll: 12/19 people @ workshop would participate	• Chicken club		• Chickens eat food scraps, near kitchens (but not too close) • Near greenhouse for mutual heating • Sight line from house for chicken protection	• 15 hens consensed (14 square feet per bird for coop and run) • No roosters • Needs year-round water • Needs power

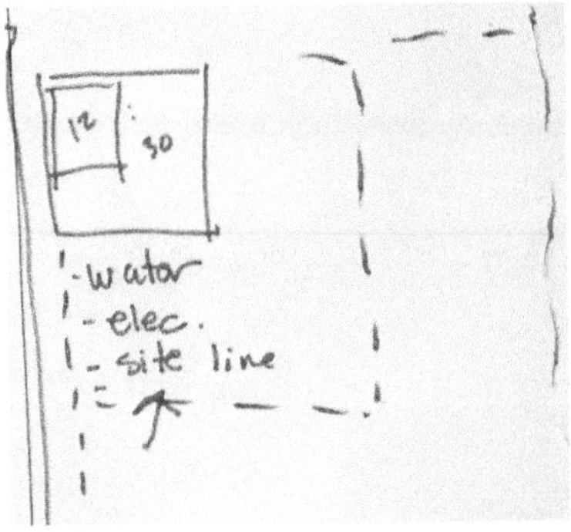

Place	Activities	Character	Relationship	Details
Greenhouse(s)	• Starting plants • Growing tropical plants • Education • Eating • Hang out • Extending the growing season	• Permaculture garden greenhouse • Tropical • Aquaculture	• Integrated into common house? And/or attached to another common space	• Phase II or III?

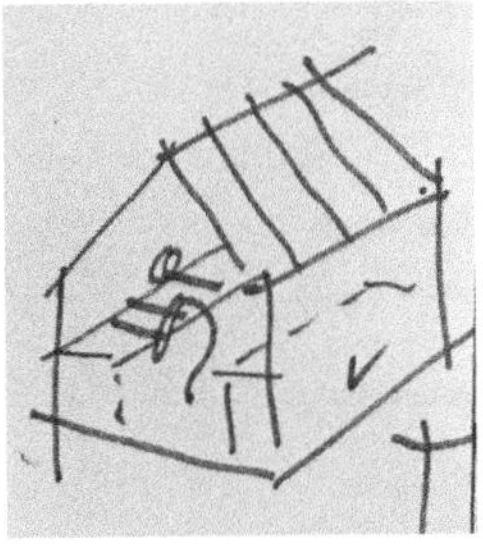

COMMENTS: ***There is a reason for each image. Two men hanging up the laundry. Something happens when it's common and visible. When you can see it from the circulation, all of a sudden, men are interested, just like when there is the more performance-like BBQ, with the big spatula in hand and the smile on his face. Over and over, in front of everyone, brainstorm how many people are actually interested in chickens, for example. In this case, the low end was 12 hens, the high end was 30. The straw poll suggested 20—and then the discussion ended on 15. The brainstorming, discussion and decision have to be definitive. It has to land. It has to be definitive and clearly supported enough to have the appropriate follow-through.***

COMMENTS: ***On occasion, it works if residents appoint a few projects to "sweat equity." But it still pays to "size it." This group wanted a bike shed bigger than a lunch box, but smaller than an aircraft carrier. And the residents will build them later.***

Place	Activities	Character	Relationship	Details
Storage		• Orderly and out of sight • Using residual space	• Private storage held for Workshop 3 • Common indoor storage held for Workshop 2 • Outdoor common storage included here	• Group storage for outdoor, recreation (canoes), and gardening tools • "Just In Time" Some at workshop, etc. • Generators, snow blowers • Kids stuff, games, toys

Place	Activities	Character	Relationship	Details
Bee Hives	• Bee keeping		• Near garden, or anywhere • 10' min. from lot line required by city	• 8 hives onsite • Near processing house (Lars has one or elsewhere in Spokane). Therefore, processing house might not be on site.

Place	Activities	Character	Relationship	Details
Fire Ring	• Visiting • Music		• At common house	• Movable

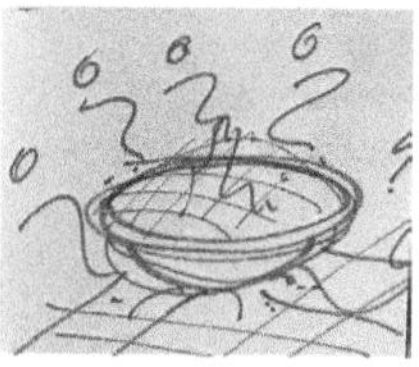

Place	Activities	Character	Relationship	Details
Hot Tub • Straw poll: 13/19 people at workshop interested	• Hot tubbing • Informal community management		• Outside • Near Common House bathroom	• 6 butt, 8 butt? • With outdoor shower • Indoor sink and bathroom (could serve meditation, sauna, garden) • Composting toilet • Would be built later by the group

COMMENTS: ***Voting is rare in community-enhanced design—instead there is brainstorming, discussion, and consensus. Unlike typical condominium or rental boards that ignore residents' needs, people in community-enhanced neighborhoods participate. The point is that people need to pay attention to the software (management) as well as the hardware (houses).***

Place	Activities	Character	Relationship	Details
Common House Orientation			• Can see people walking from cars • Don't see cars • Along circulation (en route home)	• View is to the mountains to the north • Southwest is optimal for cool-weather sun (the shoulder month) • Look to south, but block the harsh western sun

Place	Activities	Character	Relationship	Details
Pathways (accessibility)				• Make as many houses along accessible paths as possible

Location of the Common House

The most successful and frequently used common houses optimally have at least one of these three key site planning characteristics (to the extent that the site plan influences the success of the common house). They are:

1. On the way home (from parking, street, pedestrian paths). This is the most important.

2. Centrally located within the community and visible from as many front porches as possible.

3. As equidistant as possible from all houses.

All three of the above are difficult (even impossible) to achieve. However, the group successfully located the common house centrally. The two common terraces facilitate comfortable conditions in both cool and warm weather and provide a sight line from nearly all houses. In the Common House workshop, it will be important to clearly define these spaces so that activity is still concentrated at the common house so that "activity attracts activity."

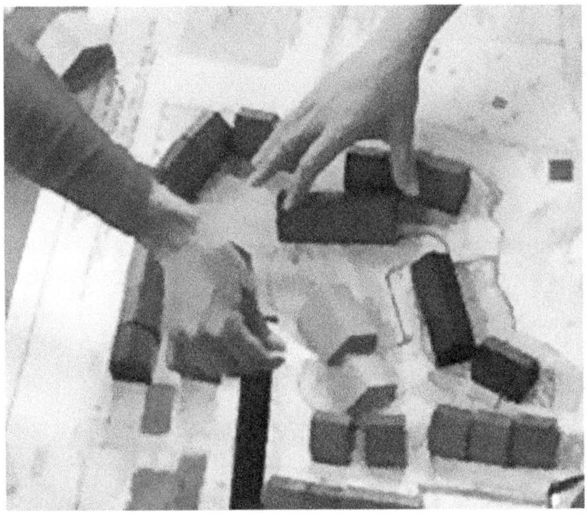

PART 4. CONCLUSION

Workshop Conclusion from Spokane

> *Our job during the Site Planning Workshop is to create the best site plan possible, embodying the individual and collective values of the group. Later we will worry about how to make this compelling vision a reality.*

These words encapsulate the tenor of an intense weekend of brainstorming, discussion, experimentation, and ultimately decision making. The result of these approximately 400 people-hours together (not to mention the logistics) are the design criteria and consensed conceptual site plan included in this program—the physical representation of the group's values and aspirations for community, consisting of the community's goals, desired activities, and planned places detailed in this document.

This is a fine program and I'm proud to say that we got to help facilitate this site layout. Let's hope it sticks. The diagrammatic site plan enclosed provides a good "test" of the design program generated at the participatory workshop and shows that the goals, activities, and places were optimally achieved. This program will morph into a final schematic design, as all of the individual elements are worked out. These elements include the specific house plans, the common house plan, the common terrace, the parking area, and so on. As these elements are worked out, this design program and this layout will be the guide and the yardstick to measure the success of the final schematic site plan.

The site imposed many constraints on the layout. The overall size of the site was ample to accommodate the program but demanded careful consideration of each square foot. The topography also drove the placement of the buildings, especially due to a desire and legal requirements to make units accessible. The existing buildings added another layer of complexity. Especially with regard to Yogashala, the group considered carefully how to create a site plan that embraced the existing building and its future cohousing residents. Finally, the three possible access points to the site yielded a large variety of possible site layouts, from which the group decided to use two to provide vehicular access where needed while maintaining a vehicle-free environment in the heart of the community. This solution was driven by many factors, but primarily the five "Cs":

1. Community: "If it doesn't work socially, why bother?" And if it does work socially, most other things can be worked out.
2. Culture: This must work for us, who we are, and who we want to become. What might be appropriate for a village in the early twenty-first century in Spokane, Washington?

3. Constraints and Opportunities Unique to the Site: Topography, access, sound, existing buildings, and adjacent buildings formed a complex matrix the group worked to address.
4. Climate: Exactly what are the temperatures, rainfall, wind, freeze/thaw cycles, etc. that are experienced here?
5. Costs: The approach of logical building deviations and less of them, and few and replicable houses plays a real role in accomplishing the group's stated goal of affordability. This will be worked out more thoroughly at Workshop 3.

Several themes emerged, which helped lead to the final consensus on a single scheme. About a dozen design solutions were tested, evaluated, and revised. These schemes ranged greatly, including clusters of houses, large courtyards, radial patterns, and street-like layouts. Primary among these themes is the relationship of privacy to community. In most modern American housing development, the private realm and public realm are clearly delineated. Cohousing reintroduces the common realm, a realm cooperatively managed to meet the needs of the community and the individual. The group carefully revised and revised again the location of the houses to ensure as best the group could that the site plan fulfilled the detailed program.

At the same time, the group ensured that the spaces between the buildings created outdoor rooms, terraces, and courtyards to support a rich common realm that supports a variety of activities, from a rambunctious party on the common terrace, to contemplative moments.

Gathering nodes were located so that almost every resident can see one from their own front porch. Also the rows of houses were arranged so that layout encourages a more or less centralized circulation patterns, which encourages community long after the honeymoon period has worn off.

The group also devoted significant effort to planning the parking, outbuildings, and open spaces like gardens, exercise, and tranquil places. In addition, the proposed parking maintains more open space near the path, and leaves the space more useful for the group and gives a more aesthetic border for the neighborhood and for visitors, should they happen along.

We have a great start at creating both community (lanes with buildings on both sides) and economy (few building types), energy efficiency (clustered buildings), and ecology (areas of the site will be left as greenspace). There is really no "one hand clapping" building—an orphan without another building across the lane.

The site plan developed in this workshop is not the only solution, but we believe that it is the best one. Now our job is to develop it further. The finalized schematic site plan will be presented at the Design Closure Workshop (after the Common House and Private House Program Workshops). And these days will be adjusted again when costs come in.

A Note About the Process from Spokane

Obviously, every space will shift. This will happen at later stages in the design process, and will be done when other objective realties step up to play a role, such as the specific house designs from Workshop 3.

Once we brainstormed and discussed, we took a straw poll and called for consensus. Once a proposal was consensed, we moved on, and hundreds of decisions were made in this manner.

However, when someone objected, we discussed and modified—or discussed and deleted—or discussed and left the suggestion as it stood—and then consensed it. I also asked everyone to be very proactive, if not aggressive, about objecting if the suggestion did not make sense to them as the best way for the group to proceed—and we had no problems with that.

In good cohousing process, once consensed, an item is the rule and we move on. On occasion, a decision is revised, but only after some percentage of the group that was in attendance when first making the decision agrees to revisit it. Haystack Heights should decide on a percentage as soon as possible (preferably before Workshop 2).

It is critical that you make any changes to this program in a deliberate fashion—perhaps a decision to revisit a given line item with agreement of two-thirds of the people present at the time of the workshop (that's typical). Reconsidered line items should be given a very tight time frame; trust each other and your decisions. Assuming each item made sense originally, and it was consensed, it is possible not to revisit a single one. For example, the Nevada City Cohousing Site Program was never modified and has proven to be an excellent guide to create an incredible and giving place for 85 people to live for more than eleven years. A few line items will be altered at the Design Closure Workshop in relation to the Common House and Private House Programs, and the site plan. But these changes will only be based on new and compelling architectural information and arguments made to improve the Site Program—not because the Program fundamentally changed. Indeed, I believe that you can successfully proceed with this Site Program and not reconsider it at all until the time of the Design Closure Workshop (based on new information). As I mentioned in the workshop on numerous occasions, the best way to prevent backtracking is to bring new members up to speed by carefully walking them through this program over coffee,

one line item at a time. Then new members get to hear a little of the back story. They get to closely connect with someone from the membership committee and begin to feel connected to the process that created the program and site plan. Ultimately, they will feel better about helping not to backtrack. By not backtracking, the cohousing group moves forward and progresses. They will feel a part of the process and the rest of the group will be happy that new people are not bringing up old stuff. And the group will be happier because they are not abruptly and awkwardly interrupting someone by exclaiming, "we've already talked about that" because they will be in the know as well.

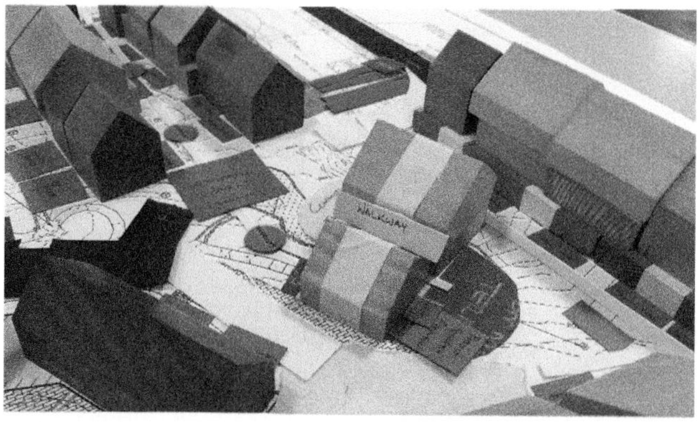

We included lots of data about how many current households would use a proposed line item (x/y hh @ wkshp chickens, x^1/y^1 hh @ wksp hanging clothes, etc.). This data was gathered by using straw polls of a representative sample: households present. Informed by this data, consensus was reached on each line item. Now that consensus has been reached, MOVE FORWARD. These uses, once consensed should live out their potential and not be reconsidered. That's how you get projects built and not move backwards.

Even once consensus has been reached on the schematic design, you will still constantly refer to the program throughout the design and construction process, and even once living there. This is how you get the details right to the extent that you can, and the process then proceeds well beyond the Design Closure Workshop.

Frankly, I use the program right through the construction documentation process, and even during construction itself, to best assure that I don't lose the richness that the group process put on the table. To be honest, we still use our program from time to time and we've been living in our community for 15 years now. The final site plan reveals the aggregate sum of the goals, activities, places and intent as originally consensed. That remains a valuable part of the group's work and history.

One last thought about the fifth "C" after Climate and Culture: Costs (see the five Cs). It's important not to lose sight of Costs. It's all too easy to allow costs to creep up until one day it's all too painfully obvious that someone or some people can't afford a house here. It takes a lot of discipline, but we know that it's very possible to build a place here that everyone loves, if we stay focused.

PART 5. SITE PLAN

Testing the Program

The following Diagrammatic Site Plan represents the plan as consensed upon at the Site Planning Workshop.

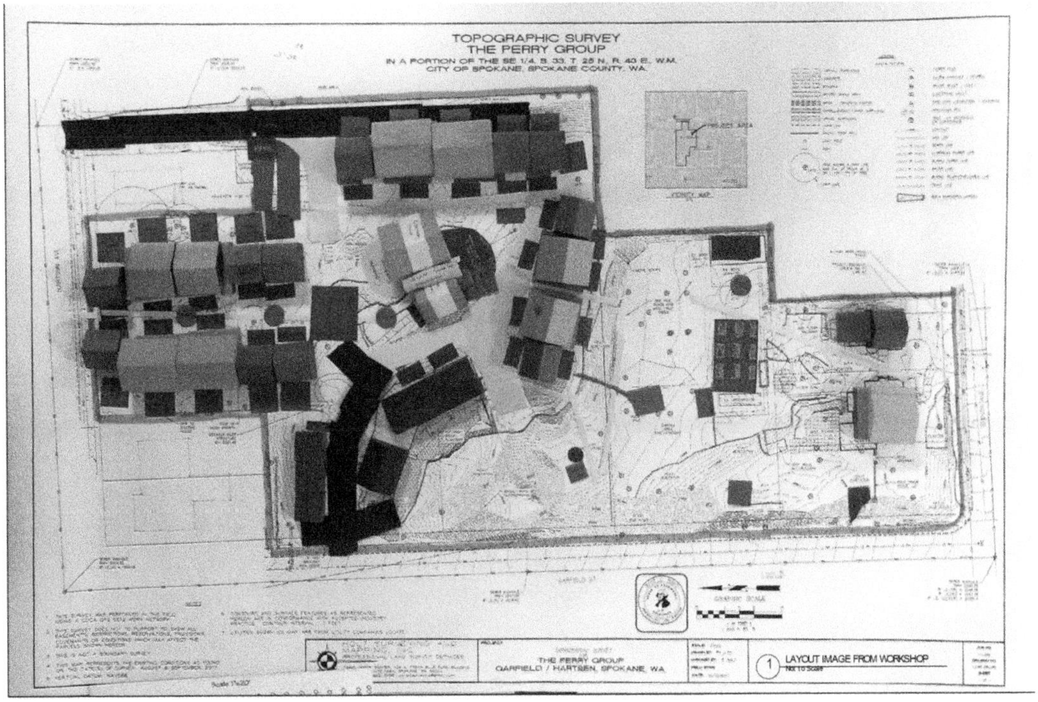

PART 6. PARTICIPANTS

At the October 21–24, 2017
Haystack Heights Site Planning Workshop,
the following participants were in attendance:

Barbara Baumgarten
Dan Baumgarten
Christie Bruntlett
John Bruntlett
Sarah Conover
Jim Dawson
Bill Lockwood
Nikki Lockwood
Mariah McKay
Pat Mertens
Chris Nerison
Ray Owens
Doug Robnett
Abby Roose
Rob Roose
Robin Roose
Sam Schneider
Bob Stilger
Susan Virnig

NEVADA CITY, CA

Great light and warmth are essential to expressing the different times and moods of the day.

NEVADA CITY, CA

Dining has to be comfortable. Some cohousing communities have dinner available in the common house every day. Most people participate two to three times each week. It's a time to catch up on what's going on, but it's not a party or a reception. We're just having dinner, centered and casual. The tables allow for two to three conversations at each table.

COTATI, CA

There's nothing more satisfying than a new common building. It's a place to discuss the issues of the day with neighbors who might not agree with you at first, nor you with them.

NEVADA CITY, CA

Inexpensive, not oversized chairs and tables play a role in people being comfortable. The architecture should say, "Get comfortable, be here." The common house is a place that people spend time voluntarily. So the difference between a 450-people-hour space and a 100-people-hour space is a combination of how inviting the space is for other activities like after-school hangouts, yoga, music, and so on. These uses are successful largely because the architecture and the smiles are inviting. Although there is a primary use, in this case, dining—the space will be used for many other activities. While it is critical that the space is flexible, it should perfectly fit the primary use of dining. It's centered, centripetal, and in every way says, "Be here now."

3

Intergenerational Neighborhood Design

Common House and Common Facilities Design

"Architecture is a social activity that has to do with the communication or places of interaction, and that to change the environment is to change behaviour."

Thom Mayne

The heart of the community, the soul of the place, and the place where you're going to stitch it all together is the common house. When right—the feel, the warmth, the sounds, the smells, the baroque light cascading here and there—the space full of ambient light, and a special sparkle of brilliance aglow. Give it all you've got, craft it, sculpt it, and be the maker; release the frozen music that it wants to be. Let it call out, "Come hither and be with your neighbor, play music, break bread." Let it be the place that calls you, the place where you feel like being, and being yourself. Make it that place, that special place that few can afford by themselves, like that gourmet kitchen that you've always dreamed of. Warm and quiet even with five people in it, with treasured concentration and laughter. You don't sweat it—we've got this—everything is where it's supposed to be. The stage is set, we're at our best.

Cohousing is a glorified dinner club really—but the dinners I've had in all three cohousing communities that I have lived in, about 3,200 dinners now have been amazing. It never detracted from the family—it enhanced it, made us feel like an extended family in a way, but not fully. And not always friends, but always fellow neighbors. We break good bread, their homemade baguettes, and dinner usually averages about $5.00 a person—but who's counting?

Giving it everything you've got to get this dinner made tonight, even if you've only had two hours after work to get everything done. You learn to do it because you're motivated to do it. Your neighbor did it for you last night and your other neighbor did it the night before that. Now, it's your turn and you want to be there for those that were there for you—and not just for making dinner. At dinner, you learned that Susan is going to have a hip replacement next month. And over the next month, you're going to organize dinners to be taken to her house, not only on common dinner nights, but every night until she's up and about again. Neighbors are often ready, willing, and able to help. The possibility to live at our potential is right there—that is, if we know and care about our neighbors. It's not religious, although it could be. It may or may not be spiritual, I'm not sure, but it is very practical. Whether it be babysitters, or temporary caregivers, otherwise having paid strangers walking around certainly isn't practical or pleasant. Eighty-year-old Leal called me at 2:00, 3:00, or even 4:00 in the morning, and said, "Chuck, please come over I need you to help me get Lloyd back into bed" because I gave her permission to call me during dinner. She said "Thanks" as she rushed back home to get Lloyd his dinner. We talked about those early mornings at subsequent dinners in the evening long after Lloyd had passed. I felt like I'm like the person I wanted to be, or at least growing in that direction, and leaning into that person because the opportunity was there.

There is more to the common house than dinner and the conversations. There are kids playing, music, dancing on occasion, planning, and being present. The life I see there is unique to small towns, villages, and high-functioning neighborhoods. Once upon a time, culture put those together, but today, it's an extremely deliberate act, decidedly conscious or "woke," as all of my millennial colleagues like to call it. I'm not a romantic here or even Pollyanna. I'm not trying to evoke what can't happen. I'm just repeating what has been observed, felt, and been nourished by.

NEVADA CITY, CA

Inviting, warm, and cozy—I want to be there.

NEVADA CITY, CA

It has to work socially. If it doesn't work socially, why bother? We're not just making real estate here.

Common: Not Public, Not Private

The wise American architect Louis Sullivan said, "A pine tree is not an oak tree." Nor is a common house a house or a public building. There is no provision in the building code for "common building." You have to work hard to get the local officials to realize that it is not a public building. A public building usually feels too cold, has too much sheetrock, has too little wood, has too little warmth, has plastic baseboards, and so on. You have to know how to respectfully discuss the realities with the building department. In the code, there are provisions to get materials and measurements altered. Of course, keep all of the accessibility stuff, in fact, enhance it. Public would be the default for most architects, because it's the most constringent—it's the "safest" from a bureaucratic point of view. But you have to be able, and more importantly willing, to debate their issues so that you can get the new neighborhood to be how they want—that is, home away from home. It's the place that is an extension of your home, a supplement to your home. For instance, if I have a 1,000 square foot home and a 4,000 square foot common house, then in effect, I have a 5,000 square foot house. However, this only really works if there is a minimum number of people-hours in the common house per week (see Chapter 14, The Details of Cohousing). This only works when it's obvious that the common house is giving and is truly a home away from home. The altogether beloved third place—that place I go to be emotionally safe and nurtured, where I can live out my life goals whether living lighter on the planet or giving and getting the support that makes a community flourish.

There are way too many cases where fire departments have made the common kitchen very inhospitable (excessively noisy, expensive, clammy—too much stainless steel), and only because the officials didn't understand this use and erred on the side of caution. The architect really needs to help here. It is not a restaurant, no one is charged for dinner, there isn't deep fat frying, and it's easy to maintain. With two or three cooks, people are not likely to leave a burner on—they are so much safer than single family houses and it's easy to prove. They do have to sanitize the dishes, mitigate bacteria, insects, and rodents infinitely better than restaurants and 99 percent of houses. This is easy for a common house to accomplish.

It's basically choreography (people and environment) based on what you hope and intend to accomplish. It's based on what I've seen successfully occur, and what I have tried to re-create. It's an art—helping craft that very special place for this very unique subculture. The reverberation, the wood finishes, the noise reduction coefficient, the sound transfer coefficient, the aspect ratio, and the coefficient of friction of the flooring are all considered. So while you're doing the contra shuffle, you won't slip and fall doing a pirouette. Learning the tango, the salsa, and some hip-hop with others is fun. And on those nights, it's the air exchanges per hour that count—at least six or seven or eight.

NEVADA CITY, CA

Open Kitchen. Kyle appreciates the accolades of his neighbors while he cooks dinner for everyone. The kitchen opens to the terrace outside, to the circulation, and to the dining room.

Kyle is the hero of the day on this evening. In a more closed kitchen with reduced apertures, the cook is the servant for the day. As an architect, it is easy to make Kyle the hero for the day or the servant for the day, one more wall or impediment and the observers are having their own conversation while Kyle is left out.

NEVADA CITY, CA

Family-style dining. When you walk in the door, it's as if your mom or dad set the table. You can just walk in and sit down without all of the churn, except we all get to take turns being mom or dad— it's gratifying.

NEVADA CITY, CA

Open Kitchen. Those interfacing with cooks in the kitchen should be outside of the kitchen. That way, a diner can acknowledge their appreciation for the cooks without being in the way.

NEVADA CITY, CA

Breaking bread together is an essential element in a high-functioning neighborhood and a timeless way to stitch a community together in the long-term. Acoustics, lighting, warmth, function, and circulation must all be just right to optimize the experience. We stress and reiterate this point because it is all too often missed.

NEVADA CITY, CA

A place for extended conversation after dinner is more or less the point. If it doesn't work socially, why bother?

BELLINGHAM, WA

Neighborhoods that work build everlasting relationships.

NEVADA CITY, CA

Done right, the experience lasts long after the meal is finished.

NEVADA CITY, CA

An assembly in the neighborhood focusing on the kids, reviving the notion that everyone benefits when they take stock in how well the children are doing.

NEVADA CITY, CA

The common house dining room is used for so much more than just dining, for example, square dancing, music, yoga, talent contests, "TED" talks, common meetings, robot competitions—you name it.

NEVADA CITY, CA

In a high-functioning neighborhood, neighbors get together from time to time to play music.

NEVADA CITY, CA

. . .making Valentine's Day/holiday cards.

NEVADA CITY, CA

The monthly management meeting generates the fifth highest use of the common house during that week. Meetings come after dining, laundry, cooking, and children hanging out in the kids' room. Next is managing the ranch collectively. In low-functioning condominium projects there is a five-person board. In apartments, independent care, or almost any other multi-family housing project, there is an owner that determines management. In a high-functioning community, every adult is on the managing board. These meetings take about two hours each month. Consense when done right makes everything go faster, makes decisions stick, and is the only way to preserve minority rights. But consent means I consent to doing it this way—it might not be how I would do it.

NEVADA CITY, CA

After hours of playing in the "wild" area one Saturday, there is a rehearsal preparing to play in a nursing home the next day.

COMMON HOUSE DESIGN

For dinner to work, it must have:

Excellent acoustics, 0.7–0.85-seconds reverberation and 65 STC between rooms.

Excellent natural light, 50–100-foot candles. More fixture lighting for cleaning.

Excellent ventilation, up to eight full air exchanges per hour.

A warm, giving, cozy feel (hyggelig) using wood and natural materials.

Excellently functioning spaces (not too big or too small) and no cross-circulation.

A LOCAL POLITICIAN INVITED TO DINNER.

NEVADA CITY, CA

No room in the community is limited to one use. Most importantly, the dining room must be a great place to dine and converse with others. At the same time, it must be a great place to make holiday cards among its many dozens of uses.

NEVADA CITY, CA

The common house should feel warm and inviting, even with the low light of dawn and even if you're the only one there. Whether it's using the gourmet kitchen, listening to the radio, or reading in the sitting room, it has to be the place that you feel comfortable and are comfortable. It evokes fond memories of last month's dance or last night's dinner.

NEVADA CITY, CA

. . .in practice. Democracy at the micro, but incubator scale—a microcosm for national politics. "Sure, we can fix that chipper, but exactly what budget line item are we using?" The Minister of Health and the Minister of Taxes lived in cohousing in Denmark. I asked him (Carsten Koch) how that happened. He said that he learned it all from living in a functioning neighborhood where they met to manage the village. That's great preparation for public management.

NEVADA CITY, CA

There are so many uses for the common spaces, and they all have to be understood in the program phase so that they can be adequately considered in the design phase. When it was understood that there would be dancing, then the right friction, slippery, but not too slippery, can be considered. A floating floor was installed, that is, a floor that gives 1/8" of cushion which is easy on the feet, the knees, and the hips. These kinds of details augment the number of people-hours both consciously and subconsciously.

NEVADA CITY, CA

The common house kitchen is always the most gourmet kitchen on the site, if not in the town. If 40 people are showing up for dinner, you want to hear that throaty sound of 15,000 BTUs of heat on the top burner (normal stove tops are 7,000 to 8,000 BTUs) when the spaghetti water isn't boiling yet and the throaty sound of a 30,000 BTU oven (normal ovens are about 20,000 BTU) when the homemade bread is not quite ready for dinner.

NEVADA CITY, CA

The oven needs 30,000 BTUs minimum so that the residents can, for example, make bread before dinner, have it come out piping hot, and ready on time.

NEVADA CITY, CA

The common house is used late into the evening by small pods of people. Make sure that the lighting makes sense whether it's 6 people or 60 people. The Danish word hyggelig is the operative concept. Cozy, warm, giving.

NEVADA CITY, CA

Game night after dinner can be most nights for whoever shows up.

NEVADA CITY, CA

. . . and often birthday parties.

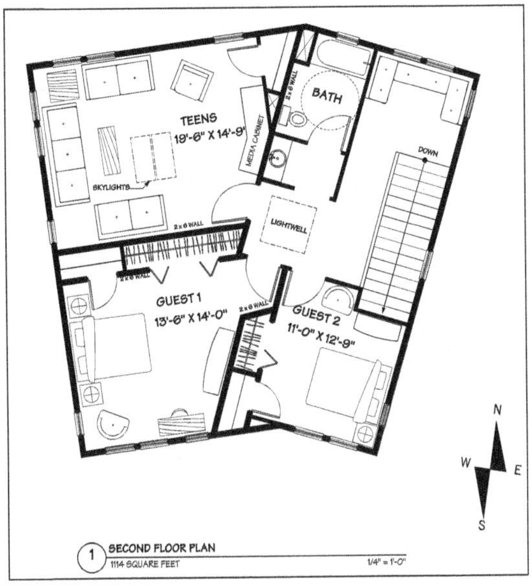

NEVADA CITY, CA

The second floor of the Nevada City common house is a refuge. Some people might assume that a teens' room near the guest rooms might be a problem. But in 15 years, it hasn't been. First of all, there is a lot of acoustic separation between them. Secondly, the teens know that they have to be quiet if guests are there. One Saturday night, I knocked and entered the teens room and there were 21 kids in the room including my 16-year-old daughter, listening to music and hanging out. Of them, 10 lived in the community and 11 did not. They were having a sleepover on the common terrace that night. Interestingly enough, the next morning the *Sunday New York Times* carried an article about raising teens safely. The article read, after listing dire safety statistics about teens, "The safest thing to do with teens is to keep them home." But teens want to be where the action is, so keep the action near home. Just pop over to the teen room and say howdy any time. Yes, high-functioning neighborhoods, neighborhood planning, and design can and should (but rarely do) address real societal issues like teen drinking, teen driving (the highest cause of death of teens in North America), and teen pregnancy.

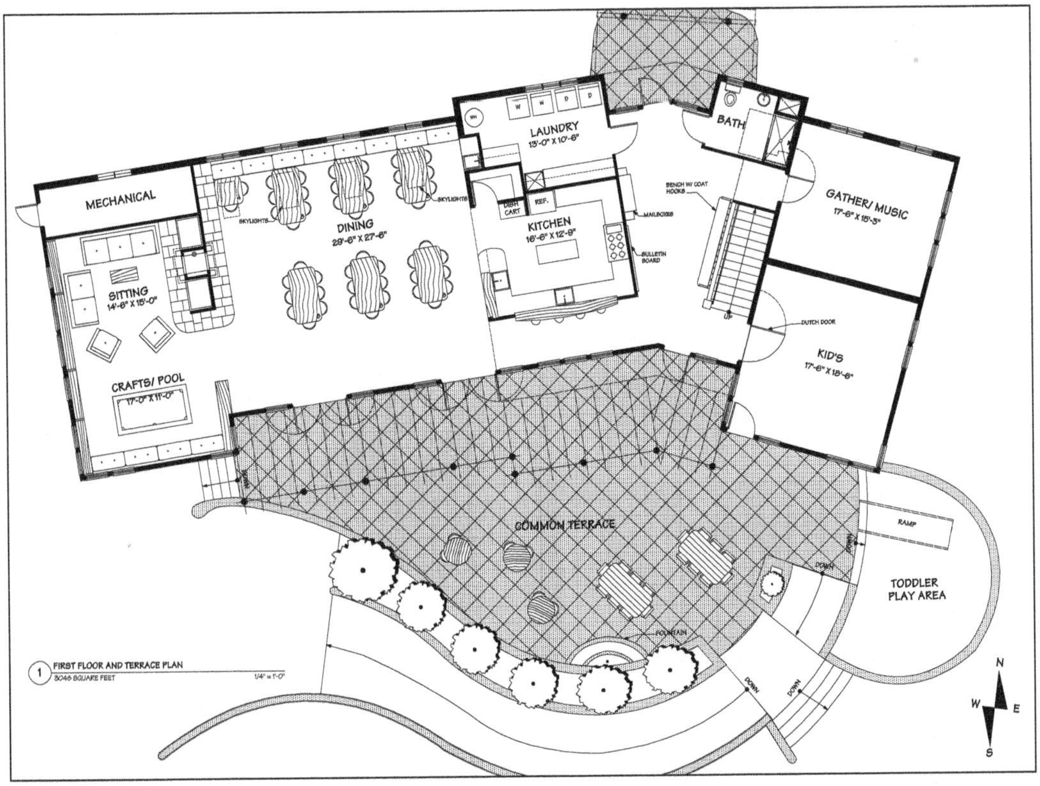

NEVADA CITY, CA

The slope of the site and the curved north property line presented both opportunities and challenges throughout the design process. One opportunity was for the building to embrace the terrace and, in doing so, the community on the south side. Every time that the common terrace is at the same height as the surrounding sidewalk circulation in the landscape, the community has complained. And it makes sense. People sitting at the common terrace always want their heads to be at least as high while sitting as people walking by, or perhaps a little higher. People sitting at the common terrace prefer a commanding view of the community. To wave, to watch the children, or to see if an 85-year-old needs help getting up the ramp in his/her walker.

NEVADA CITY, CA

Dinner at Nevada City Cohousing. It's critical that the room is the right size to function correctly. The acoustics are perfect, the lighting is cozy, the feel is warm and friendly (hyg-gelig), the circulation is not disruptive ever (no cross-circulation) and the room is clearly functional. These are all important factors in designing a successful common house.

NEVADA CITY, CA

Good acoustics in the common house starts with a rectilinear dining table. Between 2′4″ and 2′6″ is all you want the width to be; 2′4″ works well because you can speak to the person across the table with your normal voice. If you have to raise your voice at your table, then the people behind you have to speak louder as well. Then, everyone in the room is speaking loudly and wearing out their larynges. This table sits six to eight people comfortably, and there can readily be two or three conversations at the table at the same time. The best thing about 2′4″ wide by 6′8″ long and 1.75″ thick tables is that you can just purchase a flush, solid core door and then add legs. These legs are made from melted down car parts. A very inexpensive way to go.

NEVADA CITY, CA

The sitting room in the common building is where the lights go out last in the neighborhood. It's where the late night folks are watching the news together, playing pool, or having a cup of tea. It's safer emotionally to watch the news with others.

NEVADA CITY, CA

Dance performances, talent shows, and innumerable other larger neighborhood activities are best accomplished in the common dining room.

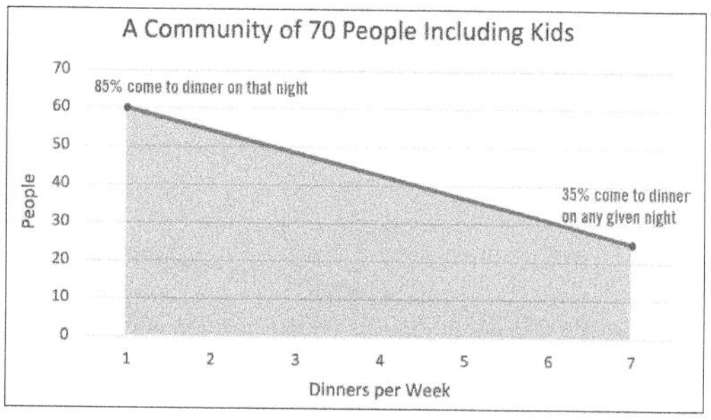

When 60 people show up, there's more noise, more chaos, more churn. That's what happens in a cohousing when dinner is only offered once a week. It's harder to have a deep and meaningful conversation. There's too much going on. Katie and I lived in a community in Denmark for six months that had dinner on the table seven nights a week for three reasons. One, they were calmer and smaller, making it easier for the cooks, and making it easier to have real conversations. Two, the cooks wouldn't have to work so hard, cooking for fewer people and more relaxed all around for them as well. And third, common dinner is the epitome of why people say that they move into cohousing. It makes life more convenient (someone else is shopping, cooking, and cleaning up and therefore I have more time), more economical (dinners run $3–$6 per night, maybe some with fresh veggies right out of the garden), makes life healthier (where you're only making dinner once a month—at least there), and more choice of community or privacy (eat at home or at the common house, the average is three times per week per person in the common house), and to make life more interesting and fun. And it does all that and more.

NEVADA CITY, CA

A future resident and co-planner of this common house made the point, "If we don't have a pool table, then the adults will never get to know the teenagers in their neighborhood." He was right. Teenagers that we all knew by name for years, but had never talked to, revealed their personalities at the pool table discussion.

NEVADA CITY, CA

Knowing that baking, chopping, and frying will be the main uses of the common house kitchen, you have to design it so that no fire department will misconstrue it for a commercial kitchen. Commercial kitchens become more expensive and will invariably create an institutional place that is not welcoming. At the same time, like everywhere else in the common house, it should be warm and giving and build community.

However, the most important aspect of creating a successful common house is that the building must be designed so that the food is on the table when the diners walk in. Too many miss this simple point. Simple is fine—salad, soup, and bread are plenty. No one complains about how simple the dinner is—good conversation will make it complicated enough. But the reality is, buffet self-service meals create so much more dropping of silverware, noise, and overall churn in the common house.

Additionally, no establishment that I have given the pre-programming talk to has installed a round table. They are not flexible and they require a second set of rectangular tables for big, around the table functions, meetings, crafts, and so on. Round tables make conversing so much more difficult. For a round table, there is either cross-talk or one person giving a speech who has to raise their voice so that everyone can hear them.

NEVADA CITY, CA

The sitting room is a great place to bring people together for the Super Bowl, World Series, NBA Playoffs, and the candidates' debates.

NEVADA CITY, CA

They started knitting at 10 a.m. and at 4 p.m. on this wintery Saturday, they were still at it.

NEVADA CITY, CA

Even the politicians like to come do their presentations in our sitting room. When rich people are the only ones with ample space, then they are the only ones heard. Thirteen schoolteachers live here, and one of them asked Tom, who was campaigning for judge, to come to the common house. That way, we might get the benefit of the doubt, should the need arise.

NEVADA CITY, CA

Goal: A place for the teens to be away from the house, but not away from the neighborhood.

NEVADA CITY, CA

Perches in the common house are just as important as perches in the site plan. People can just sit nearby when they need to, for example, a nonparent tutoring a child with their homework.

NEVADA CITY, CA

In a high-functioning neighborhood, if there is an adult that plays, others can learn to play an instrument as well.

NEVADA CITY, CA

When weather permits, this neighborhood has both formal and informal lunches or dinners outside on the common terrace.

NEVADA CITY, CA

The common terrace—a nexus, a place of continuous life, "the town square" in a high-functioning neighborhood.

NEVADA CITY, CA

One person playing a violin on the common terrace leads to others playing their violins on the common terrace, or maybe more with guitars, drums, and so on. High-functioning neighborhoods allow for an emerging culture of performing and visual arts.

NEVADA CITY, CA

The common terrace is a place of constant interest. Remember, all of these people are here voluntarily. If they wanted to be home, they would be home.

NEVADA CITY, CA

Often referred by the Danes as the backbone of the community, the common terrace certainly provides the opportunity for a lot of use every week.

NEVADA CITY, CA

When designed correctly, the common terrace never fails to be the nexus of consequence.

NEVADA CITY, CA

Dinner on the common terrace—a major source of people-hours in Nevada City Cohousing.

NEVADA CITY, CA

Outdoor neighborhood meetings during the COVID-19 pandemic. It's easy to have dining on the common terrace during a pandemic. Socially separated, but not socially isolated. At the time of this writing, there have been no cases of COVID at this cohousing.

NEVADA CITY, CA

Parking on the left, then the progression past the common house to see if the lights are on in the sitting room, the music room, the children's room, the dining room, or if there's life on the terrace. This kind of progression gives the community a heartbeat.

NEVADA CITY, CA

From the parking lot, the windows (except those to the entry) are small. The building embraces the gardens, the children, the sun, the people. The north windows should be small to conserve energy in this cold climate, and to prevent car headlights intruding inside.

NEVADA CITY SKETCH

Early sketch of the common house. When the design was finished, the common terrace was refined numerous times, but this sketch captured the essence of what it was trying to accomplish—a neighborhood gathering place. And as it turns out, this neighborhood turned into a village of sorts—it has been that successful. So, this space turned out to be the central village gathering node.

NEVADA CITY, CA

There is no end to the intercultural sharing in a high-functioning neighborhood. While the environment has to be ready, the key is to design for who residents want to be in the future. It's not that the future won't take care of itself, but it needs to be accommodated. With dining for 50 people being the number one activity on the common terrace, which by itself instills flexibility, it is the birthplace of ideas and intentions. This Day of the Dead memorial turned out to be very moving and discussion-provoking.

COTATI, CA

An after-dinner get-together in the sitting room.

COTATI, CA

Having a place to let off steam that is not in your home is central. As B.J. Brazelton says, "Don't create a 'no' environment." Rules like "don't run," "don't jump," etc. do not help children explore and grow. Give them a place to express themselves, to explore, or to explode if they have to.

COTATI, CA

Workshops play a big role in cohousing, co-living, and even affordable housing. People naturally want to get together to build stuff, repair stuff, and ostensibly save money. Although workshops are actually more for building community than building stuff.

COTATI, CA

The common terrace works best when it is embracing and when there is an obvious sense of place.

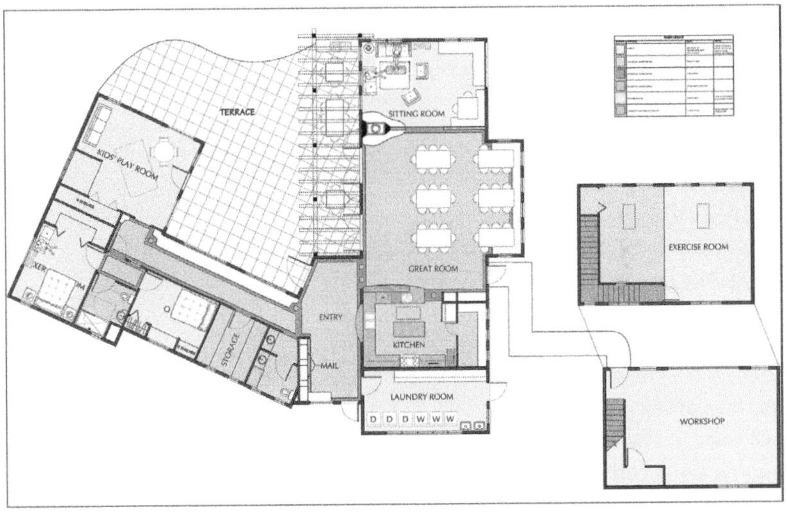

COTATI, CA

The common house often reconciles the irregular geometry on the site. The common house is infinitely more malleable than the private houses. The private houses have to stay regular in order to stay economical. If you're going to have a one-off, make it the common house.

SANTA CRUZ, CA

The common terrace and part of the common facilities are on the second floor at Walnut Commons in Santa Cruz. It is situated half a floor above street level with all of the parking below the building.

a. Kitchen
b. Dining Room
c. Sitting & Crafts
d. Ping Pong (other activities to include yoga, meditation, kids play)
e. Guest Room
f. Office
g. Laundry
h. Mail Room
i. Outdoor Kitchen
j. Common Terrace

Key dimensions are required in the dining room. Any larger and the common house loses its intimacy, people don't use it as much, it feels more vacuous, and it costs more. Any less and people feel cramped, constantly bump into each other, and don't use it as often. If it feels awkward in any way, people avoid common dinner and don't even know why—it's subconscious. Common dinners are not like restaurants because it's a special night out, or a wedding reception where the crowding is part of the fun. "We're just having dinner; I want it to be as comfortable as home or more so."

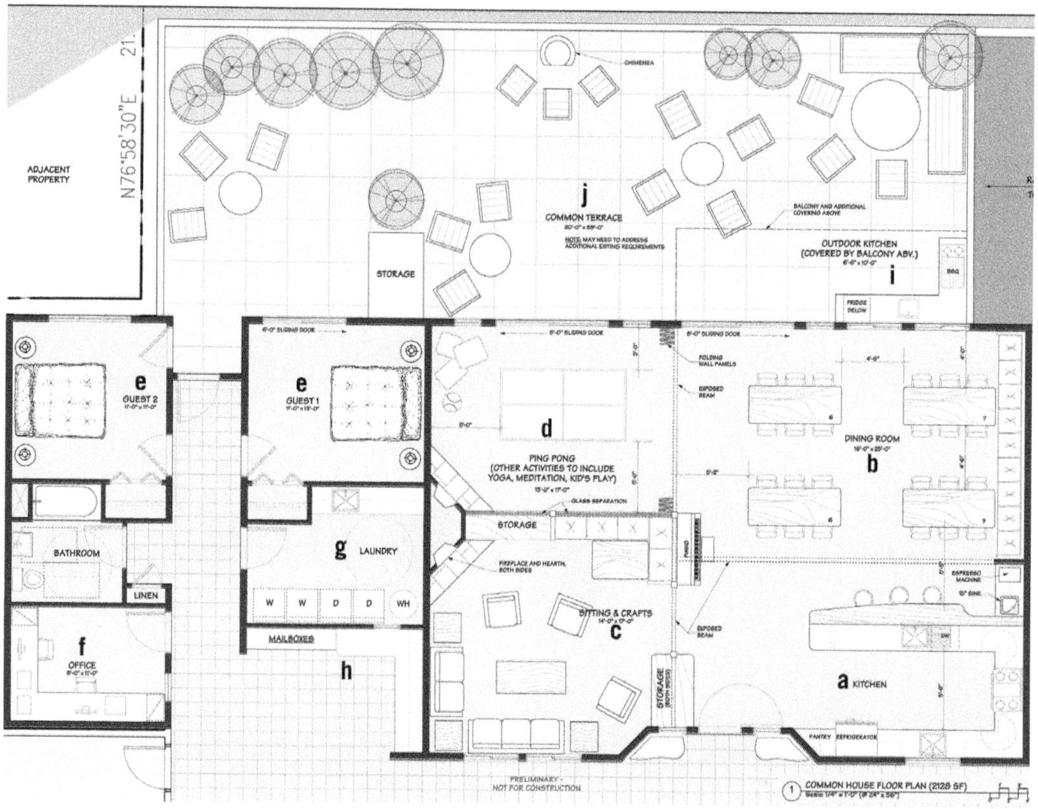

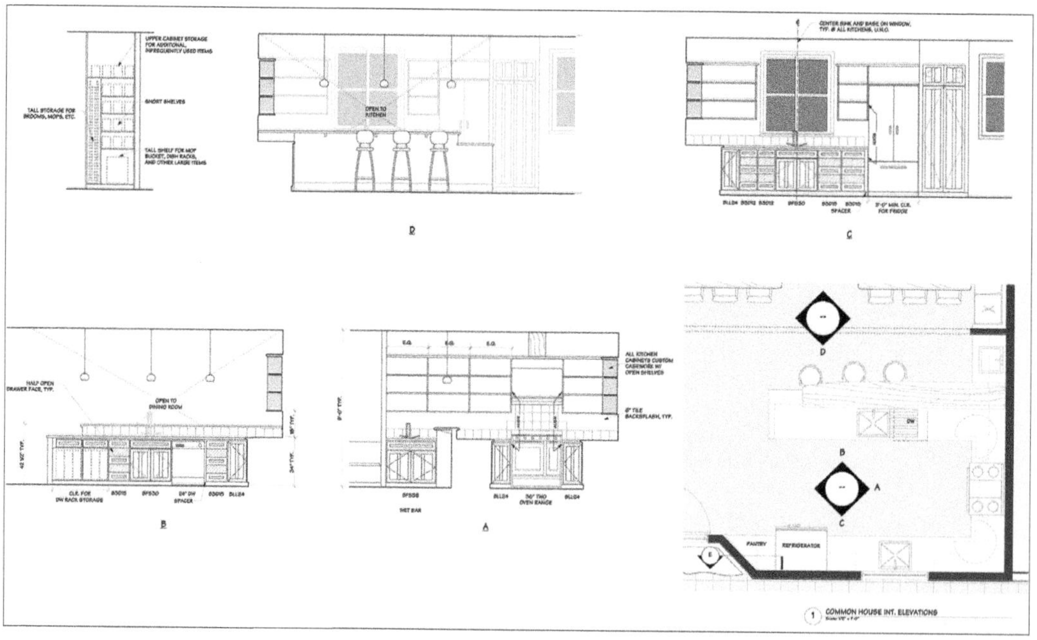

SANTA CRUZ, CA

The common kitchen for cohousing is cozy, brief, and economical, but extremely efficient. The dishwasher only takes 2.9 minutes, the refrigerator is only $7/month, the oven is 30,000 BTU, and the top burners are 7,500 BTUs. The pre-rinse makes short work of the dishes and the pull-out open shelves means that if I only cook once a month, I still know where everything is. This is as small as a kitchen can get in cohousing.

SANTA CRUZ, CA

One goal of high-functioning neighborhoods has always been to make it possible for the American middle class to consume much less, for less.

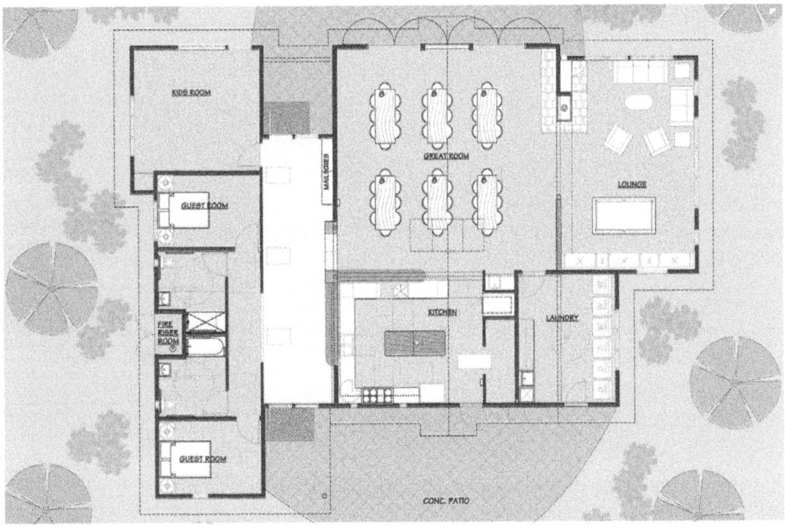

SPOKANE, WA

The all-important sitting room (on the far east/right side) is out of view to half of the houses. It's critical, because it's the last place where the lights are on at night—where people watch the news and other programs together.

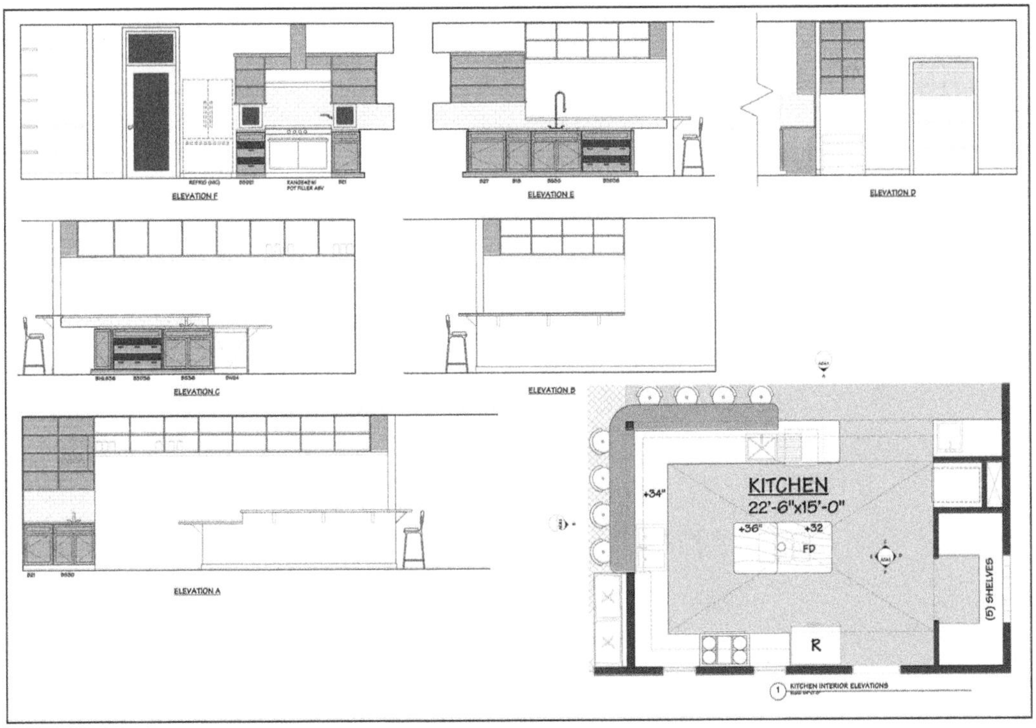

SPOKANE, WA

A better example of a bigger kitchen in cohousing.

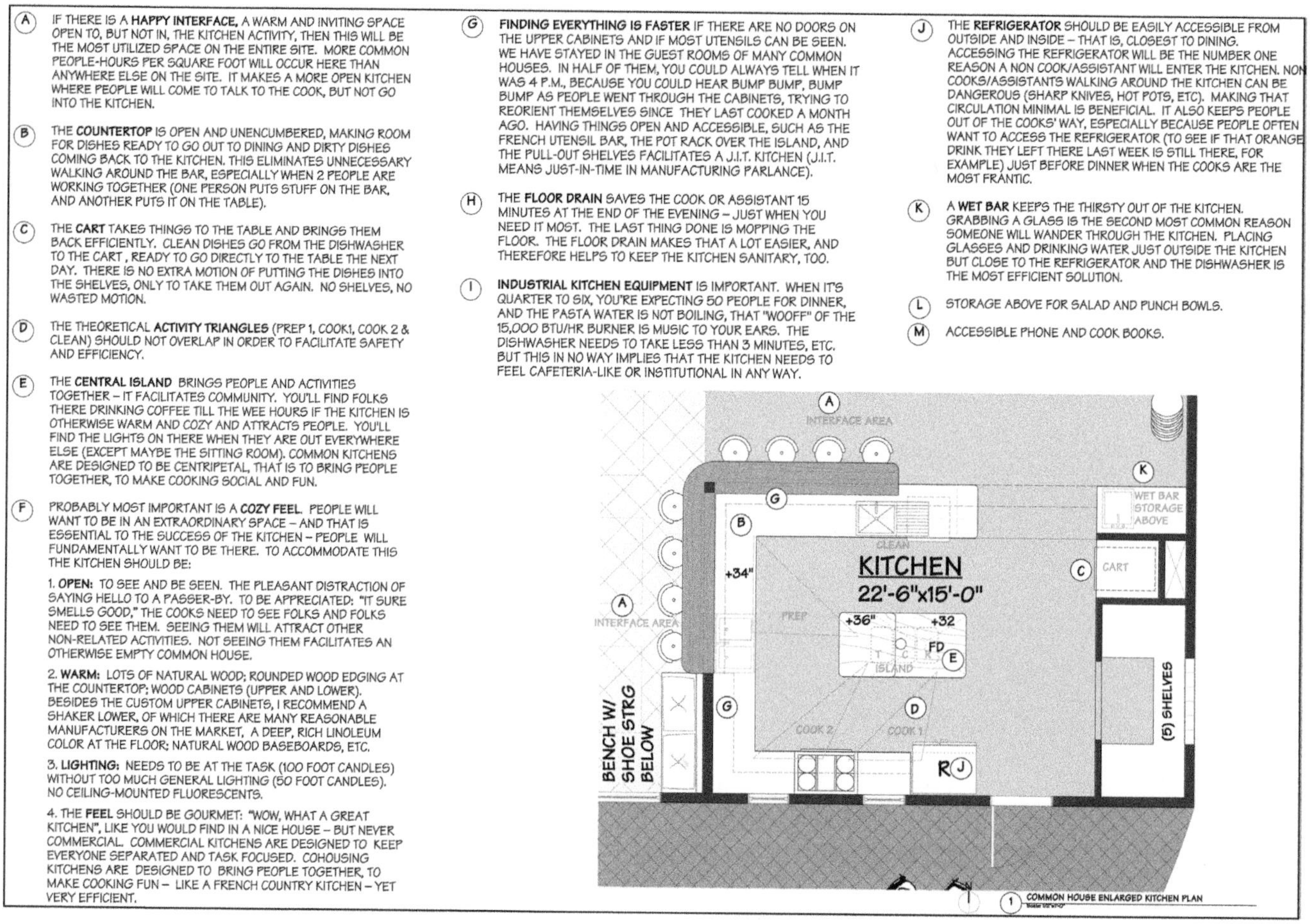

(A) IF THERE IS A HAPPY INTERFACE, A WARM AND INVITING SPACE OPEN TO, BUT NOT IN, THE KITCHEN ACTIVITY, THEN THIS WILL BE THE MOST UTILIZED SPACE ON THE ENTIRE SITE. MORE COMMON PEOPLE-HOURS PER SQUARE FOOT WILL OCCUR HERE THAN ANYWHERE ELSE ON THE SITE. IT MAKES A MORE OPEN KITCHEN WHERE PEOPLE WILL COME TO TALK TO THE COOK, BUT NOT GO INTO THE KITCHEN.
(B) THE COUNTERTOP IS OPEN AND UNENCUMBERED, MAKING ROOM FOR DISHES READY TO GO OUT TO DINING AND DIRTY DISHES COMING BACK TO THE KITCHEN. THIS ELIMINATES UNNECESSARY WALKING AROUND THE BAR, ESPECIALLY WHEN 2 PEOPLE ARE WORKING TOGETHER (ONE PERSON PUTS STUFF ON THE BAR, AND ANOTHER PUTS IT ON THE TABLE).
(C) THE CART TAKES THINGS TO THE TABLE AND BRINGS THEM BACK EFFICIENTLY. CLEAN DISHES GO FROM THE DISHWASHER TO THE CART, READY TO GO DIRECTLY TO THE TABLE THE NEXT DAY. THERE IS NO EXTRA MOTION OF PUTTING THE DISHES INTO THE SHELVES, ONLY TO TAKE THEM OUT AGAIN. NO SHELVES, NO WASTED MOTION.
(D) THE THEORETICAL ACTIVITY TRIANGLES (PREP 1, COOK1, COOK 2 & CLEAN) SHOULD NOT OVERLAP IN ORDER TO FACILITATE SAFETY AND EFFICIENCY.
(E) THE CENTRAL ISLAND BRINGS PEOPLE AND ACTIVITIES TOGETHER – IT FACILITATES COMMUNITY. YOU'LL FIND FOLKS THERE DRINKING COFFEE TILL THE WEE HOURS IF THE KITCHEN IS OTHERWISE WARM AND COZY AND ATTRACTS PEOPLE. YOU'LL FIND THE LIGHTS ON THERE WHEN THEY ARE OUT EVERYWHERE ELSE (EXCEPT MAYBE THE SITTING ROOM). COMMON KITCHENS ARE DESIGNED TO BE CENTRIPETAL, THAT IS TO BRING PEOPLE TOGETHER, TO MAKE COOKING SOCIAL AND FUN.
(F) PROBABLY MOST IMPORTANT IS A COZY FEEL. PEOPLE WILL WANT TO BE IN AN EXTRAORDINARY SPACE – AND THAT IS ESSENTIAL TO THE SUCCESS OF THE KITCHEN – PEOPLE WILL FUNDAMENTALLY WANT TO BE THERE. TO ACCOMMODATE THIS THE KITCHEN SHOULD BE:
1. OPEN: TO SEE AND BE SEEN. THE PLEASANT DISTRACTION OF SAYING HELLO TO A PASSER-BY. TO BE APPRECIATED: "IT SURE SMELLS GOOD," THE COOKS NEED TO SEE FOLKS AND FOLKS NEED TO SEE THEM. SEEING THEM WILL ATTRACT OTHER NON-RELATED ACTIVITIES. NOT SEEING THEM FACILITATES AN OTHERWISE EMPTY COMMON HOUSE.
2. WARM: LOTS OF NATURAL WOOD; ROUNDED WOOD EDGING AT THE COUNTERTOP; WOOD CABINETS (UPPER AND LOWER). BESIDES THE CUSTOM UPPER CABINETS, I RECOMMEND A SHAKER LOWER, OF WHICH THERE ARE MANY REASONABLE MANUFACTURERS ON THE MARKET. A DEEP, RICH LINOLEUM COLOR AT THE FLOOR; NATURAL WOOD BASEBOARDS, ETC.
3. LIGHTING: NEEDS TO BE AT THE TASK (100 FOOT CANDLES) WITHOUT TOO MUCH GENERAL LIGHTING (50 FOOT CANDLES). NO CEILING-MOUNTED FLUORESCENTS.
4. THE FEEL SHOULD BE GOURMET: "WOW, WHAT A GREAT KITCHEN", LIKE YOU WOULD FIND IN A NICE HOUSE – BUT NEVER COMMERCIAL. COMMERCIAL KITCHENS ARE DESIGNED TO KEEP EVERYONE SEPARATED AND TASK FOCUSED. COHOUSING KITCHENS ARE DESIGNED TO BRING PEOPLE TOGETHER, TO MAKE COOKING FUN – LIKE A FRENCH COUNTRY KITCHEN – YET VERY EFFICIENT.
(G) FINDING EVERYTHING IS FASTER IF THERE ARE NO DOORS ON THE UPPER CABINETS AND IF MOST UTENSILS CAN BE SEEN. WE HAVE STAYED IN THE GUEST ROOMS OF MANY COMMON HOUSES. IN HALF OF THEM, YOU COULD ALWAYS TELL WHEN IT WAS 4 P.M., BECAUSE YOU COULD HEAR BUMP BUMP, BUMP BUMP AS PEOPLE WENT THROUGH THE CABINETS, TRYING TO REORIENT THEMSELVES SINCE THEY LAST COOKED A MONTH AGO. HAVING THINGS OPEN AND ACCESSIBLE, SUCH AS THE FRENCH UTENSIL BAR, THE POT RACK OVER THE ISLAND, AND THE PULL-OUT SHELVES FACILITATES A J.I.T. KITCHEN (J.I.T. MEANS JUST-IN-TIME IN MANUFACTURING PARLANCE).
(H) THE FLOOR DRAIN SAVES THE COOK OR ASSISTANT 15 MINUTES AT THE END OF THE EVENING – JUST WHEN YOU NEED IT MOST. THE LAST THING DONE IS MOPPING THE FLOOR. THE FLOOR DRAIN MAKES THAT A LOT EASIER, AND THEREFORE HELPS TO KEEP THE KITCHEN SANITARY, TOO.
(I) INDUSTRIAL KITCHEN EQUIPMENT IS IMPORTANT. WHEN IT'S QUARTER TO SIX, YOU'RE EXPECTING 50 PEOPLE FOR DINNER, AND THE PASTA WATER IS NOT BOILING, THAT "WOOFF" OF THE 15,000 BTU/HR BURNER IS MUSIC TO YOUR EARS. THE DISHWASHER NEEDS TO TAKE LESS THAN 3 MINUTES, ETC. BUT THIS IN NO WAY IMPLIES THAT THE KITCHEN NEEDS TO FEEL CAFETERIA-LIKE OR INSTITUTIONAL IN ANY WAY.
(J) THE REFRIGERATOR SHOULD BE EASILY ACCESSIBLE FROM OUTSIDE AND INSIDE – THAT IS, CLOSEST TO DINING. ACCESSING THE REFRIGERATOR WILL BE THE NUMBER ONE REASON A NON COOK/ASSISTANT WILL ENTER THE KITCHEN. NON COOKS/ASSISTANTS WALKING AROUND THE KITCHEN CAN BE DANGEROUS (SHARP KNIVES, HOT POTS, ETC). MAKING THAT CIRCULATION MINIMAL IS BENEFICIAL. IT ALSO KEEPS PEOPLE OUT OF THE COOKS' WAY, ESPECIALLY BECAUSE PEOPLE OFTEN WANT TO ACCESS THE REFRIGERATOR (TO SEE IF THAT ORANGE DRINK THEY LEFT THERE LAST WEEK IS STILL THERE, FOR EXAMPLE) JUST BEFORE DINNER WHEN THE COOKS ARE THE MOST FRANTIC.
(K) A WET BAR KEEPS THE THIRSTY OUT OF THE KITCHEN. GRABBING A GLASS IS THE SECOND MOST COMMON REASON SOMEONE WILL WANDER THROUGH THE KITCHEN. PLACING GLASSES AND DRINKING WATER JUST OUTSIDE THE KITCHEN BUT CLOSE TO THE REFRIGERATOR AND THE DISHWASHER IS THE MOST EFFICIENT SOLUTION.
(L) STORAGE ABOVE FOR SALAD AND PUNCH BOWLS.
(M) ACCESSIBLE PHONE AND COOK BOOKS.
INTERFACE AREA
KITCHEN
22'-6"x15'-0"
WET BAR STORAGE ABOVE
CART
CLEAN
PREP
ISLAND
COOK 2
COOK 1
FD
+34"
+36"
+32
BENCH W/ SHOE STRG BELOW
(5) SHELVES
1 COMMON HOUSE ENLARGED KITCHEN PLAN

SPOKANE, WA

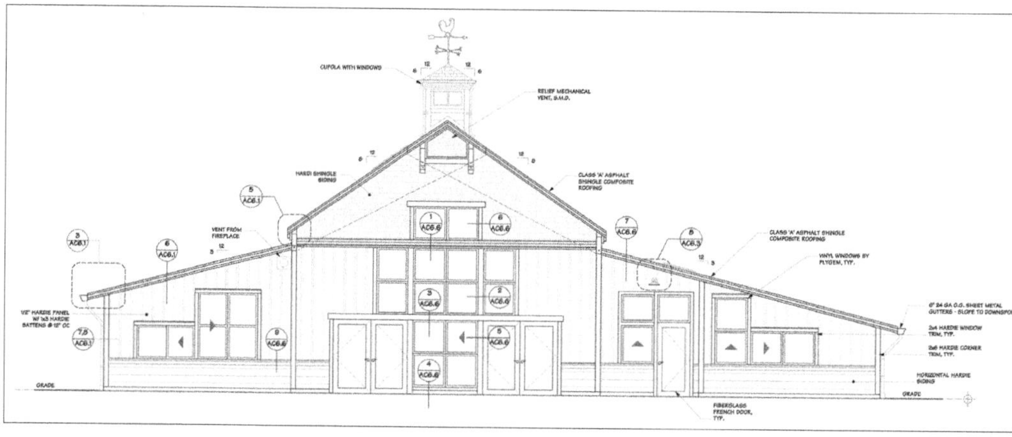

SPOKANE, WA

North elevation, reminiscent of rural culture in Washington State—the vineyards in particular.

SPOKANE, WA

Cupola with windows, essential in this case.

Once in a while, kids love getting together with other kids at dinner. They usually sit with their parents, but on occasion they sit with each other.

PLEASANT HILL, CA

One person cooking and two people entertaining. This is timeless neighborhood making.

YARROW ECOVILLAGE, B.C.

The Yarrow Common House

The common house, colorful, and in this case, at the center of the village. It is nearly equidistant from every house. Make it the flower that attracts people to go there to do laundry before dinner, and to linger after dinner. Make an attractive place for the adults, the teenagers, the kids, the cooks, the musician, the artists—everyone.

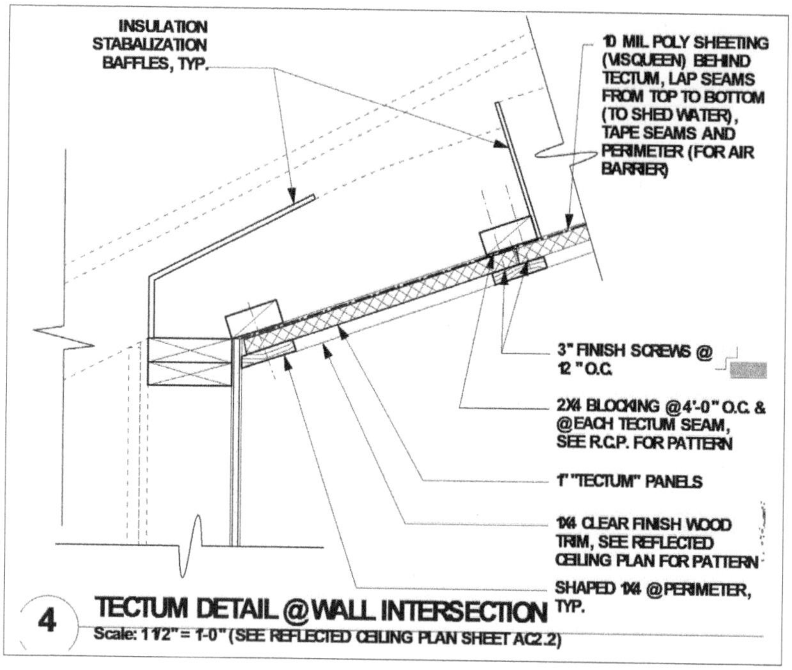

The most important detail in the common house. Sound has to have somewhere to go and something to do when it gets there. The scissor truss above the dining room ceiling makes a 3-foot-high shock absorber keeping reverberation to 0.75–0.85 seconds in the common dining room, and that is very acceptable. Over one second, the reverberation in the room is unbearable.

BELLINGHAM, WA

Workshops save the group money later on.

Legacy common house for an existing single-family-house neighborhood. This is the future—existing neighbors making a common building together. Two new common houses in the area inspired an existing neighborhood to make their own, accomplished with The Cohousing Company, capable contractors, and a lot of sweat equity.

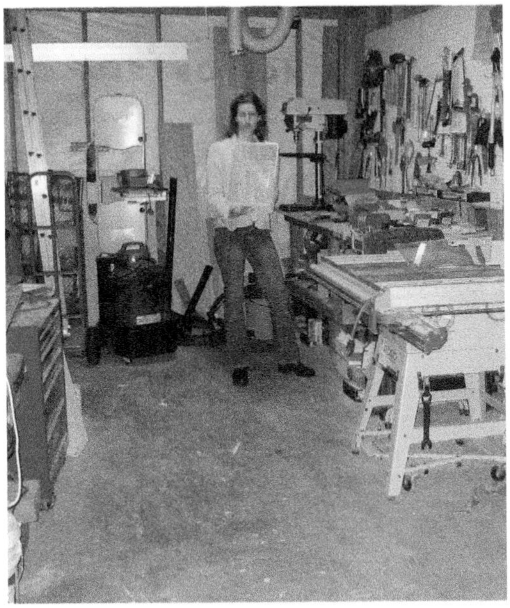

Even a one-room workshop for a 32-unit urban project can work.

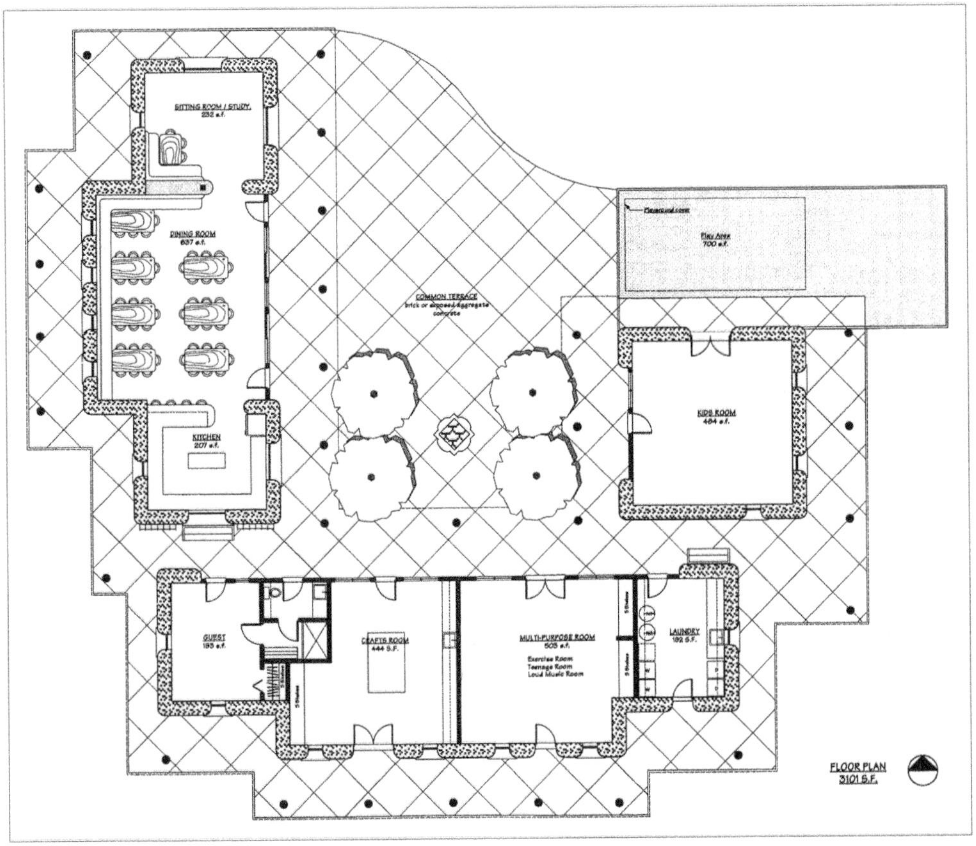

TUSCON STRAW BALE COMMON HOUSE PLAN

A perfect climate for straw bale construction. The 1,000 bales were placed by the group.

COMMON HOUSE PROGRAMMING INTRODUCTION

The only way to understand a culture is through a deliberate process of brainstorming, discussing, and deciding by consensus together, then prioritizing. There are lots of anthropological ways to understand the essence of a group's values such as bubble sorting a list or prioritizing the potential common facilities, as shown here. For example, this process could begin by comparing dining together or having a workshop—comparing them as if you could only have one. Dining together wins. Next, you would compare having a workshop or a guest room in the common house and so on until all 30 possibilities are prioritized in a clear order. Then the possibilities from 1 to 12 are built based on overlapping their costs with the budget. At this point, the group normally figures out that they can't afford them all. I rarely say to a group, "You can't afford that" because the prioritization process works that out for them. This process gets to the bottom of any neighborhood's priorities.

Haystack Heights Cohousing Common House Workshop.

Common dinner is precious.

4

Haystack Heights Cohousing

Common House Workshop

"Architecture is a political act, by nature. It has to do with the relationships between people and how they decide to change their conditions of living."

Lebbeus Woods

Besides the Danes' natural affinity for cooperation, another reason that cohousing has been so successful there is that a centered, sit-down, cozy dinner several evenings a week is such an important part of their culture. It's the time to look each other in the eyes, to appreciate each other, to talk about your day, to discuss local politics and plans for the weekend, and so much more. If the phone ever rang between 6 p.m. and 7 p.m. on any given evening, Mrs. Clausen (my host mother) would always exclaim that it's either an emergency or an American.

HAYSTACK HEIGHTS COHOUSING

www.spokanecohousing.com

COMMON HOUSE PROGRAM AND DESIGN CRITERIA

Write-up from Common House Workshop

Facilitated by Charles Durrett
Write-up by Lindy Sexton
McCamant & Durrett Architects
Spokane, Washington

December 16 – 17, 2017

Table of Contents

PART 1. CONTEXT

Background

This document comprises Haystack Heights Cohousing's program and design criteria for their Common House and other community facilities. It summarizes the desired activities, priorities, and design criteria agreed to by the resident group during a programming workshop facilitated by Charles Durrett of McCamant & Durrett Architects. Program write-up by Lindy Sexton.

This program also serves a variety of uses:

- The project's development budget allows for up to 3,500 sf[1] of common facilities. This program establishes the priorities for the use of those funds.
- As the project evolves, this program acts as a summary of the goals and design priorities of the Group.
- As new members join the community, it should be used to familiarize incoming residents with the programing and design process for the common facilities.
- This document represents the combined efforts of the future residents, culminating a deliberate process that reflects the group as a whole.
- Finally, it shows where there are overlapping interests, common concerns, and shared values; where working together makes every individual's life easier, more convenient, more practical, more economical, and more fun. By collaborating, we can have more while using less of the earth's resources.

Participatory Design Process

In summarizing the community's programming decisions, this document confirms that participants share the same expectations. During the Common House Workshop, participants went through a process to Brainstorm, Discuss, and Decide upon elements that they want to incorporate into the design of their common house and other community facilities. As the design of this project evolves, this program will be used to evaluate design alternatives and changes in the context of how they address the program goals. If the Group's goals or design criteria change, the program should be amended to reflect those changes.

Next page and Right: Common House Workshop participants.

We recommend that Haystack Heights Cohousing agree on a specific process for making changes in the program if needed. For instance, the group may require a minimum number of persons agree to reconsider an issue before it can be put back on an agenda. To reconsider an old subject, many groups require a quorum of two-thirds of the group members who were present at the original workshop. While it can be useful to consider new perspectives or insights, it is also important to respect the enormous number of people-hours and effort put into the decisions contained in this document.

Reconsidering past subjects usually happens once at most during the development of a project. That's how smart the group is the first time, when all of the collective energy, knowledge, and good will is in the room. We made these decisions at the exact right time. We struck when the fire was hot.

Prior to the Common House Workshop, the Site Program for the community was developed at a Site Planning Workshop held on October 21–24, 2017. The Site Program exists as a separate document.

The Common House Program and Design Criteria outlined here are informed by the Site Program. However, because the Site Program is subject to later changes due to the development of Private House designs, money limitations, size constraints, zoning issues, and other city requirements, the Common House may be affected.

PART 2. GOALS & ACTIVITIES

Goals for the Common Facilities

IMAGINE . . .

It is a Saturday morning in 2019 and you are sitting in the common house reading your newspaper, and waiting for the rest of the landscape committee to arrive. You muse for a few moments how this common house really meets your stated goals. What are those stated goals?

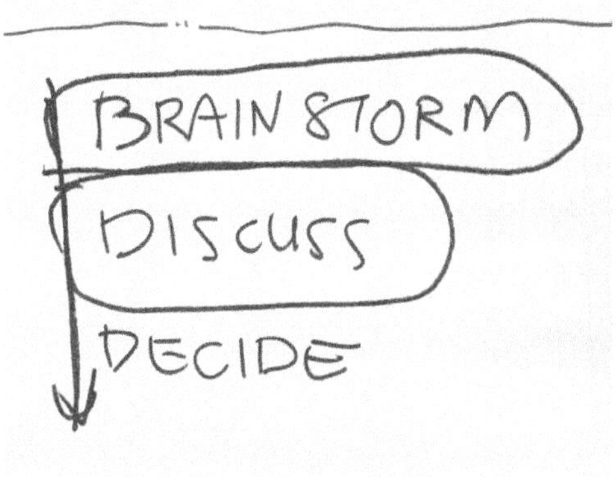

- Sense of warmth – emotional, personal
- Sense of ease
- Light
- Practical, well planned
- Convenient
- Ergonomically correct
- Comfort, extension of my living room into the common space
- Comfortable
- Welcoming and accessible
- Anticipation, like going to a concert
- Good acoustics – excellent acoustics
- Hear what you want to hear and not hear what you don't

- Spaces that are adaptable
- Nourishment – physical and social
- Accessibility to everything
- Welcoming
- Beauty, in and out
- View
- Aesthetically pleasing
- Aesthetically calming and clean
- Hub of activity
- Allowing for interaction, quick, easy, and lingering, spontaneous
- A surrounding that inspires
- Homey and cozy
- Huggelig
- Nature, lovely, small
- Redundancy of systems
- Good air quality and thermal comfort
- Invites play and playfulness
- Ease of maintenance
- Appropriate zoning or separation of spaces
- Layering of spaces
- Quiet and noisy

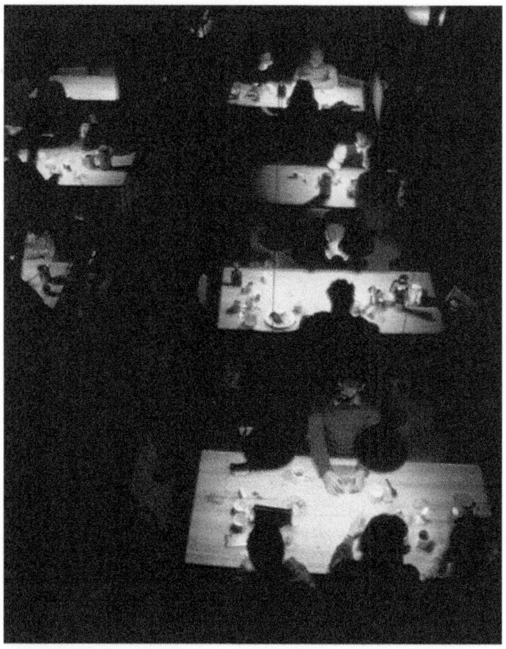

- Levels of intimacy
- Durable place that accommodates messes or rowdiness zoning to accommodate rowdiness
- Very usable
- Redundancy of systems, generator, hot water, etc.
- It looks like Spokane
- Minimum toxic
- Energy-efficient, Passive solar – Smaller carbon footprint
- The common house shall be the model of the project

COMMENTS: ***The common realm is one of the key aspects that makes cohousing unique. But common facilities cannot be separated from common management. While it doesn't belong to you personally, it belongs to people that you personally care about, that you depend on, and that you are averse to affronting.***

This table records the brainstorm. After discussion, the list of places and design criteria (see pages 10–17) were consented upon.

PROGRAMMED ACTIVITIES

Activity (verb)	Own place (to be prioritized)	# of people (early brainstorm)	When (early brainstorm)
• Heating	Yes	12	Wood fireplace
• Basking	Yes		
• Rehearsing music	Yes		
• Dining	Yes		
• Gaming	Yes		Pool table/ping pong/board games in common space
• Cooking	Yes		
• Laundry	Yes		Outdoor BBQ
• Drying your clothes	No		24/7
• Canning preserving food	Yes		
• Composting/recycling	Yes		Seasonal, decentralized, fermenting, sprouting 24/7
• Guesting/hosting	Yes		Multi-use or not
• Dancing	No		Multi-use or not
• Performing	No		
• Lecture	No		
• Reading/studying/sitting	Yes		
• Socializing	No		
• Cleaning	Yes		
• Dialoguing/talking	No		
• Crafting	Yes		Short and long term
• Arting	Yes		
• Playing music	Yes		

Activity (verb)	**Own place (to be prioritized)**	**# of people (early brainstorm)**	**When (early brainstorm)**
• Exercising	No		
• Singing	Yes		
• Sprouting	Yes		Constant and continuous
• Growing/cultivating/harvesting	Yes		
• Starting plants	Yes		Days and at mealtime
• Saunaing	Yes		
• Making, constructing	Yes		
• Studying	Yes		
• Meeting	No		5-8x/wk anytime, especially evening and weekends
• Celebrating	No		
• External communication	Yes		
• Transitioning	Yes		
• Internal communication	Yes		Mailing
• Playing	Yes		Boots, coats
• Movie Watching	No		On cart
• Lounging/sitting	Yes		Comfy chair, reading studying
• Consuming liquids	No		
• Gifting/sharing	Yes		Dining room
• Displaying	No		All the time
• Learning	No		Wherever
• Napping	No		24/7
• Printing/officing/working	Yes		24/7
• Kids being kids	Yes		

PART 3. PROGRAM PLACES

Consensed Prioritized Places

During the Programming Workshop, the community prioritized different common facility uses, consensing on the following order.

It is understood that not all common facilities will be in the Common House as some maybe work better in different locations on the property.

This list establishes the priority for uses of funds for common facilities, with the understanding that those lower on the list may not be included at all.

1. Cooking
2. Dining
3. Sitting
4. Kids room
5. Guest room
6. Laundry
7. Office
8. Guest room 2
9. Food processing
10. Making
11. Forest garden greenhouse
12. Gaming
13. Music
14. Teen room
15. Sauna
16. Meditation
17. Hot tub
18. Crafts
19. Guest room 3

Notes from Prioritized Places

1. Typical uses such as mail, lobby, and toilet rooms have been agreed upon but not prioritized, they will be put into the design by MDA.
2. Basking will be folded into sitting room.
3. Gifting will be folded into laundry area.
4. Not prioritized, but to be included: Bathrooms, Entry, Gifting, Basking.

Place	Activities	Character	Relationship	Details
Kitchen Pantry Freezer	• Facilities reuse of bags, etc. • Lots of sink space • Group cooking 2–3 • Kids supervised in the kitchen • Food Processing	• Natural light • Windows to outside • Display canned goods • Artful display	• Connection to people • Beautiful connection to dining room • Counter interfaces • Carts	• Varied height of work surfaces • Lots of counter space • JIT equipment • Optimized for flow, storing, services • Easy to sanitize • Large sink space • Organized

Place	Activities	Character	Relationship	Details
Dining Room Can accommodate 40–48 diners 6x/wk	• Allows intimate conversation • Dancing • Performing • Socializing • Dialoguing/talking • Exercising • Meeting • Celebrating • Movie Watching • Consuming liquids • Learning	• Feeling of spaciousness • Soft and hard • Sense of intimacy	• Interface with kitchen • View to outside or greenhouse? • To outside • Kids room down the hall • Close to sitting room	• Place to put boots, coats, storage • System management • Easy to clean • Accessibility • Intergenerational real tables

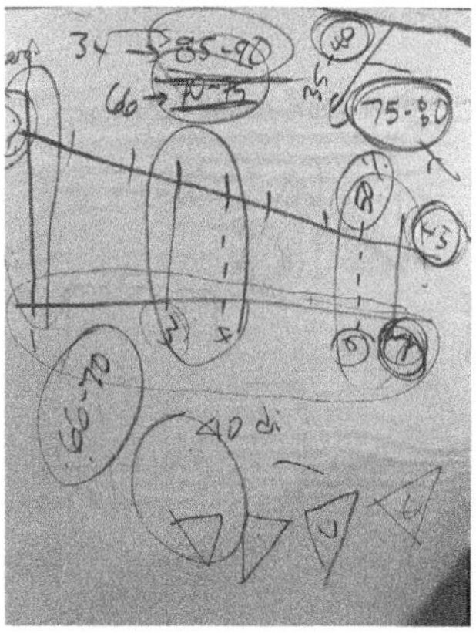

Place	Activities	Character	Relationship	Details
Sitting Room Board Games Community meeting	• Book clubbing • Nursing • Playing board games	• Super cozy after dinner	• A bit of separation to dining room • Adjacent to gaming with adequate separation (not pool, not ping pong) • See gaming • Adjacent to fireplace	• Carpet • Natural accents • Window sitting • Outlets • Convenient sitting tables • Projection on wall • Wired for sound • 1 couch, 2 chairs • Coffee table • Benches in window • Perches on front porch

Place	Activities	Character	Relationship	Details
Kids Room 4–5 kids after dinner	• Adolescents • Modular toys string castles • Could double-purpose as gaming or music space	• Open space • Flexible • Loft or enclosure • Tunneling • Closets • Little room	• Near laundry (try)	• Glass in door • Durable floor • Comfortable chair (nursing) • Open-ended activities • Cork floor • High storage, locking storage • Writable walls • Sound-resistant • Wireless video • Room to go into • Low stage or platform • Universal design

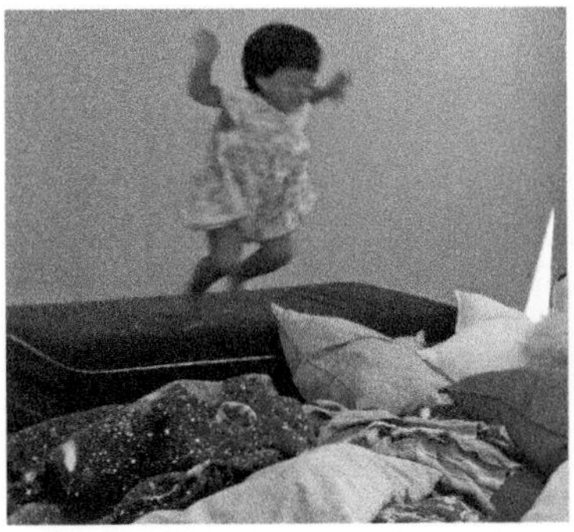

Place	Activities	Character	Relationship	Details
Guest Room 1 Size: 1.1 x GR 2 Two twin beds and blow-up mattress or similar		• Quiet • Privacy • Enclave, writers desk	• Guest rooms share bathroom and shower • Sink in room • Compartmentalized fixtures • Separate Shower? • 2–3 bathrooms in common house if split level	• Table and 2 chairs • Thermostat • Storage for linens (closet) • On accessible level • Place for suitcases • Dresser

Place	Activities	Character	Relationship	Details
Laundry	• 2 washers • 2 dryers • Gifting		• Adjacent to drying area	• Utility sink Drying rack • Mop sink • Shared detergent • Grey water • Counter space • Good lighting

Place	Activities	Character	Relationship	Details
Office			• Somewhere not noisy	• Records storage • (2) drawer file • Leave space for laser printer on top of file drawers

Place	Activities	Character	Relationship	Details
Guest Room 2 1 queen bed				• Dresser in a closet (or similar) • Closets big enough • Own thermostat (if possible)

Place	Activities	Character	Relationship	Details
Food Processing (happens in the kitchen)	• Yogurt making • Fermentation • Active food processing in common house kitchen • Active food storage on display (smaller artistic display)	• Storage of canning equipment elsewhere	• Big equipment, canning jars, and (6) freezers could be elsewhere (basement) on generator • Drain for defrost cycle	• 6×6 shelves in pantry • Outlets

COMMENTS: ***A gourmet kitchen seems fundamental to a high-functioning neighborhood. The notion that there is one place that you can easily accommodate everyone in the community, one place that you absolutely love to cook in, one place where your camaraderie with others builds quality relationships that last a lifetime and many, many quality meals.***

These program comments in the margin relate to a lot of things, but one thing that they represent for sure is the sort of dialogue that goes along with the in-person site, common areas/building, and private house workshops.

COMMENTS: ***This particular program gets very thin in detail right here. I don't recommend it. This is what happens when the subculture thinks that they know each other too well to dwell on "obvious stuff." When it comes to culture change, nothing is obvious or at least not to be taken for granted. I find that folks who consider themselves the most similar, seem to have the longest conversations later. Our community was "thin" at the outdoor laundry hanging conversation. What would normally take 15 minutes in a concentrated and facilitated conversation is still going on 18 years later.***

Place	Activities	Character	Relationship	Details
Making	• In existing shop			• To be filled in by group/committee

Place	Activities	Character	Relationship	Details
Forest Garden Greenhouse	• 600 sf			• Built later • Footings now • Able to grow a lemon tree? • Is it heated?

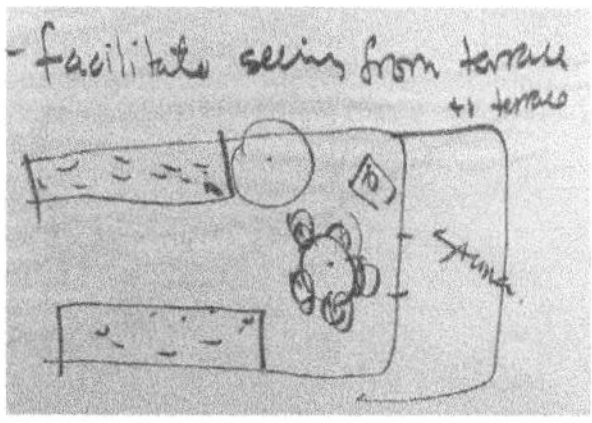

Place	Activities	Character	Relationship	Details
Glass Gallery				• Facilitates line of sight between two plazas • Easy access • Mail • Seating

Place	Activities	Character	Relationship	Details
Gaming/Pool 			• At sitting room	

Place	Activities	Character	Relationship	Details
Two story? 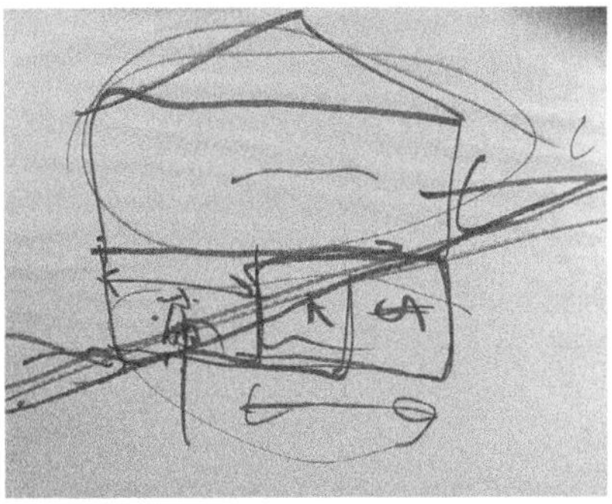				• We'll see • To be filled in by group/committee

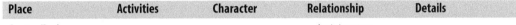

COMMENTS: ***The mail area is the nexus of consequence. That is, people bump into each other, make plans, deliver mail to neighbors, have a seat and open a couple of things, recycle, and much more. The local post office often wants the boxes out on the street. They don't seem to appreciate how important building community is, nor do they know how important it is to actually have a relationship with the mail carrier—and the mail carrier definitely appreciates it. They have somewhere to use the bathroom and to get a glass of water. In other words, community making alters the landscape, as it should.***

COMMENTS: ***There is no better opportunity to be "sustainable" than in a high-functioning community. At Nevada City Cohousing, no one had solar panels before moving in—now they all do. No one had sustainably grown lumber—now they all do.***

PART 4. CONCLUSION

Other Common House Criteria

***I. Accessibility** Successful accessibility has been a goal from the beginning. The common house will be designed to meet the current Washington Building Codes for accessibility, which is ADA accessible.*

II.* Location of the Common House** ***Per the Site Program, the common house has been located centrally to provide easy access, and good visibility from the homes and along circulation.

III.* Flooring** ***MDA will make a proposal at Workshop 5.

IV.* Sustainability** ***The group has had sustainability as a goal from the beginning. There is no better edifice to save energy (for example, one pot of boiling spaghetti water rather than 34) or better yet to create energy (note Bill McKibben's Foreword to *Creating Cohousing*).

The common house is the temple to sharing. Sharing is the key to sustainability. If we hope that a child born seven generations from now will have the opportunity we had or more, we must become more benign—community and sharing hold that possibility.

The common house is where the common history is continued and sustained for years to come. This place will play a big long-term role in the "village" at Haystack Heights Cohousing; traditions, and celebrations, and ceremony will be created. Finding a balance between privacy and community has to include a building like this with this many specific criteria, because that is how it will be used—facilitating real community (and privacy—I'll explain). And the balance of privacy and community takes us to the next workshop: the private houses.

Common House Feel

COMMENTS: ***Sometimes, community is completely misunderstood by architects. Like the dining room to the top left which feels more like a train station, or the kitchen to the bottom left which feels more like a kitchen in a battleship than in a home.***

Not an Institution

The feeling that a common house has makes a dramatic difference in how much it is used. Everything else being equal, a cold and sterile common house won't get used as much simply because there is an underlying unpleasantness to being there.

Like an Extension of Your House

The Haystack Heights Cohousing common house will be designed to be light and airy, and at the same time warm and giving. The common house should feel like an extension of one's private house; not like an institution.

COMMENTS: ***With the heightened awareness and acute focus that go on in the common realm design criteria, the weekend is a long 15-hour party, but very very efficient. When people think that they are "aware" of each other, what tends to happen is that people default to the behavior that they grew up with—just throw it into the dryer. That's why diversity in the group is useful. It makes you talk about things that you otherwise might not—it makes you turn over those rocks and to explore what you might not otherwise explore.***

Workshop Conclusion

As the Haystack Heights Cohousing community, you have the unique opportunity to plan a common house for your forming community, and to envision the common house as the hub of this new cohousing community. The outcomes of the workshop helped create a place that is an extension of the private houses and hopefully with the truest intent possible becomes the heart of the community. My experience is, if done right, the common house will supplement and extend individual possibilities, and will achieve the best of the group's common interests. And no doubt, as you will see living there, the common house will extend the physical, social, and emotional potential of probably each and every individual there, just as I have seen it do in the cohousing communities where I have lived for the last 24 years.

During the workshop, what really worked well was when folks who had a brilliant idea and it went down on paper. Then the idea belonged to the group and everyone could evaluate its merits. When the idea was good, it stayed. Sometimes it was modified by the group. Sometimes an idea turned out to be "not so good." Those ideas were removed from the paper and are not part of the design criteria. This process worked.

The workshop was a waterfall of good ideas along with buckets and buckets of good decisions. While there was a little grumbling about the prolonged discussion of a pool table, you've got to work through the chaff to get to the kernels. As long as you stay on topic—it's all relevant, until it's not. In other words, if you are looking for an avocado pit in a sprig of wheat, you are in the wrong field.

There should be little that is accidental or default about cohousing placemaking. First, we write and understand the group's story, then the pencil hits the paper and we draw it. Then we test the program, which I will present January 6, 2018.

Our collective challenge is to optimize the criteria established in the workshop so that the Common House, and therefore the community, can reach its full potential. Our next job is to test the program; that is, to see what a design for this criteria looks like. Is it too big? Can all of the adjacencies (relationships) be accomplished? What rooms should be combined (meiosis), or what uses pulled apart (mitosis)? Are some rooms too big, some too small? Which ones are just right? Answers to these questions will be based on what a schematic design shows, and the discussion that ensues.

Criteria like "centripetal" and "stop gap for the houses" are sophisticated. Criteria like that offer a lot in terms of enriching this program, and therein the final design.

In conclusion, I find the Common House design criteria workshop to be an important community-building experience, as it was here at Haystack Heights Cohousing. It is not just the discussion itself, but the memories that were created and how the decisions were reached. The overlapping values and aspirations within the group became obvious. With each discussion, the opportunity to reach our potential as individuals, and as a community, came further and further into focus. I also felt heated and even boring discussions useful. That said, there will always be opportunities to continue to learn to communicate clearly, fairly, and productively. Learning to be direct and respectful at the same time is a lifetime challenge. But I find no better incubator than this one, amongst people that you increasingly trust.

And prophetically as noted in early Haystack Heights Cohousing literature, "the design workshops will do much to bring our current members to a better understanding and appreciation of each other, and we'll continue to integrate new members along the way and strengthen our bonds."

We have further to go, but this program is a fundamental and critical step to a successful Common House and therefore to the long-term success of the community. I was particularly impressed by the passions and decisions of the group which exceeded the sum of its parts. The energy and synergy that grew from the participation, collective imagination, and the creativity of the group were a great thing to be a part of. Now, the next critical step is to manifest this program into a warm, cozy, yet also light and airy design.

A good program is necessary to make a good building, but it doesn't guarantee a good building. That is our next job and perhaps one of the most important components is the social dynamic which is almost impossible to imagine unless you've lived in a cohousing community for years.

The social is most influenced by three specific dynamics. The first is giving a damn about everyone. Wow, John is up here playing pool. He's been a recluse for months now and we're so glad to see him out, or Fred, who I've been having this super-sensitive conversation with (that John didn't notice) says, "Let's go over to my house to continue this conversation." The second is direct communication. "John, what the heck are you doing?" with tongue-in-cheek, "can't you see we're having this conversation here?" He'll see what you're saying. The third, if the sitting room is reserved for a book club meeting (this happens about 40 times per year in our community of 34 households), then nothing else happens in there during that time. That said, you still want the architecture done right the first time and we get that.

Please make sure that someone goes through this program very, very carefully with every new member. The program sets those individuals up for success and, therefore, the entire community up for success.

PART 5. PARTICIPANTS

COMMENTS: ***We've all been happier than we look in this photo. Although we had to alter our plans to save money, we are at this time quite proud of the entirely new neighborhood that we came up with.***

At the December 15–16, 2017, Haystack Heights Cohousing Common House Workshop, the following participants were in attendance:

Jim Dawson
Mariah McKay
Bob Stilger
Susan Virnig
Bill Lockwood
Nikki Lockwood
John Bruntlett
Christie Bruntlett

Anne Stephenson
Chris Nerison
Pat Mertens
Laura Mertens-Plowman
Doug Robnett
Sarah Conover
Rob Roose
Abby Roose

ENDNOTE

1. More square footage is possible within the budget because several common uses (common storage, garden shed, messy crafts, and workshop) will be built in economic garages.

SANTA CRUZ, CA

The entry.

BELLINGHAM, WA

A home doesn't have to be by itself to be a home.

NEVADA CITY, CA

Make magic happen when you can.

NEVADA CITY, CA

Dining room.

5

Intergenerational Neighborhood Design

Private Houses Design

"Architecture can be a true summation of the habits of the heart and where the heart wishes to pursue."
Charles Durrett

A house is a part of our psyche, our self-image, our day-to-day comfort—our happiness. Although you are designing a custom neighborhood, the house—while no less considered—is not a custom house. It's better than that. If basic cohousing math holds true, which it usually does, 1+1 = 3. That is, when we sit down with a group of say, six households (around ten people in total) with the intention of creating the exact same awesome dwelling, the house has the benefit of numerous creative people serving up ideas that, when facilitated well, are synthesized to realize the best of the ideas of everyone at the table. Good houses that are well proportioned and satisfying at every level can be hard to design. But I find that the real magic happens when I sit down with the ten people who are all interested in the same thing—a great house.

It's normal that some of the folks have more money than others. Those with less money help keep everyone from wishing themselves into an expensive corner. However, those with plenty of money will see that they can adequately customize their houses through options just fine, and a lot more economically than they could do with a one-off house. An option could include an additional skylight or an operable skylight with a remotely operated shade. Maybe it's some extra fancy light fixtures, a double bathroom sink, an exotic wood flooring, or a number of small customizations added after move-in. What matters is that you can afford it, you like it, and it calls you when you're not there. That you love being there, entertaining there, that the neighbors just outside the door are real neighbors. That the house takes nothing to heat and literally nothing to cool. People bring real values and experiences to the table, but they also bring aspirations and intentions. Folks who plan to live in community-enhanced neighborhoods have aspirations for living lighter on the planet, intentions to live with a diverse group of people, and to make the village work. That all comes together at the Private House Workshop.

NEVADA CITY, CA

Personality is the only way to describe each front porch. This place of close townhouses and flats make this lane interesting to walk down everyday. This is a village, not a project. This is a neighborhood, not a condominium complex. Technically, it is a condominium complex, just not a normal one.

NEVADA CITY, CA

The private house kitchen is tidy and inviting. It's very affordable, but also warm and giving. It always features a large window looking out from the kitchen sink to the common circulation outside. When one needs to talk to someone, they just knock on the window. The more affordable upper cabinets never got to the ceiling (too much construction fussiness) and it's a great place to show off your fancier platters and water pitchers.

NEVADA CITY, CA

Living room: Small, efficient homes, with no extra circulation, but warm and cozy. And the electric lights are rarely on in the middle of the day, the natural light is plenty with large, well-placed windows that go to the ceiling. More light comes in at the top of the window when it is held high.

With facilitation, we know that the 1+1 = 3 house can be fantastically functional, elegant, and cost-effective.

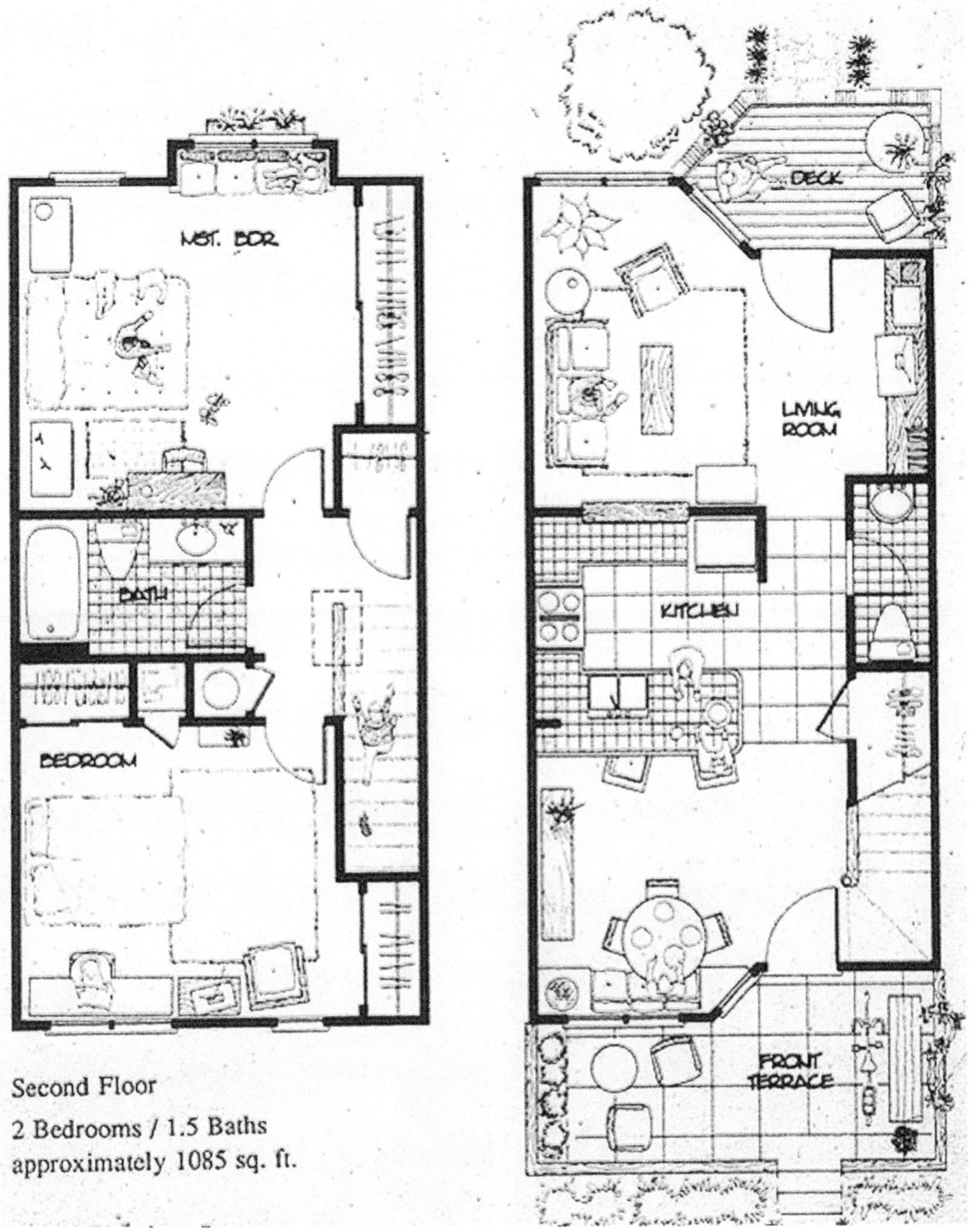

Second Floor
2 Bedrooms / 1.5 Baths
approximately 1085 sq. ft.

When done with future residents, this is where culture change happens. We start with a presentation of a 4,000-square-foot common house plan. The intent of the common house presentation here is to explain where we could not execute the common house program entirely. For example, "there were five adjacencies to the entry and we could really only accomplish four—but it still works."

FRESNO, CA

Life happens on the front porches. Pedestrians walk past each front porch on the way to the common house, and on the way to the common parking areas. As Bill McKibben is fond of saying, "What's most impressive is not how much energy is saved in cohousing, but rather how much energy is created."

FRESNO, CA

Grey days have to be mitigated, not with grey buildings, and definitely not with beige. Color brings joy and life to any environment, and is especially necessary when it's grey outside.

NEVADA CITY, CA

Kids' room in common house.

COTATI, CA

The houses above the commercial use at Cotati Cohousing are still warm and cozy, and not apartment-like.

PLEASANT HILL, CA

And here's why. "And these were opportunities that emerged in the design process that were not in the program, that we incorporated." Then the group divides up into three separate groups (no spouses together) and for 45 minutes they evaluate how well the common house met the criteria or could be improved in any way. The intent is to get the building and their evaluation and changes to it, the new lifestyle that comes with it goes into their consciousness. Then a spokesperson from each group gives a presentation about their group's findings.

FAIR OAKS, CA

Dappled light in hot climates like Sacramento helps to keep the buildings cool.

NEVADA CITY, CA

"Front porches are great places to tutor math," says the teacher to the student.

GOOD HOMES
MAKE
CONTENTED
WORKERS

13.1 Title page, *Good Homes Make Contented Workers*, Industrial Housing Associates, 1919

Extreme housing changes happened in America when this book came out in 1919. The factory managers in Chicago became empathetic of their workers because both lived downtown. So there was an extensive effort to get the managers to the suburbs, and out of town—what is now known as Chicagoland. In the foreword, Herbert Hoover wrote, "Any man who has his own house could never be a communist—he is too busy mowing the lawn and painting the fence." This is the classic Machiavelli "divide and conquer" political theory. People who are separated don't organize as much. It was the opposite of community-enhanced neighborhoods.

FAIR OAKS, CA

Use color to give the building a life.

After the discussion, the group reaches a consensus on the desired changes. Incorporating these ideas always makes for a better common house and, most importantly, it gives the future residents emotional and intellectual ownership of that space. It's this input that makes the common house especially appropriate to that subculture, and it's these changes which bring the building use to 350–450 people-hours of use per week. When the design is not refined with the future residents, common houses rarely receive more than 150 people-hours of use per week. That is not an extension of the private houses—but at 450 people-hours, it is. Then, we start the design criteria for the private houses.

NEVADA CITY, CA

There's no place like the front porch to cook exotic Chinese food. They could do it in the more private backyard, but it's more interesting to cook out front.

YARROW ECOVILLAGE, B.C., CANADA

This design has porches and decks that face the "agora" (communal space), which helps sustain relationships due to the see-through railing and porches proximate to circulation.

NEVADA CITY, CA

It's no secret that life on the front porch is a lovely variety to life in the house—even when it's a great house.

People readily want that indoor room and outdoor variety, and for it to be an easy transition. Front porches provide exactly that.

NEVADA CITY, CA

People perch there temporarily until they decide to be involved or not. During the programming phase, I measure the height of the bottom of people's buttocks. The average of these values becomes the height of the railing, otherwise known as the perch.

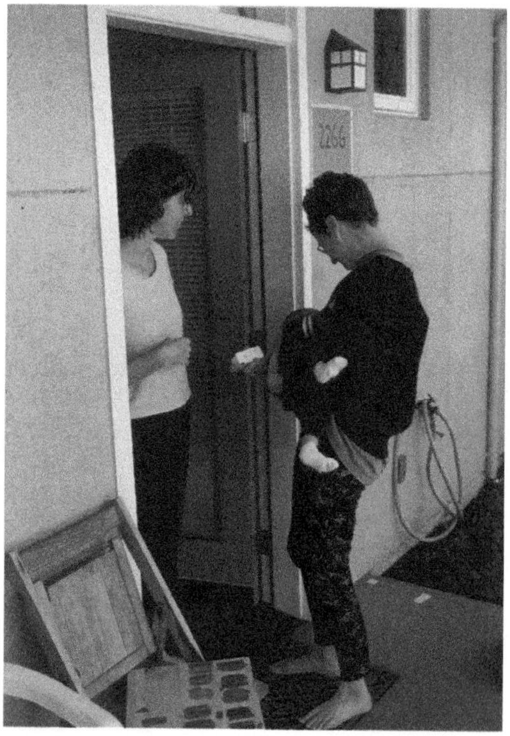

PLEASANT HILL, CA

The design criteria often say, "Easy to borrow a cube of butter from the next door neighbor, even when nursing a baby."

The most important room in the house— the front porch. Fresh air and fresh faces. You can lean or perch on the railing until you decide to join the foolery or not.

NEVADA CITY, CA

The private kitchens are ergonomic and smart from an efficiency point of view, and warm and giving to the entire floor plan from an aesthete's point of view.

The living room to the right is larger because the circulation (through the open hall) feeds the entire house, making the dining room and kitchen feel larger too.

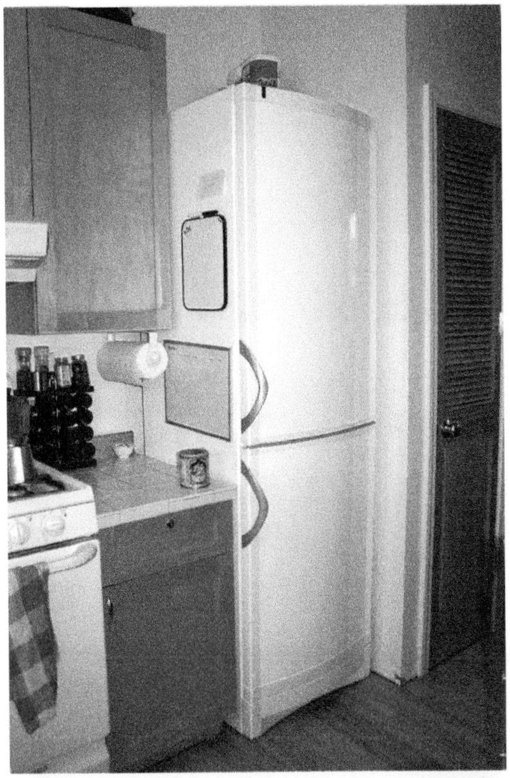

These houses are like Italian sports cars, everything can be a little downsized—but it doesn't have to be. Some folks love those big sinks and refrigerators. However, smaller refrigerators (24"), sinks (25"), and dishwashers (18") not only make your house feel more European, they also allow for more cabinet and counter space.

Custom furniture (like the bookshelves on the right) can be built by residents after move-in, articulating the open floor plan further if desired. But it's always best to start out with a kitchen/dining/living open floor plan.

A space that reflects priorities becomes the most used space. In this case, it gave Fran the face-to-face time that she wanted with her daughter. Face-to-face time with her daughter Michelle is her top priority. So whenever I looked in the window, Michelle was having breakfast, talking on the phone, or hanging out with friends; and Fran was right where she is in this photo, making breakfast, lunch, or dinner.

The floor plan reflected their priority to face each other as often as possible.

BELLINGHAM, WA

Units that cost $130,000 (in 2000) can be cozy.

BELLINGHAM, WA

Early sketch. Form follows function, two bedrooms upstairs and one downstairs leads to this shape. But this shape (two story at the bedrooms and one story at the kitchen, dining, living area) also allows for maximum daylight to the site.

BELLINGHAM, WA

We like these triplexes; we use them a lot in cohousing. This project was constructed at the impossible figure of $67 per square foot (in 2000).

BELLINGHAM, WA

Sitting room in the common house. One of the keys to achieving affordability for everyone is to have a few people who really would lose their possibility of moving in if the costs go up. Gretchen, who needed a house within her budget of approximately $105,000 in 2000, is shown here in the sitting room of the common house. Whenever she needs more room than her 900-square-foot house can offer, she has a 4,000-square-foot common house that she can use. In other words, this is a true extension of her own house.

BELLINGHAM, WA

This house is just 15 feet wide and 35 feet long, for a total at 1,050 square feet for a two-story, two-bedroom house. The front and back walls are aligned vertically with the second story—that's how you stay economical. And by burying the header into the rim joist, the window is kept to the ceiling for maximum natural light (also see page 142 detail drawing).

BELLINGHAM, WA

In Bellingham, the community-enhanced housing is surrounded by houses with prominent garage doors. These are the opposite of community-enhanced design. These are the exact houses proposed by the same developer for the cohousing site, before the group was able to secure the site.

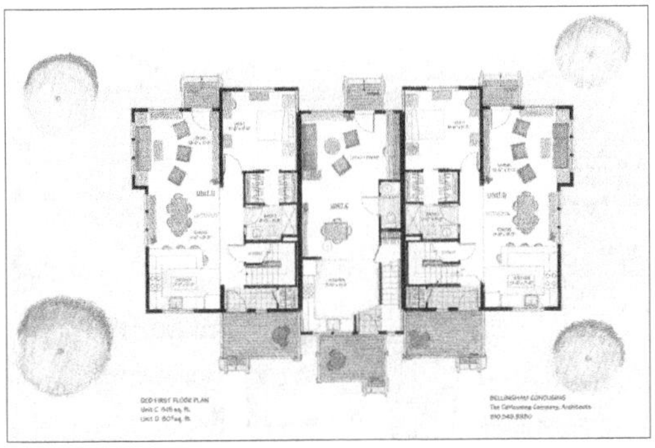

BELLINGHAM, WA

These triplexes can easily be four-plexes, five-plexes, or six-plexes with the little ones in the middle.

PLEASANT HILL, CA

And then there's the refuge, the respite, the critical private realm—the house. Warm, cozy, adequately apportioned, and appointed.

EMERYVILLE, CA

A full day of process to develop criteria together for the houses, especially where we can choose together to make them more economical. Then two days of meeting with the house types. This is the three-bedroom, two-bathroom group.

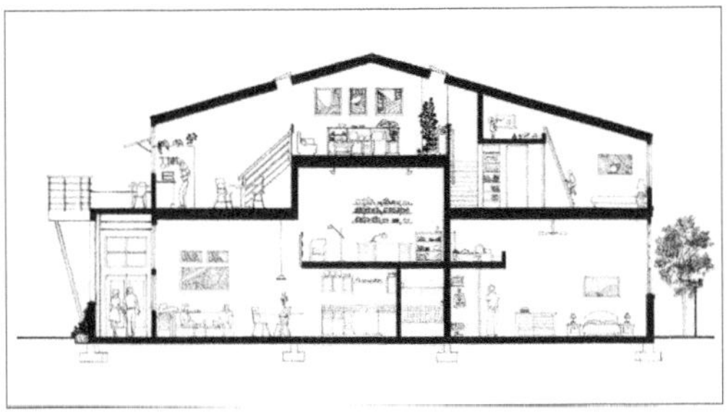

EMERYVILLE, CA

This two-story downstairs unit was once the factory. The new one-story hump-over unit rests above the downstairs unit. The hump (an old monitor) made for easy house zoning.

EMERYVILLE, CA

The upstairs unit, resided in by the author of this book and his family for 12 years.

EMERYVILLE, CA

The unit, especially above the factory can be as clean and modern as you desire.

KIDS' ROOM IN COMMON HOUSE.

Too often, the kids' room in a typical house is their only world. That's why the kids' room in the common house is so important and seriously affects the kid's bedroom design.

NEVADA CITY, CA

Back porches are for all of the private events and the privacy that you want.

NEVADA CITY, CA

Backyards and back decks are just as important as front porches.

EMERYVILLE, CA

This is the warmed up interior of a dwelling unit inside a rehabilitated factory.

Private backyards don't have to be big to be effective.

Closets can be the office, and often are.

Warm the place up with features like this simple but textured wood—sustainably grown pine, of course. They are so cheap in fact, that sometimes we have to paint them white because there are too many knots. Regardless, it costs the same and we just decide at delivery—and of course future residents are involved; we let them know that we might need to do it. A lot of simple inexpensive touches are important—you don't want just another gypsum board box, although you want it to cost as if it were.

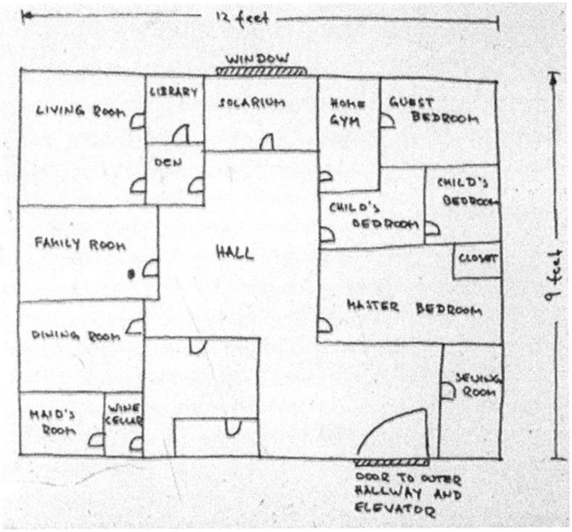

While we know that it's good to have folks involved in the design of their houses—it can go astray without good facilitation. Without facilitation, the self-designed house is too often similar to this one.

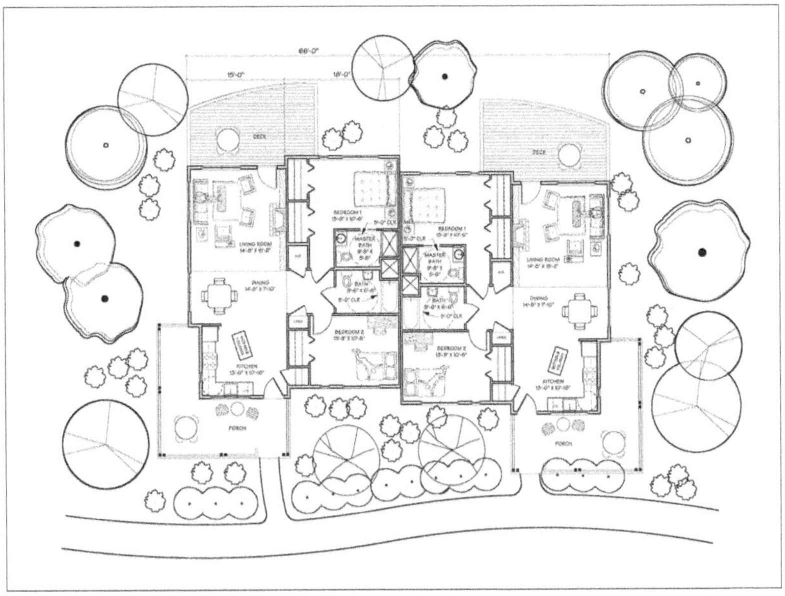

A well-facilitated house plan.

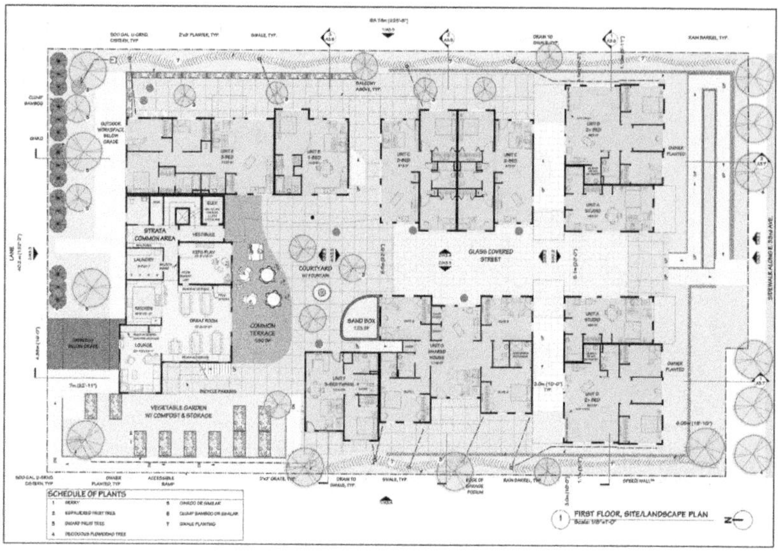

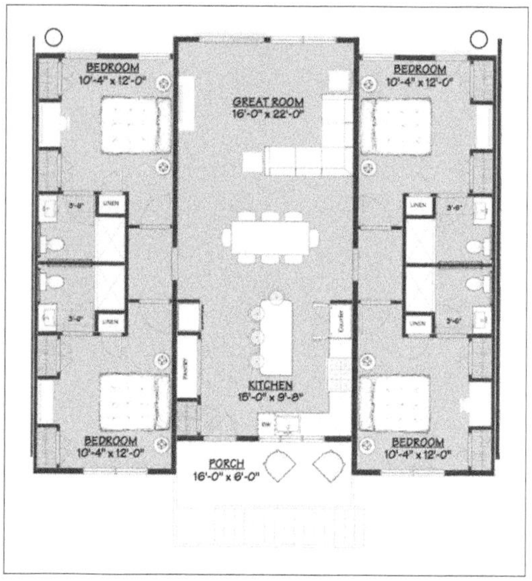

VANCOUVER COHOUSING, CANADA

This dense site needed a variety of house plans to make the Rubik's Cube work. The 31-unit Vancouver Cohousing took the place of two single-family houses on 0.61 acres. It is located on a street with a prominent bus line in a previously low-density neighborhood, just down the street from a fledgling commercial neighborhood center.

Good urban design and consideration always play a role in the design of new cohousing. The group bought two sites with two houses each (shown below) and combined them to be one site with 31 houses after rezoning.

When affordability is paramount, we often recommend a house something like this. In the case of Vancouver Cohousing, a 29-year-old resident was able to muster the down payment with a lot of help from her family. She rented the other three bedrooms to help pay her family back, and to make the mortgage. This is very doable in a community because, in this case, Vancouver Cohousing has a 6,100-square-foot common house to take the pressure off the private houses. You can have dinner there, your friends are there, and you can often get some privacy there too—the spaces are, of course, not always occupied. In other words, shared houses are different in a community, they act differently—and they offer affordability.

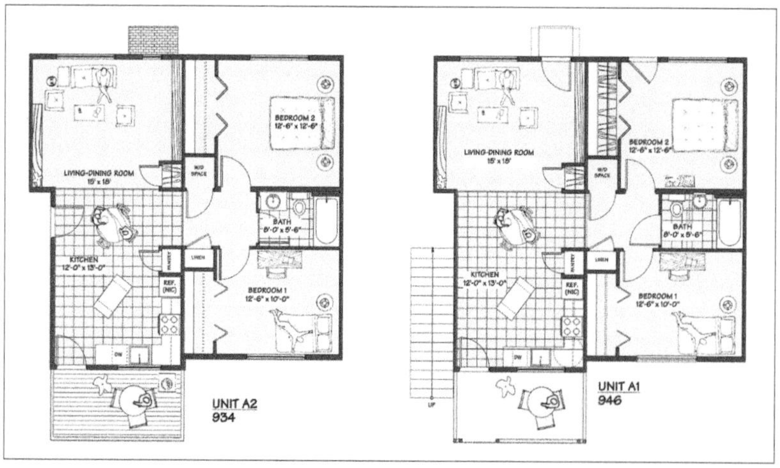

FAIR OAKS, CA

Unit A

When designing affordable community-enhanced units, the key is the gracious decks that face the community.

Downstairs they have a private patio on the back and a front porch on the front, and upstairs they have a deck that works for both privacy and community.

Great natural lighting, even with a single aspect house (a house with light from one of its four sides only). This makes a lot of houses very economical.

A typical private house building plan. The unit types from left to right are: large townhouse, small townhouse, one-story flat, large townhouse.

SPOKANE, WA

NOVATO, CA

Unit C First Floor Plan.

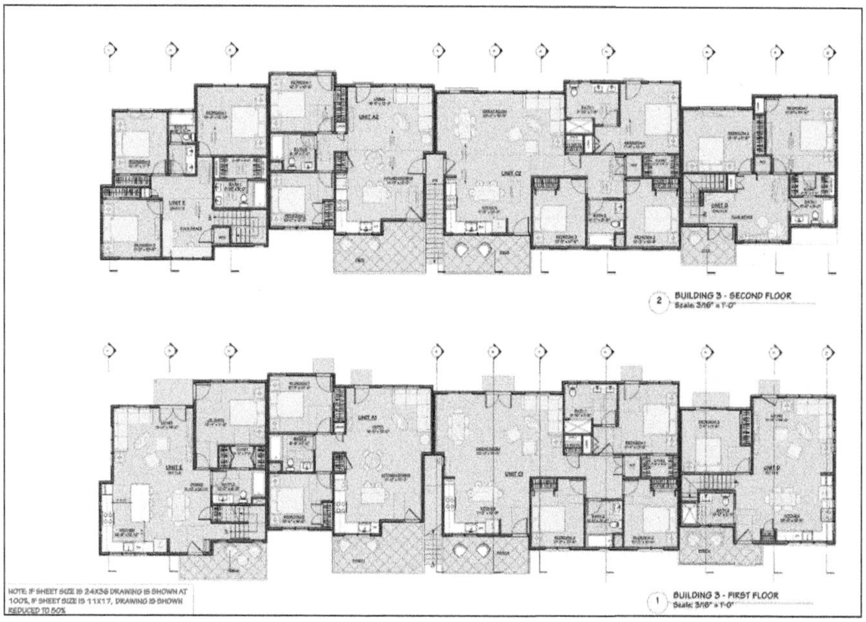

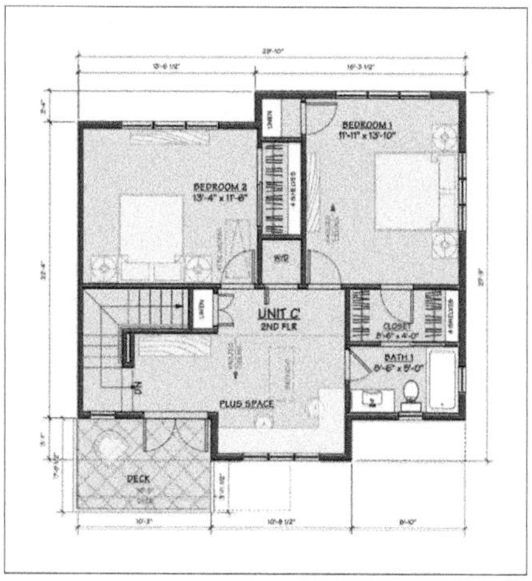

NOVATO, CA

Unit C Second Floor Plan.

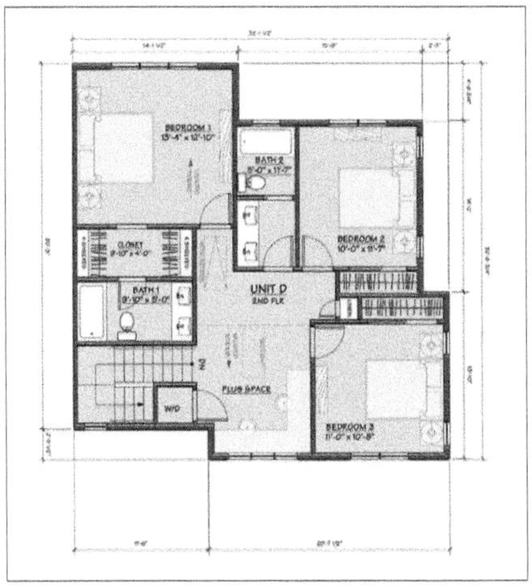

NOVATO, CA

Unit D Second Floor Plan.

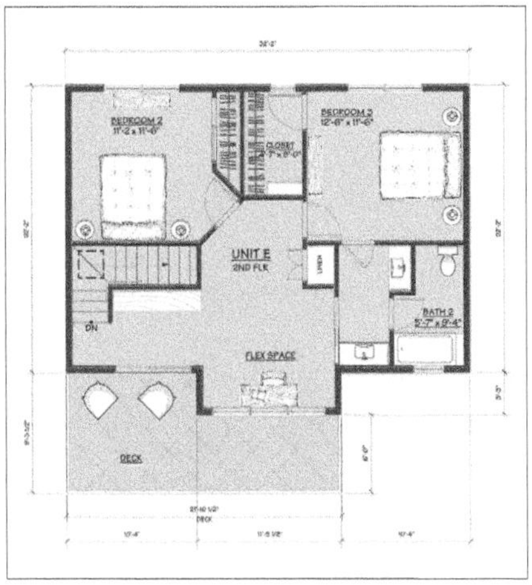

NOVATO, CA

Unit E Second Floor Plan.

NOVATO, CA

Unit F Second Floor Plan.

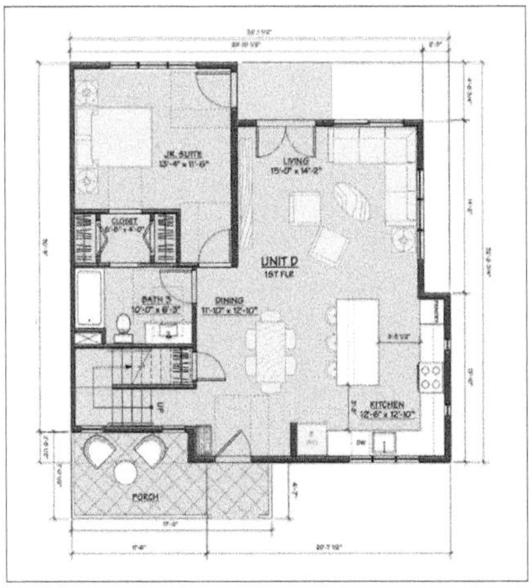

NOVATO, CA

Unit D First Floor Plan.

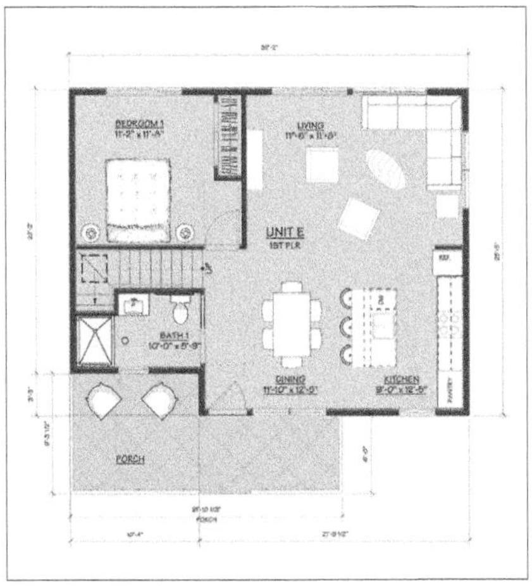

NOVATO, CA

Unit E First Floor Plan.

NOVATO, CA

Unit F First Floor Plan.

NOVATO, CA

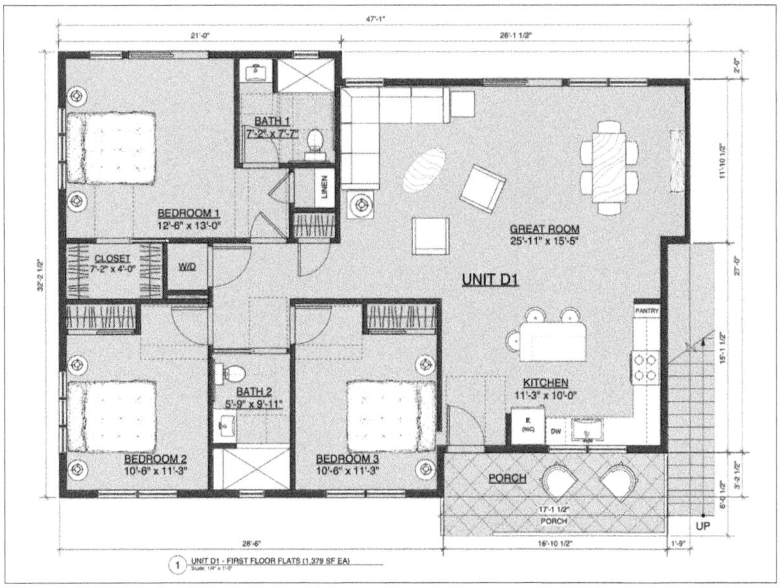

A large flat in Novato Cohousing.

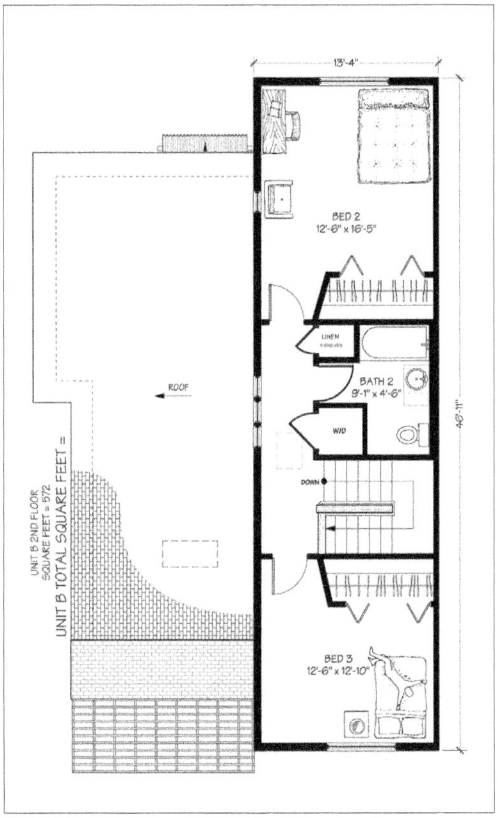

FRESNO, CA

Unit B Second Floor Plan.

A typical exterior for affordable architecture.

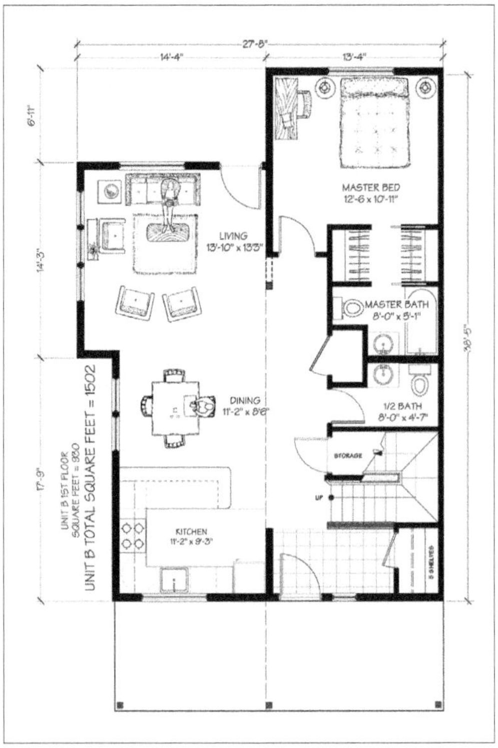

FRESNO, CA

Unit B First Floor Plan.

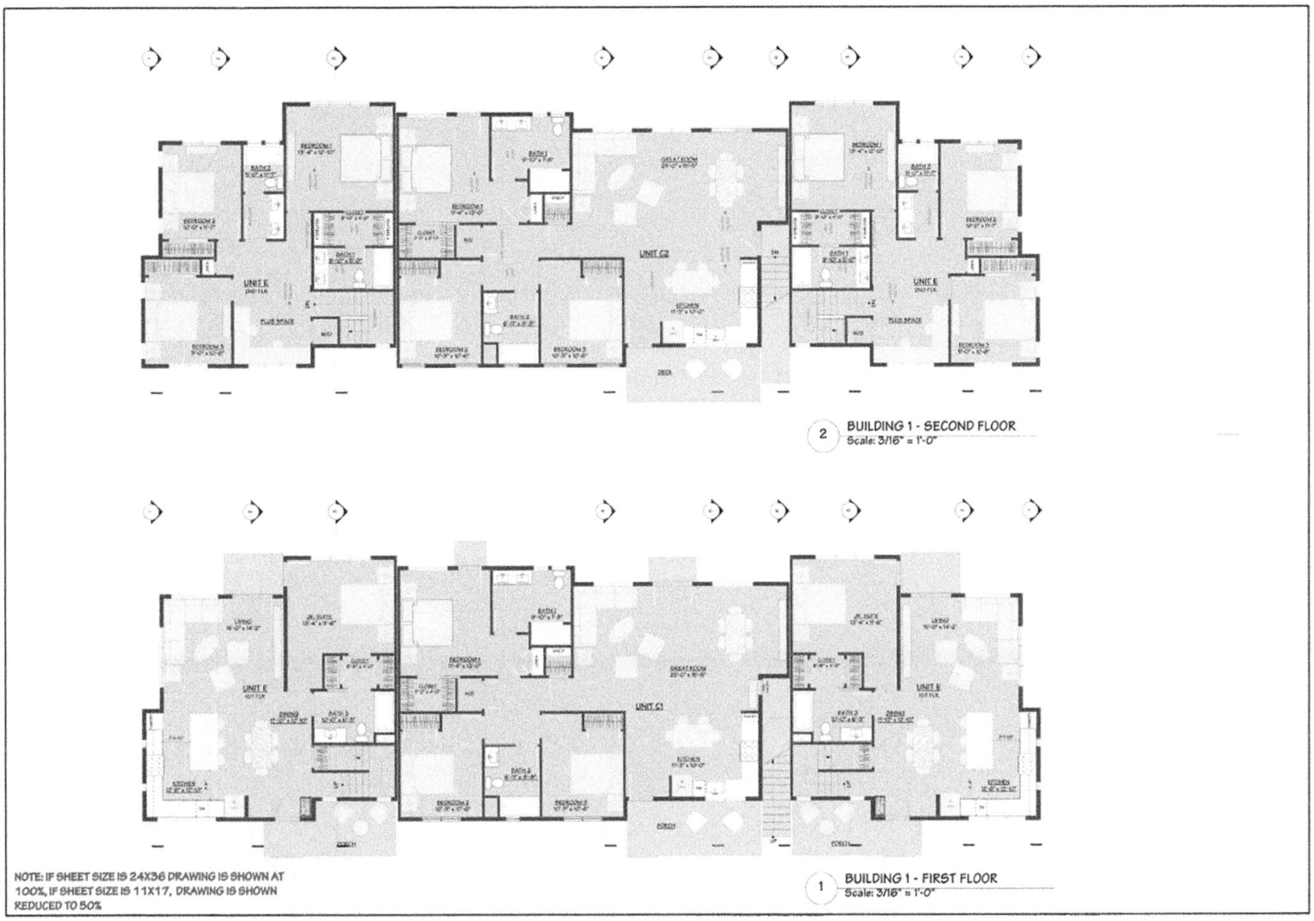

NOVATO, CA

When sites are tight and groups are eccentric.

FAIR OAKS, CA

Large flats.

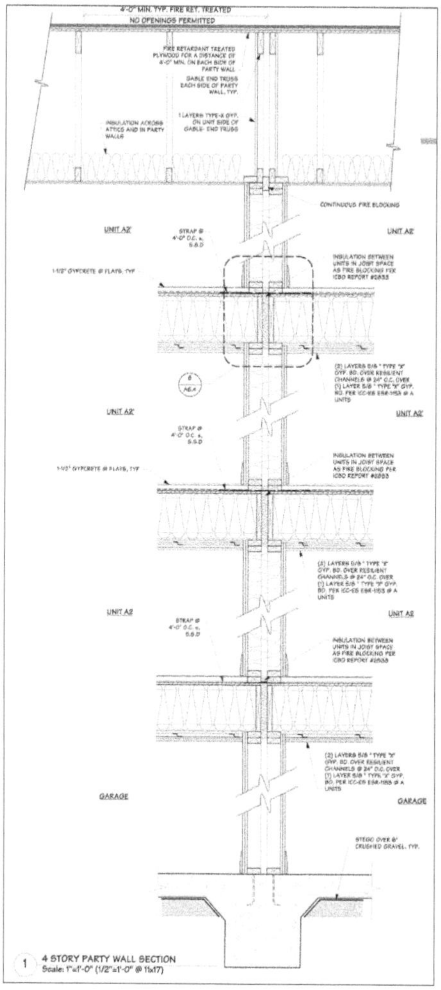

The environmentalists of the future will be the acoustic engineers who figure out how to help Westerners live closer together, and happily. This above drawing is the cheapest way that we have found to do it right.

Advanced framing—just use as much wood as you need in the exterior walls—saves volume for insulation and saves money. Most construction, even production construction, uses about 25 percent more wood than necessary.

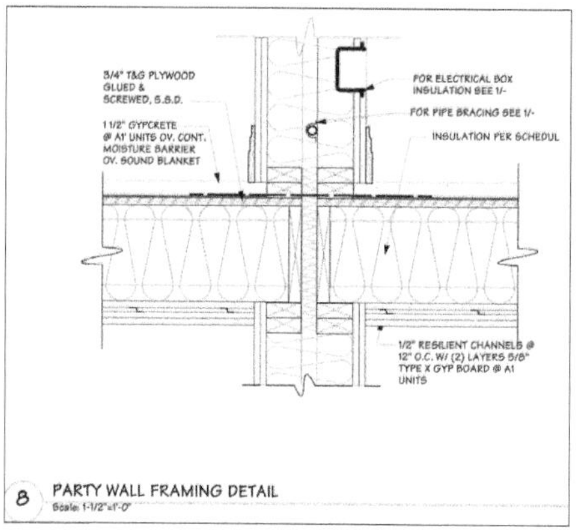

Party Wall Framing Detail (Section)

Details that matter. Neither the walls nor floors are connected, except for straps to tie the entire building together.

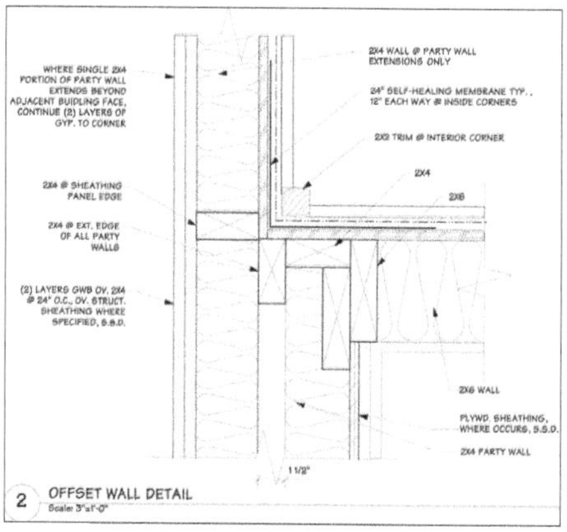

Offset Wall Detail (Plan View)

The extra gypsum board (sheet rock) plays a huge role in both sound mitigation and passive cooling as a "thin mass." The only place that different dwelling units are connected (with one 2 x 4) is at the extreme edge.

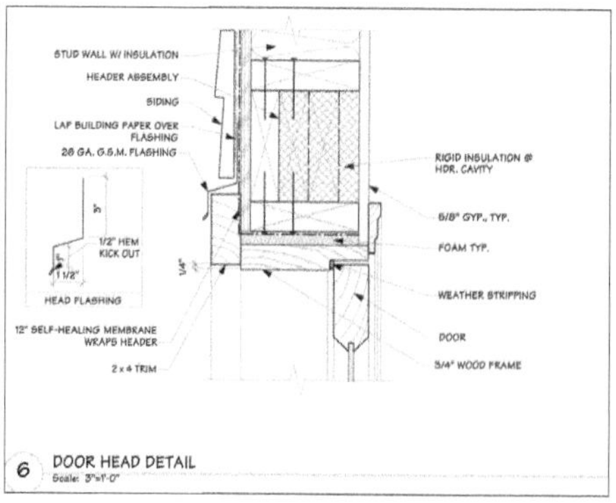

NEVADA CITY, CA

Extra skylights and especially wooden niches are easy to add later, but both make the construction a lot more expensive to bid and to build when the project is first constructed.

Appointing the houses is easy and economical if done by just putting a plug there and letting the owner do it later. There are so many finishing touches that go into a house, and can readily be options in order to keep the prices down for everyone.

NELSON, B.C.

There are so many myths about cohousing in North America. Myth number 26, there are no young people involved. Nelson B.C. Cohousing was probably a 35-year-old average.

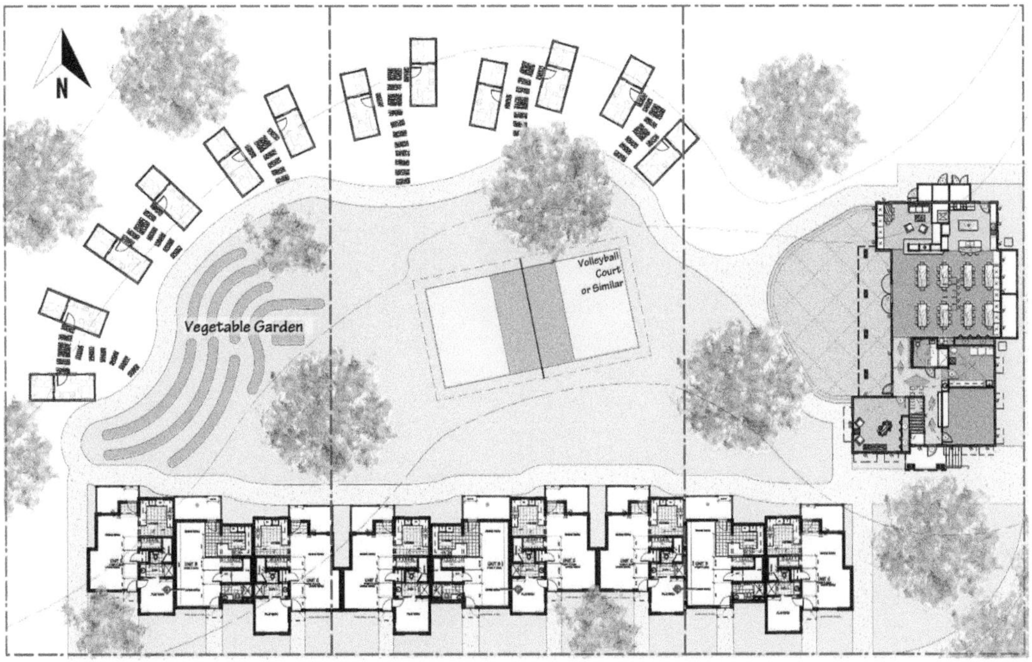

PARADISE, CA

Twelve tiny houses, thirteen flats and town houses, and a 2,000 square foot common house for three previously burned-out single family lots in Paradise California.

Haystack
Heights Cohousing

Co-development can be straightforward and fun; you're designing your future neighborhood together.

Spend the time to understand, evaluate, critique the common house in three separate groups. Come together, consense all changes, and the building will fit like a glove (one hour total).

6

Haystack Heights Cohousing

Private House Workshop

"The residents, the users, on whose behalf we plan, should have a chance to meet each other and be together about something."

Søren Nielsen, Danish Architect

The private home design must start with the group's "design refine" of the common house. Split into three groups, they review and refine the design, and each of the three groups presents their findings to the other groups afterwards, and, after discussion, they reach consensus on the changes. The private house floor plans are generated with the group over three days (the eighth, ninth, and tenth days) of the full 12 days of the design workshops.

HAYSTACK HEIGHTS COHOUSING

www.spokanecohousing.com

PRIVATE HOUSE PROGRAM AND DESIGN CRITERIA

Write-up from Private House Workshop

Facilitated by Charles Durrett and Gary Burke
Write-up by Lindy Sexton
McCamant & Durrett Architects
Spokane, Washington

January 6 – 8, 2018

Table of Contents

PART 1. COMMON HOUSE DESIGN FEEDBACK

Group Feedback on the Common House Design

The common house design was intended to embody the Common House Program to the fullest extent possible. Dozens of designs were tried. Of these, the design presented to the group optimally embodied the program.

The common house presented in the back of this program shows the changes that the group suggested and consensed as changes to be made. For the most part, we are collectively headed in the right direction. This common house will breathe life into the community, like no other building can, no doubt.

Feedback and discussion from the three groups included:

- French door into greenhouse or light at side of door.
- File cabinet next to bathroom, with possible printer over it.
- Bring bathroom wall in on Main Floor (to make room for file cabinet).
- No shower in bathroom on Main Floor.
- No work benches in greenhouse.
- Rain/snow cover on North deck?
- Add bench seating/storage on South deck.
- Keep bench seating/storage on North deck.
- Add stackable chair storage.
- Grills at entries.

- To figure out location of music/MP rehearsal. (MIA)
- Consider moving guest bedroom, opt for multipurpose?
- Dining room big enough?
- Guest room upstairs?
- Pull down screen/TV.
- Print/copy over file.
- Grow 6" for rock on the fireplace.
- No entryway directly into dining room on East side.
- Cart and pantry locations specified in kitchen.
- Sidelight at door into greenhouse.
- Sidelight at door at North deck.
- No shower, replace with storage in bathroom.
- Flip Laundry and Kids' room?
- Kids' room too big?
- Do we truly need shower on main floor bathroom?
- Move deck east adjacent to dining area.
- Why entry between kitchen/sitting room?
- Delete shower, move W wall in, extend sitting area/lounge South for quiet area.
- If possible, put freezer room in Potential Storage in basement.
- Separate toilet and sink in bathroom?
- No door leading from bathroom to guest room 1 in basement.
- Mark pantry and cart locations in kitchen.

We discussed all of the feedback and all that was consensed was incorporated into this revised design or improvements to the extent that it could be. Line items that are repeated in the feedback listed above (from three separate groups) are not all duplicated in this document.

COMMENTS: ***The third group, hard at work. This process is what helps people realize that if cost cutting has to happen, it's better not to happen in the common house. Let it happen at the private house workshop because the common house makes all of the houses bigger.***

PART 2. CONTEXT

Background

This document comprises Haystack Heights Cohousing's program and design criteria for their private houses. It summarizes the desired goals, priorities, and specific design criteria agreed to by the resident group during a programming workshop facilitated by Charles Durrett and Gary Burke of McCamant & Durrett Architects. Program; write-up by Lindy Sexton. Where criteria are not fully developed here, they are delegated to the individual house type design.

This document also serves a variety of uses:

- **To outline the design criteria**.
- **To evaluate proposed designs**.
- **To summarize the goals** and design priorities of the resident group (Group) as the project evolves.
- **To familiarize incoming residents** with the programming and design process for the private houses and the Common House as new members join the community.

This document represents the combined efforts of the future residents, culminating in a deliberate process that reflects the Group as a whole.

Once the design is complete, and consensus has been reached by the Group, the private house drawings will reflect and also supersede this program. The drawings will then reflect the programmed information as well as any new information. Subsequent design development information will further clarify the feasibility of programmatic and schematic designs.

Introduction

Creating the house of your dreams. . .

. . .a house that fits in the context of a custom community, in the context of a budget, in the context of a site. Within these contexts, the goal is to create houses that meet members' dreams, aspirations, and budget.

"To make something, anyone can do that. But to make it so appropriate that the entire larger place would feel remiss without it, that's the trick."

–Pat McDermid, The Mountain House

What's unique about cohousing is the community focus. But respite and privacy are the yin to the yang of the energy and support of the community.

The common house is really A PART of each private house. It is an extension of your private house and supplements your house, where you go every day. The more the common house is useful, used, and necessary, the healthier your cohousing community will be. I use my common house four or five times a day to get the mail, to have dinner or breakfast on occasion, to sit by the fireplace to do my homework (like this program), to have a meeting about the garden, and to do my laundry (because it's more ecological than to do so in the private house). The acoustics, the feel, and the lighting in the common house will be what makes it a place that you want to go, and do go on a daily basis.

Participatory Design Process

In summarizing the Group's programming decisions, this document confirms that participants share many of the same expectations for the project. As the design of this project evolves, this program should be used to evaluate design alternatives and changes in the context of how they address the program goals.

The members of Haystack Heights should agree on a specific process for making changes to the program, such as requiring a minimum number of persons who want to reconsider an issue before it can be put back on the agenda. While it can be useful to consider new perspectives or insights, it is also important to respect the enormous number of resident hours and effort put into the decisions that are expressed in this document. What moves cohousing projects forward is moving forward. Moving backward rarely makes a better community. Moving backward usually creates delay and sometimes unnecessary acrimony.

Some groups request that two-thirds of those present be consulted as to whether it can even get back onto the agenda. Usually, in that process, it is explained why it went that way. But most importantly, everyone's time has to be respected. If someone was there when the decisions were made, but can't be there when the decisions were revisited, they will become really annoyed.

Prior to the Private House Workshop, the Site Program for the cohousing community was created with the group at the Site Planning Workshop. The Common House Program was created at a Common House Workshop. Each of these workshops have been documented separately in their own program documents.

The Private House Program and design criteria outlined here are informed by the previous workshops. Previous design iterations of both the common house and site plan are subject to changes due to private house designs, budget limitations, zoning issues, size constraints, and other city requirements. Each step forward requires some reconsideration of decisions made previously. This is an iterative process where each designed line item must be brought up to parallel the others.

McCamant & Durrett Architects intends to adhere to the program outlined herein as close as possible. The designs will be evaluated at the Design Closure workshop.

COMMENTS: ***As mentioned earlier, the 12-day program design process is the best way to accomplish culture change. The process of discussion among future neighbors is critical for considering and making decisions like, "Should we have a common laundry for affordability, community, and sustainability?" They consider what's going to be standard per house, what's going to be an option, what will be done by the owner later, and what won't be discussed further in these workshops. This conversation has no room for making people right or wrong, but just getting to the correct decision for this group. And what will be done later by the owners.***

COMMENTS: ***The common laundry turns out to be the only place to economically recycle greywater via the landscaping, get ultra-low water use machines and use biodegradable detergents (bought at 1/3 off the original price), have less noise in your house, have less construction for your house, and disturb your neighbors less by washing at midnight when compared to having individual laundry units in the individual houses. There is so much cultural consideration in these conversations with hundreds of other points—especially if most people come to the table with open minds about issues like where the cars are parked. These conversations lead to really deep, if not profound, cultural considerations. This is brought up here, because it is here that people have the hardest time deviating from the norm. I want the group to do what they want to do, but after they have considered all possible alternatives.***

The Culture of Living in Cohousing

With a high-functioning common house in cohousing, you need less in your private house. Guests prefer to stay in the common house with its palatial amenities and more privacy. Big cooking projects can be done in the common house, and are easier because it is so well designed and outfitted. In the common house, laundry can be done more quickly and easily with several machines side-by-side, and the common house laundry room can be state-of-the-art.

Rather than focusing on the typical American Dream (a big house with a bigger garage), consider the life you aspire to having. Rather than the "Dream," we need the Great American Awakening. What do you need to best support that vision?

A life in cohousing is different from a life in a typical suburban home (which is why most cohousers choose cohousing). For instance, cohousers spend 80 percent of the time, spent in their yards, on their front porch; while in a typical suburban home, 80 percent of yard time is spent on the back porch, as you have heard me say. Therefore, in cohousing, a front and back porch might very well be designed differently. This is just one of many examples of differences in the cohousing lifestyle that likely should be reflected in the design of the houses.

Pleasant Hill Cohousing

Because of shared common space, private houses in cohousing are ample, yet more modest than typical single-family houses. They provide a balance of privacy and community.

Oakcreek Community

Workshop Topics

We discussed different aspects of the private house design criteria, such as:

- Kitchen design
- Open floor plan
- Storage
- Accessibility
- Natural light
- Natural ventilation
- Sound proofing
- Affordability
- Front porches
- Built-ins to create hierarchy
- Use of wood
- Customization
- Backyards
- Ceilings
- Thermal comfort

And we discussed what will come up at Workshop Five—the materials.

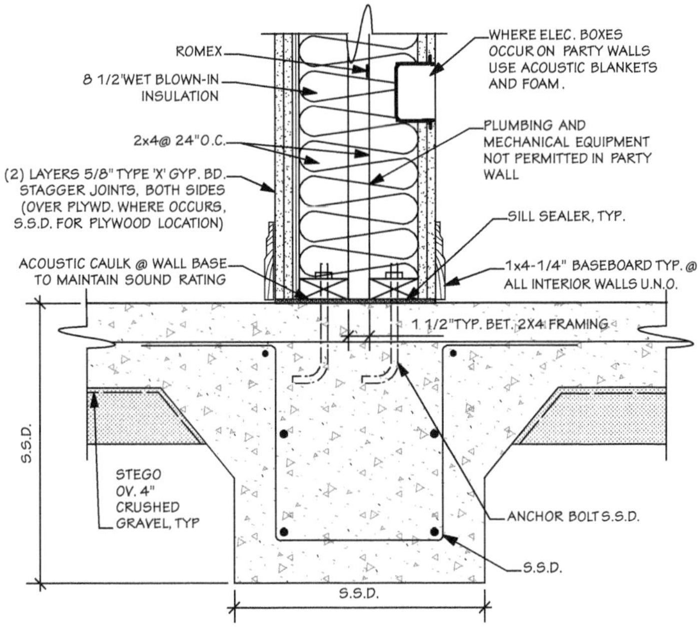

Construction detail at party wall: reducing sound transfer is a priority in the buildings.

Other Topics

It is sometimes difficult to stay with house planning issues. Folks often feel compelled to inject amenities (i.e., "my grandmother had tile counter tops, I've got to have them or I'll just die"). We will discuss those amenities further and prioritize them later (Workshops Five and Six). The priority now is to get the floor plans designed—to get the bones just right.

What will be standard amenities (A), what are options (B), and what will be custom and after-the-fact (C) will be addressed in Workshop Six.

COMMENTS: ***What we normally default to is what we are used to doing.***

The advancement of culture change is reviewing what a functional neighborhood is and how it is formed. However, like any emerging technology or invention, there is a lag in the acceptance.

But what designers like most about these design workshops is that right before your eyes, you see a reemergence of the timeless if not ancient understandings for what makes sense as common, and what makes sense as private. No blurring of the border, but an interlocking that becomes as natural and obvious as two hands clasping together.

PART 3. PROGRAM

Goals for the Private Houses

Imagine you come home one late afternoon, in 2020, and when you walk through the front door, you say to yourself, "Wow, I just love my home. The houses are optimized and we met most of the goals for our houses."

What do you love about it? What were and what are those goals for your houses, your refuge?

- High windows
- Outside merging w/inside
- Light
- Warm and cozy
- Natural materials
- Just big enough
- Easy to navigate
- Come be here
- Sign of entrance
- A smart transition
- Quiet
- Sense of stillness
- Good display
- Affordability
- Beauty
- Great kitchen
- Open floor plan
- Facilitate aging in space
- Place to be a family
- Intermediate places
- A place to be private
- Just right storage
- Accessible
- Easy to clean
- Visitability—visit
- Customize ability
- Private outdoor space
- Public outdoor space
- Built-ins
- Looks like Spokane
- Sense of spaciousness
- Consciousness of transitions
- Thoughtful—composting, etc.
- Outdoor living
- Ambiance
- Ventilation

A Highly Facilitated Private House Unit Matrix

A poll of group members present at the workshop led to the formulation of five unit types (A1, A2, A3, B, C). The distribution below reflects the decision of those five types. The exact bath types and sizes were developed in small groups for each unit type over two days. The floor plans at the end of this program illustrate the consensed plans for the three unit types.

Unit	Beds	Baths	Type	Size (sf)	Quantity
A1	2	1	Flat	866	4
A1′	2	1	Flat	854	4
A2	2	1 3/4	Flat	983	2
A2′	2	1 3/4	Flat	970	2
A3	2+	2	Flat	1,089	2
A3′	2+	2	Flat	1,074	2
B	2+	1 3/4	Townhouse	1,204	3
C	3+	1 3/4	Townhouse	1,468	8
			Total:	**30,468**	**27**

COMMENTS: ***Affordable housing has three to four unit types, unless you're on a really tight site like this one. In this case, the number of unit types often goes up to distribute the overall costs, as seen in the matrix.***

Programming the Pieces

All units are designed with attention to natural light and transitions from public to private space, or "soft edges," such as front porches. The Group together decides which elements will be standard or customized. Details such as built-ins and custom woodwork will be discussed further in the Design Development Workshop. Additional zoning or layering of the all-room can be facilitated if an owner feels necessary by custom furniture.

House Zoning

All-room concept: The kitchen, dining, and living room are to be open and easy to communicate between. It is the ability to "borrow" space from the adjacent room(s) that makes smaller spaces feel more generous.

Various methods can then be used to personalize and create hierarchy within the open plan. Rugs provide no physical separation but significant visual differentiation. Furniture can separate the space physically. Floor-to-ceiling casework can be used to close off an area almost completely. Custom woodwork can warm up any environment—even an already warm one! The all-room provides maximum flexibility for a diverse range of personal styles and uses.

Interior Spaces

In western terms, house areas come in three types: functional (living room, kitchen, etc.), circulation (hallways), and access (an area, say, in front of a bookshelf). In open floor plans, rooms often have all three characteristics—making them feel more gracious. An open floor plan saves space by creating areas that can have multiple uses. The living room in effect "borrows" space from the circulation to make it, in fact, larger. Spaces for circulation may be used for gathering and activities, and may expand into other "rooms." Outdoor spaces, like the front porch and windows between indoor and outdoor space, help small interior rooms feel larger than they really are. Moveable furniture can be used to create semi-separate open spaces.

Exterior Architecture

The exterior architecture will be reviewed carefully at design closure, but the point of departure will be the visual preference study.

Living Room

To be worked out individually per unit type.

Private House Front Porches

Front porches include room for a table and chairs. Programmed at 7' deep in the Site Design Workshop.

Kitchen

- Kitchen to be "L," "U," "Galley," or "Country" depending on what works best for each individual unit type.
- Kitchens will face the front of the house, whenever possible, with the kitchen sinks at the window looking toward the common area (whenever possible).
- Dining table should fit in kitchen in some units (a country kitchen).
- Upper cabinet discussed at 14" above counter top. No one objected to the 14" counter to upper cabinet dimension.
- Range width to be 30".
- Dishwasher to be 18" (but probably an option, see Workshops Five and Six).
- Sink size to be 25" wide.
- Refrigerator size to be 24."
- Island per kitchen to probably be option (see Workshop Six).
- Pull-out cutting boards.
- Sill height to be 2'8" to 2'11" on regular living room or bedroom windows.

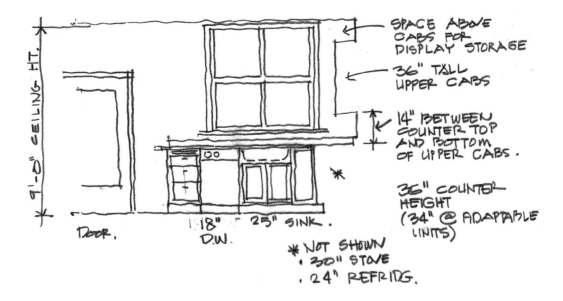

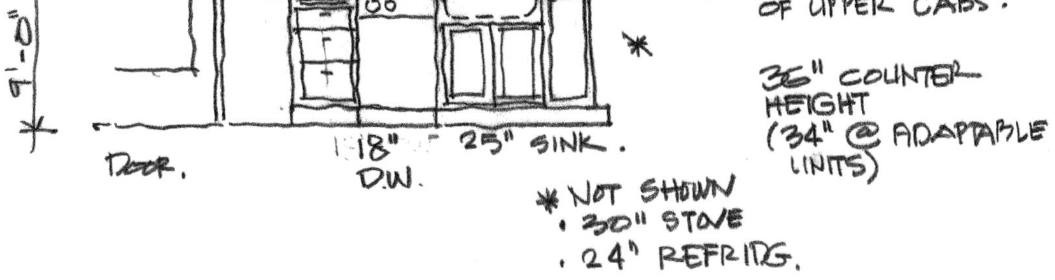

Storage

Storage for each unit was discussed in the house type meetings.

Closet Door

There are no perfect closet doors. The ones that seem to "get out of the way" best and allow the most texture are the bi-fold or slider. To be worked out per house type by architects and presented at Workshop Four.

Other Programmed Pieces

- Sloped ceilings where possible.

Washer and Dryer

All units will have a designated closet that may be plumbed and vented for a stacked washer and dryer (Workshop Six). The washer and dryer and their plumbing will probably be an option, unless more than 80 percent or so of households want it—then they will probably be standard in all units where they fit. If you don't have a washer/dryer in your home:

- The closet can be used for storage instead.
- You won't have noisy machines in your home.
- Humidity in your house will be reduced.
- The walk to the common house laundry is easy and enjoyable and is third, only after common cooking and eating, in terms of giving people an excuse to go there.
- Common laundry washers and dryers tend to be state-of-the-art in efficiency, and common detergent tends to be ecological—at wholesale prices in the Common House.

COMMENTS: ***Sketches the architect drew while planning the private houses with the group.***

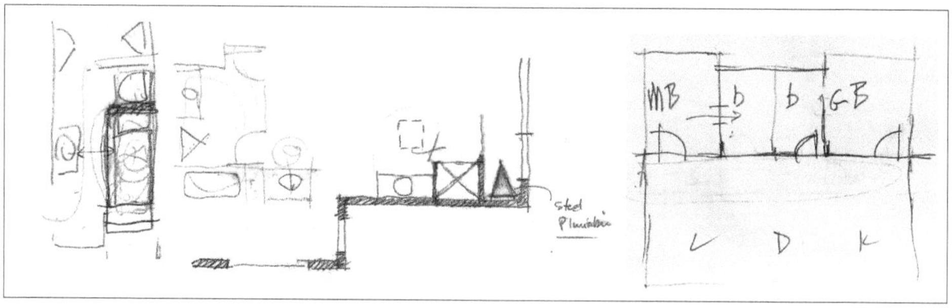

The private kitchen is a simple, beautiful, and quiet place where you can cook intimate meals.

In the kitchen, drawers help access goods.

The bathroom is to be adaptable or optional (universal) as finalized in Workshops Five and Six. On the left: accessible sink. On the right: accessible shower.

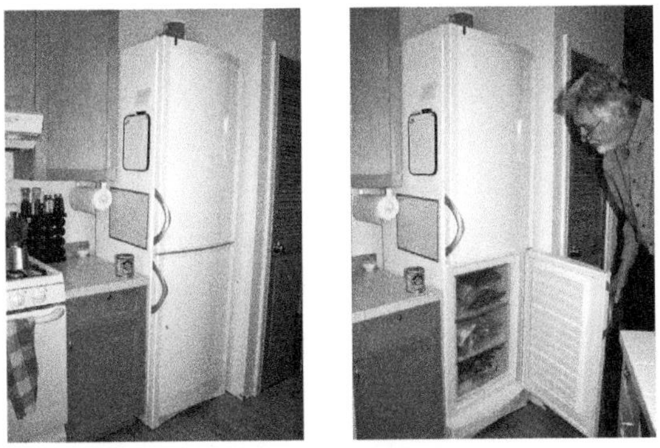

Rightsizing your life. When you eat dinner in the common house a couple of times per week, in town once a week, at a friends once a week; an energy-efficient 24″ refrigerator in your private house is enough. These refrigerators are quieter and allow for more counter and cabinet space.

Universal design helps eliminate the need for special devices by making everything easy to use by everyone.

Later, but during construction, organized options make it easy to personalize the houses.

COMMENTS: ***This survey is done in person with everyone ranking them at the same time. As I put each image on the screen, I asked them to rate the "look" from 1 to 5, 5 being the top—i.e., I like this a lot, and 1 being the bottom—i.e., I really, really don't like this. Those numbers are averaged, and the final ranking is derived from 1 through 54. As we mentioned, we basically amalgamated the top 20 rankings to come up with the unique Spokane Cohousing look at the workshop.***

Architectural Preferences

Following are the top responses of the architectural style survey that the Group took. These prioritized 54 images (some are from Spokane, some are not) will be the basis for the architectural style of the project.

Rank		Score	Rank		Score
1		**4.5**	6		**4.2**
2		**4.5**	7		**4.2**
3		**4.3**	8		**4.2**
4		**4.3**	9		**4.1**
5		**4.2**	10		**4.1**

Rank		Score	Rank		Score
11		**4.1**	16		**3.7**
12		**4.0**	17		**3.7**
13		**4.0**	18		**3.6**
14		**3.9**	19		**3.6**
15		**3.8**	20		**3.5**

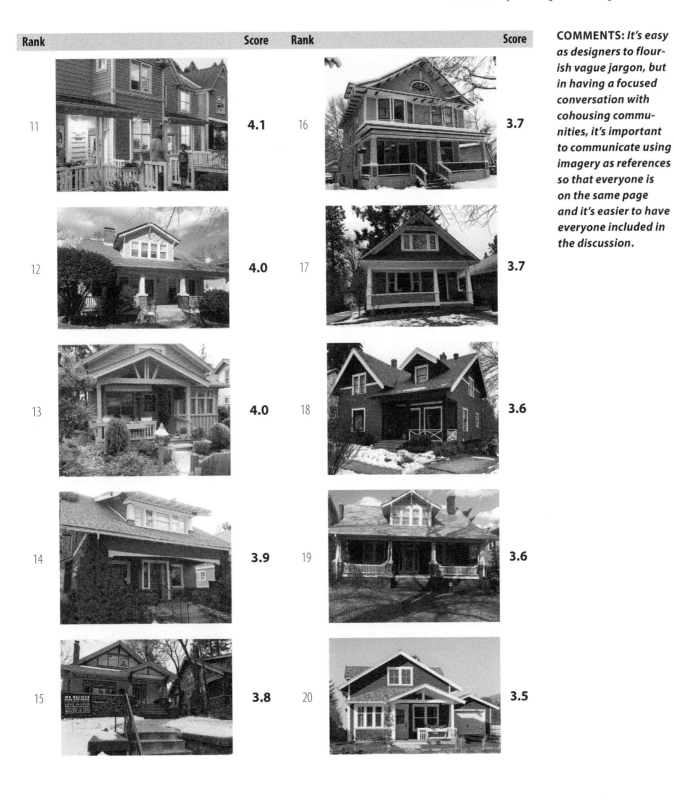

COMMENTS: ***It's easy as designers to flourish vague jargon, but in having a focused conversation with cohousing communities, it's important to communicate using imagery as references so that everyone is on the same page and it's easier to have everyone included in the discussion.***

Rank		Score	Rank		Score
21		**3.5**	26		**3.2**
22		**3.5**	27		**3.2**
23		**3.4**	28		**3.2**
24		**3.2**	29		**3.1**
25		**3.2**	30		**3.0**

Rank		Score	Rank		Score
31		**3.0**	36		**2.8**
32		**2.9**	37		**2.8**
33		**2.9**	38		**2.8**
34		**2.9**	39		**2.6**
35		**2.8**	40		**2.6**

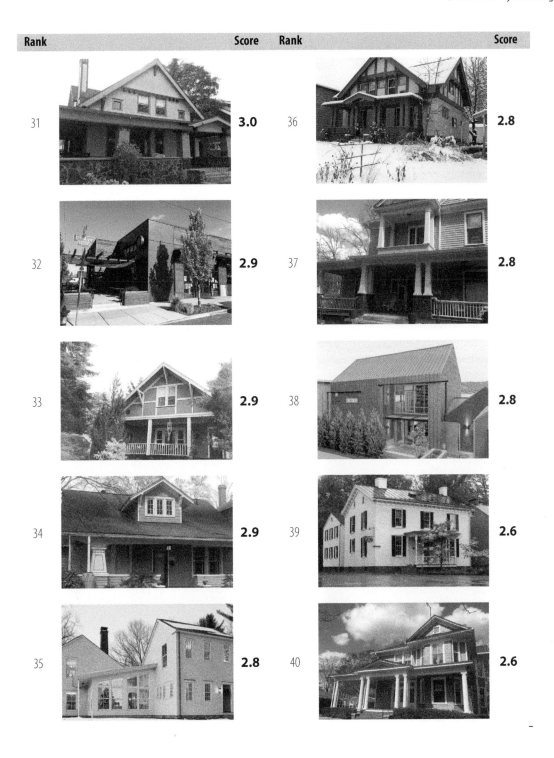

Rank		Score	Rank		Score
41		**2.6**	46		**2.4**
42		**2.6**	47		**2.3**
43		**2.5**	48		**2.2**
44		**2.4**	49		**2.1**
45		**2.4**	50		**2.1**

Rank		Score	Rank		Score
51		**2.1**	53		**1.8**
52		**1.9**	54		**1.6**

PART 4. CONCLUSION

Workshop Conclusion

The house design effort in the small groups is where most of the house schematic design is refined and developed. Each design is a function of the small group meetings held for each unit type. And the plans will also be improved upon as MDA fits them into the rationale and structure of the larger buildings, the site, and the style preferences of the Group.

As we refine the private house plans, please keep the ABC list in the back of your mind. In other words, think about amenities (A list), options (B list), and customization (C list). These items will play a role in the feel of the homes and the final design, but will not be part of the immediate conversation. They will be discussed during Workshops Five and Six.

Specific materials, from doorknobs and kitchen sinks to windows and flooring, will be determined during the Design Development Workshop (Workshop Five), but they are not a part of what is required for the final schematic design. That said, the schematic design must be one that has been thought through.

I'm particularly happy with the elegance of the solutions that we came up with, if perhaps not always the grace by which we came up with them. The private houses are absolutely the most difficult of the components of this custom-made neighborhood. The folks who join later will profit immensely from your hard work. The Private House Workshop (Workshop Three) reconciles the deeply personal notion of home with the concept of supportive community. Basic cohousing math (1+1 = 3) played out in spades here—that is, she had an idea, then he had an idea, and they combined ideas so that the house turned out better than it would have with either idea alone.

Sincerely,

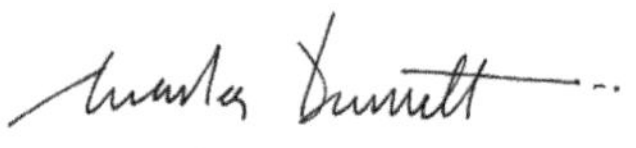

Charles Durrett

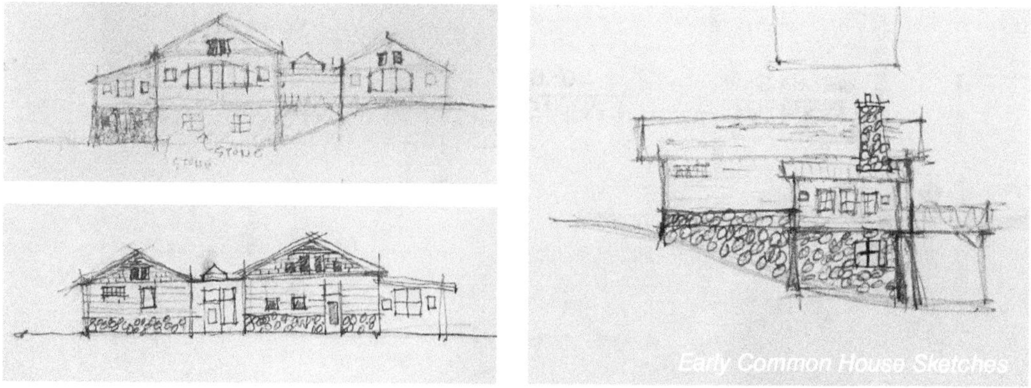

Early Common House Sketches

Next Steps

Design Closure (Workshop Four)

The next workshop is the Design Closure Workshop, where we present and explain to the Group the entire proposed schematic design. We will have aggregated the house types into buildings, located the buildings on the site, and adjusted the site plan accordingly. We will present drawings of the building elevations that include proposed exterior materials, front porches, and key design details. After this step, the decisions made will not be revisited unless an outside source requires a change. This is key for budget, schedule, and quality. A little backtracking can lead to a lot of unraveling.

The final goal is for all of the necessary design drawings to start the base sheets for all of the other professionals involved in design development and formulation of construction documents that go to the city. The civil engineer, the mechanical engineer, the structural engineer, etc.

Design Development (Workshop Five)

The Design Development Workshop is where we consider all of the materials, from the front doorknob and the kitchen sink to the rear porch light.

Prioritization (Workshop Six)

The Prioritization Workshop is where costs that exceed basic construction are prioritized. Some amenities will go into every house; some will become options; and some will become custom work done later by the homeowner (for example, custom woodwork).

PART 5. APPENDIX

At the January 6–8, 2018
Haystack Heights Private House Workshop,
the following participants were in attendance:

Jim Dawson and Mariah McKay
Bob Stilger and Susan Virnig
Bill and Nikki Lockwood
John and Christie Bruntlett
Anne Stephenson

Pat Mertens and Ray Owens
Doug Robnett and Sarah Conover
Rob and Abby Roose and Robin Roose
Chris Nerison

MUNKSØGÅRDS, DENMARK

Why do they have communal dinners five nights per week? Because they can. Because everything else goes easier when they break bread together, both individually and collectively—"I'll always give you the benefit of the doubt if you cook for me." Relationships, management, everything. Although a very affordable senior cohousing—one mistake they made here is undersizing the common terrace. Still, it works.

WOLF CREEK LODGE SENIOR COHOUSING

There is no judgment for seniors who want to live out their lives with other people that they relate well with—all they often want is to talk about their lives and all of the things they have learned along the way.

PART

2

Senior Cohousing Design

Seniors deserve to be respected, not just housed. It seems that the only way to make sure this happens is to authentically involve them in planning the project. The more days the better, but twelve days of co-design has proven to work well. It also doesn't pay to set them up, or to do everything for them. Being able to ask your neighbors "Hey, what's for dinner tonight?" "Who's mowing the lawn?" "Can you help me fix this please?" "Do you want to go camping together this weekend?" is a much nicer way to live out your life. Let's go to the store and get some snacks for tonight's party.

MUNKSØGÅRDS, DENMARK

Even in a senior housing project, the vehicles are remotely parked. No noise, no smell, no danger—just human interaction.

MUNKSØGÅRDS, DENMARK

This group worked for years to make this project. It wasn't until the watershed evening when the architect and the builder in unison suggested that there's only one way to get this done. And that was if they put 10 (exact 2B1b) dwellings downstairs and 10 upstairs—rather odd for a senior housing project. But this way, they could afford it. In addition, they felt it was better than the unsuitable single-family houses that they were moving from. Plus, they made the agreement that if you lived upstairs and needed a roll-in downstairs unit, someone downstairs would change houses with you. The upstairs units were more popular anyway. Cooperation supersedes architecture. As the residents put it, "the buildings are just the picture frame, the life between the buildings is the picture."

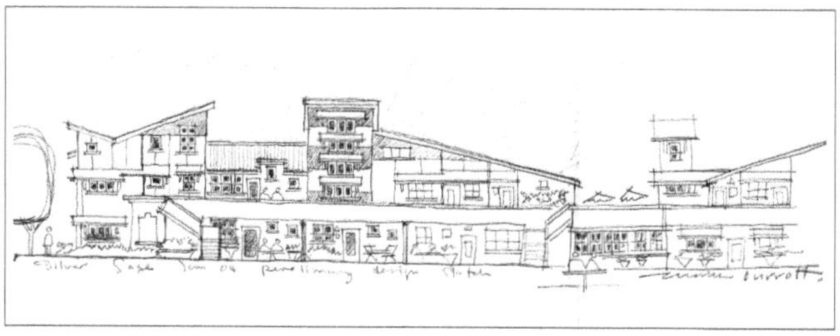

SILVER SAGE, BOULDER, CO

Early sketches tell you what's attractive, what's possible, and what's practical. Study your intentions until you know for sure that you will like it. There's nothing worse than getting a building half-built and saying to yourself, "Whoops."

MUNKSØGÅRDS, DENMARK

The life between the buildings is palpable when done right, and to accomplish that at all, it must be affordable. If convalescence is necessary for a knee or hip operation or similar, they could move into the one-story common house for a couple of months.

7

Senior Neighborhood Design

Site Design

"Architecture and architectural freedom are above all a social issue that must be seen from inside a political structure, not outside it."

Linda Bo Bardi

How do you optimally design a community site plan for seniors? You pull it all together. Have tighter, more old-timey circulation, like a tight medieval passage, and gathering nodes on every lane. Then, pull it all apart. Make the parking remote, for example. Meg, at 90 years old, picked the house furthest away from her car (700 feet away) because, in her words, "my relationship with my neighbors is more important than my relationship with my auto." And I can attest to the hundreds of seniors who say that their trek to their automobiles (while often pulling a little canvas wagon) keeps them young and definitely keeps them connected. Furthermore, it leads to deep relationships that lasted for the rest of their lives. Once people get used to a car-free zone, they love it. Even so, a few do live near their cars and there are always backup plans—like being able to take the car or an electric golf cart to the house under extenuating circumstances.

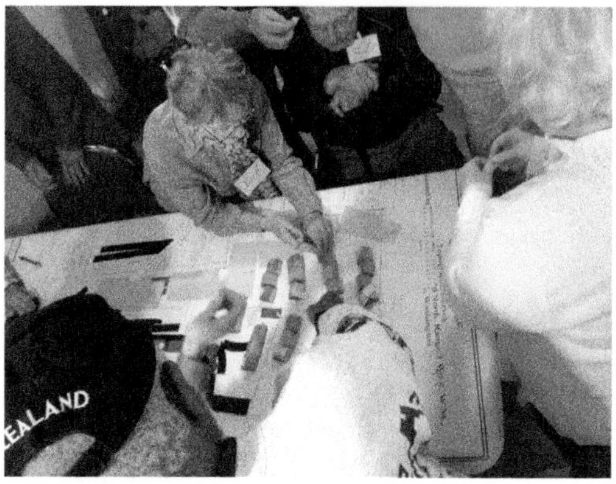

QUIMPER VILLAGE, WA

How do you make a twenty-first-century northwest village? You start with the people and their discovered criteria; you start with the culture. Let's try this one. . . what if we moved the houses this way? How does that better fulfill the criteria. . . or detract from the stated criteria prominently posted on the walls?

QUIMPER VILLAGE, WA

This is what matters—this is the real test. Does the site plan actually do what it was intended to do?

QUIMPER VILLAGE, WA

This is the overall drawing, the main design closure document along with a hundred others. That is, once the site plan had been concurred, the common house, and its location, and all three of the house plan designs had to be coalesced and synthesized. This was the synthesis.

I really can't mention cars without talking about Sardinia, Italy, and Okinawa, Japan. Both are known as two of the five "blue zones" around the world (regions with a higher-than-average life expectancy). Sardinia, for example, has 17 times more centenarians than North America—17 times more per capita people who live to over 100 years old. Of the many books about blue zones, their advice for living past 100 years of age boils down to three main things:

1. Eat right, mostly light.
2. Stay active, mostly low impact.
3. Stay connected (i.e., community).

SILVER SAGE, BOULDER, CO

Everyone can see the common dinner in the springtime. "I might not have signed up this time, but I will next time."

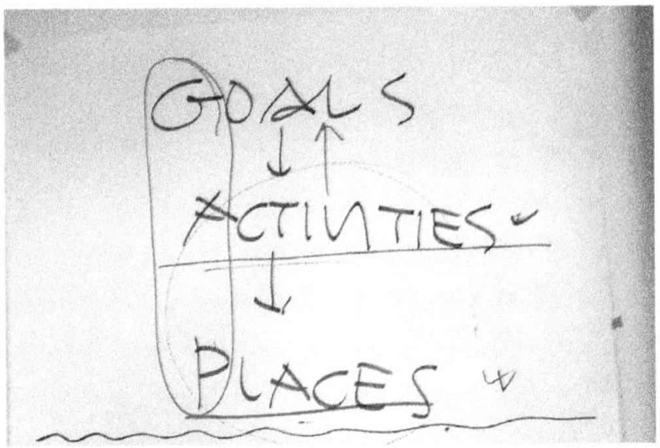

STILLWATER, OK

The goal of the design criteria process is to fill the GAP between what we have and what we want.

WOLF CREEK LODGE, CA

Go ahead and tell the story—explain the environment that you are proposing. However, don't do it from above in some isometric, bird's-eye view—use an experiential point of view to capture the life.

STILLWATER, OK

Group 2 at work in a different room. Left to their own devices and to evaluate the design criteria they developed two days ago, lots of ideas are flying. It's not like working with a bunch of architects worrying about whether it will be published or not while apparently contemplating their next move like a chess game. These folks have one job, "how do we make a great neighborhood that I will love and that these precious people around me will also love?"

Genetics are often mentioned; when Sardinians move to the United States, their average life expectancy drops below what is expected in Sardinia.

When I was sailing around the Mediterranean with Jan Gudmand-Høyer, every time we came to port in the evening in Greece or Turkey, we would be greeted with the timeless view of a group of seniors sitting on the wharf at portside. Retired folks want to talk about their lives and all they've learned along the way. Even in intergenerational enhanced communities, seniors usually spend their time mentoring each other. Give this to them—make this happen if you can.

In self-developed projects like cohousing, there are so many opportunities to break the mold. Zoning was invented in the early twentieth century, and it was designed to keep people of color out of white neighborhoods. In 1916, the first zoning code in the United States in Berkeley, California, explicitly

STILLWATER, OK

The two separate groups came up with two separate site plans. The groups then collectively evaluated each site plan separately, around four–five times. Through careful conversation, they basically asked themselves over and over, "OK, which aspects of our goals, activities, and places does Scheme 1 address best?" and "OK, now what aspects does Scheme 2 address?," and so on. This happened over and over for about an hour until we had a merged and agreed scheme, which we built. One hour of time to run through this exercise is time well-spent when dealing with a plan that will be there forever.

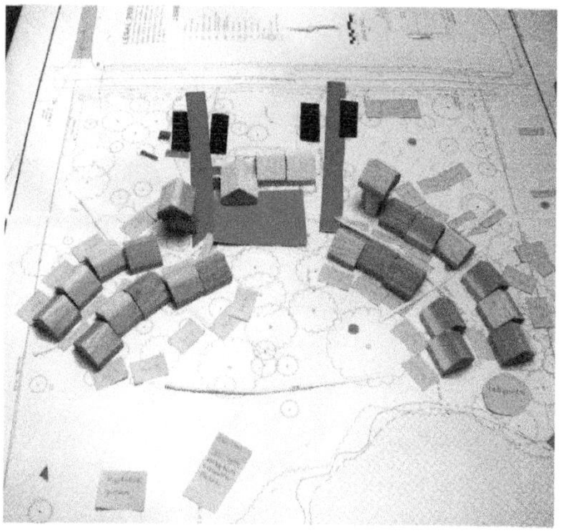

STILLWATER, OK

Elevate the table and look down the lane one at a time; each person gains perspective and a sense of scale. Each vignette is studied by everyone. Squint a little and you can see the life between the buildings.

contained a proponent reading: "we have to keep the multi-family housing with Negros and Asiatics out of the white, single-family neighborhoods." This was largely enforced by a developer, Duncan McDuffie, who pushed for single-family zoning after fearing a black-owned dance hall would be able to move to a subdivision next to his neighborhood. He created covenants with the intent to exclude non-whites from living or purchasing in many of the prominent neighborhoods he developed. Zoning was used as an institutional means of keeping the white suburbs separate from people of color. As an architect who has designed thousands of housing units, I have never seen any other means of combating that blatant racism and classism as well as cohousing does. Cohousing is very much the magic bullet. That is—over and over again, when you bring citizens to the table who can make the decision makers (city council, planning commission, etc.) familiar with the real people involved, they have a very difficult time saying no—if not impossible. Of the 55 cohousing projects we have done, only one stopped due to conservative decision makers, and that was in Marin County, California. In other words, I have seen that when we introduce the people involved with a cohousing project to the decision makers, city council, planning commission, they tend to agree with our plans. If I don't have the group with me, it's back to brand x as far as the city is concerned. Consider, in the case of Stillwater, Oklahoma, the group went to a long-established single-family house neighborhood, bought a house for less than $400,000, and remodeled that into the common building. Of the 24 units, the group absolutely needed six units to be $150,000, given their population and budgets. And unfortunately the cost of construction was no less than elsewhere in the U.S.—the area had the same surge in construction costs due to the financial market crash of 2008. However, the group's initiative and empowerment were able to persuade the city council to rezone the parcel of land from single-family to multi-family—enabling the six affordable units to be built to their budget. This was possible because Stillwater had scores of "Cultural Creatives."

"Cultural Creatives," as described by Paul Ray, one of the authors of the book by the same name,[1] are the people who move into community-oriented neighborhoods with the intention of growing older in a different way than their parents did. Pat Darlington explicitly stated, "I'm moving into Still-

STILLWATER, OK

"You could put 20 seniors on a boat, and take them out to a deserted island, and together they will do a better job of providing for themselves than any institution we have yet invented." To provide for individuals appropriately, you have to do it with them.

water Senior Cohousing, because I have no intention of growing older like my father did, left to his single-family house, unable to drive and therefore isolated, lonely, and consequently of ill health for far too long." These Cultural Creatives were able to express these realities to the city council and the planning commission, both in private and public hearings. Consequently, they received a 5–0 vote of approval at the planning commission and 5–0 at the city council. Solving our mutual needs as we age couldn't be more overlapping—it's a good time to live in a real community. As the prolific author Bill Thomas likes to say, "You can put 20 seniors in a boat and take them out to a deserted island, drop them off, and they will do a better job of providing for themselves than any institution that we have yet created for them. Armed with legions of PhDs in gerontology—we can't come close."

The discovery and championing of intergenerational cohousing as a model for senior cohousing is what jumpstarted senior cohousing in Denmark. Intergenerational cohousing had proven that proximity—in combination with the intent of creating a highly functional neighborhood—played a key role in people knowing each other, caring about each other, and supporting each other over time. And, by 1985, many seniors lived in intergenerational cohousing. Some liked living with all the kids, some did not—and so senior cohousing started. This was a pivotal moment for senior housing in Denmark. Focus groups started in earnest for every new community-enhanced senior housing project. There are those who say that every senior housing project made in Denmark today has been marked by the success of cohousing (housing that is designed to be extraordinarily successful from a community point of view); from focus groups and extensive common facilities, to remote parking, and on-going organization—all with an emphasis on what can we do together and what activities can we share (like walking to the store together) that can make our own individual lives more convenient, more practical, more economical, healthier, and more fun.

MOUNTAIN VIEW, CA

Programming the site plan. Establishing the criteria for two days before moving the wood blocks.

VILLAGE HEARTH, NC

Seeing your landscape fall into place is fun, and it builds strong bonds at the same time. Would this LGBTQ group of future residents be able to make a neighborhood that made them feel safe individually late into their elderhood? Not by themselves, but with others? Of course. The future residents were clear—we need a place where others will understand us, accept us, and know our shared history.

Whether those legacy projects are apartments, single-room occupancy, housing hotels, multi-family of many different sorts, co-living, or even seniors living in single-family house neighbor-hoods; these ideas and concepts enable folks to get organized easily, making their lives more engaging and lively.

The mission statement of this senior cohousing reads simply: "we intend to have as much fun in our second 50 years as we did in our initial 50." Started by five couples in their early 50s, and move in with five teenagers.

STILLWATER, OK

How hard is it to buy a single-family house in an upscale neighborhood and get it rezoned to 24 dwelling units? Never discount this possibility. Never negotiate against yourselves. As this group showed, anything is possible. And the result is a warm and glowing community, not a 90-year-old dying alone in a single-family house—as is what occurred in the house that they bought and converted.

MOUNTAIN VIEW, CA

Even in one building, the negative space (the outside) can be, and should be, embraced by the built environment.

The inception of senior cohousing in Denmark in 1985.

MOUNTAIN VIEW, CA

Beauty is its own reward. Sculpture, if you will. Models help make architecture happen, and really help the users know what it will feel like to come home.

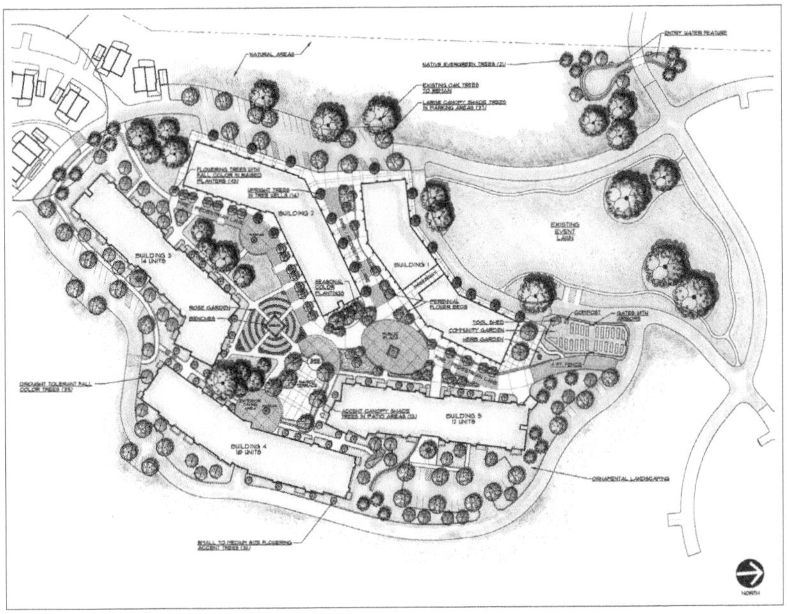

LEGACY—RINCON DEL RIO, CA

Commercial below makes it feel like a medieval village.

QUIMPER VILLAGE, WA

The larger neighborhood shut this previously proposed senior housing project down for the same site. They already had a monolith/impersonal behemoth in their neighborhood. They wanted another neighborhood in their neighborhood—we gave them a village and the project was approved.

QUIMPER VILLAGE, WA

The Port Townsend group successfully relied on future residents to go through the designs, program, and agreements with all potential future residents throughout construction. That's how you help make a culture of cooperation. There's an entire world out there if you don't want to cook for your neighbor. Occasionally, here we do.

QUIMPER VILLAGE, WA

"If you want to get another senior housing project approved, don't design a behemoth." That was the advice of the land seller. Not a desirable project in the background.

QUIMPER VILLAGE, WA

Deep down, village making is in all of us. We know how to do it, it's in our genetic code. We just have to unleash it, remember it, and feel it. At the same time, it is an intellectual act—and therefore requires an extensive write-up of your intentions (a program).

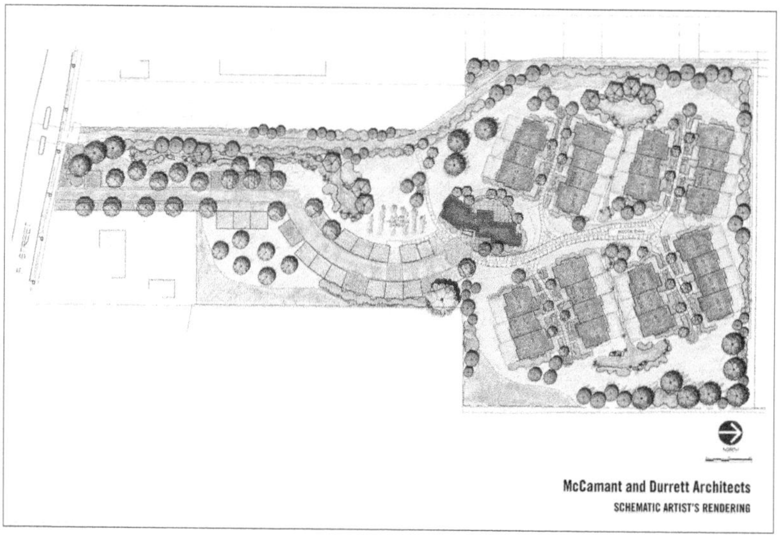

QUIMPER VILLAGE, WA

In this northwestern climate, it's good to have lots of big windows facing the south.

QUIMPER VILLAGE, WA

Senior Cohousing Site Plan

Two days of creating site plan criteria, followed by two evenings of moving blocks in order to best test and optimally achieve the desired criteria.

One can easily see if the lights are on in the common house (to the left), and can easily decide when to connect there.

QUIMPER VILLAGE, WA

A village feels like a village.

QUIMPER VILLAGE, WA

After three thorough workshops, this design closure sketch carried the day with the future residents and the city council.

QUIMPER VILLAGE, WA

In the grey and drizzly world under the dense and cloudy skies, the greenhouse plays a huge community role. It reminds me of Birmingham, England. When the sky opened up a little or a lot and rained, the community members would retreat into the greenhouse and still be in warm company.

SILVER SAGE, BOULDER, CO

Often, it's just a gate (that can be easily walked around) that signals that someone lives here, someone cares about this place, and "we ask that you do too." Silver Sage working drawings finished and construction administration by Bryan Bowen.

SILVER SAGE, BOULDER, CO

The bicycle shed, in action. Be very silly in the design process so that you don't need to be while living there. It's critical to have active participation in order to get people's priorities straight. It doesn't take long into the development process, just a few weeks, before everyone realizes that community is the real priority.

SILVER SAGE, BOULDER, CO

Design Closure: Physical cardboard models are often necessary to get the design approved, to help let everyone know where the design is, including the group, the city, and the design team. This is the rough draft of the construction. Now is the time to fix things, especially roof problems—not during construction.

SILVER SAGE, BOULDER, CO

The same project as the model. The streetscape is important because the cityscape you present becomes your identity, if not your role, in the neighborhood.

SILVER SAGE, BOULDER, CO

Silver Sage, a compact senior cohousing built on 0.83 acres in North Boulder, Colorado. You can make a village here as well as anywhere else, as long as the common spaces are embraced.

SILVER SAGE, BOULDER, CO

When done right, even urban environments can feel like a village.

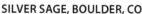

SILVER SAGE, BOULDER, CO

The street façade. That and a few residents at the podium in City Hall got this project approved in one night. For context, this never happens in Boulder.

SILVER SAGE, BOULDER, CO

Architecture is its own reward. Remember, if it's worth building it, it's worth designing it. Try not to build anything that doesn't fit the setting. Design it as if the entire place would be remiss without it.

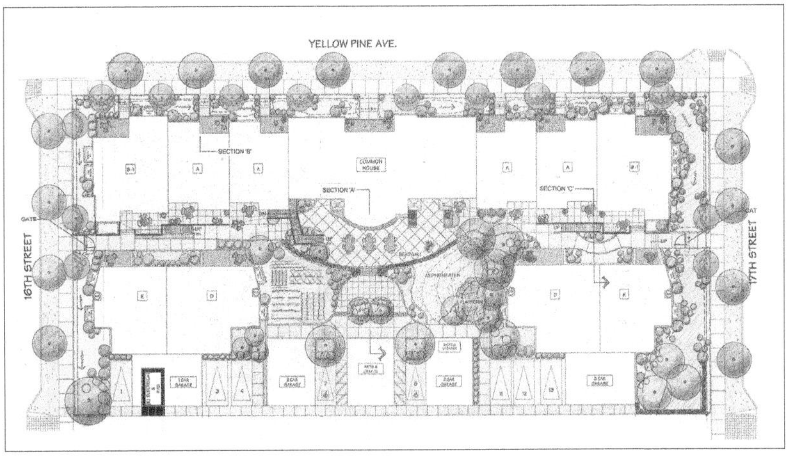

SILVER SAGE, BOULDER, CO

While designing this site plan with the group, they made it clear that as many houses as possible should be able to see the bicycle shed from their kitchen window. That way, if they see someone that they haven't seen for a while going for a ride, they can join them. This is so that if you see that Susan is going for a bike ride, "Hey, if she can do it, just recovering from illness, then I can too," or "Margaret's going as well, and I haven't spoken to her for a while."

SILVER SAGE, BOULDER, CO

A front porch that embraces the landscape, the passers-by, and the common house to the right.

SILVER SAGE, BOULDER, CO

Colorful architecture helps everyone celebrate and feel good about their accomplishments.

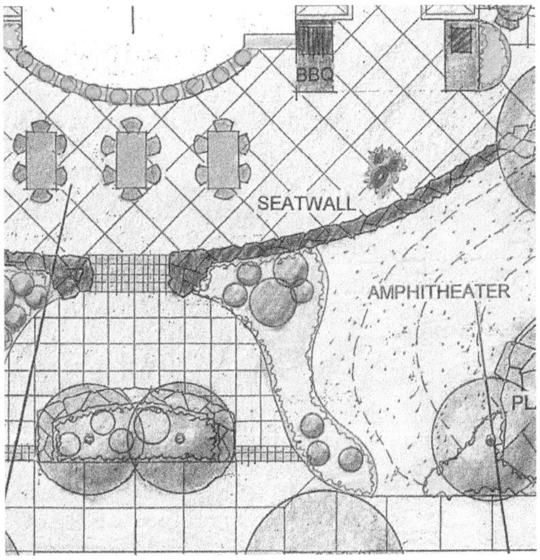

SILVER SAGE, BOULDER, CO

There are so many opportunities in the design process to fulfill the group's priorities and to add features. Here, the winter flood drainage becomes an amphitheater for summer use.

SILVER SAGE, BOULDER, CO

The common house is in the center on the bottom floor. Like the common terrace, the garden, the amphitheater, and the bicycle shed, it is embraced by the houses.

WOLF CREEK LODGE, GRASS VALLEY, CA

Early sketches, after programming. These are essentially feasibility sketches.

WOLF CREEK LODGE, CA

On a street with otherwise grotesque setbacks, "hold the corner" was our battle cry in order to bring pedestrian interest and walkability to the street, and therefore more "eyes on the street." The Head of Planning said that no one else was "holding the corner," to which we replied, "let it begin with us." Over and over, it appears that the zoning code is the nemesis of good land use. Therefore, you have to be the advocate of good land use and challenge both the zoning code and the officials. Repeatedly, we're surprised how pleasant and happy the officials are that we were able to do it a better way. Most professionals realize that setbacks are a setback, the world needs no more boxes sitting in a pool of asphalt. People prefer a streetscape with definition, color, texture, and character—not the butt-end of a bunch of cars. Architects, be the activist—be prepared to do the right thing. The French have their activist doctors (Doctors Without Borders), the Americans have their activist lawyers (ACLU), and in Denmark, there are many activist architects. That is, they challenge what a practitioner sees as something that can be done better and lobbies for the planet and for healthier environments. I'm very happy with how often bureaucrats change their minds and ultimately appreciate the improvement. Challenge height limits, density, parking, and definitely setbacks. Over and over again, it seems that the zoning code will lead you astray if you're motivated to make a great neighborhood. But you can do it.

WOLF CREEK LODGE, CA

Final Site Plan

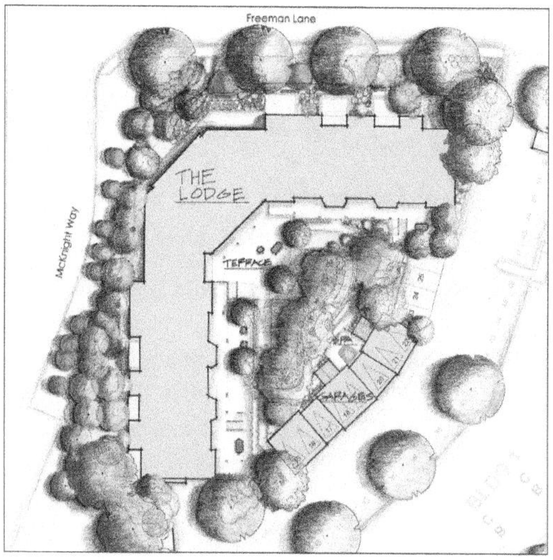

WOLF CREEK LODGE, CA

Sketches can be so realistic these days. It proves more economical, when considering possible delays, to invest in good graphics so that you have less backtracking.

WOLF CREEK LODGE, CA

Completed in 2012, the Wolf Creek Lodge in Grass Valley, California, embraces the sun and the culture. Make the single-loaded corridor lively, as if you are progressing through a landscape of front porches, and as if it's a continuous room where continuous life happens.

WOLF CREEK LODGE, CA

Rendered sections make the anatomy of the buildings understandable.

STILLWATER, OK

With real lives, real values, and ever-emerging values in the context of listening and empathizing with others, I find that a well-facilitated neighborhood creation process makes the absolutely best neighborhood that you can find anywhere—whether measured in shared people-hours or smiles per half hour.

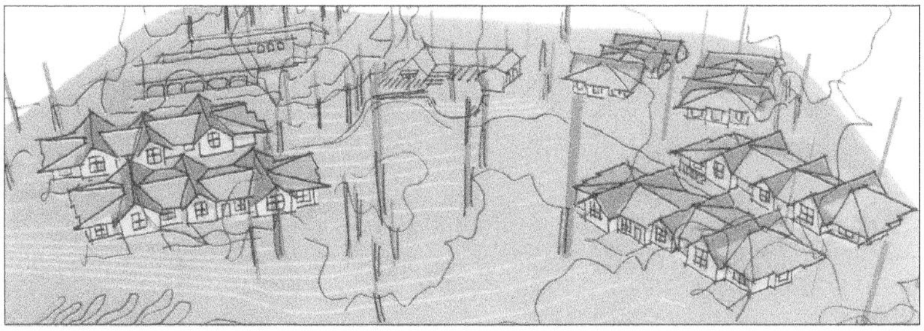

STILLWATER, OK

The final village was built more or less like this. The white building in the middle is the former single-family house turned common house. The residents moving from single-family houses, condominiums, and rental apartments spent two days bringing their various viewpoints to the table which resulted in this site plan on the third and fourth day. The residents placed every one of these blocks on these locations. Together we all criticized the final plan based on how well that they fulfilled the criteria from the all-day Saturday and all-day Sunday criteria-making collaborations. With the entire group and myself, we modified it to bring it into perfect alignment with the criteria. Every different group must come up with their own unique criteria so that they can come up with their own site plan.

STILLWATER, OK

The future residents provided the first test of the program via the facilitated block discussion. This is the second test layout, based on the first test by the group. It's a sketch of the suburban house creating a new village. The single-family house to common house conversion is in the center.

STILLWATER, OK

With Group two in another room, the two groups are doing the best they can to reflect the design criteria that they developed together (shown on the back wall).

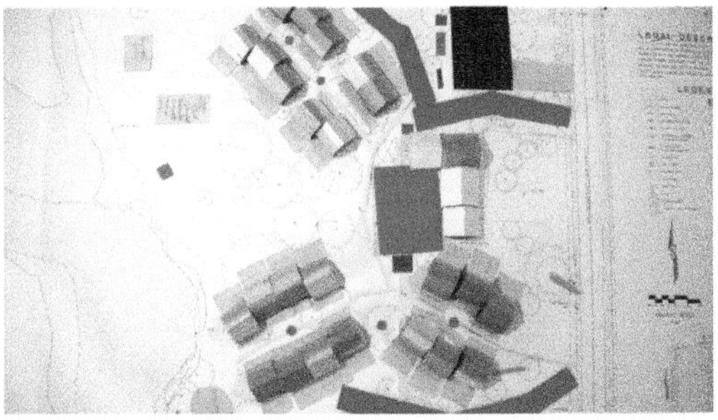

STILLWATER, OK

Two days of criteria, then two evenings of blocks. Six of these brand new houses had to come in at $150,000, which took everything that we had. But it is extremely doable, and often, extremely necessary. We certainly couldn't have done it without these people's participation and dedication. This is Group one.

STILLWATER, OK

They made it, and you could feel their sense of ownership. There was no stopping them, although as developers they had bought a single-family house in one of the best neighborhoods in town and rezoned it to a new 24-unit neighborhood—something typical designers can rarely do. But at this point, and in this case, it was personal, so the city voted to approve it 5–0 (planning commission) and 5–0 (city council).

STILLWATER, OK

As presented to the city planning commission (approved 5–0) and to the city council. Remember, this is a site in a single-family house-zoned neighborhood rezoned to a neighborhood with a newly minted design for 24 units.

STILLWATER, OK

Gathering nodes have a self-explanatory purpose. Every lane should have one. Each gathering node should be seen by as many porches as possible. When done right, things like this happen often.

STILLWATER, OK

This is where the site plan settled. After the blocks came the architects, then the civil engineer, and so on. We did not, nor would we ever, ask the city—because the city's opinion gives us what they want—which is just more of the same. What we need is imagination, creativity, and the value of real life that brings about a real vision for a better future, and a better neighborhood.

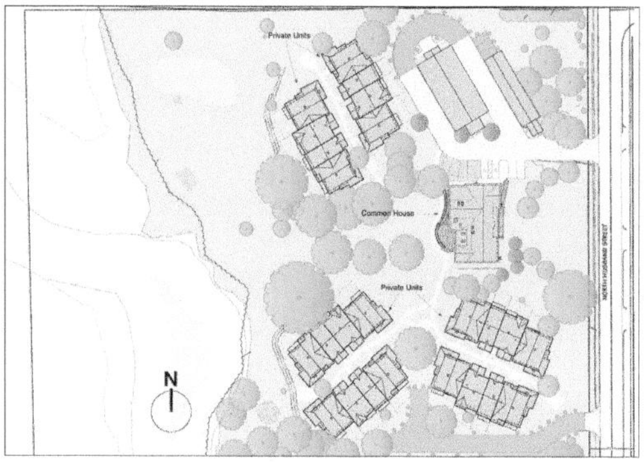

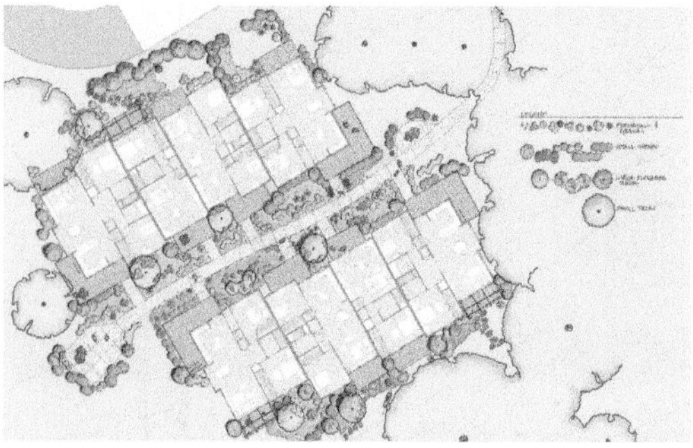

STILLWATER, OK

The gardens and the structures together make up an environment that make us happy, and fulfilled.

MOUNTAIN VIEW, CA

Perches of every sort have to be factored into the design of a one-building single-loaded corridor solution, like here at Mountain View Cohousing.

MOUNTAIN VIEW, CA

Reviewing the group-generated design criteria.

MOUNTAIN VIEW, CA

Design closure

Now, what are we getting? It's looking something like this, and this is what we plan to go to the city council with.

MOUNTAIN VIEW, CA

Mountain View on the horizon. The back side also gives something to the neighborhood—color, texture, life, richness, and character. The group not worrying about subjective questions like these of which there are four or five is asking to set the group up for failure.

MOUNTAIN VIEW, CA

On a single exterior walkway, build every detail so that it feels like more than just a walkway.

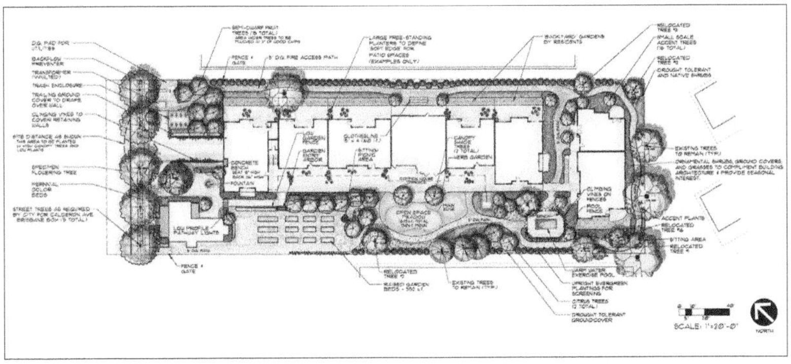

MOUNTAIN VIEW, CA

How do you make a village with a one-building solution? While it's not by nature "embracing," there's always a way to create a sense of place. Whether with trees or a minor outbuilding, physical elements can play a role, lots of quality gathering spaces inside and outside of the building also help.

MOUNTAIN VIEW, CA

The building must feel like home both day and night. The original single-family house (white building on the left) was the sole structure on the 0.9-acre site. We added a 19-unit cohousing in the backyard. In this case, the only way that the fire department would allow it was if all 19 units were all a single building—and it turned out to be the best solution for the site, neighborhood, and pocketbook. All of the parking is located below the building. Note the garden— typical for a garden right at move-in for a community-enhanced project. Having the gardens in place allows people to start getting to know each other right off the bat. People can get started the day after they move in. When this is a calling, like it is for some folks—you are not home until you put your hands in the dirt.

MOUNTAIN VIEW, CA

Models communicate the design better than just sketches so that the architect can make improvements along the way. And the city and the future resident group can see what we have in mind.

MOUNTAIN VIEW, CA

Especially in a single-family neighborhood, the streetscape takes on considerable importance as a strategy to descale the building.

VILLAGE HEARTH, NC

The program is clearly on display in the background, the block manifestation of that in the foreground. This LGBTQ group felt confidently that they would never feel safe without each other as they grow older. Because of their historical status in society, especially in the South, they articulated the way that a lot of seniors feel when there is not a good history of LGBTQ population moving to traditional assisted care or a nursing care facility.

VILLAGE HEARTH, NC

An old fashioned village, with the inviting village green right in the middle.

VILLAGE HEARTH, NC

An extremely diverse group, but still much in common—it took no time at all for the blocks to fall into place because the design criteria (on the wall behind them) was so thorough.

VILLAGE HEARTH, NC

Nothing is more exciting than the design closure workshop. Were the community members listened to? How well did we make ourselves clear? How well was the facilitation accomplished? Did the architect get that tricked-out barbeque into the project that we specified? There are thousands of other details to make sure they are addressed. I thought it was a good sign when the future resident on the left wept as we unveiled the final design—and it was.

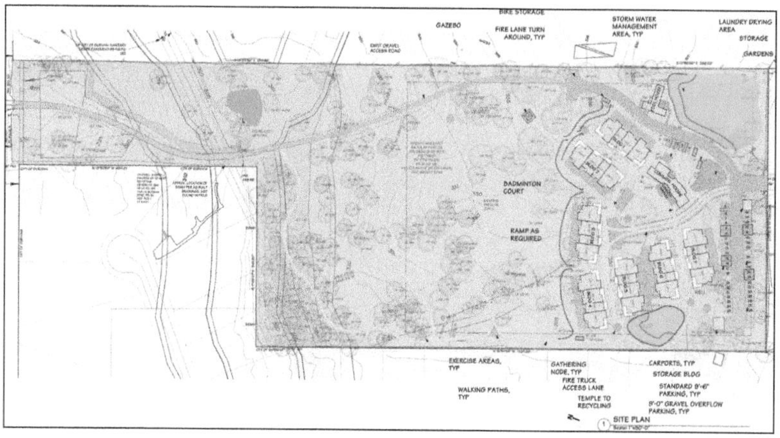

VILLAGE HEARTH, NC

The future residents of Village Hearth had 15 acres to work with. They chose to make a tight-knit village on 4 acres and to keep the rest as wooded open space. Done traditionally, this would have been more single-family homes and subdivision like all of the surrounding neighborhood.

VILLAGE HEARTH, NC

. . . And they moved in right in the middle of the pandemic. Socially distanced, but not socially isolated.

VILLAGE HEARTH SENIOR COHOUSING, NC

VILLAGE HEARTH, NC

This is how you get a cohousing project built—through ownership—emotional ownership. "We own this place." Through all of our codesigning and codeveloping efforts, and now, we're going to build it. The failed single-family house under construction on the site (upper right) is now replaced by 28 houses for this senior LGBTQ allies community. They believe that they have nowhere else better to go than this caring and loving community that they helped make.

SHEPHERDSTOWN, WV

The best neighborhood makers are those who plan to live there. There is so much heart that they bring to the table. I've never seen it with developers or architect co-designers, and of course not bureaucrat designers. But when with those who intend to live out the balance of their days here, you see them pruning their roses, and having iced tea on the porch. You see it through their eyes.

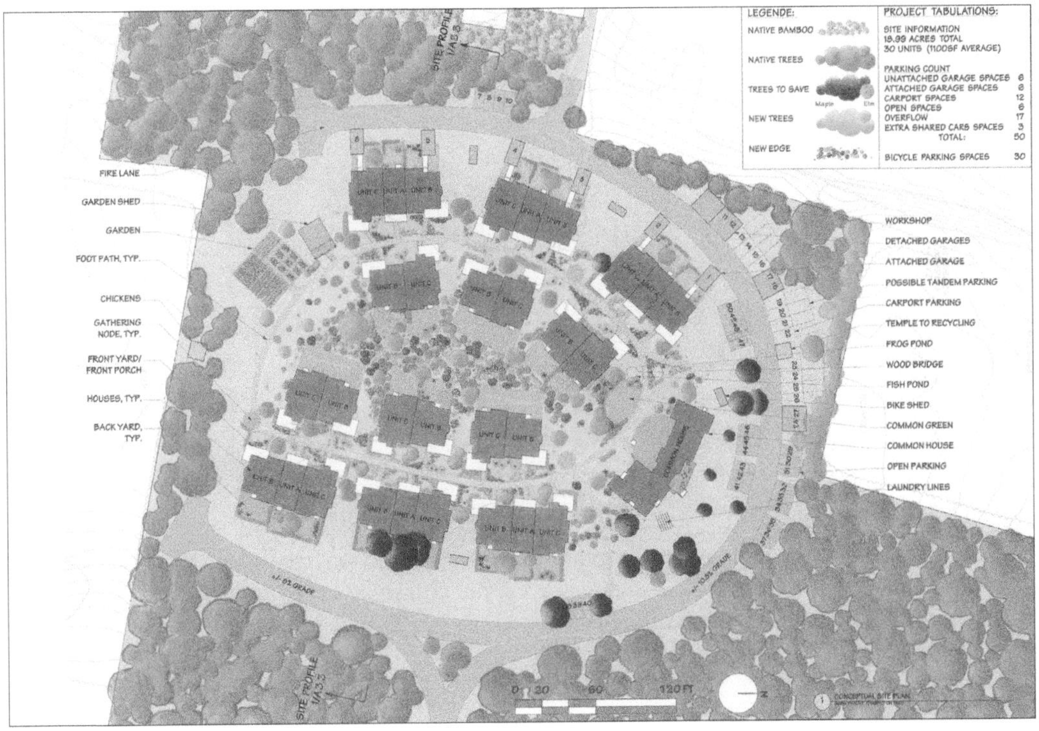

SHEPHERDSTOWN, WV

Reminiscent of the Iroquois and other tribes of the Shenandoah Valley.

SHEPHERDSTOWN, WV

PUYALLUP, WA

Double cohousing feasibility

Very preliminary feasibility sketch for a new double cohousing community in Puyallup, Washington. Cohousing associated with farms and extensive vegetable gardens are increasingly popular in Denmark, and we expect it to become more and more common in North America.

LEGACY

Green house projects like this are very common in Sweden especially for senior cohousing as well as communities that utilize multiple floors in a high-rise building of 80 units per acre or more. These projects are very energy-efficient. See Chapter 14 on density.

LEGACY—RINCON DEL RIO, CA

Housing above, commercial below. Old-world, medieval town villages are on the way back. What's old is new again.

LEGACY—SACRAMENTO STREET SENIOR HOUSING, BERKELEY, CA

This 41-unit senior housing above the commercial below feels like a community. This scale is the future if we are ever to make cities walkable and interesting.

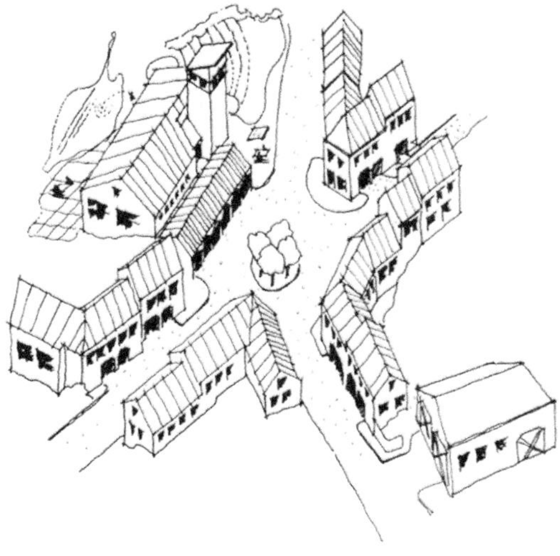

LEGACY

The medieval "planning" above is along the lines of how people naturally flow through a space. By nature, it is foot-driven and relationship-driven sequencing. When doing a larger project, especially with a cohousing and a commercial component like Rincon del Rio, I start with a very pedestrian-oriented land use prototype—such as when walking was the main mode of transportation.

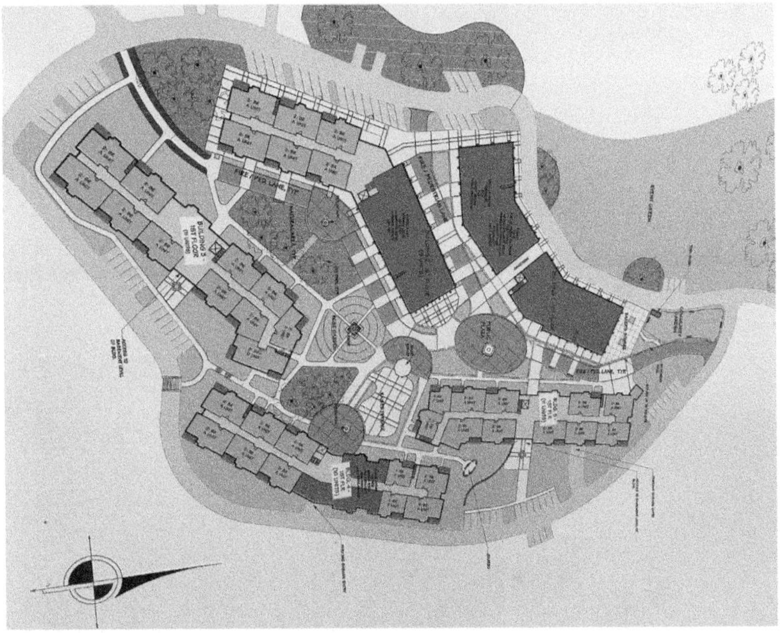

LEGACY—RINCON DEL RIO HOUSING ABOVE

The medieval town plan works well for community-enhanced design. Commercial below and condos above. This will be a rich pedestrian environment that has the bones of a highly functional pedestrian-oriented neighborhood.

LEGACY—SACRAMENTO STREET SENIOR HOUSING

Café below, housing above.

LEGACY—RINCON DEL RIO, CA

Centripetal design, design that brings people together.

LEGACY—RINCON DEL RIO, CA

Community design is big on front porches.

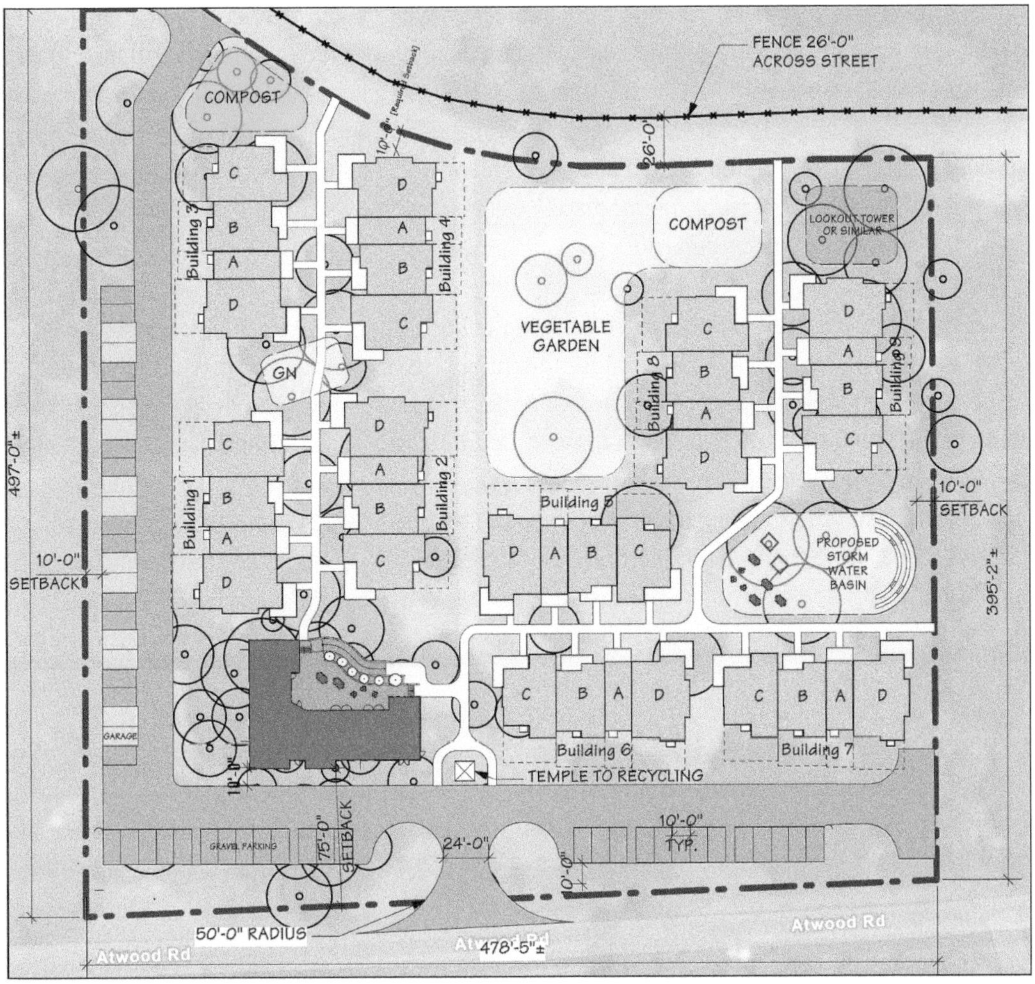

Placer County feasibility sketch.

Next Steps and the Future

Placer County in California has entered into an Exclusive Right to Negotiate Agreement (ERNA) with The Cohousing Company. County officials have been to other cohousing communities in the area and strongly believe that a community like this in their town of Auburn would create a fantastic, high-functioning neighborhood and prove to be a model for future suburban development. In plain sight, it is obvious why they want one in their town—kids playing, parents chatting—cohousing is a high-functioning neighborhood at its best and it's palpable. It's the kind of neighborhood that every town aspires to be. County officials reaching out to an aspiring new high-functioning neighborhood is new in America, but very common in Denmark. It seems obvious that the county could play a significant role in positive neighborhood making and they can. In Denmark, it is not uncommon for the county to reach out to help an aspiring group of future residents—this is the first cohousing for this to happen in the U.S. In Denmark, they have realized that there are so many "services"— elder care, childcare, after school, music lessons, and saging in general that are best provided at the neighborhood level. And there they manage a community garden, meals on wheels, recreation, rides to the grocery store, entertainment, and more. In other words, if you look at all of the health and welfare institutions established at the county level, it's clear that in an organic fashion the neighborhood can do it better. The county is always there as a backup, but not for the everyday quality of life necessities. To begin a real community invokes a sense of belonging, a sense of accountability, and a sense of ownership—"this is my neighborhood and I will help by reacting to aberrant concerns," everything from litter to suspicious behavior.

When Kathryn McCamant and I started building cohousing in the U.S., many people asked us why we didn't create a non-profit, because that might make it easier for counties to participate at this level. In the U.S., the average non-profit project takes seven years to get a project built, and that's longer than most cohousing groups will stick around. And with the homelessness crisis in the U.S., we can't expect middle-class or even lower middle-class groups to get financial support—even if that might make fewer people become homeless. Too often as a country, we wait until it's too late and then we might or might not do something. Usually counties can't help new high-functioning neighborhoods because they are too busy having to remedy the pathologies in low-functioning neighborhoods. High functioning neighborhoods like cohousing are a dynamic way of averting a crisis by housing lower middle-class people in adequate housing.

The reason that the Danish counties and cities are quick to help is because they realize how much the county will save by having high-functioning communities in their midst. Nevada County, California, for example, spends over $1 million in transportation per year getting 2,500 seniors to where they need to go—the pharmacy, the doctor, the physical therapist, even the all-important friend's house. Sixty-four thousand trips are provided by big lumbering buses. That's 25 trips per year per senior. Some say it's too many, some say it's too few. In either case, it's over $500 per senior per year, or $41 per trip. In contrast, senior cohousing communities never require this cost, or meals-on-wheels, rarely nurses on-the-go, or hundreds of other services that counties end up providing. Hospice care is real and at some point does become professionally administered. For one senior cohousing development in the county, the fire department wanted $1 million (as it was a much larger project than a normal cohousing community). When asked what their number one call was, Jerry, the now retired fire chief, said pick-up and put-back calls. We said that we would self-perform that requirement unless there was a serious injury, and saved most of that million dollars.

Placer County existing site initial visit.

Legacy: The WELL Single Room Occupancy (SRO) Co-Living Community

Amidst a global pandemic and health crisis, the onset of COVID-19 has rippled across many different sectors and populations. Among the most vulnerable were seniors, seeking safe, resilient, and connected housing solutions. Contrary to disconnected suburban communities reliant on cars or massive senior living complexes that lack dignified space, the future must turn to building resilient communities, forming valuable relationships, and engaging profoundly with one another. According to research on living richer lives, "dozens of studies have shown that people who have satisfying relationships with family, friends, and their community are happier, have fewer health problems, and live longer" (see Harvard HealthBeat). For seniors, especially in times when health precautions fray many of these relationships, it is critical that they are part of a community that can support them. More specifically to senior health, countless studies have shown that eating right (mostly light), exercising often (mostly low impact), and staying connected with community are crucial to living longer and healthier. Considering these criteria, do single-family houses or nursing homes truly check all of the boxes? How would you describe your perfect place of living out the rest of your years? WELL is taking the first steps into exploring these questions and the potential of community-enhanced senior co-living to address these issues inspired by cohousing communities.

Common Facilities Program

Goals:

- Thrive in community while aging in place
- Safe physically and emotionally
- Maintain purpose and meaningful experience
- A place to get to know each other, to care about each other, to support each other, and to look out for each other
- And more...

Activities:

- Sharing ideas
- Dancing/partying
- Meditating
- Helping one another
- Hosting guests
- Lounging
- Relaxing by the fireplace
- Sitting in the sun
- Exercising
- And more...

The WELL SRO Co-living Project is a prototype consisting of a single five-story building complete with 196 suites, multiple common houses, parking, management offices, small street-level retail, and recreational spaces. This project aims to create long-term, wellness-focused housing that is family-

Project cross-sectional diagram.

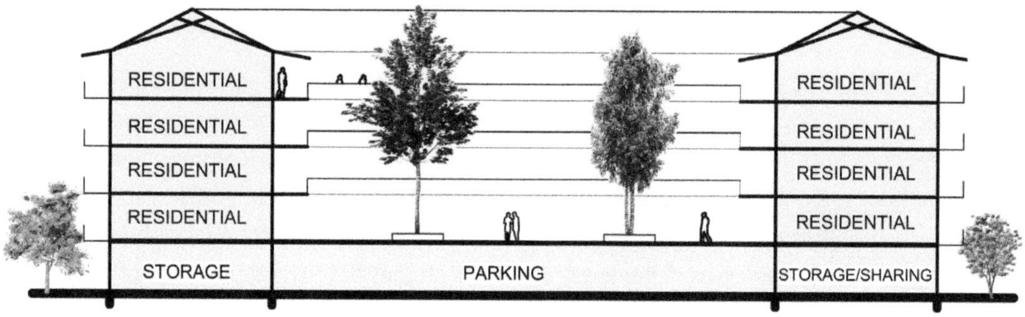

supportive, senior-friendly, energy-efficient, and sustainable. In designing and developing this prototype, the goal is to demonstrate the efficacy of the concept both socially and economically. By creating a replicable model of community-enhanced senior co-living, it can be modified and adjusted to address senior living across the United States. For those familiar with cohousing and other community-enhanced living formats, the critical factor is the community engagement process of each project as they are replicated in varying contexts and geographical locations. As one can imagine, the base program of the prototype will play a crucial role in the success of these communities. If done right, it will ensure that the design of the buildings is conducive to facilitating strong, resilient communities. As no residents were identified at the outset of the project, and therefore it is obviously not cohousing, it is even more important to empathize with those future community members in the most serious manner possible. As an expert in cohousing and community culture, The Cohousing Company referenced its communication with other senior cohousing communities to compile a prototype program in the WELL SRO Co-Living Project.

While this project represents the potential of community-enhanced living to address unsolved concerns with housing in the United States, there are many hurdles in implementing this

Project building/ podium plan.

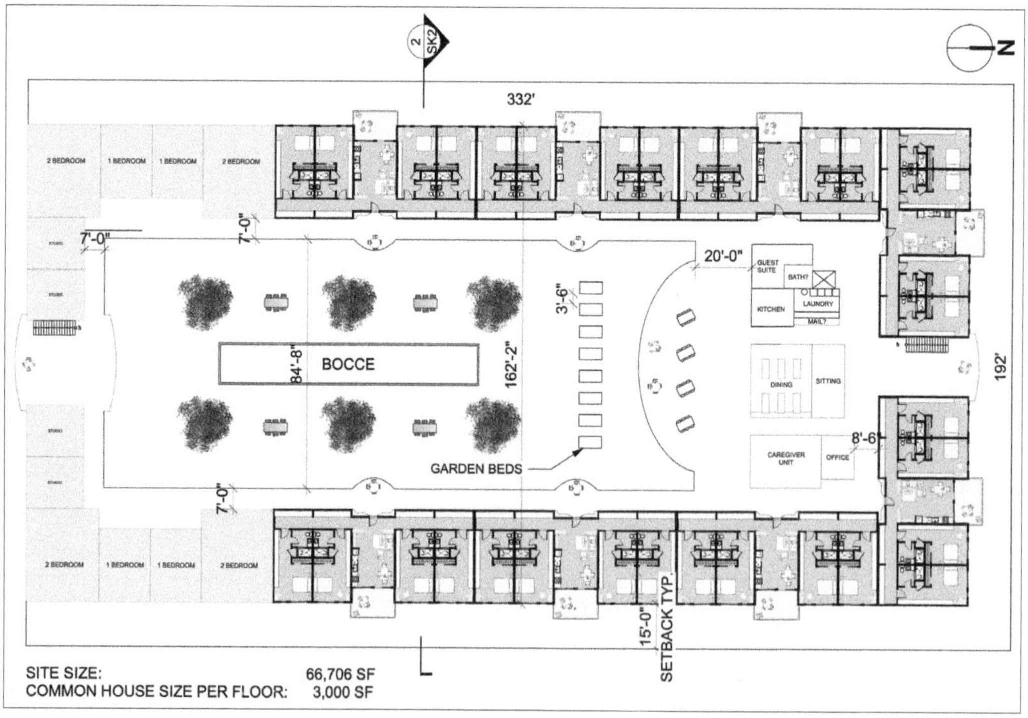

Common Facilities Program

Places:

- Dining space
- Kitchen
- Caregiving space
- Lounge
- Laundry
- Guest room
- Mail room
- Office/Business center
- Bike repair/maintenance/workshop
- Storage
- Exercise room
- Unisex bathroom
- Arts & crafts space
- Music space
- Garden storage
- And more. . .

emerging typology in senior housing. One of the primary concerns is the willingness of investors to fund a project that has no analogous proof of concept to reference. Of course, similar projects have been completed abroad and similar concepts have achieved success in North America, but this specific proposal type has not been commonly seen since the turn of the twentieth century when single-room occupancy developments were more common. Originally, this typology aimed to accommodate new immigrants or young women moving to the big city until they were established in society. These projects were designed for low-income, low-middle-class, and the missing middle-class who wanted (and frankly needed) a place that was fun, not cast adrift, and not lonely. To create a modernized iteration of this typology today, it may take a more incremental approach of introducing it to the market, before it is replicated at a larger scale. Ultimately, buildings that feel like neighborhoods is the goal—where people can and do help take care of each other.

The WELL SRO Co-living Community may be the first of many to iterate upon the cohousing model to create housing in the United States that unifies communities, weathers difficult times, and revolutionizes dignified, affordable housing.

Valley View Senior Homes

Valley View Senior Homes is very affordable senior housing (the residents all live on Social Security) inspired by cohousing and the belief that humanity can take care of seniors who might

"Lombard Street" solution. Because of the nature of the site, the single-box appeared the most appropriate and cost- effective option. A significant challenge was to create what some have referred to as a "hill town" solution. In abandoning the one-building form, we adopted the hill town possibility.

otherwise be homeless. We expect that there will be more legacy cohousing projects like this one in the U.S. and Canada in the future than actual cohousing projects.

Owned and managed by Satellite Affordable Housing Associates (SAHA) developer, that believes in community first, Valley View features small homes with small courtyards, all things on a human scale, and all things as connected to the earth as possible. Its design facilitates people knowing one another and developing positive relationships with one another.

Valley View Senior Homes is influenced by a 1936 collection of articles by John Steinbeck called *The Harvest Gypsies*. In these articles, Steinbeck shared the story of cottages and agricultural towns spanning from the Northern Californian town of Redding to San Diego in Southern California. Steinbeck observed how powerful social bonds help individuals persevere through adversity. In this spirit, Valley View Senior Homes is designed to get seniors talking to each other and knowing each other, so they can do a lot for themselves by helping each other.

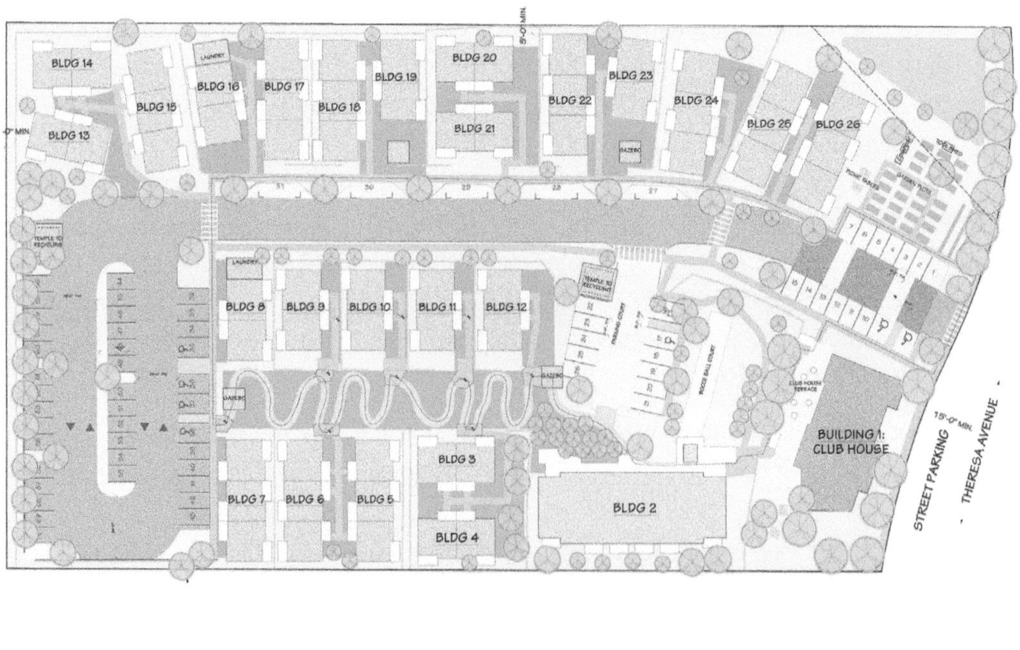

Schematic site plan.

You must appreciate the city of American Canyon, in particular, the head of community development, Brent Cooper, for seeing that community first is even more important than "housing first." Valley View Senior Homes is reminiscent of community-oriented affordable senior housing projects built in Denmark since 1985, when the first Danish senior cohousing community was completed. Started under unique circumstances, six women joined forces to establish the fact that the primary characteristic that needed to shift in senior housing was that there absolutely needed to be a major upgrade in the reality of community. And the community aspect has to be real. It's not enhanced because we say it is, it must be obvious. Since then, senior housing in Denmark has become a participatory process, utilizing focus groups and smart design with a front porch, pedestrian-oriented atmosphere, and where people obviously connect.

Per the Housing and Urban Development (HUD) 2015 statistics, there are about 3.5 million homeless people in America. At about 1 percent of the country's population, it's a number too big to ignore. Although Valley View Senior Homes is officially low-income senior housing, homeless veterans and others in similar situations take advantage of projects like these. These small, economical housing developments are in critical demand across the country.

Many of the units first went to homeless veterans, then otherwise senior homeless (one resident per household to be at least 55 years old to qualify), previously homeless, and at risk of becoming homeless. It was designed to be a community to the fullest extent possible in the absence of working with the future residents. Step one, jettison the previously proposed one-building solution.

Valley View Senior Homes is located at 1 Natalie Lane, in the city of American Canyon. The 3.5-acre parcel is zoned as a medium density residential subdivision. The 56-foot hill on the property slopes from west to east. And the site is set in a rural, semi-rural, and increasingly suburban context.

It's important to note that the residents were not involved in the planning of this project, but the project did not progress any faster because of this. It took 10 years, start to finish, to complete Valley View Senior Homes. By contrast, a well-facilitated cohousing project typically takes about two to three years to complete. And future residents participations for homeless housing projects also make them happen in two to three years. Put simply, a group of future residents generates an urgency, and because they have a personal stake in the outcome they are motivated to move the project along quickly. What strikes me as odd is how afraid most agencies are of future residents participation, "They will demand too much; they will talk too much; they will make it take longer; they will make it cost more; they will suggest indecorous designs." We have designed over a hundred participatory projects now—and none of that has been the case. Just the opposite is true

ENDNOTE

1. Paul H. Ray and Sherry R. Anderson, *The Cultural Creatives: How 50 Million People Are Changing the World* (New York: Three Rivers Press, 2000).

Quimper Village

Site Plan Workshop
When it comes to neighborhood making—everyone has an architect in them. They bring real values, experiences, and good ideas to the table.

All hands on deck make for a great site plan, based on a clear and well thought out design criteria.

8

Quimper Village

Site Planning Workshop

"There is a yearning for a community of neighbors where one can recognize everyone, where numerous casual encounters occur each day, and where a sense of ownership and control allows subtle modifications to be made to the shared environment as community needs change."

Clare Cooper Marcus

Senior Cohousing Site Plan Programming doesn't always have to be done by architects, but good programming is like anthropology—"who are these people anyway, and where do they want to go?"—this is where we really get to understand the group. Some of the most successful community-enhanced developments were programmed by architects, skilled at facilitating a clear design criteria with future residents—not a default program, and certainly not a program "based on my long years of practice."

QUIMPER VILLAGE

www.quimpervillage.com

SITE PROGRAM AND DESIGN CRITERIA

Write-up from Site Planning Workshop

Facilitated by Charles Durrett
Write-up by Erik Bonnett
McCamant & Durrett Architects
Port Townsend, Washington

January 31 – February 3, 2015

Quimper Village Vision Statement

We are a group of couples and individuals planning a cohousing development that addresses our needs for living and aging successfully in community while enriching our private lives.

As we move along this path, we are endeavoring to maintain respect and consideration for one another, understanding that building community is a fluid, evolving process to which each of us contributes. We look forward to many discoveries and course corrections, and plan to do this with healthy consensus, growing grace and good humor.

Table of Contents

*** Some images were not taken during the workshop. They depict other cohousing communities and do not suggest the building style that will result in Quimper Village. Each photo shows a desirable situation, activity, or programmed place that was accommodated in a way that was appropriate for that specific community in which it exists. The design of Quimper Village will be specific and appropriate to the unique needs and desires of this group, while drawing inspiration from the successful design of other communities. The group above, however, is Quimper Village.**

COMMENTS: ***While The Cohousing Company was looking at the climate and key feasibility questions, the future residents were studying the realities of getting older and why bother with this whole new community making in the first place. They set up two sessions of Study Group One (SG1).***

PART 1. CONTEXT

The following summary was prepared to help us familiarize ourselves with Port Townsend. It may be useful to share with future residents who might not be familiar with the town and its many amenities and also may be interesting for current residents to see a characterization of your community.

Port Townsend City Facts

County: Jefferson
State: Washington
Latitude: 48°07′N
Longitude: 122°47′W
Elevation: Sea Level to about 200 feet
Land area: 7 square miles
Population in 2010: 9,100 people
Population density: 1,300 people per sq. mi.

Local History

Port Townsend received its name from Captain George Vancouver in 1792. By the late 1800s the town was believed to be destined to become one of the largest western seaports. It was during this boom that the Victorian architecture that characterizes the downtown historical district and nearby landmarks was erected.

However, as the Depression struck, plans were scrapped to extend the railroad to Port Townsend in favor of eastern Puget Sound ports. Capital moved on and through the mid-1900s the paper mill south of town was the economic mainstay.

Economy and Demographics

Today the paper mill continues to be the largest private employer, but a vibrant tourist economy along with the public sector has brought economic stability and cultural vitality to the community.

The most notable aspect of the demographics of Port Townsend is the median age: 53, which is reflective of the large retiree population in the city. Additional significant facts include (compared to state average):

- Lower median household income ($41,000)
- Higher housing prices ($300,000 per unit)
- Lower rate of multi-family housing (21 percent)

- Lower rates of immigrant populations and racial diversity
- Over 1 in 6 persons below poverty line

In aggregate, the demographic suggest a large opportunity for Senior Cohousing in Port Townsend: affordable, multi-family housing for older residents.

Local Culture and Events

Port Townsend was founded because of its relatively sheltered harbor and commanding position at the entrance to Puget Sound from the Strait of Juan de Fuca. This unparalleled access to open waters and protected bays set off by stunning views of the Cascade and Olympic Mountains makes the backdrop for the town's cultural and tourist activities.

Port Townsend has long been known among mariners as a center for high quality craftsmanship, especially in the trade of wooden boat building. Today the city has two active marinas as well as a ferry port. The Northwest Maritime Center curates a vibrant culture of seafaring, offering classes, displaying exhibits, and organizing numerous events including the annual Wooden Boat Festival. For the old salt, Port Townsend is an ideal home.

The town also offers numerous cultural events like art walks, an international film festival, a writer's conference, and music festivals. Also a vibrant farmer's market is a hallmark of the region's local food and economic resilience values.

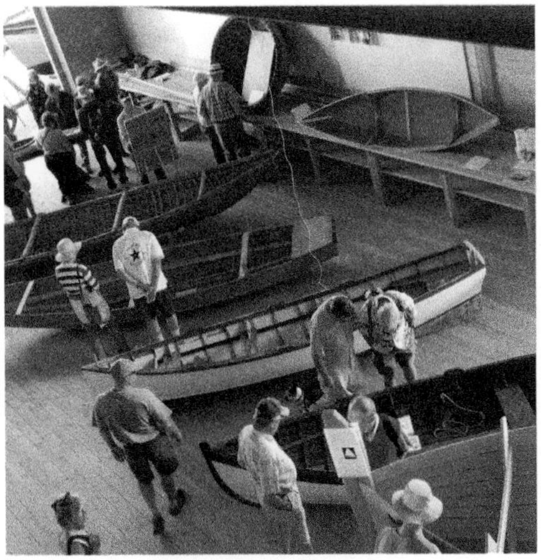

Climate and Design

Climate Synopsis

Port Townsend's weather is controlled by three major factors: its maritime location, the general seasonal trends of the Pacific Northwest, and the rain shadow of the Olympic Mountains. As a maritime city, Port Townsend experiences relatively mild cool temperatures year round, frequent breezes, and occasional storms. Overall the climate is similar to much of the Pacific Northwest in that the summers are almost completely dry and sunny, while winter brings frequent cloudy and rainy weather. However, because of the Olympic Mountains to the southwest, Port Townsend receives a small fraction of the rains that nurture the nearby temperate rain forests. Rainfall is half that of many communities east of Puget Sound. Along with its culture and picturesque location, the regionally admired climate is part of what makes Port Townsend a desirable place to live.

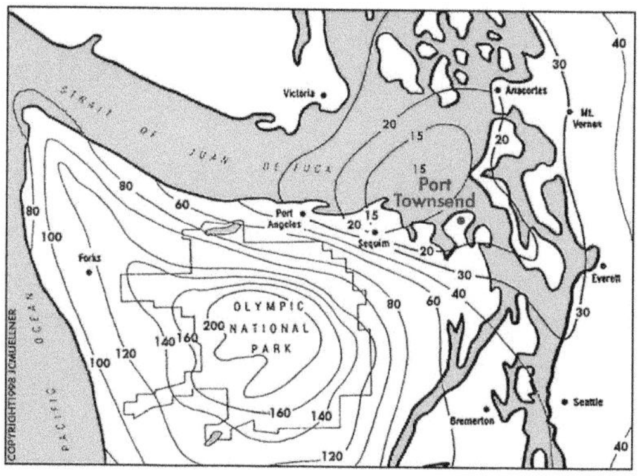

Climate as Form-Giver

Several aspects of the Port Townsend climate suggest specific design responses. These responses will improve the energy performance of the project, increase thermal comfort, bolster community resilience, and also contextualize the architecture—making it relevant and meaningful in this specific place.

The most immediately obvious and important characteristic of the climate is its consistent cool weather. While hot record temperatures have reached 100°F, average summer highs only hit the mid to low 70s.

With these low temperatures, along with the welcome presence of sun (about 250 days per year with at least some sun), buildings can respond with:

1. **Tight construction.** Avoiding inadvertent leaks and controlling introduction of fresh air into the buildings will keep heat inside.
2. **Ample insulation.** Although cold temperatures are rare, the persistent coolness makes the climate similar in heating demand to a place like Salt Lake City, which experiences much colder extremes.
3. **Unshaded windows.** Overheating is rarely if ever a problem; sunlight and heat are usually welcome inside.
4. **Small and compact units** will minimize heat loss through the building envelope.
5. **Wind-protected sunny outdoor spaces.** Providing shelter from the frequent breezes will significantly increase comfort and usefulness of outdoor spaces.

Applying these strategies will deliver comfortable indoor conditions for about one-third of the year without the use of a mechanical heating system.

By the Numbers

Average July–Aug Daily Max: 71°F

Sunny or Partly Sunny Days[a]: 264

Heating Degree Days[b]: 5233

Cooling Degree Days[c]: 5

Average wind speed[d]: 5–10 knots

Design wind speed: 85 mph / 110 mph gust

Average Summer Sea Temp[d]: 52°F

a) Data for Sequim.

b) Heating Degree Days are a measure of the need for heating, in this case heating to 65°F. (5233 is the sum of the differences between the average outdoor temperature and 65°F for each day of the year).

c) Cooling Degree Days are the inverse of Heating Degree Days, in this case measuring the need for cooling to 70°F.

d) Based on NOAA Buoy PTTWW1 located in the ferry harbor.

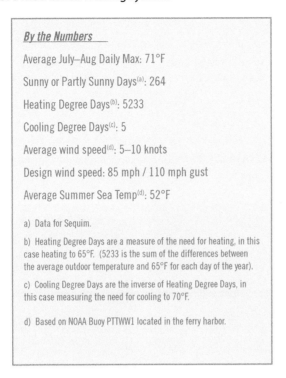

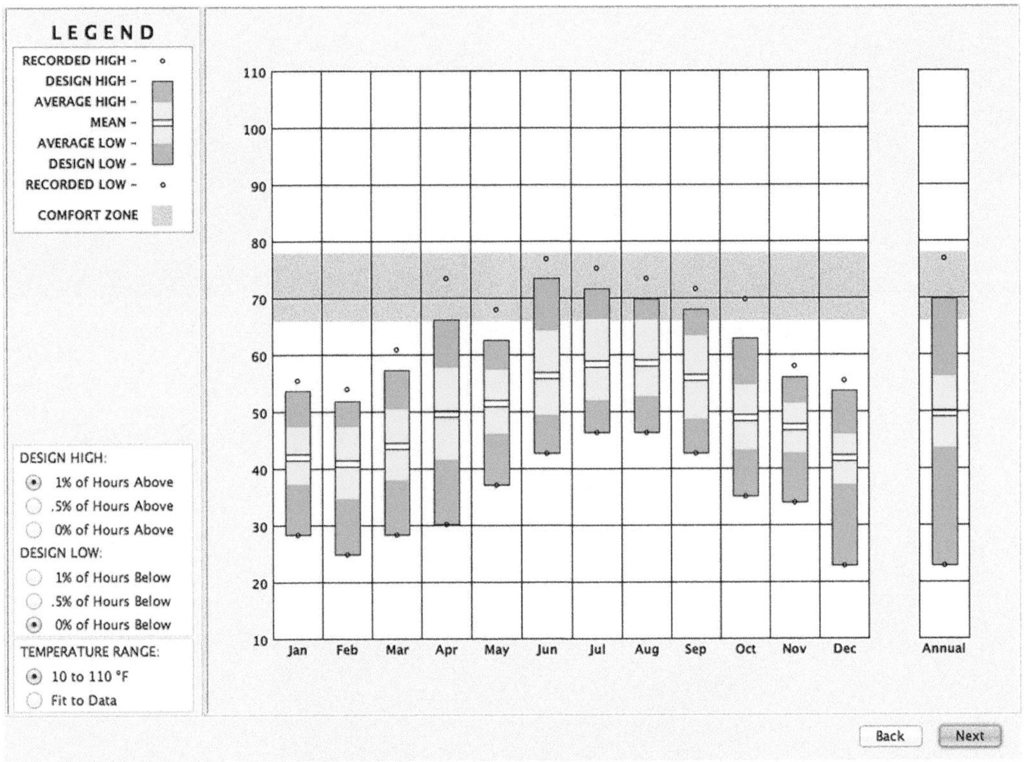

With the exception of summertime highs, temperatures are below the comfort range for the inside environment. (Visualization of Whidbey Island Typical Meteorological Year data).

Site Context

Quimper Village will be located in a residential and agricultural neighborhood less than a mile from downtown Port Townsend. Shops, restaurants, coffee shops, and grocery stores are all within walking or easy bicycling distance. Also within a mile of the site is Fort Worden State Park offering numerous recreational and cultural activities. Several other parks including Kah Tai Lagoon Nature Park are within walking distance as well. The waters of the Puget Sound are also close by to the northeast and southeast.

The site itself is set back from F Street with a panhandle lot. A pedestrian path runs through the site and connects to a system of paths and dirt roads extending all the way to the Strait of Juan de Fuca.

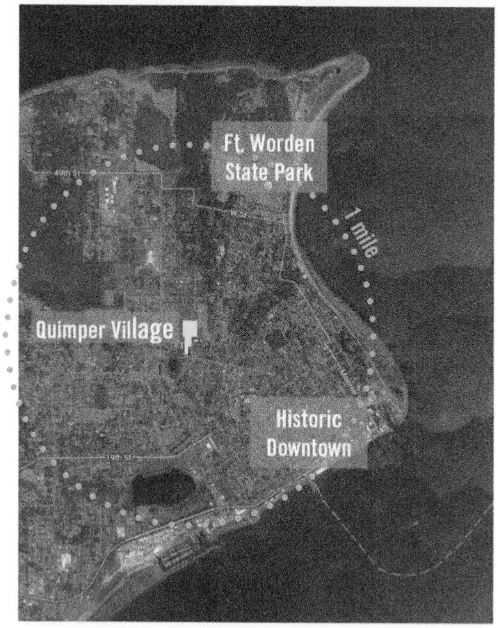

Project Description

The Quimper Village LLC currently has an option on the 6.3 acre site (on F Street near the intersection with Redwood Street). The site is currently an open field bordered primarily by small fields, gardens, and houses, as well as two senior housing facilities. Twenty eight homes will be built, optimally creating a sustainable and cooperative community. As of the January 31–February 3 Site Planning Workshop, there was a core group of about fifteen committed households!

PART 2. DESIGN PROGRAM

Outline of Process

Brainstorm

- Generate ideas (as freely as possible)
- Get creative juices flowing
- Ensure the opportunity for everyone to be heard
- Provide a fast and fun way to get started on a new topic
- Avoid discussion and judgment

Discuss

- Have goal in mind
- Debate merits of an issue
- Clarify issues
- Put forth proposals

Consensus

- Break question down to lowest common denominator
- Ask for objections and ask for consensus
- State the decision

Site Design Goals

- Connection
- Clean
- Natural/Cozy
- Pleasant landscape
- Friends are there
- Easy
- No visible cars
- Attractive/Pretty
- Combination of privacy + community
- Inviting
- Close proximity
- Quiet
- Colorful
- Birds
- Joy/Fun
- Not isolated/Connected to community
- Accepted/Inclusion
- Sheltering/Supportive place
- Walkability
- Openness
- To feel like a part of the PNW
- To feel like it belongs
- Physically and emotionally safe
- Feels solid
- Feel proud
- Feels appropriate/Good value/ Not gratuitous
- "Was worth it"
- "We did it together"
- Feeling of "vision"
- Ecologically appropriate

ACTIVITIES BETWEEN BUILDINGS

- Cooking and dining
- Dancing/music
- Drinking and happy houring
- Wine and conversation
- Sing along
- Producing entertainment
- Holding plays (acting, watching)
- Watching movies
- Book clubbing
- Playing games (cribbage, poker)
- Crafting
- Raising the flag
- Enjoying the fire
- Pressing cider
- Preparing for emergencies
- Yoga
- Bocci
- Getting exercise (machines)
- Blowing bubbles
- Flying kites
- Watching sunsets and stars
- Walking
- Dog walking
- Bike riding
- Wheelchair racing
- Hauling the groceries
- Getting the mail
- Doing photography

- Reading a book
- Sitting and chatting in small groups
- Gardening
- Landscaping
- Bird watching
- Deer abatement
- Composting
- Woodworking
- Doing repairs
- Sharing work
- Hot tubing
- Kids playing
- Storing stuff
- Hanging cloths and doing laundry
- Holding yard sales
- Disposing of garbage, recycling
- Parking cars
- Washing and charging autos

*** The activities on this list will be 'optimally' accommodated. Some will have their own place. Other activities will be accommodated at other designated places on the site. This will depend on site conditions, economics, and group choices. Large cost items will be prioritized at the Common House Workshop.**

PART 3. PROGRAM PLACES

Place	Activities	Character	Relationship	Details
Garbage/Recycling/ Compost	• Taking out the trash	• Beautiful	• Easy to fetch • At Parking	• 7 bins including recycling, trash, and yard waste

Place	Activities	Character	Relationship	Details
Garden	• Gardening • Composting • Arboriculture (deferred)		• By garden • Convenient to house and to garden	• Raised (waist level) • Has water • 1.03/hh garden beds (29 beds for 28 households) • Compost, 10'x10', rat proof, closed

Place	Activities	Character	Relationship	Details
Open Space	• Yoga • Bocci • Getting exercise • Blowing bubbles • Flying kites • Watching sunsets and stars	• Hardscape • Some grass • Openness • Sculptural shape	• Beyond the common terrace	• Bocci OK on grass • 30'x50'

Place	Activities	Character	Relationship	Details
Parking	• Personal vehicles • Shared vehicles • Guest vehicles • Recreational vehicles	• Open (DG) • Garages with storage, 16 for 28 households (9 of 16 now) • Carports with storage, 11' wide, 2 for 28 hh (1/16 now)	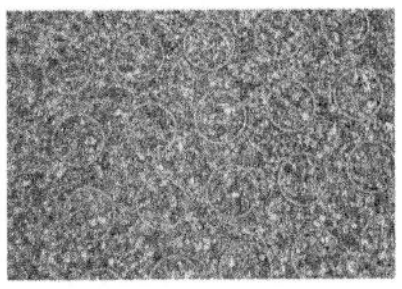 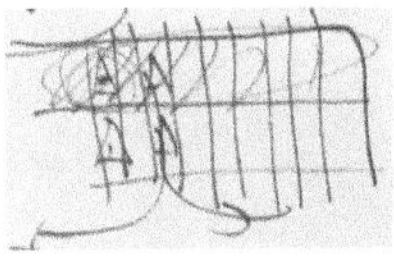	• 1.3 total spaces per household • 30 cars amongst 16 households now (1.88/hh) • 19 cars expected amongst those present (1.19/hh) • Will use neighbor-hood on-street parking for rare large gatherings • Overflow parking on grass OK • Rec. vehicles: 3 now (0.19/hh) • Shared cars: 2 • Golf carts: 1 initially, 2 possible • Some house-hold tandem OK • Asphalt drive isle

Place	Activities	Character	Relationship	Details
Hot Tub		• Open	• Yonder • Close to common facilities (to keep costs down) • Close to shower	• 8 person • Low maintenance

Place	Activities	Character	Relationship	Details
Front Porch				• 8′ front porch • 15′–33′ door to door

Place	Activities	Character	Relationship	Details
Front Yard				• 10′ deep

Place	Activities	Character	Relationship	Details
Backyard				• 8′ front porch • 15′–33′ door to door

Place	Activities	Character	Relationship	Details
Common Terrace	• Cooking/ dining • Dancing/music/ movies/theater/ entertainment • Drinking and conversation • Games/crafts • Raising the flag • Enjoying a fire	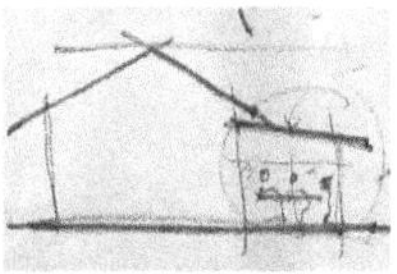 	• 15'–33' door to door	• 35 people (based on 2 meals/week) • Temporary coverage (deferred) • Wind screen (deferred) • Radiant heat • Pavers • Accessible

Place	Activities	Character	Relationship	Details
Storage (Bikes)	• Bike storage 0.86/hh (17 bikes now, 14 anticipated in current group)	• Could be same as a garage • Note: different storage shed types harmonious, attractive, cute	• Near tools/ workshop	• With electric service for electric bikes
(Boats)	• Kayaks 0.25/ hh (4 now)		• Could be on exterior wall of garages	• 17'–24' long
(Garden Shed)	• Potting	• Could be same as a garage	• Near garden • Probably near vehicular access	
(Shared Storage)	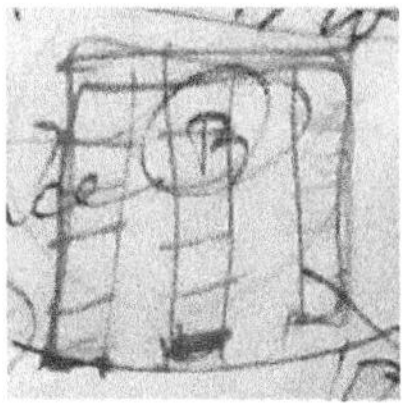	• Two two-car garages		
(Personal Storage)	• Other options for personal storage: attics, garages		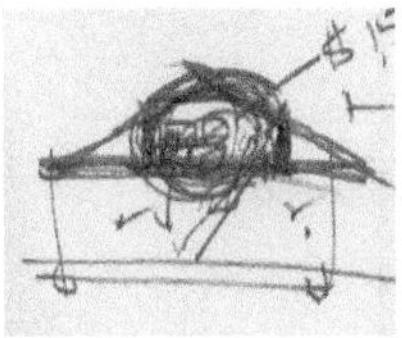	

COMMENTS: ***Of the dozens of participatory exercises done with the group at the site design stage, this one (below) is probably the most important. Here, the residents are separated into two lines, face-to-face, 110 feet apart. No spouses are across from one another. The residents start 110 feet apart because that is the typical distance between front doorknobs in one of Port Townsend's downtown 1920's neighborhoods (the heyday of American neighborhood making). The scenario: imagine that Sunday night was a common dinner. After dinner, you got into a prolonged conversation with one of your neighbors that you had grown close to. She mentioned that later that night she would be having a tough phone call with a grown child about a serious topic, like a breakup or an aberrant grandchild. Now, imagine that it is Monday morning and you're both leaving your houses across from each other on the same lane. You care about this person, so you wonder how the call went. You don't want to pry, but hopefully you will know the mood. If she appears extremely down, you might call her later and ask her to share a pot of tea. This is neighborhood making as if people care about each other, as opposed to just***

Place	Activities	Character	Relationship	Details
Outdoor Workspace		• Easy to drop off materials	• Adjacent to parking • Next to garbage • Less noise	• Space for (2) pickups

Place	Activities	Character	Relationship	Details
Hanging Clothes	• Hanging out the laundry • Conversation	• Look OK/Aesthetic • Convenient	• Right outside the door from the common laundry • Near garden • Be sensitive to neighborhood • Concentrated in one area • Could be screened	• Covered with acrylic • 8'x40'

what the bureaucrats, bankers, and business people want. Now, I ask each pair to walk toward each other until one of them stops, then both stop. That's how far their front doors will be from each other—door knob to door knob.

You cannot tell what mood someone is in at 110 feet apart. You can tell at 33 feet—the group's chosen maximum separation.

Place	Activities	Character	Relationship	Details
Children's Play	• Storing toys (grandparent's closet) • Riding bikes, trikes, roller skates • Swinging		• Can also take bus, car, or bike to beach	

Place	Activities	Character	Relationship	Details
Gathering Places	• Hanging out the laundry • Conversation	• Natural Shapes	• Sunny • Enough of them that everyone can see one from house • One is secluded • One in garden	• Don't have to worry about furniture in the rain • Great pavers • Round Table • Low wall • Build a couple to begin with • Can see the sky • One is covered

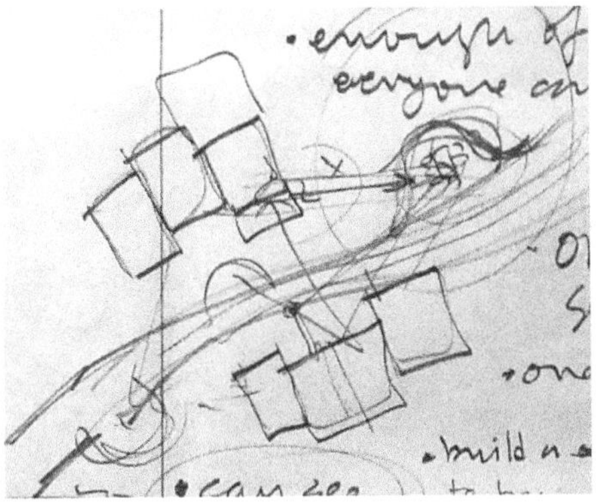

COMMENTS: ***If you wanted to do a post-occupancy "how successful is the site plan" evaluation, these are the metrics: life between the buildings and people-hours outside. This takes a team of folks to run around on a weekday and a weekend—the trick is to be the fly on the wall. See people-hours and smiles per half hour in Chapter 1 and Chapter 14. In suburbs, you find the numbers to be lower. In high functioning neighborhoods, these numbers are much higher.***

Location of the Common House

The most successful and frequently used common houses have three site planning characteristics in common. They are:

1. On the way home (from parking, street, pedestrian paths)

2. Centrally located within the community

3. As equidistant as possible from all households

All three of the above are frequently difficult to achieve. However the group located the common house centrally between the parking and most units. The trade-off with this location is the common terrace is generally on the north side of the common house, so it will receive less sunlight. To address this, the group oriented the common house so that the main terrace will receive afternoon sunlight, and proposed a second "front porch" facing southeast where residents can take advantage of morning sun with coffee or tea in hand.

Relationship to Larger Neighborhood

- Invited guests only
- Easy to invite neighbors in
- Details signal private vs common vs public
- Definitive interface
- Invited public access
- Strangers don't walk "willy nilly"
- Limited public access
- Obvious way finding
- Make it clear that it is private property
- Eyes on all common outdoor spaces

Access to be defined primarily with environmental design, rather than No Trespassing signs.

Design of the public trail uses environmental design, along with tasteful signage to delineate appropriate uses.

The group sought to balance openness and privacy in the relationship to the larger neighborhood.

COMMENTS: ***Usually, the group comes up with a variety of site plans, compares them to the program, and then contrasts them with the two separate teams coming up with two separate site plans. Then the two site plans merge into one. That's what happens 9 out of 10 times. At Quimper Village, they did not use the evolution methodology. They generated a dozen possibilities and compared each one to the detailed program. Then, with guidance by the architect, they decided which site plan best reflected the two days of criteria, and chose that one.***

PART 4. CONCLUSION

Workshop Conclusion

Imagine a grey Saturday morning in early spring. You are waiting for a few friends to join you. You have a warm beverage in your hand and as you look around you think, "Wow, we achieved our goals."

What are those goals?

Our job during the Site Planning Workshop is to envision this reality, to create the best site plan possible, embodying the collective values of each member of the group. Later we will worry about how to make this compelling vision reality.

These words encapsulate the tenor of an intense weekend of brainstorming, discussion, experimentation, and ultimately decision-making. The result of these approximately 600 people-hours are the design criteria and consensed conceptual site plan included in this program—the physical representation of the group's values and aspirations.

This is a fine program and the diagrammatic site plan provides a good "test" of the participatory workshop. Ultimately this program will morph into a final schematic design, at the Design Closure Workshop, as all of the individual elements are worked out. These elements include the specific house plans, the common house plan, the common terrace, the parking area, and so on.

With ample gently rolling land, the site did not dictate how to lay out the buildings. Sixteen design solutions were tested, evaluated, and revised. These schemes ranged greatly, including clusters of houses, large courtyards, radial patterns, and street-like layouts.

Several themes emerged, which helped lead to the final consensus on a single scheme. Primary among these themes, is the relationship of privacy to community. In most modern American housing development, the private realm and public realm are clearly delineated. Cohousing reintroduces the common realm, neither fully public or private, cooperatively managed to meet the needs of the community. The group carefully revised and revised again the location of the houses to ensure each house had access to private space.

At the same time the group ensured that the spaces between the buildings created outdoor rooms, terraces, and courtyards to support a rich common realm. Gathering nodes were located so that

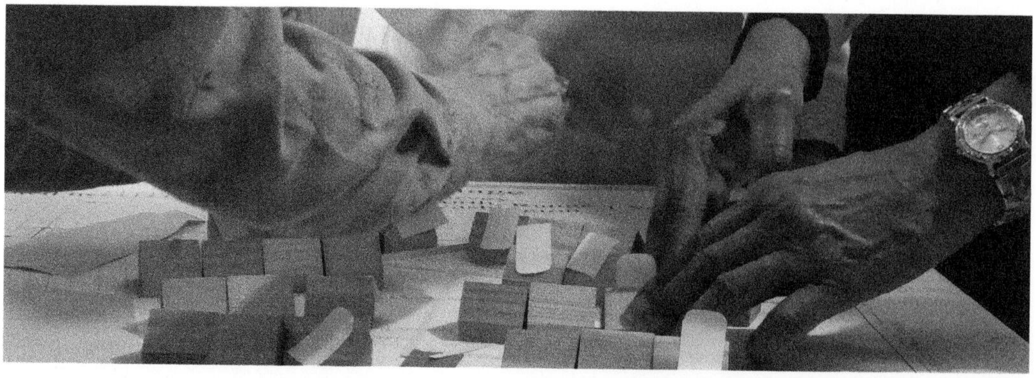

The group took a straw poll of preferred units to test the quality of the site plan. Preferred units were widely distributed, indicating a high-quality plan. Chuck stated that he could "live in any unit."

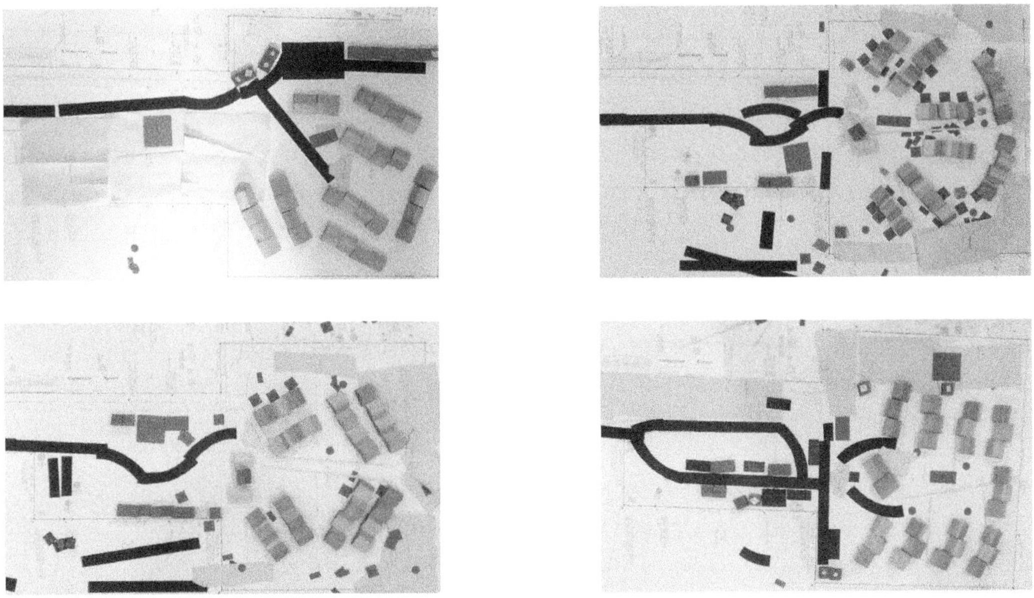

Four of the sixteen distinct site plans that were brainstormed and discussed.

each house can see one from the front porch. Also the rows of houses were arranged so that all houses could see either the common house or the central outdoor space adjacent to it.

The group also devoted significant effort to planning the parking and outbuildings. Axial, windy, arced, and looped access roads were all proposed and evaluated. The arced drive, which was decided upon, provides an entry sequence that is formal but not wholly automobile-dominated. In addition, it maintains more open space near the public path, leaving the space more useful for the group and more aesthetically giving to the broader neighborhood.

The site plan developed in this workshop is not the only solution, but we believe that it is the best one. Now our job is to develop it further. The finalized schematic site plan will be presented at the Design Closure Workshop (after the Common House and Private House Program Workshops).

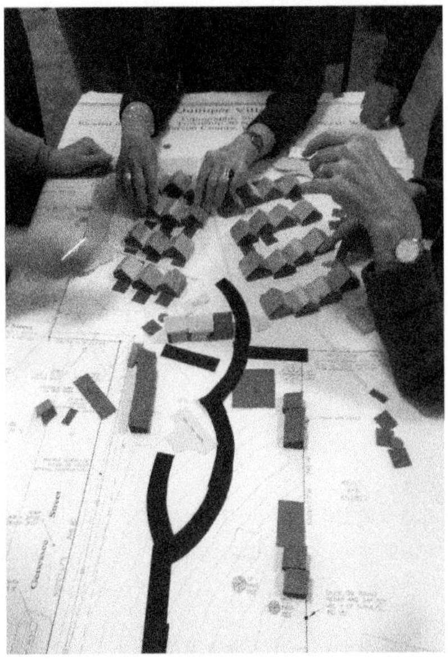

Members work to incorporate yards and paths into the site plan concept which was eventually consensed.

Early on, members adjust the house blocks seeking to provide both clearly defined private and common space.

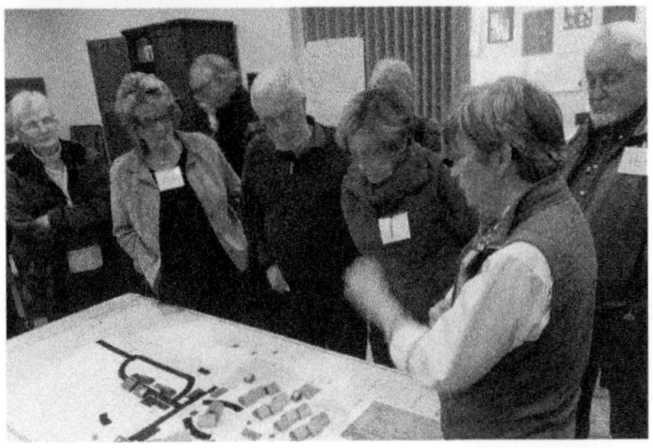

Members discuss the merits and shortcomings of a particular site plan concept in relationship to the consensed program.

COMMENTS: ***It only takes two things to get a project built: a vision of what a real community might be in your mind, and a clear set of steps to getting there.***

Miscellaneous Topics

Several meetings were held outside of the workshop sessions pertaining to the broader process of creating Quimper Village, such as construction cost and the development of house options. To address some of these issues, Chuck reviewed the steps of creating cohousing and emphasized the financial and labor savings associated with doing the steps in the right order and at the right time. Several issues arose which related more directly to the site program and are listed below:

- As a part of the land purchase agreement, the group had previously agreed to retain at least twenty-five percent (25 percent) of the total acreage of the property as open space in one contiguous piece of land: Quimper Village may use such open space for storm water control, gardens or similar uses.
- Propane to be made available. Decision on which houses, which service company, and which configuration to be made based on group desires in Workshops 2–5.
- The consented program herein (e.g., storage, hot tub, workshop) will be prioritized for inclusion or exclusion from project during Workshop 6, Prioritization.

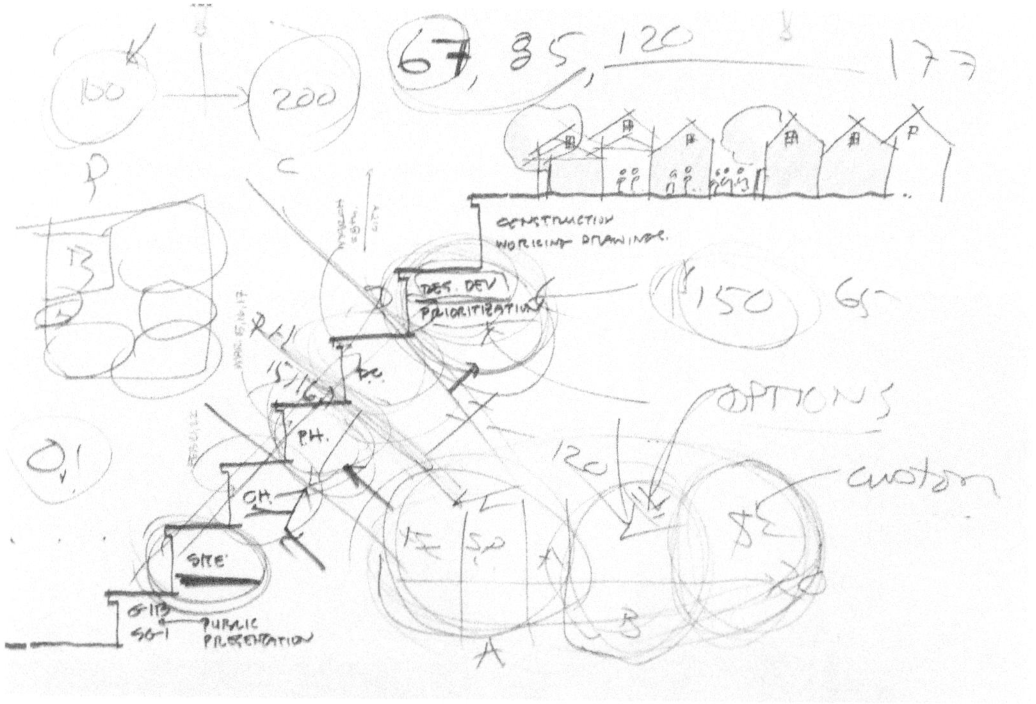

The steps of creating cohousing. It is important to keep the process deliberate, and therein efficient. Staying on topic at each step is the best way to assure realization of the group's collective vision.

A Note About the Process

Several spaces will need more distinct siting or programming. Not to worry, this will happen at later stages in the design process.

When I asked, does anyone object to, or does anyone have a problem with any given proposal or feel it is not appropriate, and no one objected, we had consensus on that suggestion and moved forward.

However, when someone objected, we discussed and modified—or discussed and deleted—or discussed and left the suggestion as it stood—and then consensed it. I also asked everyone to be very proactive, if not aggressive, about objecting if the suggestion did not make sense to you as the best way for the group to proceed—and we had no problems with that.

In good cohousing process, once consensed, an item is the rule and we move on until we reach consensus on an alternate proposal.

It is critical that you make any changes to this program in a deliberate fashion—perhaps a decision to revisit a given line item with agreement of two-thirds of the people present at the time of the workshop. Reconsidered line items should be given a very tight time frame; trust each other and your decisions. Assuming each item made sense originally, and it was consensed, it is possible not to revisit a single one. For example, the Nevada City Cohousing Site Program was never modified and has proven to be an adequate guide to an incredible and giving place to live for 94 people. A few line items were altered at the Design Closure Workshop in relation to the Common House and Private House Programs, but only when new and compelling architectural information improved the Site Program—not because the Program changed. Indeed, I believe that you can successfully proceed with this Site Program and not reconsider it at all until the time of the Design Closure Workshop (based on new information). The best way to prevent backtracking is to bring new members up to speed by carefully walking them through this program one line item at a time. By not backtracking the cohousing group moves forward and progresses.

Even once consensus has been reached on the schematic design, you will still constantly refer to the program. This is how you get the details right to the extent that you can, and the process then proceeds well beyond the Design Closure Workshop.

Frankly, I use the program right through the construction documentation process to best assure that I don't lose the richness that the group process put on the table. The final site plan reveals the aggregate sum of the goals, activities, places, and intent as originally consensed. That remains a valuable part of the group's work and history.

One last thought about the third "C" after Climate and Culture: Costs. It's important not to lose sight of Costs. It's all too easy to allow costs to ebb up until one day it's all too painfully obvious that someone can't afford a house here. It takes a lot of discipline, but we know that it's very possible to build a place here that everyone loves, if we stay focused.

PART 5. WORKSHOP SITE PLAN

Testing the Program

The following Diagrammatic Site Plan represents the plan as consensed upon at the Site Planning Workshop. The full group agreed to combine aspects of each subgroup's final block layout. They agreed to use the house layout of Group Two, moved to the location of Group One. Group One's parking layout was agreed upon. The common house location was extremely similar in both layouts, so the group agreed to work out any differences during the common house workshop.

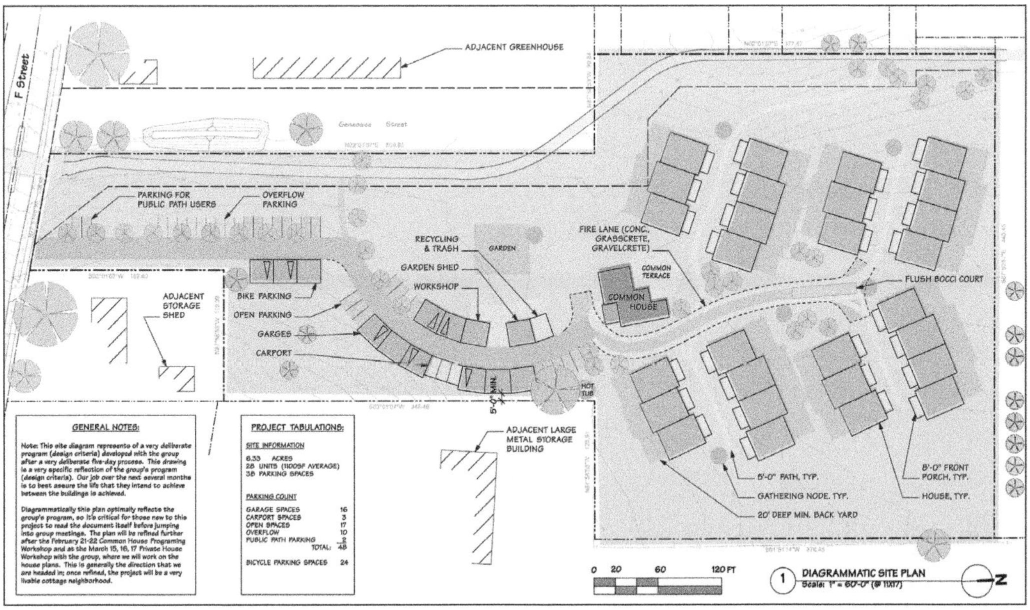

PART 6. PARTICIPANTS

At the January 31 – February 3, 2015,
Quimper Village Site Planning Workshop,
the following participants were in attendance:

Barbara and Mack Boelling
John and Pam Clise
Deborah Steele and Dennis Daneau
Michael and Linda Holbrook
Anne Holman
Kathleen Holt
Pat and David Hundhausen
Leon and Diane Lopez
Jerry Spieckerman and Bobbie McMahon
Sharon Moller
Ingelisa and Poul Oxenbol
Janet Palmer
Steve and Pat Resende
Nancy Richards
Carolyn and Jack Salmon
Robert "Woody" Woodward

STILLWATER, OK

Neighbors messing around in the Stillwater common house. Neighbors let their hair down, as you can do comfortably with neighbors that you know over time, in a warm and cozy place that you helped define. You own it literally of course, but more importantly, you own it emotionally. This ownership, this intensive use, and this warmth all stem from the participatory programming and design process.

MOUNTAIN VIEW, CA

Each group evaluated the common house plans by assessing how well they met the criteria they came up with, deviated, and improved on it. The evaluations happened in three separate rooms, then presented by a spokesperson from each group, and then brought together by a facilitated discussion and consensus for a single well-thought-out solution. Pull it apart, then pull it together.

9

Senior Cohousing Design Concepts

Common House Design

"My dream is to see a society of equal opportunities, without the stark social segregation, without poverty, hunger, homelessness, and where women can walk around anywhere and everywhere as safely and freely as men."

Ar Anupama Jundoo

Never am I more excited about community-enhanced design than when I watch 40 seniors spend two full days to decide which common amenities outside of their houses and shared with the entire neighborhood will make their personal lives more practical, more social, more healthy, more convenient, more supportive, more economical, more interesting, and more fun. This is real cultural evolution among seniors—those who you might think would get stuck in their ways.

"It's just a building!" No, it's a reflection of who we are—it's a reflection of our culture, and it's a reflection of who we want to become. We want to swim in beauty and stem the heating of the planet. We want to build and sustain a viable society, and there are few devices accompanied by a healthy process that are more likely to successfully get you there.

VILLAGE HEARTH, NC

You couldn't ask for a more inviting and giving world to commune with your fellow neighbor.

Besides sustainability, the main function of breaking bread together is to figure out who wants to do something after dinner, like go for a walk.

QUIMPER VILLAGE, WA

Open, centered, giving, warm, cozy, and comfortable.

The Danes would say that if you ask 100 seniors at random if they would be interested in senior cohousing, maybe one would say yes. But if you ask 100 seniors who have explored the advantages of growing older with others who know you, care about you, and that support you—then at least 40 would say yes. There are a number of established training workshops that help seniors explore these advantages with each other. Study Group I (SG1), often referred to as Aging Successfully, is a 10-week course of learning, dialogue, and discovery, two hours per week. Participants learn the

QUIMPER VILLAGE, WA

The cooks are, as usual, the heroes of the day.

importance of becoming aware and conscious of the issues involved in aging, out of denial, and proactive. The course covers the following 10 topics: aging in place and aging in community; the group process, working together efficiently, and nonviolent communication; the physiological realities of getting older; co-care (what you will and want to do) and outside care; co-healing (someone to talk to in times of need); the economics of getting older; philosophy, spirituality, and mortality; aging and growing into elderhood; embracing risk; and case studies. In other words, you can't just design a village and hope that people will live out their days in a village-like manner—you need to help them see the advantages and means of accomplishing village life as well.

While working with Quimper Village in Port Townsend, Washington, we were also working with two other senior cohousing groups to create new custom senior neighborhoods. Quimper Village was by far the easiest of the three to work with because they had taken SG1 twice, as they had thoroughly discussed the issues and had both feet in the future, individually and as a group. The project went smoothly and it became a state-of-the-art cohousing. The group that took SG1 once worked well, but there was an issue of new people joining and not being ready for the future, compared to the group that took it twice. And with the group who did not take it all, they had to work through many more issues during the design process. Throughout the development they had conflicting ideas about their capacity as a group—with clearly one foot in the future and one foot in the past. Study Group One is germane to a smooth process. For a full discussion of SG1, see Chapter 7 of *The Senior Cohousing Handbook: A Community Approach to Independent Living*.

Study Group One, Port Townsend, WA. Here are 20 seniors analyzing, studying, and discussing the issues that will have everything to do with their lives being more than fulfilling.

Reviewing all of the group-generated criteria during a break.

MOUNTAIN VIEW, CA

Looking in from outside makes anyone want to be invited to dinner.

STILLWATER, OK

Stillwater common terrace. Neighbors being neighborly.

MOUNTAIN VIEW, CA

There was enough adversity with a difficult city approval process—which seemed trivial later—but it made these common dinners feel like you were part of a rugby team that had just won the national championship, sitting in the local pub relishing their win.

STILLWATER, OK

Out on the common house terrace with grandkids who want to be at this senior community because this is where the action is.

STILLWATER, OK

The common terrace of the common building is where neighbors hang out, but it also gets a lot of use beyond the common gatherings. It's in a sweet location, with the best sun exposure in the winter, the best shade in the summer, and the best view. It should also be seen by as many houses as possible.

Because of the group's goals, Village Hearth was designed to feel like a lodge. I like it when someone says "I feel like I'm on vacation all of the time" when they are in the village.

MOUNTAIN VIEW, CA

Make a place: a village and a common house that feels like a family that you belong to. Find your tribe and be inclusive—you'll be surprised how big your family really is.

VILLAGE HEARTH, NC

The common house is now ready for people to have dinner together.

MOUNTAIN VIEW, CA

It's almost time to break bread together tonight at Mountain View Senior Cohousing. In this senior cohousing community, there are common dinners twice a week. Neighbors take turns making dinner for those who attend— about 75 percent of the 30 people that live there each night. There's also the Friday night potluck, and numerous other dining-centric activities.

VILLAGE HEARTH, NC

Evaluating the proposed common house plan in three separate groups. How close does it follow the program? Do the circulation and other architectural considerations make sense? and so on.

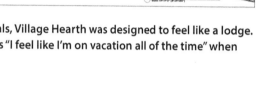

QUIMPER VILLAGE, WA

Prioritizing the long list (about 25 items) of possible common spaces. Do this in three separate groups (without spouses in the same group) and then meld them into one. The discussion building the criteria, the discussion prioritizing, then the discussion melding all three groups' ideas usually tells you who this group is and who they want to be in the future.

QUIMPER VILLAGE, WA

These workshop participants are evaluating the architect's common house plan and discussing whether it fulfilled the common house program. What was pointed out in the architect's presentation that could not be achieved in the program? What opportunities presented themselves during the design process that were not already in the program or the design criteria? What could not be accomplished? For example, we committed to having five rooms off of the entry, but there were only four. Nothing set this common house up for success or gave it the strong foundation of a solid design criteria like instilling ownership in the group. They carefully created that criteria, and just as carefully, they evaluated how well we fulfilled it. The group had set up 400–500 important decisions in the program. In other words, it could only get better from there. This same process has worked for The Cohousing Company with multi-family housing, subsidized housing, shared housing, dormitories, town planning, childcare centers, community-enhanced condominiums, community-enhanced single-family neighborhoods, cohousing, and co-living developments.

QUIMPER VILLAGE, WA

Here was the mark-up from one out of three groups. Proposed changes were presented by a spokesperson for each group that portrayed their concerns. There was a great deal of overlap between the three groups. It was being done thoroughly and therefore only took a couple of hours. This evaluation and analysis process and overlap serve as a reminder of what was proposed to happen in the common house and clearly stated what the group had together—at that point, they were ready to start designing the private houses.

QUIMPER VILLAGE, WA

In several groups, the community discusses and decides all of the activities of the common house (dining, cooking, yoga, etc.). Which activities need their own space? Dining does. Cooking does. Yoga doesn't. In this case, yoga would be done in the dining room.

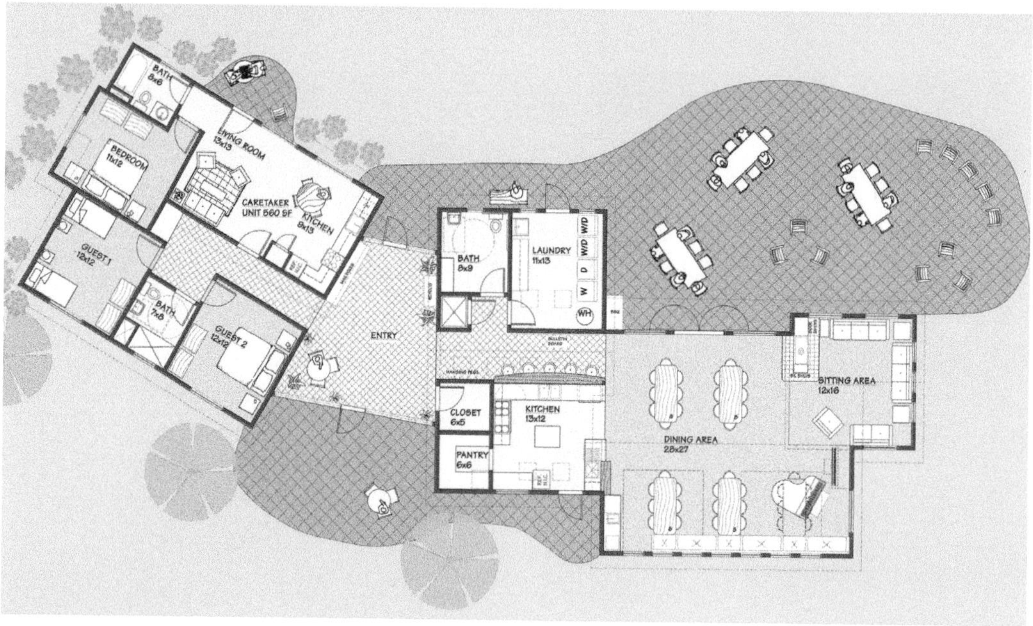

QUIMPER VILLAGE, WA

The Port Townsend common house terrace is unique. It has two fronts and two backs, but they are interchangeable. Sometimes the west side is bustling at 4 p.m. because of the afternoon sunshine (especially in fall and spring); and sometimes it has high use on the east side, for early morning coffee while watching the sun rise. They both work out.

QUIMPER VILLAGE, WA

A place that we have together is a feeling that must be evoked. This neighborhood has places where residents can gather, manage the ranch, discuss the issues of the day, learn more about each other, and learn from each other. There are places to plan for the spring garden, have afternoon tea, or debate. An extension of the house, and an extension of the neighborhood at the same time. Neither would be whole without the other. And it works that we belong here.

QUIMPER VILLAGE, WA

Feel the inviting warmth, the openness, the access to appreciating the fellow neighbors who are cooking dinner.

QUIMPER VILLAGE, WA

Family-style dining. When you walk into the common house at 6 p.m., dinner is ready—just like how mom or dad used to make it.

QUIMPER VILLAGE, WA

An open relationship between the kitchen and the dining facilitates communication. "Hey, we're behind schedule—can you chop some carrots for us?"

QUIMPER VILLAGE, WA

Yes, everywhere is a gathering node of sorts, but that's if everywhere is giving and warm, with good acoustics and lighting. Most importantly, the environment must have people that you grow used to, just like a village: just like a high-functioning neighborhood.

QUIMPER VILLAGE, WA

Good acoustics, good lighting, good functionality, and no cross-circulation. This dining room is where it is supposed to be and as big as it should be for cooking, dining, conversing, and relaxing. "How was your day?," and "Would you consider running for mayor?"

QUIMPER VILLAGE, WA

Design for the day-to-day—make that work first and foremost. I hear architects (who have never lived in cohousing) say one after another, "What we need in this space is a big stage." Those types of activities almost never happen. One extra unnecessary space after another, and then all of the sudden, the day-to-day is not comfortable—and there's no one there to plan the extraordinary events.

QUIMPER VILLAGE, WA

Perches, perches, perches. In senior cohousing, make it easy to sit down here, there, and everywhere. You cannot depend on a quality social episode to last only as long as people can stand. It needs time to develop, to remember what you wanted to say, and to let the conversation circle back to what you really wanted to bring up.

QUIMPER VILLAGE, WA

The three heroes of the day—"It wasn't hard."

QUIMPER VILLAGE, WA

Hanging around after dinner shows a high functioning neighborhood. Beside more specific measurements like total people-hours, how early people come to dinner and how late they stay after are some basic litmus tests for a high functioning common dining room.

QUIMPER VILLAGE, WA

Howard moved into cohousing reluctantly. But now he enjoys hanging out at the edge of the kitchen watching the cooks and being recruited to do chopping for the neighborhood dinner. It is a special place to promote this helpful, generous kind of behavior.

QUIMPER VILLAGE, WA

A neighborhood management meeting in the common house.

QUIMPER VILLAGE, WA

The personal storage room in the free-standing personal/common storage building, open so that it can be seen by neighbors. "Hey, are you using your luggage this weekend? Are you using your golf clubs?" It may seem invasive, but if you like and trust these people, you're happy to help.

QUIMPER VILLAGE, WA

Twenty-one-year-old professional caregiver Charlie (left) assists 80-year-old resident Suzie (right), who really appreciates and needs the help. It's fun for Charlie to be around a lot of other people that also take care of Suzie. This more natural and organic method of caring for each other is reminiscent of any high-functioning village that you might find in Southern Italy, Southern France, Eastern Africa, or anywhere else in the world. They made a room in the common house as a caretaker apartment. This gerontology, or nursing, student might care for Jim 14 hours per week and Jill 14 hours per week while going to school.

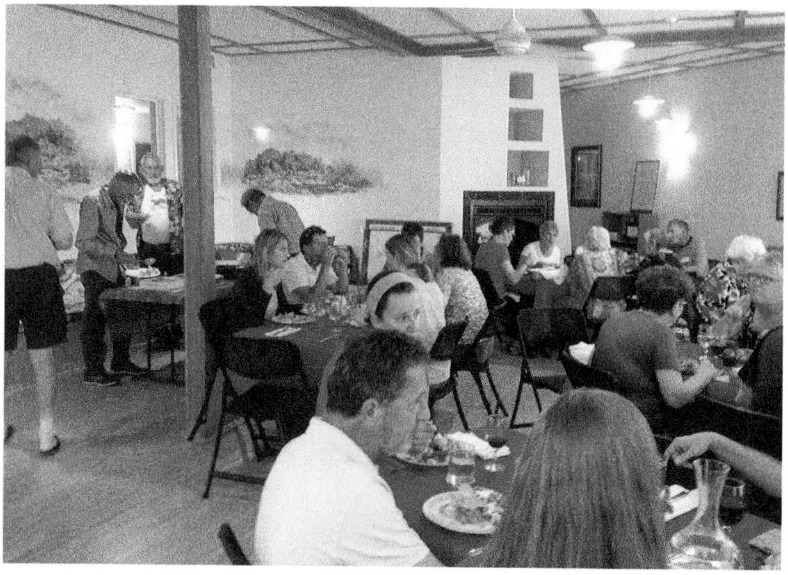

WOLF CREEK LODGE, CA

The common house at Wolf Creek Lodge: a 30-unit senior cohousing community.

WOLF CREEK LODGE, CA

Evaluating the common house schematic design before starting on the private houses. The common house program was established at the last meeting, and they will start on the private house programs later today. But it's best to know the common house intimately before starting the private houses. "Maybe I don't need that extra bedroom, the common house has two." "Maybe I don't need that gourmet kitchen, the common house has one." This is true for both multi-family and cohousing projects.

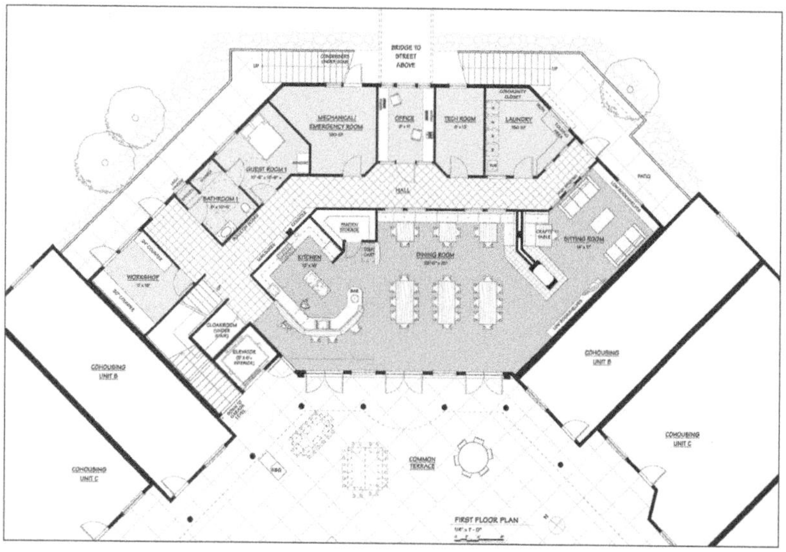

WOLF CREEK LODGE, CA

The first floor of the common house.

WOLF CREEK LODGE, CA

Evaluating the common house plan.

WOLF CREEK LODGE, CA

As I sat down for dinner one night as a guest at this cohousing community, feeling pleased and comfortable, I marveled at the sumptuous vegetable platters placed in the middle of the table. Design a place where the love is palpable, and where people are motivated to do something like this for their neighbors because someone else made something similar for them the day before. In other words, all of the small moves that you make to bring people together will reveal themselves. Sustenance is part of the milieu of community. If the space is well designed, then dinner will probably be well designed too.

WOLF CREEK LODGE, CA

The interface between a passerby and a cook: "Yum, that looks good," "Thanks for cooking," and so on.

WOLF CREEK LODGE, CA

Socially distanced, but not socially isolated during the COVID-19 pandemic.

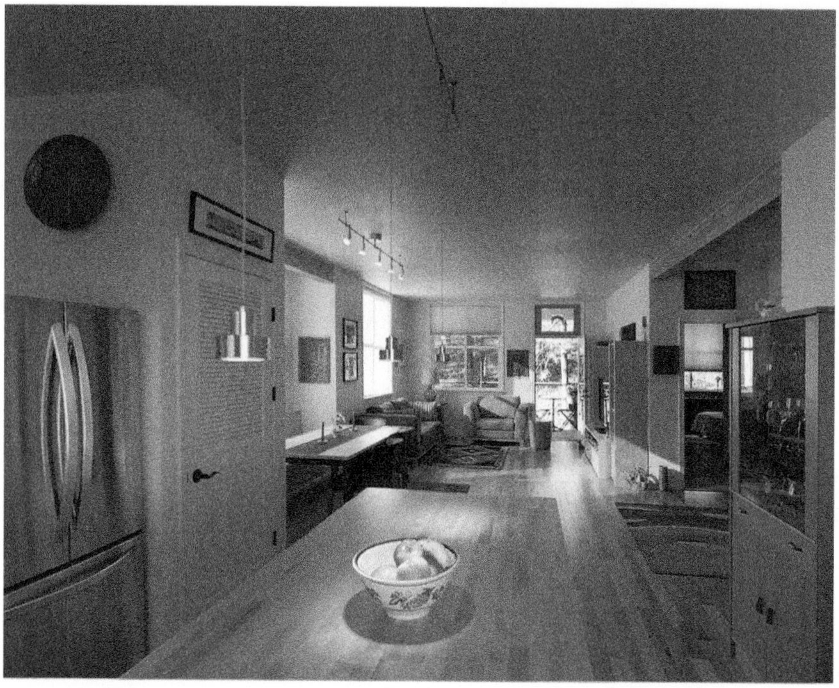

WOLF CREEK LODGE, CA

WOLF CREEK LODGE, CA

The common house.

WOLF CREEK LODGE, CA

The sitting room, used for games, reading, conversation, and more. Often there are school-age kids here in the afternoon. The residents make it available for homework and tutoring by the elders that live there.

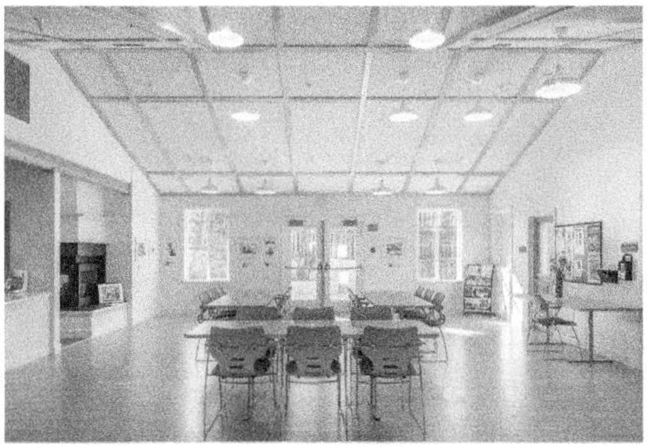

LEGACY—VALLEY VIEW SENIOR HOUSING, CA

The common dining room.

LEGACY—VALLEY VIEW SENIOR HOUSING, CA

The common house at Valley View. A lot of veterans live here, so there are three soldiers (lighted dormers) at attention, with one fallen comrade (not lighted dormer) on the left.

LEGACY—VALLEY VIEW SENIOR HOUSING, CA

The fireplace made from repurposed slate.

LEGACY—VALLEY VIEW SENIOR HOUSING, CA

The common house.

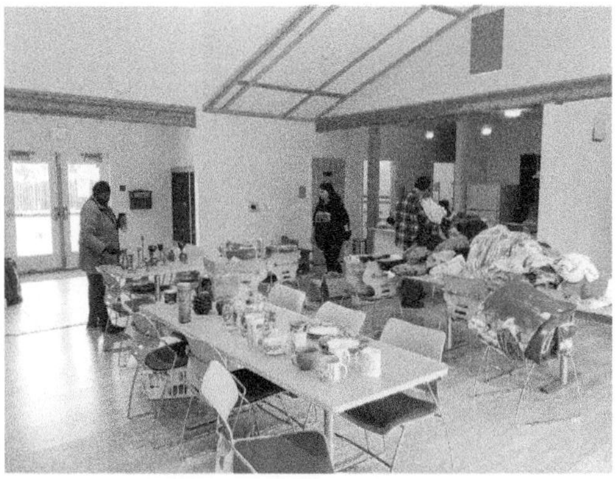

LEGACY—VALLEY VIEW SENIOR HOUSING, CA

Most of the residents at Valley View Senior Housing were formerly homeless, who needed these considerable donations to set up a home.

LEGACY—VALLEY VIEW SENIOR HOUSING, CA

The sitting room.

LEGACY—
CASA VALASCO, CA

The Cohousing Company took a three-story brick telephone switchboard station (built in 1921) and turned it into a five-story senior community, exclusively for folks on Social Security, with a new basement (for common laundry, mechanical, etc.) and a new common house penthouse.

LEGACY—CASA VALASCO, CA

Residents used to wait for paratransit for an hour on their own. Now they wait for fellow residents to walk to the store together two blocks away. That shift and 18 other adjustments came from the three evenings of community building workshops. Before the workshops, people would never open their doors to visitors—now they welcome them in. Relationships led to trust, and trust led to major shifts in behavior.

Acoustics: Sometimes ear muffs are the tell-tale signs of bad common house acoustic design.

LEGACY—CASA VALASCO, CA

The penthouse common building was never used during the first month after move-in. Subsequent to the three community building workshops after move-in there are people in there every day.

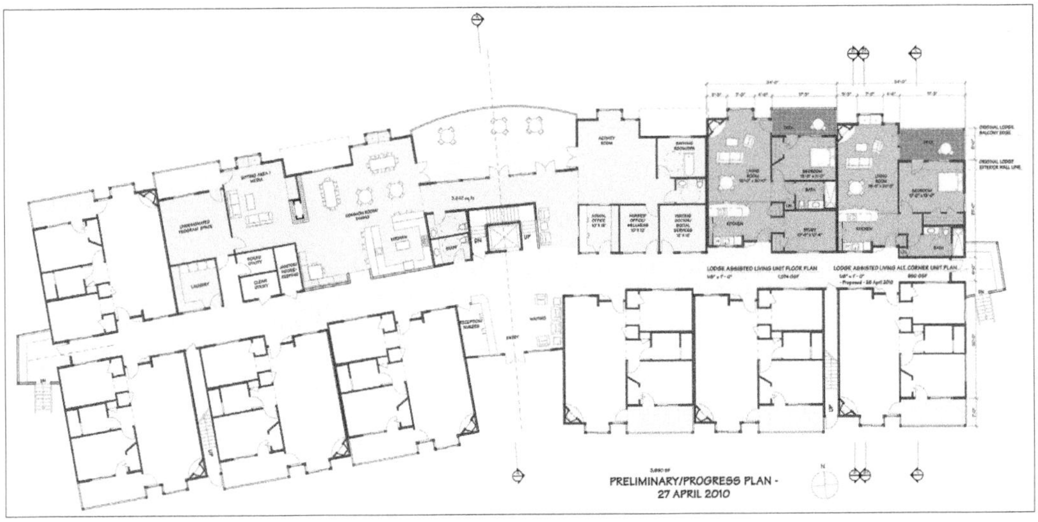

LEGACY—RINCON DEL RIO, CA

Learning from cohousing, The Cohousing Company has gone on to make lots of cohousing-inspired communities like this two-story 15-unit building. Every apartment has a bedroom with its own bathroom, kitchenette with sink, under-counter refrigerator, two-burner stove, and four-person dining table. This is very much the missing market housing. Housing for folks without a lot of money, but who still want to live a happy life and know that they need the wonder of community to accomplish it. We have also had great luck getting cities to reduce their development fees for projects like these, as many essential services for seniors are reduced.

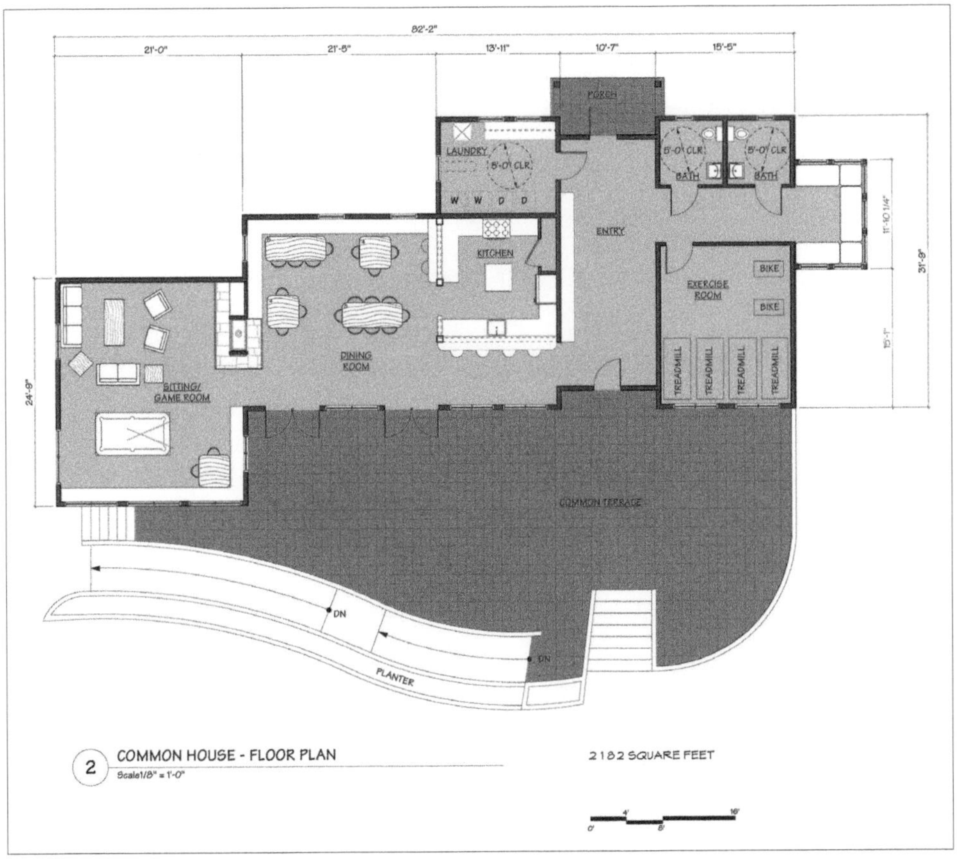

LEGACY—RINCON DEL RIO, CA

A new housing development for seniors with a 20-unit cohousing community and extensive common facilities.

LEGACY—RINCON DEL RIO, CA

The common house.

QUIMPER VILLAGE, WA

Common House Workshop. Two days total in creation. About 450 people hours went into the design and creation of their future common house. This dig-deep programming and thorough design discussion lead to a very successful common house that has accumulated over 36,650 people hours over the last 10 years they have lived there.

QUIMPER VILLAGE

Bubble sorts are an extremely effective means to understand the values and priorities of a new group of people.

10

Quimper Village

Common House Workshop

"In my professional life, all the design, design research and guideline writing that I've done has gradually moved towards "social change" rather than "environmental improvement". For those of us who want our work to move this way, it rings false to separate social relationships from physical environments; they are part of the same fabric."

David Chaplin

The main complication in doing an anthropological-based design in the context of growing toward community-enhanced design is that it's not only about who they are now, but who they hope to become. When it comes to prioritizing the spaces in the common house, number one and two are always cooking and dining. It impresses me how such a big commitment—eating with your neighbor three to five times per week—seems to become a natural conclusion in the quest to figure out what will make my life better.

QUIMPER VILLAGE

www.quimpervillage.com

COMMON HOUSE PROGRAM AND DESIGN CRITERIA

Write-up from Common House Workshop

Facilitated by Charles Durrett
Write-up by Erik Bonnett
McCamant & Durrett Architects
Port Townsend, Washington
February 21 – 22, 2015

Table of Contents

COMMENTS: ***Eight locals came to our initial organizing meeting for Nevada City Cohousing. One couple that we had not seen before—a Native American (Nisenan) couple—came to the meeting. After brief introductions they said nothing for the rest of the night. As we were walking out I approached them and asked, "Howdy, are you thinking about joining this effort?" "Oh no," he said, "but we are impressed that you folks are proposing something akin to a condensed village." He continued, "You white folk generally build houses equidistant across the landscape and consume a lot. We just want you to know that you can let us know if we can help in any way." That meant a lot to us.***

This could have been the case in Port Townsend as well, where Native Americans traditionally built compact villages and where now the European emigrants built their houses distant from each other.

PART 1. CONTEXT

Background

This document comprises Quimper Village Cohousing's program and design criteria for their common house and other community facilities. It summarizes the desired activities, priorities, and design criteria agreed to by the resident group during a programming workshop facilitated by Charles Durrett of McCamant & Durrett Architects. Program write-up by Erik Bonnett. This program also serves a variety of uses:

- The project's development budget allows for up to 3,500 sf[1] of common facilities. This program establishes the priorities for the use of those funds.
- As the project evolves, this program acts as a summary of the goals and design priorities of the group.
- As new members join the community, it should be used to familiarize incoming residents with the programming and design process for the common facilities.
- This document represents the combined efforts of the future residents, culminating a deliberate process that reflects the group as a whole.
- Finally, it shows where there are overlapping interests, common concerns, and shared values; where working together makes every individual's life easier, more convenient, more practical, more economical, and more fun. By collaborating, we can have more while using less of the earth's resources.

The Participatory Design Process

In summarizing the community's programming decisions, this document confirms that participants share the same expectations. During the Common House Workshop, participants went through a process to Brainstorm, Discuss, and Decide upon elements that they want to incorporate into the design of their common house and other community facilities. As the design of this project evolves, this program will be used to evaluate design alternatives and changes in the context of how they address the program goals. If the group's goals or design criteria change, the program should be amended to reflect the changes.

We recommend that Quimper Village Cohousing agree on a specific process for making changes in the program if needed. For instance, the group may require a minimum number of persons agree to reconsider an issue before it can be put back on an agenda. Many groups also require a quorum of

A common house used by the Klallam First Nation, who previously inhabited the land now occupied by the City of Port Townsend.

Historic Port Townsend.

COMMENTS: ***If you're going to approach design from an anthropological point of view, it's critical to understand the culture of the town to the fullest extent possible. All of the group's needs become obvious. This group happens to be very active, and they want to accommodate that in their design. Obviously, the town's culture is a foundational part of the planning.***

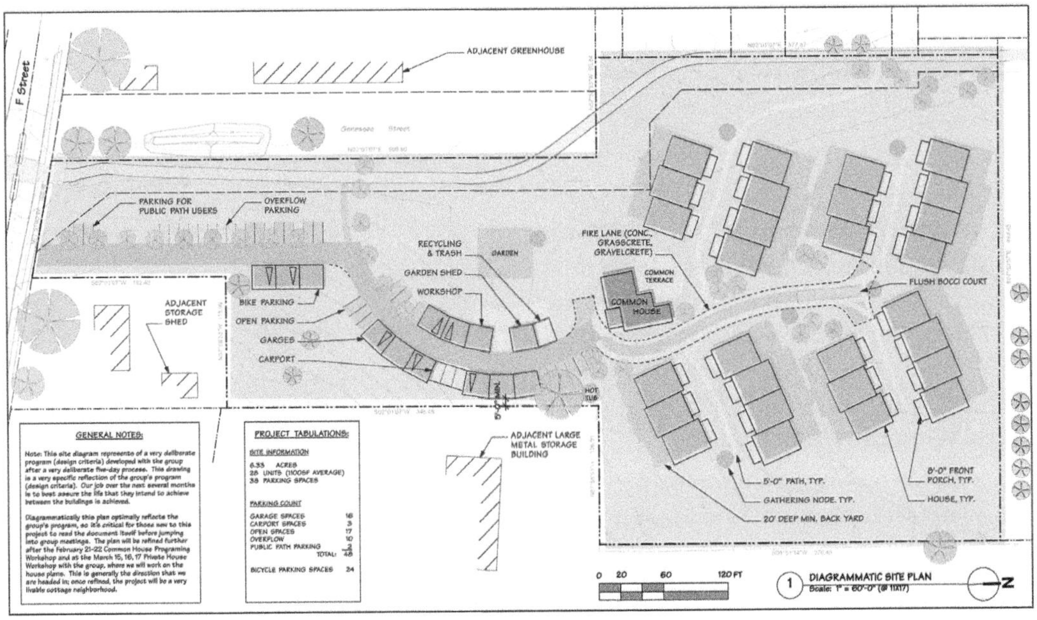

The Site Plan generated at the Site Planning Workshop.

two-thirds of the group present to reconsider an old subject. While it can be useful to consider new perspectives or insights, it is also important to respect the enormous number of people-hours and effort put into the decisions contained in this document.

Reconsidering past subjects usually happens once at most during the development of a project. That's how smart the group is the first time, when all of the collective energy, knowledge, and good will is in the room. We made these decisions at the exact right time. We struck when the fire was hot.

Prior to the Common House Workshop, the Site Program for the community was developed at a Site Planning Workshop held on January 31–February 3, 2015. The Site Program exists as a separate document.

The Common House Program and Design Criteria outlined here are informed by the Site Program. However, because the Site Program is subject to later changes due to the development of Private House designs, money limitations, size constraints, zoning issues, and other city requirements, the Common House may be affected.

COMMENTS: ***People-hours in the common house per week are directly proportional to the thoroughness of these programs and how reflective they are of this group's real life and aspirations.***

PART 2. GOALS AND ACTIVITIES

Goals for the Common Facilities

IMAGINE . . .

It is a Saturday morning in 2017 and you are sitting on the common house terrace reading your newspaper and waiting for the rest of the landscape committee to arrive. You muse for a few moments how this common house really meets your goals. What are those goals?

- To manifest the community that we have developed
- Beauty and comfort
- A welcoming home
- Invites each and every one of us in some way
- Easy maintenance
- See sunshine
- Good acoustics
- Capture and take advantage of the sun
- Connect
- Facilitates the ability to grow and adapt
- Serve our different interests
- Facilitates togetherness

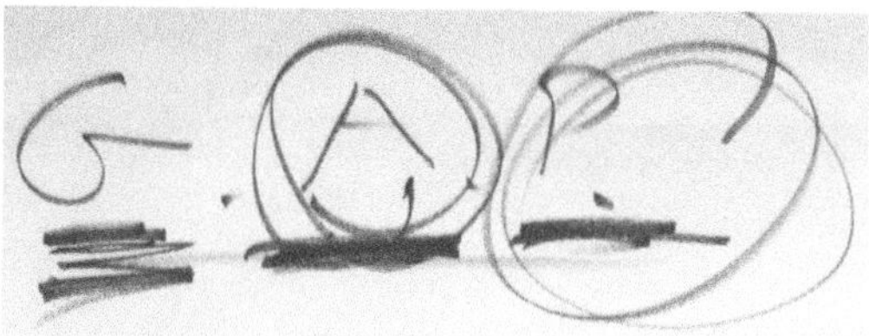

- Looks and feels like the Northwest
- Accessible to all of us
- Hallmarks the best of the spirit of here
- A variety of opportunities
- Natural light
- Comforting in all seasons and weather
- Effectively welcomes
- It feels like we live it
- Physically and emotionally sustaining (Feeds our bodies and souls)
- Cozy
- Richer and less solitary life
- Is hospitable, be hospitable
- Is neighborly, be neighborly (into the larger neighborhood, i.e., not a cloister)
- Secure
- Serves the practical side of life
- Gives us a practical excuse to get together
- Levity
- Cultural enrichment
- Cultural and practical sharing
- Supports health

Programmed Activities

This table records the brainstorm. After discussion, the list of places and design criteria (see page 264) were consented upon.

Activity	Own Place	# of People	When
• Garage saling	No	?	1x/year
• Sitting/gazing at the fire	No	Varies	Daily
• Meditating	No (at home)	-	Daily
• Conversing	Yes	50	4–8x daily, 8–10p.m.
• Hot tubbing	Yes	6–8	3x/week, 8–10p.m.
• Creating (quilting, crafting, sewing, writing)	Yes	12	3–4x/week, 10–3p.m.
• Sitting in the sun	No	All	As possible, 3–4 p.m.
• Poker / games	No	-	-
• Exercising (with weights and equipment)	Yes	10	Daily
• Dining	Yes	40	2–3x/week, 5–9p.m.
• Performing	No	40	
• Watching movies / common football	No (2)	Lg: 30, sm: 5	Daily
• Cooking	Yes	3	Daily
• Sewing	No	2–8	1x/week
• Tai chi / yoga	No	6–12	2x/week, a.m.
• Hosting guests	Yes (2)	1–4	All day
• Doing Laundry	Yes	3	Daily

COMMENTS: ***This is the first common house that we designed that had two full common house terraces—an east and a west. One for where the sun is in the morning and one for where the sun is in the afternoon (if there is any sun at all). In a climate like this which is often cloudy, people follow the sun.***

It's not normally a good idea to have two terraces because it might dilute the energy that people are looking for when they meander up to the common house. However, in this case, all you need to do is to follow the sun and you will find the people, and that's where you want to be. It's always better to listen to the culture and the climate when coming up with an appropriate design response. In other words, in design there are no rules—only principles.

Activity	Own Place	# of People	When
• Relaxing/lounging	Yes	Varies	Daily
• Dancing	No	?	1x/week
• Picking up mail, newspaper	Yes (mailboxes)	28 households	Daily
• Playing music	Yes (Shared)	?	?
• Reading & exchanging (book club)	Yes (bookcase)	?	?
• Meeting	No (shared)	≤ 28 households	Several x/week
• Managing (files, storage)	Yes (small office)	1–2	5x/week
• Classes/discussions/learning	No	≤ 28 households + guests	3x/week
• Roasting	No	-	-

Activity	Own Place	# of People	When
• Brewing/wine making (drink everywhere)	No (in kitchen)	-	-
• Smoking and/or curing food	No	-	-
• Downcycling (Downsizing)	No	-	-
• Compost collection (composting in garden)	No (in kitchen)	-	-
• Recycling collection (storage and pick-up outside)	No	-	-
• Crafts (messy, knitting/crochet, scrapbooking)	Yes	10-15	Daily
• Drinking	No	≤ 28 households	Daily

Activity	Own Place	# of People	When
• Painting (Oil, VOCs, smelly)	Yes (not in C.H.)	-	-
• Wood carving	No (in woodshop & common terrace)	Small number	?
• Toileting	Yes (2)	1 at a time	Lots of x/day
• Exhibits	No	-	-
• BBQing	Yes (outside)	-	-
• Parties	No	-	-
• Canning/Preserving	No (kitchen)	-	-
• Renting the building	-	-	-
• Computing	No	-	-
• Storing (food, utility, cleaning)	Yes	0	Daily
• Emergency preparedness	Yes (closet)	7	1x/month
• Media	No (storage alcove)	7	10–12 hrs/month
• Caretaking	Yes (apartment)	7	-
• Accommodating kids and families	Yes (studio B)	7	Familiy visits lots
• Sharing/community closet	No (Laundry room)	-	-
• Helping one another	No (everywhere)	Everyone	Always
• Stargazing	No (outside)	-	-

PART 3. PROGRAM PLACES

Consensed Prioritized Places

COMMENTS: ***This is one of the most essential, if not crucial, exercises in community-based design. This bubble sort only ever considers two spaces (or amenities) at a time. In this case, the bubble sort is very much an anthropological act. "Would you rather visit the in-laws this weekend or go to a football game?" In other words, you can use this method to figure out where any culture is in terms of their activities and values. You consider 26 items like that and prioritize them from A–Z, and you have a very good idea what the values are ingrained, some conscious, some unconscious—just like the effects on any individual in the context of a culture.***

During the Programming Workshop, the community prioritized different common facility uses, consensing on the following order.

It is understood that not all common facilities will be in the common house as some may work better in different locations on the property.

This list establishes the priority for uses of funds for common facilities, with the understanding that those lower on the list may not be included at all.

1. Dining Room
2. Kitchen
3. Bathroom 1
4. Caretaker
5. Sitting Room
6. 6 (tie). Laundry
7. 6 (tie). Wet Bar (espresso bar and more)
8. Guest Room 1
9. Workshop
10. Guest Room 2
11. Storage 1 (programmed at Site Workshop)
12. Garden Shed
13. Craft Room (messy crafts to be combined with Garden Shed in the same "2-car garage," clean crafts to be absorbed into sitting and dining)
14. Emergency Prepared Response (at Storage garage)
15. Hot Tub (programmed at Site Workshop)
16. Storage 2 (additional garage)
17. Music (to be combined with Dining Room)
18. Exercise

Not prioritized but to be included:

- Office (alcove)
- Entry

Place	Activities	Character	Relationship	Details
Dining Room (can accommodate 30 diners 3x/week) (can accommodate 48 diners 1–2x/year)	• Dining • Not cooking • Sharing • Community • Camaraderie, reengaging with friends, laughter • "Captive audience" • Continuing the conversation • Meeting • Playing music, dancing, performing • Focus, lectures, classes, discus-sions, learning • Parties • Yoga • Clean crafts	• Smell of food • All my senses being engaged • Beautiful room • Color • Good lighting • Candles, wine • Background music • Wonderful acoustics • Just the right amount of "live" acoustics • Comfortable aesthetic	• Audience	• Comfortable and stackable chairs • Tables: conducive to conversation, easily movable, consider collapsible

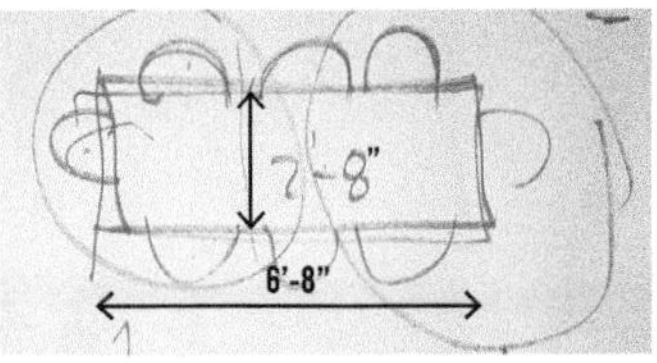

COMMENTS: ***In the case of Glacier Circle, the entire community hired a full-time assistant within two months—a single mom. But she did so much more than check in on Mr. Jones and Mrs. Jespersen every day. She made soup for lunch or dinner on occasion, she made common dinner for all on special occasions, did the community books, helped clean the common house, and gave people rides to the doctor. All in all, it was a 30-hour per week job.***

The caretaker unit becomes obvious to most senior cohousing groups, especially those like Quimper Village that took SG1 twice, "Hey, turns out that I might continue to get older." If they don't recognize this need, I just make one suggestion—go to visit a nursing home—then we'll decide.

Place	Activities	Character	Relationship	Details
Kitchen with Pantry (3 butt kitchen)	• Cooking • Conversing • Roasting • Brewing / wine making • Smoking and/or curing food • Recycling and compost collection • Parties • Canning / preserving • Storing food		• Direct relationship to BBQ, briquets • Close to door to outside (for garbage, groceries, outdoor BBQ, etc.) • Bussing without going into the kitchen	• Lots of counter space • One lower & one higher counter • Pull-out drawers • Storage for pots, pans, knives, silverware • Open upper shelves • Obvious and easy storage • Commercial appliances • Gas stove (48", 6-burner) • Induction stove • Convection double electric oven • Bar • Prep island • Separate prep sink • Pre-rinse • Dishwasher (1) • Instant hot water • Floor drain • Carts/rolling • Efficient garbage and recycling • Good ventilation • Adequate lighting

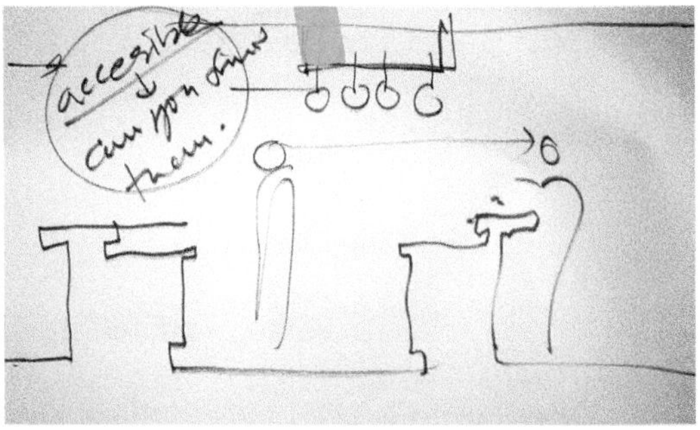

Place	Activities	Character	Relationship	Details
Caretaker Unit (2 guests /caretakers)	• Long-term guest room initially • For use by care-taker as needed	• Comfortable • "Everything space" for privacy • Keep it simple • Efficiency	• Separate entrance	• Long-term guest room • Complete kitchen (later)
Place	**Activities**	**Character**	**Relationship**	**Details**
Sitting Room (10–12 sitters comfortably) (20 sitters possible)	• Sitting • No TV at construction • Portable TV later • Clean crafts	• Cozy • Warm • Great color 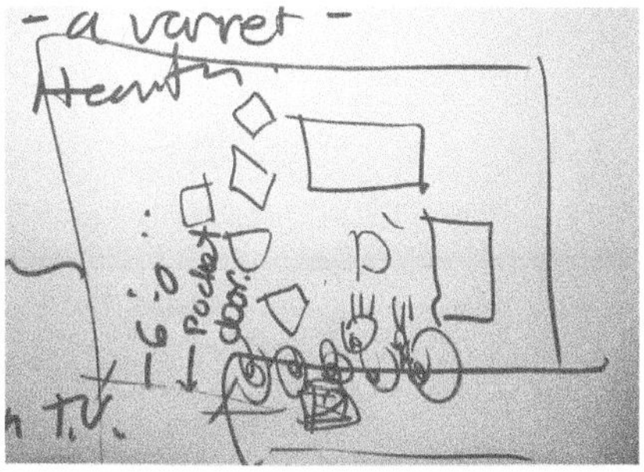		• Gas fire • Couches • Comfortable • Nice carpet • Good for reading • Bookshelf • A place for a TV • Afghans • Ottomans (2) • Variety of seating • Hearth
Place	**Activities**	**Character**	**Relationship**	**Details**
Laundry (for 21 estimated households) (11 of 15 households at workshop would do laundry at CH at least partially)	• Hanging clothes • Folding 		• Access to outdoor clothes drying • Near espresso bar • Near bathroom • Near entry	• 3 washing machines • 3 dryers • Solar dryers (racks) • Hanging space • Utility sink • Area for carts • Good ventilation

COMMENTS: ***Glacier Circle built a caretaker unit above the common house. Since then, a single woman has taken over that job. How much does this affect design? Immensely. Is it an additional unit? Yes. The community builds the space and those that need care pay for the care. And in the case of Glacier Circle, the entire community pays for the activities (like making common dinner) that serve them all.***

COMMENTS: ***Houses are smaller and less costly because they have two guest rooms in the common house. One for a grandchild visiting from college, and another for everyone else. It's often hard for the younger seniors to imagine grandkids visiting from college—but if you live in a cool enough place, it will happen.***

A big misconception at first is, "Why should I help pay for the workshop, I'll never use it?" That fades when you start to see that the great equalizer is 24/7. That's what we all have in common. I might not use the workshop, but I'll be using something else. And that you might break a chair while moving in and someone else might offer to fix it in the workshop, and you'll trade them some computer consulting. In other words, everyone sees that everything evens out.

Place	Activities	Character	Relationship	Details
Wet Bar	• Espresso	• B.Y.O.B.		• Espresso machine (Satellite brand coffee system, heats water) (later) • 5'–6' long • Little sink • Instant hot water • Under counter refrigerator (milk/wine) • Boxes of tea • Cups • Glasses (wine, etc.) • Small bussing cart

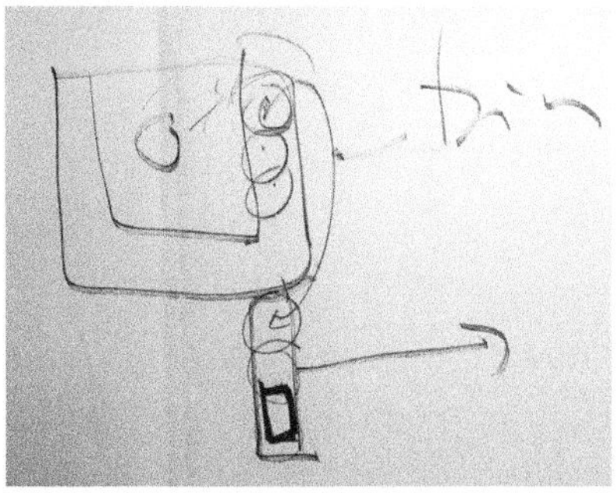

Place	Activities	Character	Relationship	Details
Guest Rooms (guest room 1 and guest room 2)	• Sitting next to a window (bed elsewhere)	• Not a motel room • Different from each other • Comfortable	• To long-term guest quarters • Separate • Shared bath	• Two @ 12' x 14' • End table • Reading light • One with twin bed • One with queen bed • Suitcase holder • Hanging some stuff

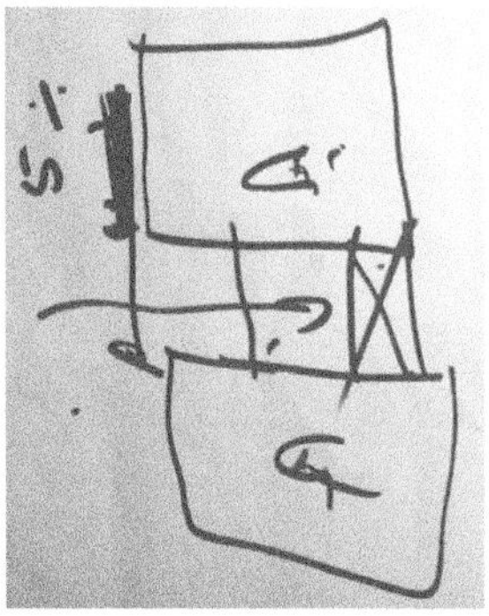

Place	Activities	Character	Relationship	Details
Workshop	• Painting • Sewing • Scrapbooking • Terra-cotta Sculpture • Kiln & wheel • Messy crafts @ NE light (clean crafts @ C.H.)			• Space for adjacent lean-to future addition

Place	Activities	Character	Relationship	Details
Storage (programmed during Site Workshop)				• 7′-0″ high garage door • 10′-0″ clear height to trusses

Place	Activities	Character	Relationship	Details
Garden and Craft Shed		• Two-car garage	• One garage for messy crafts and gardening	• 22′ x 22′ • Insulated and heated • To be subdivided later • Hot water • 1/2 bathroom (also used for workshop) • Utility sink • 110v • 220v • 7′-0″ door • 10′-0″ clear height to trusses

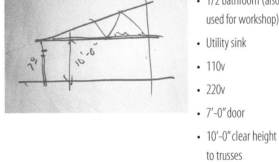

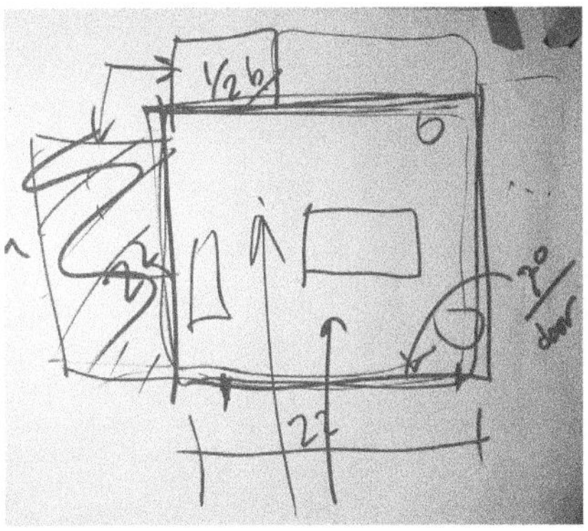

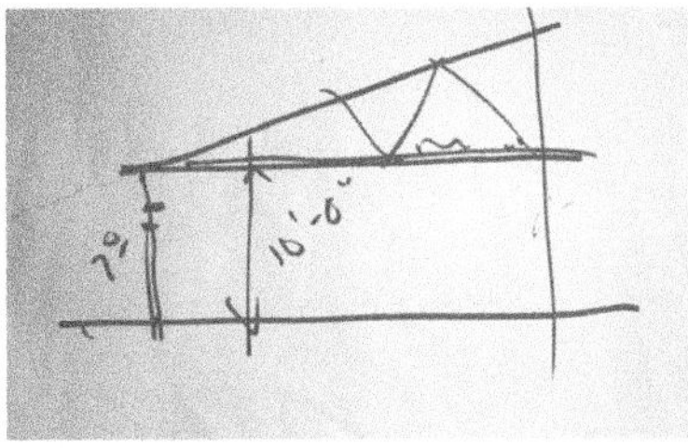

Place	Activities	Character	Relationship	Details
Clean Craft Room	• Sewing • Beading • Scrapbooking • Card making • Print making • Knitting, crochet • Quilting • Ironing • Classes			• Drawing table • Cutting table • Storage accommodated throughout

Place	Activities	Character	Relationship	Details
Exercise Room				• Multi-exercise on site • Multi-gym

Place	Activities	Character	Relationship	Details
Office	• Storing records			• 8′ closet • Shared equipment

Place	Activities	Character	Relationship	Details
Entry	• Entryway • Storing coats • Changing jackets • Changing shoes • Recycling	• "Back door" • "Utility door" • "Postman's door" (drop-off, not a long-term door) • "Front door" • Art work • Facilitate, not dramatize temp. change	• Umbrella holder (@ porch OK) 	• 6′–7′ aperture to dining room • Hooks, pegs (up and down • Mail boxes/cubbies, package shelf, newspapers • Bulletin board • Wet, muddy shoes • Bench

PART 4. CONCLUSION

Other Common House Criteria

I. Accessibility

The common house will be designed to meet the current Washington Building Codes for accessibility.

II. Location of the Common House

Per the Site Program, the common house has been located centrally to provide easy access and good visibility from the homes.

III. Sun Catching

During the workshop, it was stated over and over: "good natural light, good artificial light, good acoustics." We made this a blanket criteria for every relevant place—so it is not stated throughout the program.

Furthermore, with summer highs only in the low 70s but also 156 sunny days, it is recognized that the activity "sitting in the sun" is most often accomplished indoors in Port Townsend. Thus, the common house will embrace the sun when it is present, but will also be designed to function well during the 146 days annually with precipitation.

(Data from bestplaces.net.)

COMMENT: ***This program was written along the same time as Haystack Heights' Program (Chapter 4). Even though they are for two different projects, the purpose of both is to instigate a culture change that is universal to both intergenerational and senior cohousing neighborhoods. It is important that every one of our clients sees this, reads this, and understands what we can accomplish together as a community.***

Common House Feel

Not an Institution

The feeling that a common house has makes a dramatic difference in how much it is used. Everything else being equal, a cold and sterile common house won't get used as much simply because there is an underlying unpleasantness to being there.

Like an Extension of Your House

The Quimper Village common house will be designed to be light and airy, and at the same time warm and giving. The common house should feel like an extension of one's private house; not like an institution.

Workshop Conclusion

As the Quimper Village cohousing community, you have a unique opportunity to plan a common house for your forming community, and to envision the common house as the hub of this new cohousing community. The outcomes of this workshop will help create a common house that is an extension of the private houses and truly becomes the heart of the community. The common house will supplement, extend, and even exceed an individual's possibilities, and will achieve the best of the group's common interests. And no doubt, as you will see living there, the common house will extend the physical, social, and emotional potential of each and every individual, just as I have seen it do in the cohousing community where I live.

During the workshop, what really worked well was when folks had a brilliant idea and it went onto a piece of paper. Then the idea belonged to the group and everyone could evaluate its merits. When the idea was good, it stayed. Sometimes it was modified by the group. Sometimes an idea turned out to be "not so good." Those ideas were removed from the paper and are not part of the design criteria. This process worked.

The workshop was a waterfall of good ideas along with buckets and buckets of good decisions. While there was a little grumbling about the prolonged discussion (by maybe a minute) of the pegs vs. hangers methodologies of hanging a coat, you've got to work through the chaff to get to the kernels. As long as you stay on topic—it's all relevant, until it's not. In other words, if you are looking for an avocado pit in a sprig of wheat, you are off topic.

There should be little that is accidental or default about cohousing placemaking. First we listen and understand the groups' story, then the pencil hits the paper.

Our collective challenge is to optimize the criteria established in the workshop so that the common house, and therefore the community, can reach its full potential. Our next job is to test the program; that is, to see what a design for this criteria looks like. Is it too big? Can all of the adjacencies (relationships) be accomplished? What rooms should be combined, or what uses pulled apart? Are some rooms too big, some too small? Which ones are just right? Answers to these questions will be based on what a schematic design shows, and the discussion that ensues.

Criteria like "continuing the conversation" and "just the right amount of live acoustics" are sophisticated. Criteria like that offer a lot in terms of enriching this program, and therein the final design.

In conclusion, I find the common house design criteria workshop to be an important community-building workshop, as it was here in Port Townsend. The overlapping values and aspirations within the group became obvious. With each discussion, the opportunity to reach our potential as individuals, and as a community, came further into focus.

We have further to go, but this program is a fundamental and critical step to a successful common house and therefore to the long-term success of the community. I was particularly impressed that with clear, direct, communication, the group exceeded the sum of its parts. The energy and synergy that grew from the participation, collective imagination, and creativity of the group was a great thing to be a part of. Now, the next critical step is to manifest this program into a warm, cozy, yet also light and airy design. A good program is necessary to make a good building, but it doesn't guarantee a good building. That is our next job.

Chuck Durrett

PART 5. PARTICIPANTS

At the February 21–22, 2015
Quimper Village Common House Workshop,
the following participants were in attendance:

Barbara and Mack Boelling
John and Pam Clise
Pam and Jim Daley
Deborah Steele and Dennis Daneau
Michael and Linda Holbrook
Anne Holman
Kathleen Holt
Pat and David Hundhausen
Leon and Diane Lopez
Jerry Spieckerman and Bobbie McMahon
Sharon Moller
Ingelisa and Poul Oxenbol
Janet Palmer
Steve and Pat Resende
Nancy Richards
Carolyn and Jack Salmon
Mhaire Merryman and Timothy Singer

"Livet er ikke det vaerste man ha'.
Og om lidt er kaffen clar."
Life isn't the worst that one can have.
And in a little while, the coffee will be ready.

ENDNOTE

1. More square footage is possible within the budget because several common uses (common storage, garden shed, messy crafts, and workshop) will be built in economic garages.

WOLF CREEK LODGE, CA

Interior: This kind of architecture is the easiest to reach a consensus on by all—simple, sans decoration (arches and such), Scandinavian and Shaker style.

QUIMPER VILLAGE, WA

Houses that make sense and look good are all we are usually looking for.

11

Senior Cohousing Design Concepts

Private Houses Design

"I don't think architecture should only be about shelter... It should be able to excite you, to calm you, to make you think."
Zaha Hadid

Who knew that your final home would be the most bespoke and well designed? Designed with the wisdom of a cohort of people with your lifestyle needs in mind, such as having the kitchen oriented toward the pedestrian circulation so that you can summon a passerby's attention just by tapping on the window. "Hold on, I'm going to come out to say hello." The kitchen at the front and a thousand other small details accomplish the gift of cohousing, and that is staying connected to your neighbor.

Then imagine that your other goals for the private houses that you set out with your compatriots were also accomplished. Warm, giving, small, compact, well designed, easy to maintain, and easy to clean. And imagine that it sat lightly on the planet, used little energy, was built with sustainably grown wood, and accomplished what you have been hoping for, but needed colleagues to actually accomplish your dream.

It's nearly impossible to do all of those things with a single-family house. But it's possible in cohousing and other high-functioning neighborhoods; where community, sustainability, and beauty bear fruit. A cozy and warm home sandwiched by a front porch, an appropriate interface with the community, and a back porch for outdoor privacy. If you care about the big picture—seeing community grow and thrive into the future—it's best to accomplish that now. Community is important, but no more than how much I need refuge, my respite. It's an entirely symbiotic relationship. *Psychology Today* is clear that, when people look at a house they usually consider the kitchen, the bathrooms, and the storage. But they should also be asking, "where do the neighbors meet?", and in a community-enhanced neighborhood they will have places for that. But there is no good reason that they won't love their home as well—and with the help of smart neighbors and a good architect, they will love it more than anything they could come up with on their own. People who live in communities, neighborhoods, and villages that work do not need a large house. There are a lot of opportunities outside to build pergolas, gathering spots with seats around a fire, or sandboxes for toddlers—especially if you don't use it all up with roads and driveways as too often happens. All of the sudden there is a park and playfields appearing out of nowhere. Homes that have driveways use well over 1,500 square feet of asphalt per house, but parking at the periphery of a neighborhood uses less than 500 square feet per house. For more about these kinds of line items, see Chapter 14. For practical, emotional, and spiritual reasons the house means so much, but in the context of a functional neighborhood—it's a different kind of space than we are used to.

SILVER SAGE, CO

Jenny moved into her new house at Silver Sage at 83. She said that her husband had died 10 years previously, and in that time living alone she was noticeably losing her words. Moving in to cohousing meant that someone could see her through the glass front door (shade up) and knock on the door, like Scott, and come in to talk.

MOUNTAIN VIEW, CA

Open floor plans make all of the rooms feel more generous.

WOLF CREEK LODGE, CA

After the full-day private house program, two subsequent days go into the design of the private houses—then that's it. And they are better houses than those that regular developers spend months to finalize. I've heard a lot of senior cohousing groups say this, but not as often as this one, "Chuck can you hurry this along? I don't ever buy green bananas." Virginia to my right said it the most, but you can see her brother Wayne, buying a separate home to her right, say it in his body language. The gentleman to the left is blind, but he pushes his lovely wife's wheelchair in the striped shirt. She's a quadriplegic but she can guide him along the way.

WOLF CREEK LODGE, CA

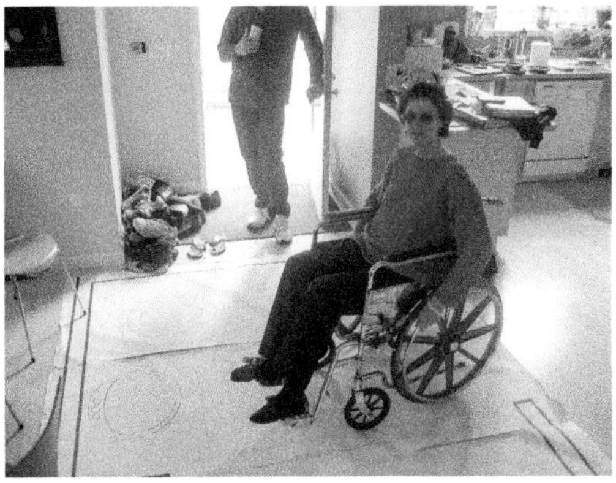

WOLF CREEK LODGE, CA

Mock it up. Even if you don't need a wheelchair today— you might someday. This Wolf Creek resident had a full-scale bathroom plan to roll around in to understand the design of the space. When one day, she may need the space.

WOLF CREEK LODGE, CA

A typical "front porch" at Wolf Creek: Comfortable, textured and with character; even with a single-loaded corridor, continuous circulation/front porches that access the houses on one side.

WOLF CREEK LODGE, CA

First Floor Plan: A very efficient way to make a community in one building with common house in the middle.

Second Floor Plan: Generous front porches, even in a three-story building.

Third Floor Plan.

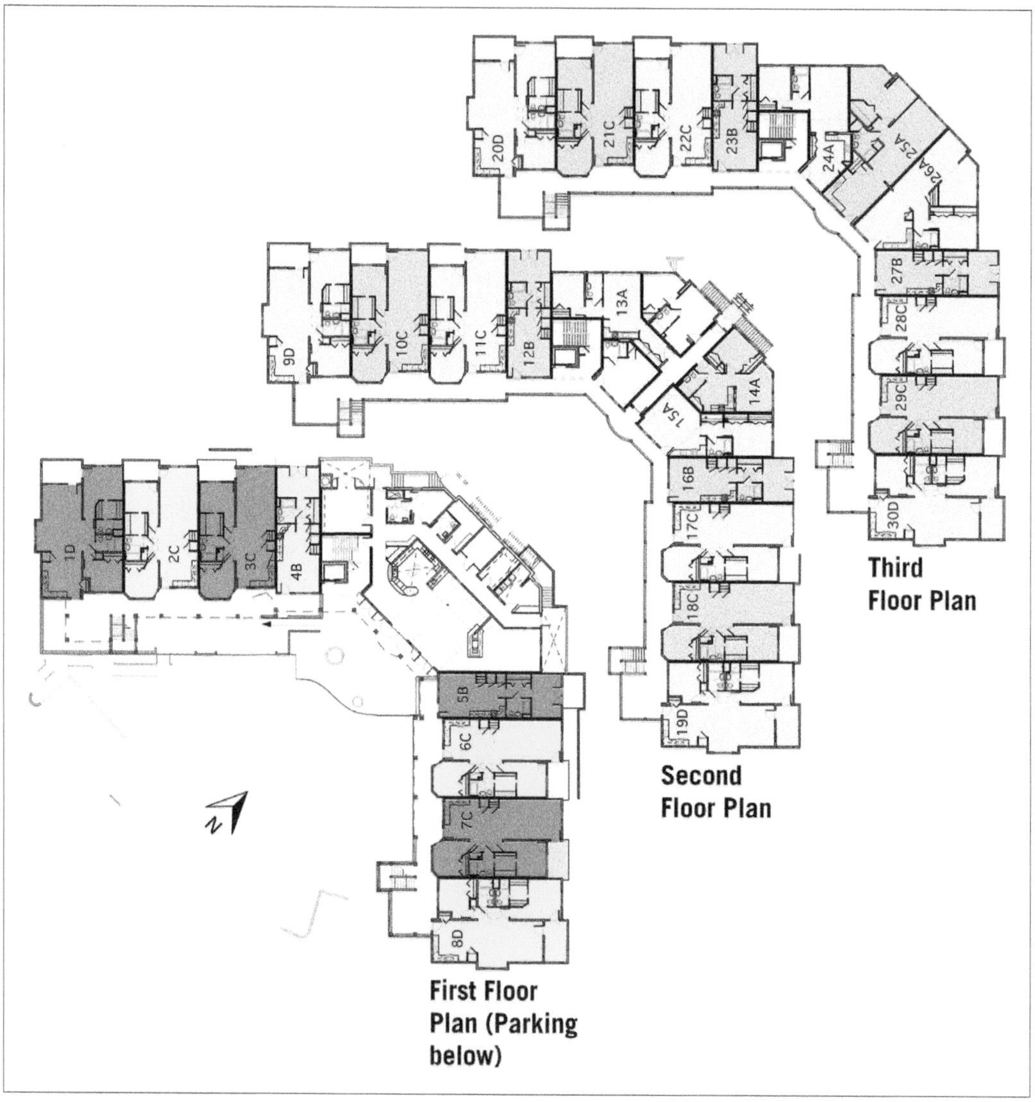

QUIMPER VILLAGE, WA

After my initial meeting with the 1-bedroom and 1-bathroom unit group, I hand the scribble to an accompanying draftsperson—in this case Erik Bonnett. Then I meet with the next group, the 2-bedroom and 1-bathroom group, and so on. Then the next morning I start over with the 1-bedroom and 1-bathroom group with a crisp new computer print-out of a floor plan. This routine starts the day after the general and the specific criteria making with the group. General: warm, cozy, etc. Specific: 14 inches between the kitchen counter and the bottom of the kitchen wall cabinets, and so on.

WOLF CREEK LODGE, CA

Richard and Gail looking from their front porch.

QUIMPER VILLAGE, WA

A 12-foot-wide room, with light coming from both ends and (2) skylights. Even as "interior house," with houses on each side, there should be enough natural light for the lights to be off during the day.

QUIMPER VILLAGE, WA

The kitchens are small, but highly functional—like a small boat's galley. However, Americans do have a hard time downsizing the refrigerator: the most expensive appliance in the house to run and the noisiest if too big.

QUIMPER VILLAGE, WA

The front porch is the least expensive but the most luxurious room of the house with the best fresh air and the best connection to the community at large.

QUIMPER VILLAGE, WA

This is how the house design seminars look after understanding the goals, activities, and places the day before. The architect spends 1.5 hours with the 1-bedroom and 1-bathroom group, then the plan is handed off to the accompanying draftsman. They revisit the plan again the next day for another 1.5 hours or until there is consensus from all 7 or 8 households. Then the 2-bedroom and 1-bathroom, 2-bedroom and 2-bathroom, and 3-bedroom and 2-bathroom groups take turns meeting with the architect.

QUIMPER VILLAGE, WA

There is so much pride in participation. The pride of the emotional ownership goes a long way to jumpstart a high-functioning neighborhood, getting it approved by the city, financed by the banks, and attracting others who want to be part of the excitement. In this image, Quimper Village just finished the second 1.5 hours of unit "C" (3-bedroom, 2-bathroom) design, which usually works out as one bedroom and two offices in senior cohousing. The larger units usually make it easier to afford the smaller units, which cost more per square foot to build than the larger units.

QUIMPER VILLAGE, WA

There are three unit types (A, B, C) and two building types in total (ABBC, ABC). This is what production construction looks like, and how you make sure that you keep the cost down and everyone in the project. The costs were $50–$90 per square foot in the 1990s, $100–$125 per square foot in the 2000s, $125–$150 per square foot in the 2010s, and $150–$200 per square foot since 2020.

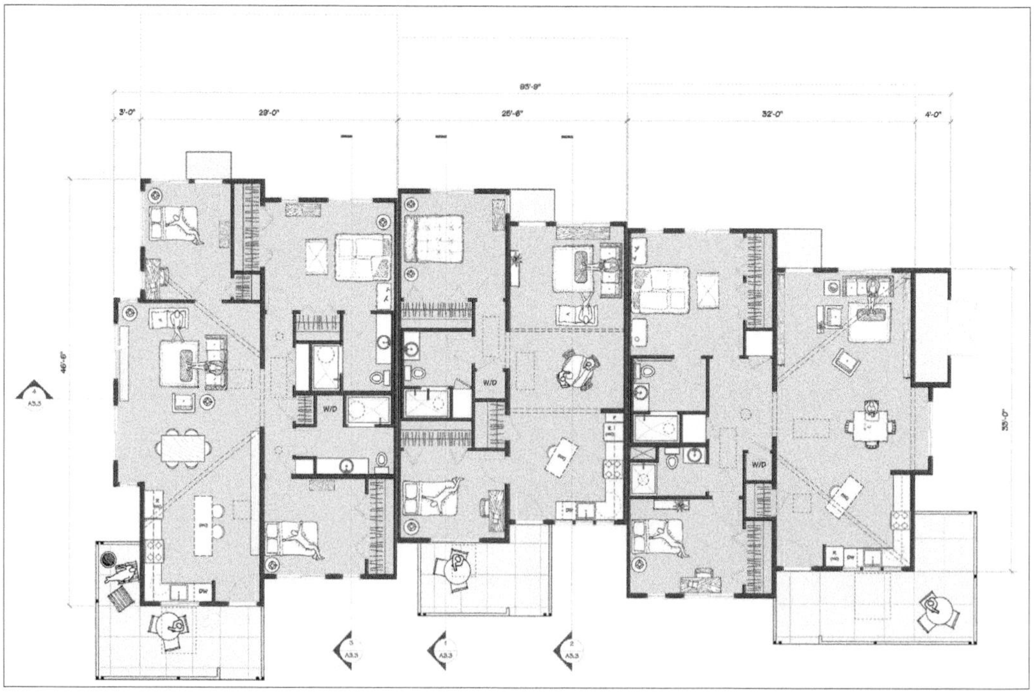

QUIMPER VILLAGE, WA

It never fails to amaze me how elegant yet highly functional these houses can be. They fit like a glove, not like a grocery bag.

STILLWATER, OK

Start the three-day private house design by carefully considering and evaluating the common house design. The architect goes through what worked (per program), what didn't, and new found opportunities. Then one person of each of the (3) groups presents that group's proposal changes, then the architect facilitates an amalgamation of the three critiques, and the changes and final solution are consensed. The group will have another opportunity to check it at the design closure workshop.

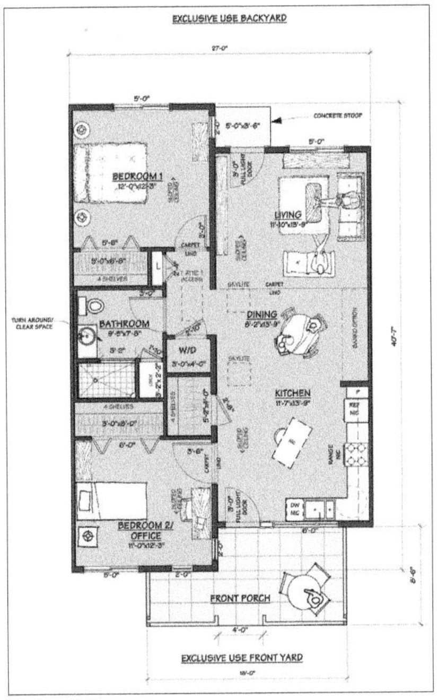

VILLAGE HEARTH, NC

Two-bedroom and one-bathroom unit.

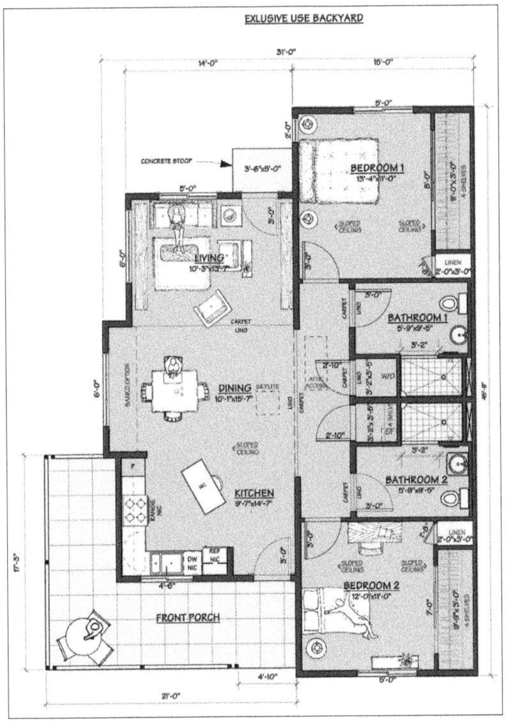

VILLAGE HEARTH, NC

Two-bedroom and two-bathroom unit. An easy house for two couples to share if costs are an issue.

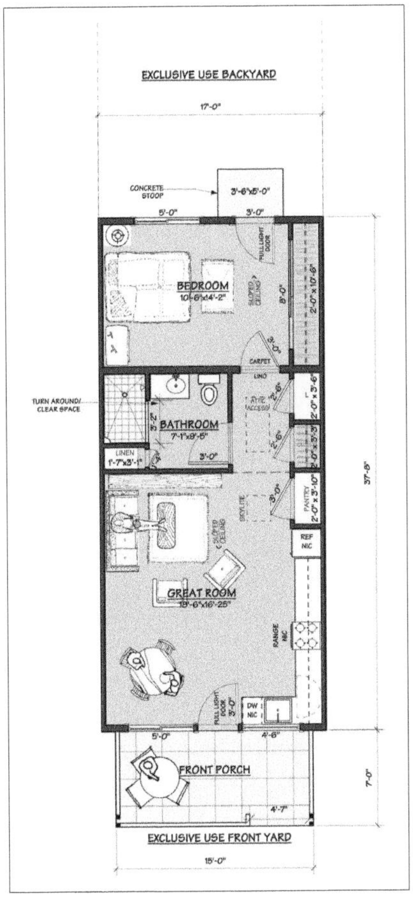

VILLAGE HEARTH, NC

A very cost-effective one-bedroom and one-bathroom condominium unit.

MASLOW'S HIERARCHY OF NEEDS

Self-fulfillment does not mean laboring on your house all day, especially if I've already spent 15 percent of my waking hours shopping, cooking, and cleaning up, and got the apron that said so. It might mean rubbing shoulders with others that are having similar life experiences as you, whether it is raising a family or winding one down. Set yourself free via cooperation.

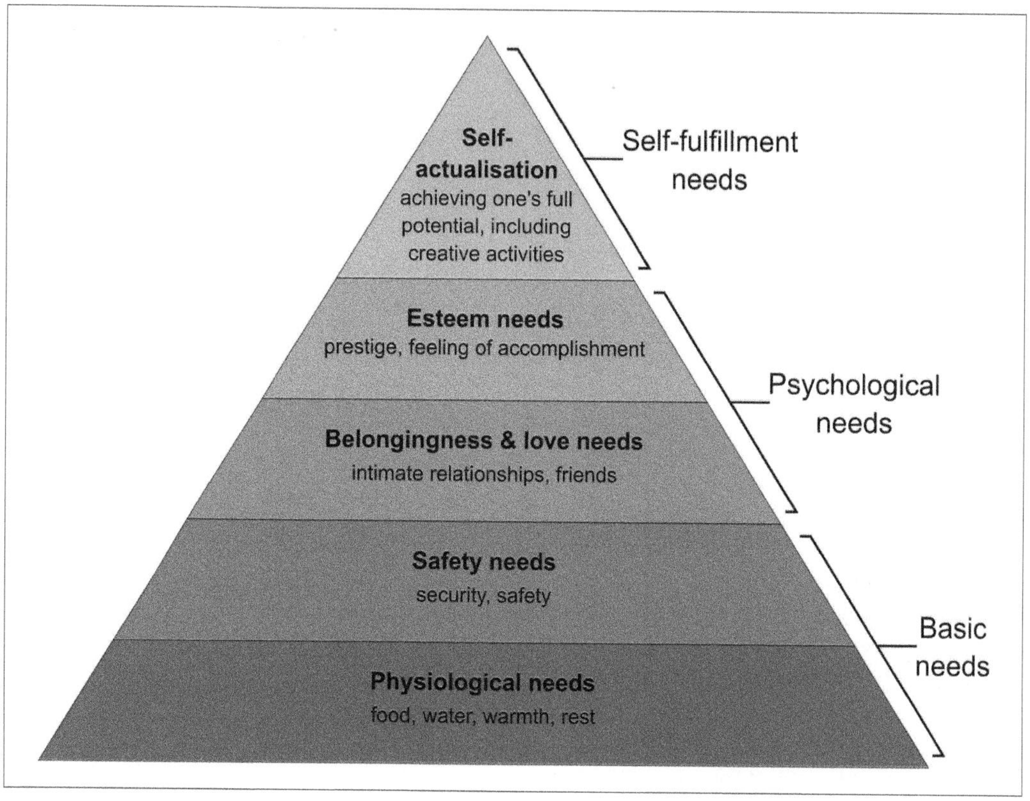

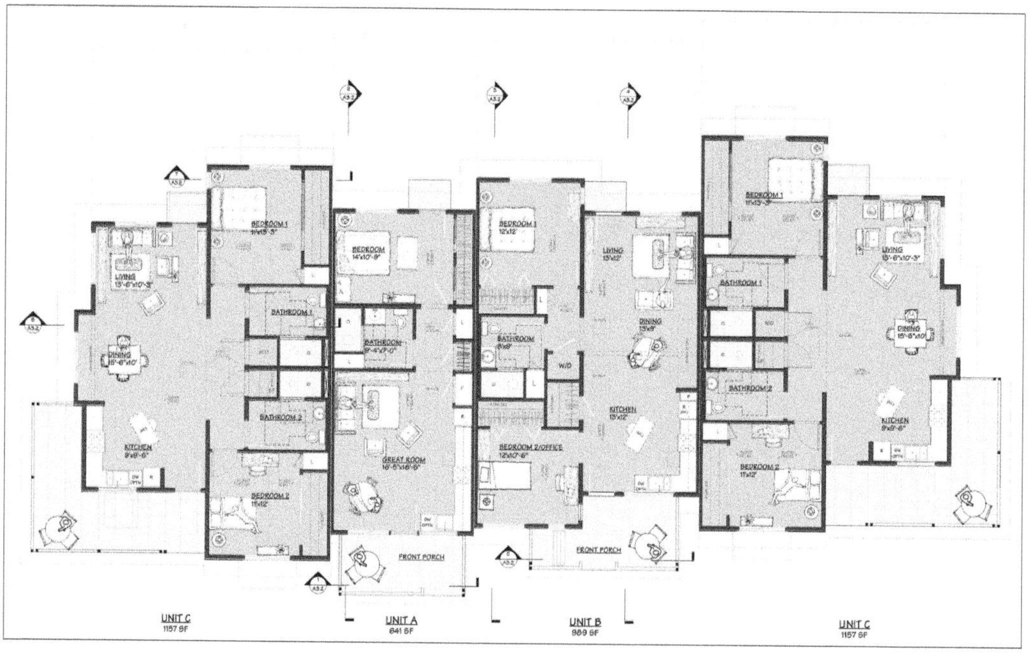

VILLAGE HEARTH, NC

Whole building design. This is about as economical as you can make housing, the four units are exactly the same in all seven buildings of the project.

Prioritizing: Reconciling Costs and Cultures

Prioritizing has everything to do with culture work. What you get in cohousing, over and over again, is a champagne taste for a beer budget. However, this means using opportunities to prioritize along the way—whether it be amenities in the houses or entire spaces in the common house. Although there is often a dichotomy in our wishes for the budget, it is reconcilable through prioritizing. Prioritization happens like a normal bubble sort: only two items are considered at a time.

STILLWATER, OK

Costs prioritized. To my amazement, this group prioritized ground source heat pumps as the number one amenity at $4,500 per house, using a considerable amount of the discretionary money set aside for amenities. As one person in the group said, "Chuck, that's what we do here in Oklahoma—we drill." In this case, two hundred tubes, almost 200 feet deep. It was a big move by the group designed to save considerable fossil fuel over the years, but with a considerable upfront investment. Over and over again I find that if I'm going to rezone a site (saving this group about $1 million), or remote parking or ground source heat pumps or 100 other big moves, I must work with the future residents, because I need them to get through the city council and the planning commission and so on.

Common facilities that best actualize your goals are an important place to prioritize. Time and time again, people who have never lived in cohousing brainstorm so many beautiful things/spaces/activities/common facilities during the design process that could make their lives better. However, even if you could afford them all, would you use them all? These ideas need to be prioritized according to what best reinforces the future residents' goals of affordability. While two-thirds of the things/spaces/activities/common facilities are normally built, the other third are not lost because they are attributed to higher-priority spaces. For example, while yoga rarely gets its own room, it's always accommodated in a higher prioritized space (dining or music, for example).

One way to afford more amenities or even make the development affordable at all is to get the site rezoned—typically from single-family to multi-family, commercial to multi-family, or low-density to higher density. If we begin the rezoning process after the design and vision have been finalized by the group, we are usually able to get more of the groups' amenities than what people assume is possible. That is, rezoning normally saves the group hundreds of thousands of dollars, and rezoning is more possible with cohousing. This is simply because cohousing brings many aspirational and motivated people together. When these folks know exactly what they want and why they want it—the officials see it too. We need their passion and drive to get through the city council, the planning commission, the planning department, the banks, the civil engineers, the building department for rezoning, and everyone else that prefers to design with the rearview mirror as their guide rather than the future. Over and over again we make it through the rezoning process with success. After we rezone a development to make it more affordable, the worst part of my job is when the mayor, neighbors, and numerous others come up to me at the grand opening to say "we can't believe that we ever fought this rezone at all—this environment feels as if the entire place would be remiss without it."

Of all the workshops, the sixth and last of the design workshops is the most interesting. For one, the group has worked together so everyone knows how to process information efficiently and with clear, direct, diplomatic, and respectful dialogue. And there is no judgment for what people are advocating for. During these discussions, extra sound transmission mitigation between houses and enhanced energy-efficient houses (a ten-item package) are usually the first and second priorities. But the next 20 items are a crapshoot of ideas based on what people came up with during the three-day private house design workshop and the three months before that, such as "my grandmother had tile counter tops, I'll die if I don't have tile counter tops." They go onto this list and get prioritized in this six-hour workshop usually three or four weeks after the house design workshop, so that we can realistically price the amenities per house. If it's a high priority it will go into each house, and it will be cheaper that way. If it is within midway priorities, it will probably be an option, such as a more costly skylight. If it's within the last third of the priorities, it will probably never be discussed again. From a cultural point of view, this is the most value-laden workshop. For sure, this is where there is a considerable amount of understanding for who the group is and what is important to them. People forget about the tile counter tops so that percolates down to last on the list because the person that was going to "die" doesn't really care about it anymore. At this point, the future residents often begin to favor the sound package (blown-in insulation, acoustically isolated plumbing pipes, extra-thick extra-dense sheetrock, a dozen-item package, and other acoustic features), sustainable materials (certified sustainably grown lumber, no toxins in glues and finishes, and at least a ten-item package), all of which has a considerable impact on energy efficiency and conservation. There is no judgment. If you want to make a case for how a common hot tub will make subsequent management go easier, then do it. Even when it comes to energy efficiency, the desires of the group is what makes things happen. Opinions about community are just as important as everything else, maybe more so—since they are the only magic bullets in the community. (I lived in two different cohousing communities that got a common hot tub two years after move-in. The common meetings took less time once the hot tub was in place.) Whether it's a school board, church elders, or a city council talking about a new walking street, this method of prioritizing in a bubble sort always gets things done and clarifies what is important to this group and their long-time and newly found list of priorities. I've done this drill with new and existing low-income multi-family housing projects and found it to be an incredible community-building exercise, that made the residents lives more practical and safe. The new on-site activities changed the nature of the social structure from nobody cares or knows each other, to I know everybody and care about them.

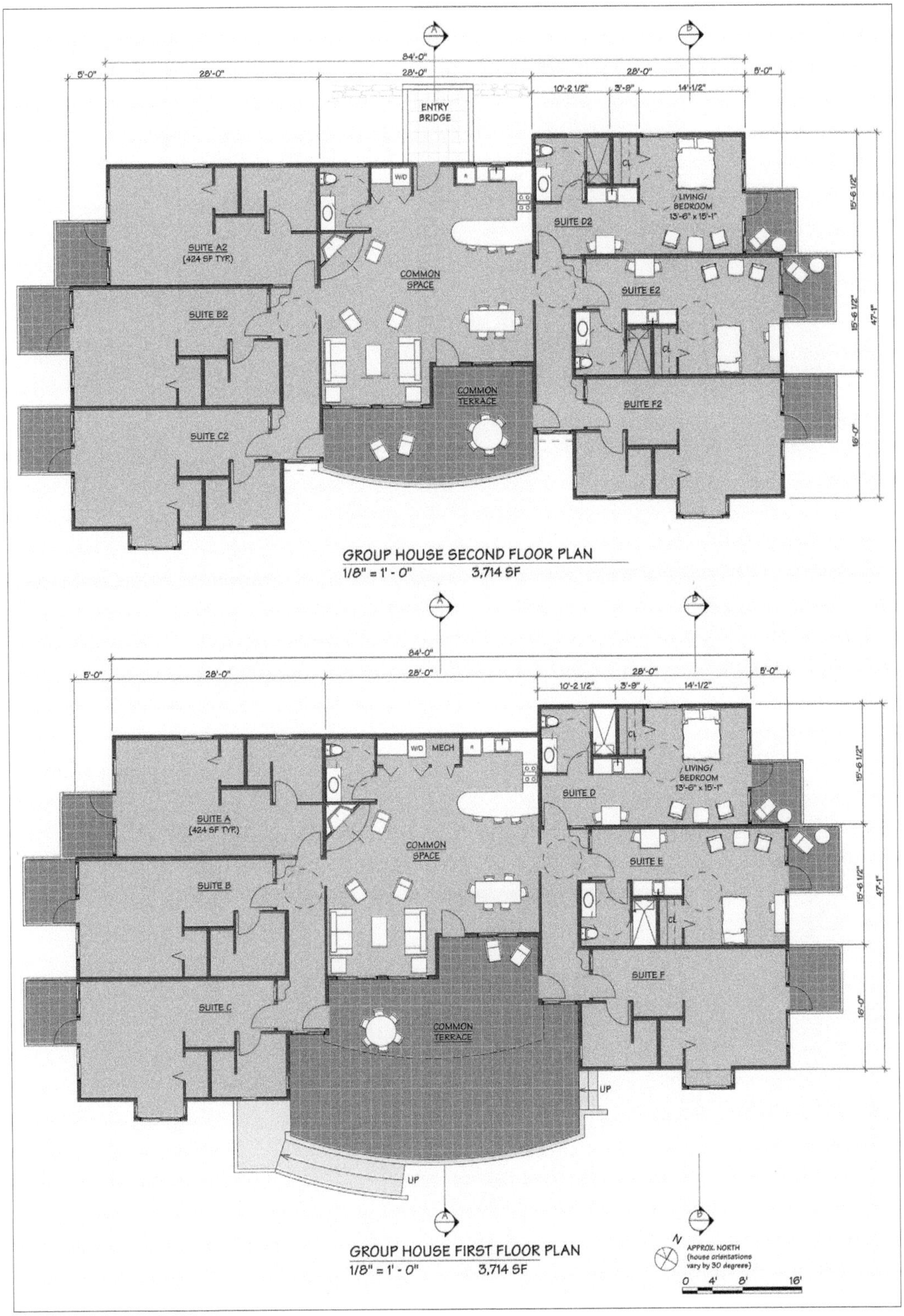

LEGACY—RINCON DEL RIO, CA

The common facilities at Rincon del Rio: Designed to bring people together for fellowship and community, yet give them their own place for respite and refuge. A two-story plan (six suites with bedroom/ bathroom on each level) with two shared living areas (with kitchen, dining, and living) for 12 suites in total. This building could comfortably serve 24 people or more, but the acoustics would have to be handled exceptionally well.

LEGACY—VALLEY VIEW SENIOR HOUSING, CA

This is lovely. A very affordable new village in Napa County for folks previously without housing, or at risk. Now she is "whole" as she would put it.

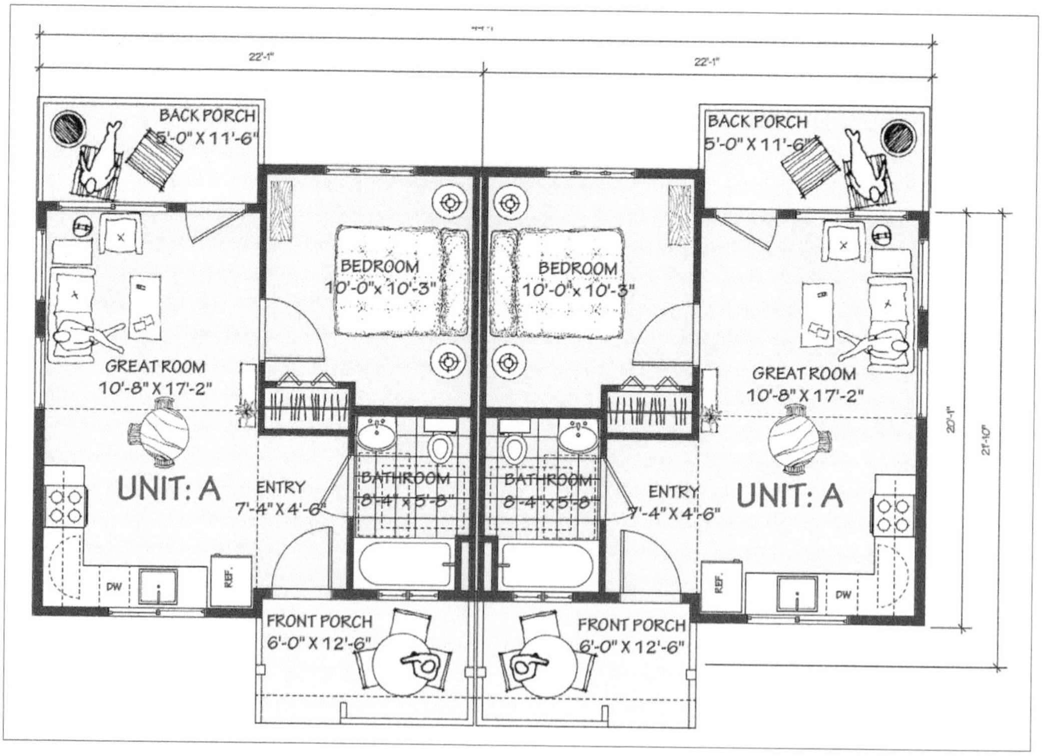

LEGACY—VALLEY VIEW SENIOR HOUSING, CA

QUIMPER VILLAGE

Private House Workshop.

QUIMPER VILLAGE

Design Closure Workshop

O.K., last chance to tweek before we take it to the city. This is an entire day workshop—and the group has never changed anything of consequence. But they understand it, and can speak to it—and that is why these projects make it through the city or county so rapidly.

12

Quimper Village

Private House Workshop

Innumerable social and physical clues communicate to visitors and residents alike a sense of home and neighborhood. This is a place that people are proud of, a place that children will remember in later years with nostalgia and affection, a place that just feels "good."

Clare Cooper Marcus

The private house design experience is one of listening carefully to what the future residents have to say. The house is such an important place of self-expression, self-confidence, political representation, self-worth, taste, and intention. It is also a place where you can be part of the solution to whatever the problem might be.

QUIMPER VILLAGE

www.quimpervillage.com

PRIVATE HOUSE PROGRAM AND DESIGN CRITERIA

Write-up from Private House Workshop

Facilitated by Charles Durrett
Write-up by Erik Bonnett and Mathilde Berthe
McCamant & Durrett Architects
Port Townsend, Washington

March 15 – 17, 2015

Table of Contents

COMMENTS: ***This program was written along the same time as Haystack Heights' Program (Chapter 6). Even though they are for two different projects, the purpose of both is to instigate a culture change that is universal to both intergenerational and senior cohousing neighborhoods. It is important that every one of our clients sees this, reads this, and understands what we can accomplish together as a community.***

PART 1. CONTEXT

Background

This document comprises Quimper Village Cohousing's program and design criteria for their private houses. It summarizes the desired activities, priorities, and design criteria agreed to by the resident group during a programming workshop facilitated by Charles Durrett of McCamant & Durrett Architects. Program write-up by Erik Bonnett.

This document also serves a variety of uses:

- To outline the design criteria.
- To evaluate proposed designs.
- To summarize the goals and design priorities of the resident group (Group) as the project evolves.
- To familiarize incoming residents with the programming and design process for the private houses as new members join the community.
- This document represents the combined efforts of the future residents, culminating a deliberate process that reflects the Group as a whole.

Once the design is complete and consensus has been reached by the group, the private house drawings will reflect and also supersede this program. The drawings will then reflect the programmed information as well as any new information. Subsequent design development information will further clarify the feasibility of programmatic and schematic designs.

Introduction

Creating the house of your dreams. . .

. . .a house that fits in the context of a custom community, in the context of a budget, in the context of a site. Within these contexts, the goal is to create houses that meet members' dreams and aspirations.

In cohousing, the community is the focus. But respite and privacy are the yin to the yang of the energy and support of the community.

The common house is really A PART of each private house. It is an extension of your house, where you go every day. The more useful, used, and necessary the common house is, the healthier your cohousing community will be.

The acoustics, the feel, and the lighting in the common house will make it a place that you want to go, and do go on a daily basis. However, you also have to have good excuses to go there. Excuses like eating dinner, doing the laundry, getting mail, sampling the latte or beer of the day, and more.

> "Me. We."
>
> *– A poem by Muhammad Ali*

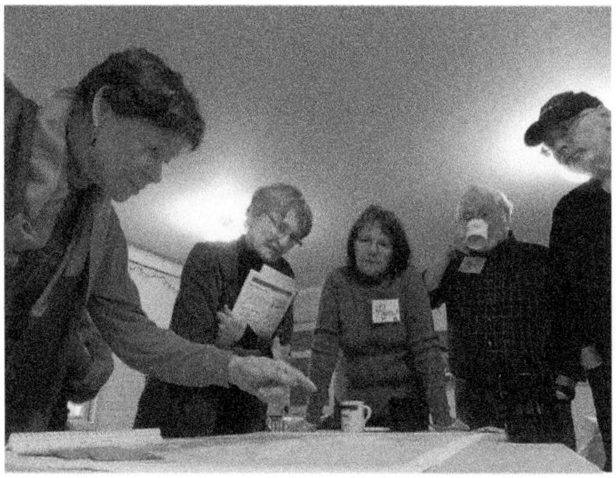

Participatory Design Process

In summarizing the group's programming decisions, this document confirms that participants share the same expectations for the project. It also identifies areas that need further discussion. As the design of this project evolves, this program should be used to evaluate design alternatives and changes in the context of how they address the program goals.

The members of Quimper Village should agree on a specific process for making changes to the program, such as requiring a minimum number of persons who want to reconsider an issue before it can be put back on the agenda. While it can be useful to consider new perspectives or insights, it is also important to respect the enormous number of resident hours and effort put into the decisions that are expressed in this document.

Prior to the Private House Workshop, the Site Program for the cohousing community was created with the group at a Site Planning Workshop. The Common House Program was created at a Common House Workshop. Each of these workshops have been documented separately in their own program documents.

The Private House program and design criteria outlined here are informed by the previous workshops. Previous design iterations of both the Common House and Site Plan are subject to changes due to Private House designs, budget limitations, zoning issues, size constraints, and other city requirements. Each step forward requires some reconsideration of decisions made previously. This is an iterative process where each designed item must be brought up in parallel to the others.

McCamant & Durrett Architects intends to adhere to the program outlined herein as close as possible. The designs will be evaluated at the Design Closure workshop.

The Culture of Living in Cohousing

With a working common house in cohousing, you need less in your private house. Guests prefer to stay in the common house with its palatial amenities. Big cooking projects can be done in the common house, and are easier because it is so well designed and outfitted. In the common house, laundry can be done more quickly and easily with several machines side-by-side, and the common house laundry room can be state-of-the-art.

Rather than focusing on the typical American Dream (a big house with a bigger garage), consider the life you aspire to having. Rather than the "Dream," we need the Great American Awakening. What do you need to best support that vision?

A life in cohousing is different from a life in a typical suburban home (which is why most cohousers choose cohousing). For instance, cohousers spend 80 percent of the time spent in their yards on their *front* porch; while in a typical suburban home, 80 percent of yard time is spent on the *back* porch. Therefore, in cohousing, a front and back porch might very well be designed differently. This is just one of many examples of differences in the cohousing lifestyle that likely should be reflected in the design of the houses.

Because of shared common space, private houses in cohousing are ample, yet more modest than typical single-family houses. They provide a balance of privacy and community.

Workshop Topics

We discussed what people need in their house. The group agreed to let the house design come out of this discussion, within the context of the project budget and the site. These are the kind of things we discussed:

- Kitchen design
- Open floor plan
- Storage
- Accessibility
- Views
- Natural light
- Natural ventilation

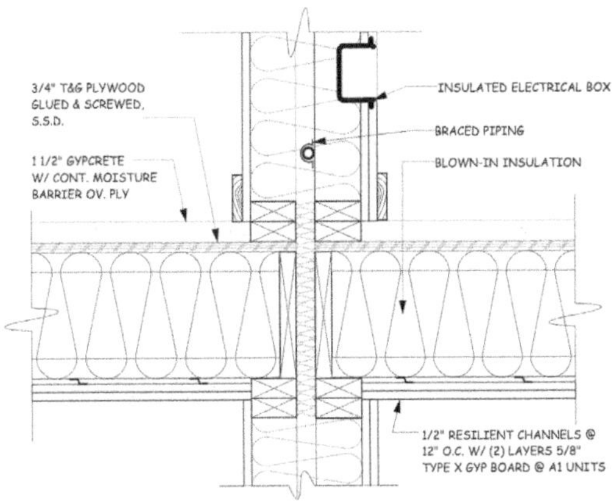

Construction detail at party wall: reducing sound transfer is a priority in the buildings.

The front porch in cohousing facilitates informal interaction. Most people in cohousing spend the majority of their outdoor time on their front porch.

COMMENTS: ***This detail is one of the most important details in this book. The environmentalists of the future will be the acoustic engineers that help Americans live closer together.***

- Sound proofing
- Affordability
- Front porches
- Built-ins to create hierarchy
- Use of wood
- Customization

Other Topics

It is sometimes difficult to stay with house planning issues. Folks often feel compelled to inject amenities (i.e., "my grandmother had tile counter tops, I've got to have them"). We will 'brainstorm those amenities' further and prioritize them later (Workshops Five and Six). The priority now is to get design documents to the city, and to meet your lifestyle desires in the floor plans.

COMMENTS: ***The priority of affordability is almost always discussed at length and during the private house discussions, priorities are built in. Buy the land cheap. Have diligent feasibility done. Keep the number of unit types down. These details (among many others) contribute to keeping the costs down (see Village Hearth in Chapter 11, where the group built seven buildings exactly the same).***

PART 2. PROGRAM

Goals for the Private House

Imagine you come home one late afternoon, in 2017, and when you walk in the front door, you say to yourself, "I just love my house." What do you love about it?

- Great natural light and artificial light (e.g., skylights)
- A feeling of spaciousness
- A place for everything, everything can be put away
- Clean lines, uncluttered design
- Balance in terms of design
- No wasted space
- "Makes me feel comfortable"
- Space is well used
- Cozy
- Flexibility in room (furnishing)
- Bookcases, art on the walls
- Warmth in texture and materials
- Can see from one end to the other
- Warm and welcoming
- Pretty woodwork
- Organized / Multiple uses
- Niche for business activities with a view
- Aesthetic, beautiful
- Interesting
- Good lighting for artwork
- Changes in ceiling height (low, high)
- Window sills
- Gas fireplace
- See backyard from front door, be able to see a lot
- Warm colors
- Cat box is hidden

Private House Unit Matrix

A straw poll of group members present at the workshop led to the formulation of three unit types. The distribution below reflects the proportions of interest in those three types. The exact bath types and sizes were developed in small groups for each unit type over two days. The floor plans at the end of this program illustrate the consensed plans for the three unit types.

Unit	Beds	Baths	Type	Size	Quantity
A	2	3/4	Cottage	910	12
B	2	3/4+3/4	Cottage	1,196	8
C	3	3/4+3/4	Cottage	1,335	8
				31,168	**28**

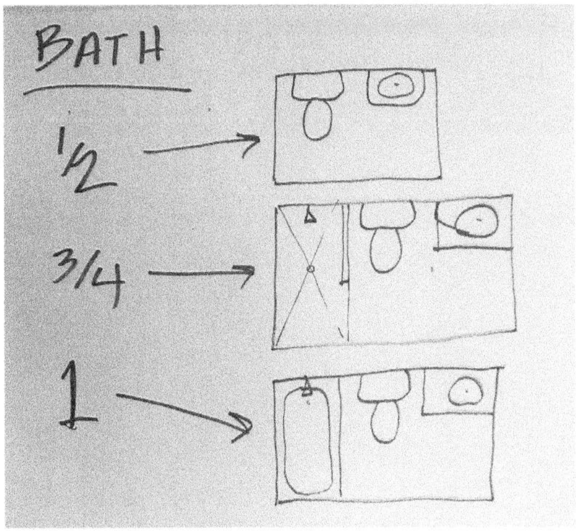

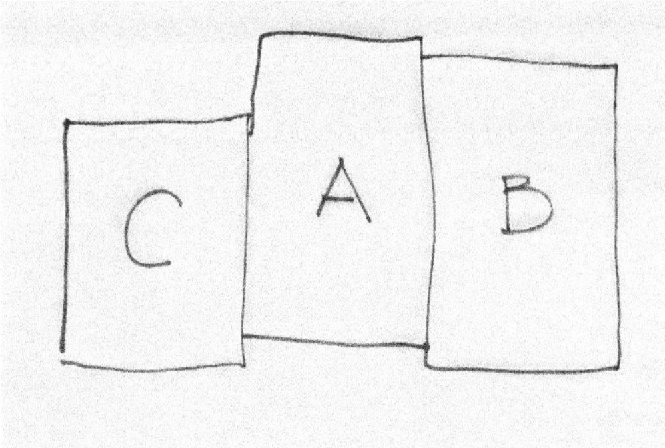

COMMENTS: ***In general, when affordability is important, the difference between custom construction and production construction is that you can make production construction feel custom. Production construction means that it doesn't require a lot of trained skills to build. On the other hand, custom construction means that someone is standing around with a hand on their hip saying, "Joe, what do you think we should do here at this corner?" In production construction, less detail is added in order to make it easier to build.***

COMMENTS: ***To the right is Damien, blind, but neighbors stop by regularly to chat.***

Programming the Pieces

All units are designed with attention to natural light and transitions from public to private space, or "soft edges," such as front porches. The group together decides what elements will be standard or customized. Details such as built-ins and custom woodwork will be discussed further in the Design Development Workshop.

House Zoning

All-room concept: The kitchen, dining, and living room are to be open and easy to communicate between. It is the ability to "borrow" space from the adjacent room(s) that makes smaller spaces feel more generous.

Various methods can then be used to personalize and create hierarchy within the open plan. Rugs provide no physical separation but significant visual differentiation. Furniture can separate the space physically. Floor-to-ceiling casework can be used to close off an area almost completely. Custom woodwork can warm up any environment—even an already warm one! The all-room provides maximum flexibility for a diverse range of personal styles and uses.

COMMENTS: ***Our role as architects, designers, and consultants is to guide the group to realize their intentions. For example, if they express the goal to "live lighter on the planet," we often reframe the approach to say "this architecture facilitates living lighter on the planet" and "this does not."***

Interior Spaces

In western terms, house areas come in three types: functional (living room, kitchen, etc.), circulation (hallways), and access (an area, say, in front of a bookshelf). In open floor plans, rooms often have all three characteristics—making them feel more gracious. An open floor plan saves space by creating areas that can have multiple uses. Spaces for circulation may be used for gathering and activities may be expanded to other "rooms." Outdoor spaces, like the front porch and windows between indoor and outdoor space, help small interior rooms feel larger than they really are. Moveable furniture can be used to create semi-separate open spaces.

Exterior Architecture
The exterior architecture will be reviewed carefully at design closure, but the point of departure will be the visual preference study.

Private House Decks
Decks include room for a table and chairs. Programmed at 8′ deep in the site workshop.

Storage
Storage was fit into each unit in the house type meetings.

Closet Doors
There are no perfect closet doors. The ones that seem to "get out of the way" best and allow the most texture are the bi-fold.

Washer and Dryer
All units will have a designated closet that may be plumbed and vented for a stacked washer and dryer. The washer and dryer and their plumbing will probably be an option, unless more than 80 percent or so of households want it—then they will probably be standard in all units where they fit. If you don't have a washer/dryer in your home:

- The closet can be used for storage instead.
- You won't have noisy machines in your home.
- Humidity will be reduced.
- The walk to the common house laundry is easy and enjoyable and is second only to common cooking and eating in terms of giving people an excuse to go there.
- Common laundry washers and dryers tend to be state-of-the-art in efficiency, and common detergent tends to be ecological—at wholesale prices.

Kitchen

- Kitchen to be "L", "U", "Galley," or "Country" depending on what works best for each individual unit type.
- Kitchens will face the front of the house, whenever possible, with the kitchen sinks at the window looking toward the common area (whenever possible). Some dining rooms may also be at the front of the house.
- Countertops discussed to be 34" or 36" high. Following the workshop the city clarified that either counter height will be allowed.
- Upper cabinet discussed at 14" or 16" above counter top. Height to be consented upon during design development workshop.
- Range size determined for each house type.
- Dishwasher size determined for each house type.
- Sink size determined for each house type.
- Refrigerator size by house type.

Living Room

To be worked out individually per unit type.

Other Programmed Pieces

- How and to whom gas will be provided is held to workshop five.
- As many sloped ceilings as possible.
- Slab-on-grade construction proposed due to 30–40k in cost savings per unit.

COMMENTS: ***Why would showing the Group a bunch of photos of some architectural types be critical? Because everything goes easier when the Group is comfortable with the architecture.***

Architectural Style

Following are the top responses of the architectural style survey that the Group took rating each image on a scale of 1 to 3, 1 being "I like this", 2 being "Eh, maybe", and 3 being "I don't like this". These 20 images will be the basis for the architectural style of the project.

Rank		Score	Rank		Score
1		**1.52**	2		**1.63**
3		**1.67**	4		**1.72**
5		**1.89**	6		**1.93**
7		**2.04**	8		**2.04**
9		**2.04**	10		**2.04**

Rank		Score	Rank		Score
11		**2.11**	12		**2.11**
13		**2.19**	14		**2.22**
15		**2.22**	16		**2.34**
17		**2.37**	18		**2.37**
19		**2.37**	20		**2.38**

COMMENTS: ***In some projects, I have had general contractors tell me, "Chuck, if you need the construction at this price, then there will be no carpenters on the site." Amazingly, we were still able to pull it off, still making warm and giving homes in the context of production rather than custom constructions, and getting homes built at prices that the future residents could afford.***

PART 3. CONCLUSION

Workshop Conclusion

The house design effort in the small groups is where most of the house schematic design is refined and developed. Each design is a function of the small group meetings held for each unit type. And the plans will also be improved upon as MDA fits them into the rationale and structure of the larger buildings, the site, and the style preferences of the group.

As we refine the private house plans, please keep the ABC list in the back of your mind. In other words, think about amenities (A list), options (B list), and customization (C list). These items will play a role in the feel of the homes and the final design, but will not be part of the immediate conversation. They will be discussed during the Prioritization Workshop (Workshop Six).

Specific materials, from doorknobs and kitchen sinks to windows and flooring, will be determined during the Design Development Workshop (Workshop Five), but they are not a part of what is required for the city submission. It is essential to get a schematic design to the city so that they can start their review process. That said, the schematic design must be one that has been thought through well enough that the Group can stand behind it.

Sincerely,

Charles Durrett

Next Steps

Design Closure (Workshop Four)

The next workshop is the Design Closure Workshop, where we present and explain to the group the proposed schematic design that will be submitted to the city. We will have aggregated the house types into buildings, located the buildings on the site, and adjusted the site plan accordingly. We will present drawings of the building elevations that include proposed materials, front and rear porches, and key design details. After this step, the decisions made will not be revisited unless an outside source requires a change.

COMMENTS: ***There are often four or five people who will get priced out of the project if it goes over budget. Nothing helps the group stay disciplined more than knowing that they could lose four or five people that they care about if they fail to stay on budget. These are people who went to the public hearings, who knocked on neighbors' doors, and who made their payments on time to date. To help get the folks with more money from pricing others and themselves out of the picture, it takes people with little money. It takes knowing that your own happiness will be more influenced by Suzie staying in the group than having a tile countertop. You can always put the tile in later, which you won't anyway, because you'll be hiking the High Sierras with Suzie instead.***

The final goal is for all of the necessary design drawings to go to the city for PUD approval, and to start the base sheets for all of the professionals involved in design development and formulation of construction documents.

Design Development (Workshop Five)

The Design Development Workshop is where we consider all of the materials, from the front doorknob and the kitchen sink to the rear porch light.

Prioritization (Workshop Six)

The Prioritization Workshop is where costs that exceed basic construction are prioritized. Some amenities will go into every house (enhanced soundproofing, for example); some will become options; and some will become custom work done later by the homeowner (for example, an extra skylight).

PART 4. APPENDIX

Group Feedback on the Common House Design

The common house design was intended to embody the common house program to the extent possible. Dozens of designs were tried. Of these, the design presented to the Group best embodied the program. However, some program line items were not accommodated. Also, other opportunities arose as well during three-dimensional exploration of the program. The following list includes these opportunities and alterations, as presented to the Group:

- The refrigerator space is smaller than programmed to accommodate more natural light in the kitchen. However, space for an additional refrigerator is provided in the pantry.
- The aperture between the design room and sitting room was not reduced to 6′–8′ as per the program. Such a small opening felt pinched in the context of the proposed volumes.
- The office closet is larger than programmed due to an opportunity that arose from the overall geometry of the building.
- The stove may be bigger than is needed.
- Kitchen may be bigger than is needed.
- The common house may appear small at first, but when also considering the outbuildings, the common facilities are gracious.

Feedback from the group included:

- Programmed craft and sewing storage not provided. *(MDA will revise to provide).*
- Is the dining room large enough? *(Programmed size is provided. The group will consider an upright piano which will allow for more seating space).*
- Are the guest quarters disproportionately large?
- There is an interest in providing more light in the common house dining room. Would a single larger clerestory more economically provide more light?
- Which wall will be used for presentations/movies?
- Many group members are happy with kitchen size.
- Stove could be 36″ wide.

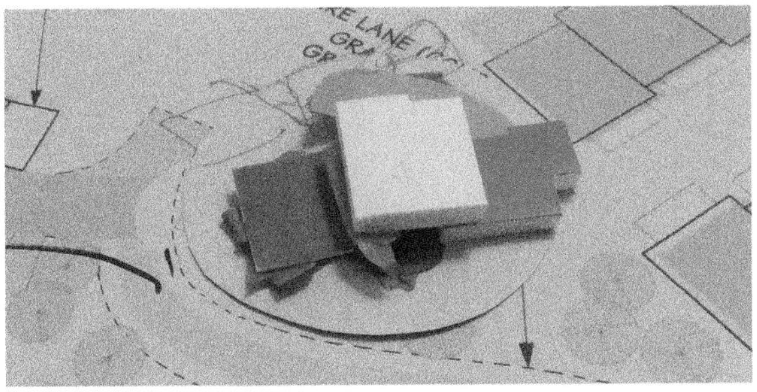

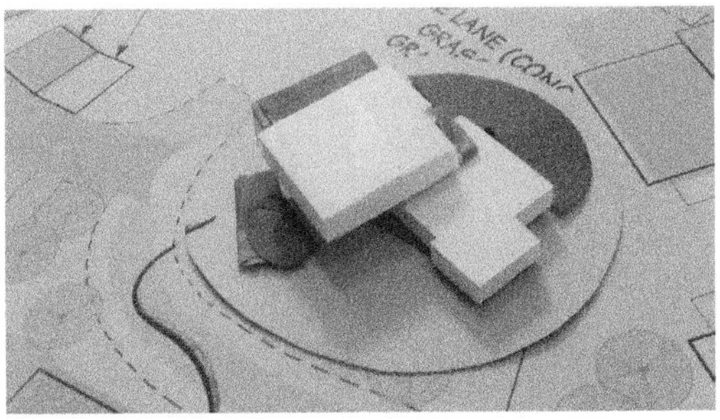

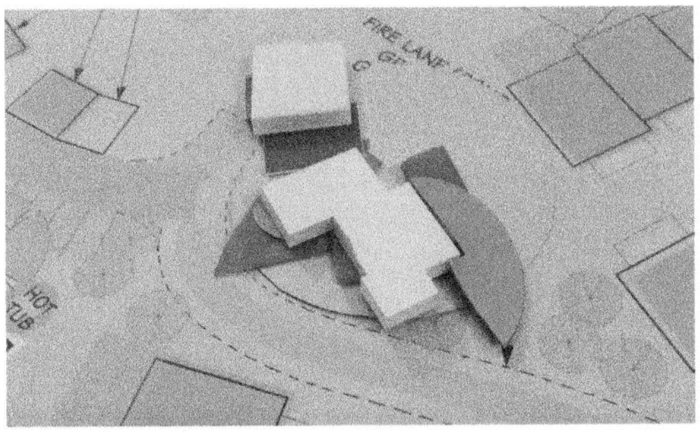

Above: Three common house siting designs brainstormed by the subgroups.

A representation of the mirrored scheme consented to by the whole group.

Placement of the Common House

The siting (placement and orientation) of the common house was intentionally not presented as a singular solution. This ambiguity was created so that the group could participate in optimizing siting of the common house. Three subgroups were formed and the future residents experimented with three-dimensional models representing portions of the common house. Siting priorities that emerged from this exercise included:

- Access to afternoon sun on the common terrace.
- Using the sitting room as a light house or beacon of activity in the common house. (The sitting room should face the center of the community.)
- The ability to easily see activity on the common terrace and within the common house on the walk from parking to the private houses.
- Some privacy for the caretaker unit and guest rooms.
- Privacy for the adjacent private house backyards.
- Two-story designs were explored, but discarded due to increased cost and decreased accessibility.

The Group agreed that the common house design should be mirrored, while making sure the common terrace has exposure to both the afternoon sun and the community.

At the March 15 – 17, 2015
Quimper Village Private House Workshop,
the following participants were in attendance:

Pam and John Clise
Jack and Carolyn Salmon
Pat and David Hundhausen
Jerry Spieckerman and Bobbie McManhon
Janet Palmer
Mike and Linda Holbrook
Debbi Steele and Dennis Daneau
Anne Holman

Nancy Richards
Diane and Leon Lopez
Ingelise and Paul Oxenbol
Steve and Pat Resende
Sherry Moller
Kathleen Hold
Timothy Singler and Mhairi Merryman
Jim and Pam Daly

BELLINGHAM, WA

Strong relationships are what make neighborhoods work over time, but the design plays a huge role in fostering or detracting from creating and sustaining relationships.

PART
3

The Rest of the Story

Architecture is the picture frame; the community is the picture. In cohousing, the picture frame influences the living picture—just like a forest or the sea influences the life there. The stage set means a great deal to helping us all design our own roles in this sometimes seemingly mindless urban drama. It's more fun if it works, if you can afford it, and if your house does not make you feel guilty about over-consumption. As you have seen so far, designing a prosocial/functional neighborhood is a deliberate act—it is not random. Make it worth everyone's while—make it right!

VANCOUVER COHOUSING, B.C.

29-year-old Britta (lavender sweatshirt), a key initiator helped make a project that she and acquaintances could afford. Then she helped get it approved.

13

Affordability

"Architecture that is not affordable, does not serve, but takes away."
Charles Durrett

The critical question of affordability is a common theme throughout this book. When it comes to affordability, it is a new day everyday because the market is constantly shifting. Prior to 2007, the cost of construction was going up predictably between 4–4.5 percent per year, but it depended on the number of Hurricane Katrinas and Sandys that had their way with us. Katrina shot plywood cost up from $20 per sheet to $30 overnight. The Great Recession of December 2007–June 2009, determined by the International Monetary Fund to be the largest economic downturn since the Great Depression of the 1930s, resulted in almost 100,000 builders in the U.S. going out of business or retiring early, and skilled labor was lost in droves. Then lumber mills shut down, banks stopped lending, and when the economy picked up again years later there were too few people to build anything. Costs went through the roof. Today in 2021, the costs of construction are double to what they were in 2008. Instead of 3 percent inflation annually 1994–2007, it has been about 6 percent annually since. In the last year, the price of lumber in Northern California increased by 200 percent due to the incessant forest, rural, and suburban fires in Washington, Oregon, and California. On top of that, there are also tariffs on lumber coming from Canada; mills shut down due to Covid and are just now starting up again.

Put the houses in one place and keep them close together to make them feel like a village, but keep some open space for farming. If the group does not work out as farmers (it's harder work than it looks), then lease it out to a young farmer family just starting out. This is the project that won The Cohousing Company the World Human Habitat Award presented by the United Nations. The root cause of difficult development in the third world is the overdevelopment of Western countries—land consumption and sprawling in particular. Keeping the houses closer together is an important way to save money. When we explain the costs of separation (a more sprawling solution), the group always moves the blocks closer together.

Inexpensive garages: 1.0 KW per house equals almost zero energy bills.

Cohousing Communities: Designing for High-Functioning Neighborhoods is written foremost to make designing communities achievable for young architects and future residents. This book also addresses the important issue of affordability when designing communities.

Global warming will be one of the greatest causes of housing cost increases in the future. According to scientists, the next disaster will be flooding, and likely more fires. There are clearly more challenges ahead. Creative housing solutions such as modular homes, shipping container houses, straw bale and cob homes might offer some possibility for reductions, but not in multi-family construction, as it will likely shift to timberframe or to IFC or many others. But to create major cost reductions for building community housing, major changes such as rezoning and smaller changes like waste will need to be addressed.

Prioritizing is where you get to the bottom of what their culture is, and who they want to become. We learned this exercise from anthropologists in Denmark who use it to determine the design of government buildings for small towns, where roads might go, and definitely in making new neighborhoods.

Residents install their own tile work (otherwise known as sweat equity) in the common house. These recycled tiles were free. A few of the 10 residents who helped clean, cut, and install the tiles had done so before, but wanted to learn more. The activity helped bring the community closer together.

It is critical that architects learn how much engineering, consultants, and materials cost and what will save money for their projects. It is also important that groups hire architects experienced in building communities to ensure their project is affordable.

PROCESS

The Difference Between Yes and No

The number one way to reduce costs, and often make the project happen is to have a clear and predictable process. When I became involved with the Yarrow Ecovillage, the group was seven years into the project, $700,000 in debt, had built only four of the 33 houses, and had not begun building the common house. Luckily a new person to the group, Yonus Jonkind, a systems engineer, knew that the group's problems stemmed from the lack of a clear system, and hired The Cohousing Company because he knew that they had a system. Random haphazard behavior never works with development. After employing a clear system, the group was able to move in two years later with no debt. In a different project, a group had worked with three different architects over four years and wasted considerable money. They then hired The Cohousing Company to start the design process from scratch and Cohousing Solutions to completely restructure their development scenario. They were done with the design and submitted their planning application to the city in six months. Up the stairs one stair at a time, but moving forward works much better than any other method. We recommend the following process devised of the following 10 steps.

Public Presentation: Get the word out in a deliberate fashion. We have done hundreds of these presentations and others have too. This is how you catalyze a new interest group in your area. This is key feasibility—is there a client? Is there momentum? That's how projects get built.

GETTING-IT-BUILT WORKSHOP: The GIB workshop (see Afterword) is crucial to saving money. More cohousing has started and had a successful launch with a GIB than any other means. Use a clear strategic plan to keep the project on track.

Groups knowing how to work well with each other is key. When it comes to affordability, smart groups know process exceeds all else. You can have money and land, but if you don't have process, you will not accomplish a high-functioning neighborhood.

1. **Public Presentation**

   Have someone like Katie McCamant or myself come to town to do a public presentation. Advertise broadly, if 50–300 people come, you probably have a project. Do not grow the group in dribs and drabs—get it started with momentum, traction begets traction.

2. **Getting-It-Built Workshop**
   - Which consultants to hire?
   - When to get the LLC in place?
   - Approval Process
   - When to apply for bank financing?
   - Group Process
   - Construction contact?
   - And much more
   - Two days to get this critical info (see Afterword)

STUDY GROUP 1: This is where seniors start to see a much more economical and fun future.

. . . then you get houses that you like and can afford.

Process the private house program with the people planning to live in that house type.

Process, process, process, one step at a time builds the most beautiful and the most appreciated places. Beautiful because, if deliberate, the architect can spend more time making it beautiful because they are not chasing inconclusive labyrinths. And, consequently, it's more appreciated by the group, because it feels like it suits them like a pair of custom and supple fine-fitting Italian leather gloves.

Use a site design process that makes the entire neighborhood work.

3. **Study Group One (SG1)**
   See Chapter 7 of the *Senior Cohousing Handbook* (10 weekly sections)
4. **Site Design Criteria Program Workshop** (four days total)
5. **Common Facilities, Design Criteria/Program Workshop** (two days total)
6. **Private House Program and Schematic Common House Plan Critique Workshop Design Criteria/Programming** (three days total)
7. **Design Closure Workshop** (one day)
8. **Design Development Design Criteria/Workshop** (one day)
9. **Prioritization**
   What can we afford to build? (one day)
10. **Physical Plant Maintenance Process** (at move in) (one day)

The Design Closure Workshop: It's a party most of the time.

VANCOUVER, B.C.

Design Closure Workshop: invested people is how you get impossible/intelligent projects approved.

The roll-in "snail shower" is very popular amongst seniors, and probably the most custom-built thing in the house—with a solar tube in the shower and a light fixture in the solar tube for evening showers.

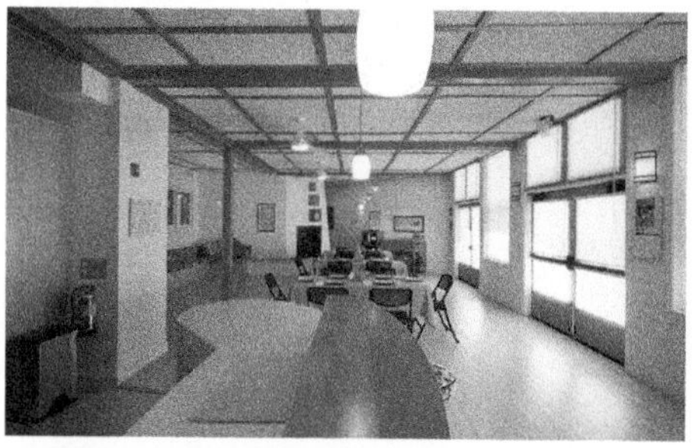

Common Facilities: Kitchen to dining relationship—open and easy, helps to entertain people in the kitchen and the dining area.

BELLINGHAM, WA

Site: Extremely economical construction made these buildings cost only $67 per square foot to construct in 2000.

Common Facilities: The construction of a neighborhood common building.

Kitchen: The galley kitchen can be the most economical solution. It looks expensive, but it's not.

Common House Facilities: If done right, they are the apex of community buildings and everything to do with making individual lives more economical, convenient, practical, interesting, healthier, and fun.

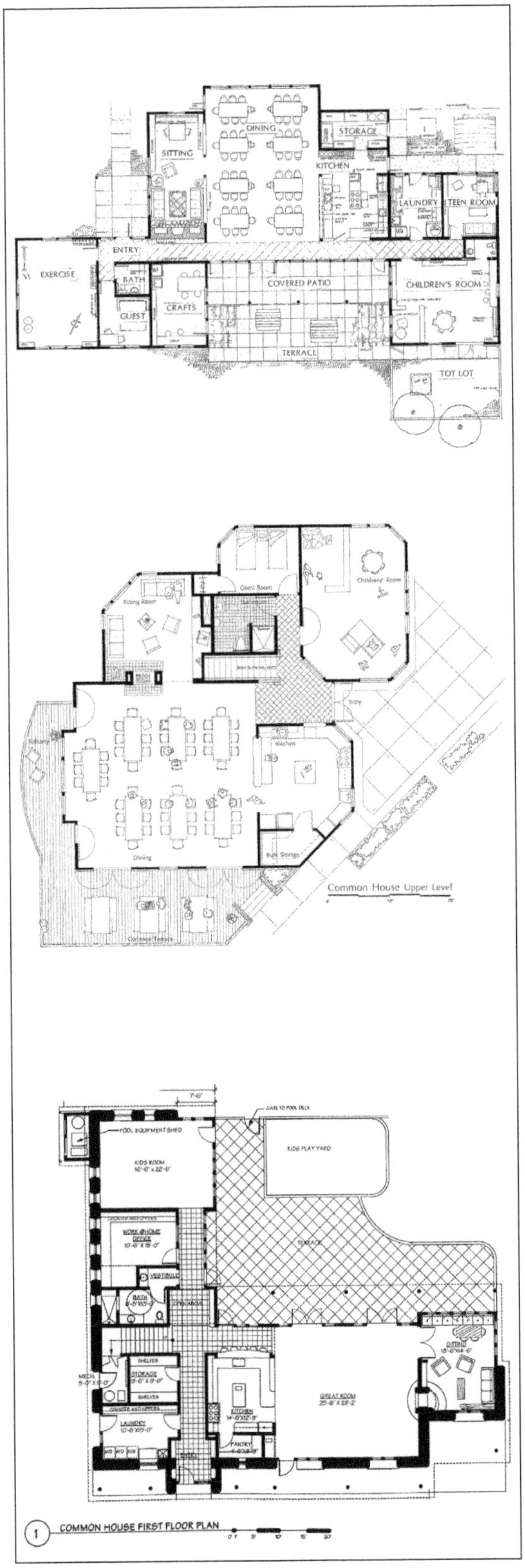

Common House Plans: Sample common house floor plan designs.

Design Development: The right siding, the right windows, and the right lighting all make a difference.

Design Development: Inexpensive construction does not have to be without color and character.

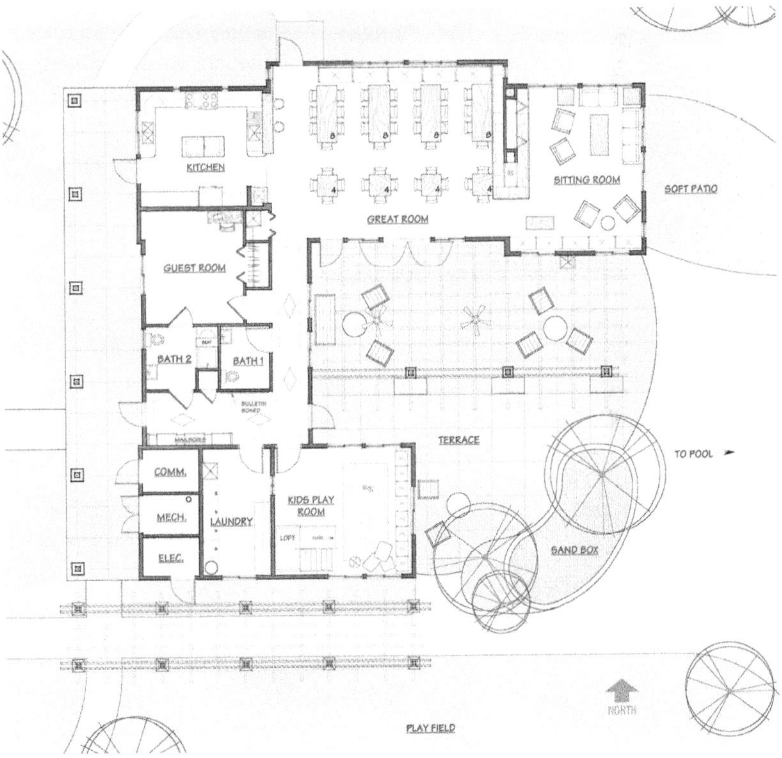

Fresno, CA. Common House. When a group presents the design that they helped create and therefore fully understood, then the city understands it, appreciates it, and approves it.

Hand sketches help everyone see it.

VANCOUVER, B.C.

Rezoning two single-family lots (in the middle of a single-family house neighborhood) to 31 dwelling units was the only way to build this project affordably. Of course, the neighbors objected initially, but now kids come over to play with the resident kids and their parents come over for a cup of tea.

COHOUSING PREVALENCE

Education and Awareness

When starting a new high-functioning housing project, it is crucial to make the literature and awareness available to as many people as possible. Cohousing sometimes takes too long in the early stages, which can also result in it not being built. Cohousing is more than a term—it is a slightly more complex way of living, but infinitely more gratifying, and certainly a little more complex than watching TV. I worked in Southeast Africa for a year and found village life to be more intricate. But when I looked closer I noticed that once you get used to living in a village, it's actually less complicated than going in alone. Driving a car is more complicated than walking, but walking across a country is more complicated than driving across a country. There is a lot to digest in the beginning stages of developing a cohousing group, but supplying people with the additional information helps move the project forward. This was particularly evident in Anchorage, AK, where a new cohousing project was prompted by a public presentation that drew 300 attendants. Efficiency plays a key role when it comes to affordability, and workshops like Study Group I or the Getting-It-Built workshop or the 500 Communities Programs (see Afterword) help the future residents develop key skills to design a community, making it easier to get the job done. Today there is also extensive writing about cohousing that newly formed cohousing groups can benefit from, especially *Creating Cohousing* and *The Senior Cohousing Handbook*.

Stillwater, OK

The Big Rezone

The biggest single move that new cohousing groups can do to save a considerable amount of money is to rezone a desired site. This concept is discussed throughout the book (see Chapter 7), but here are the dollars and cents of it. The Stillwater group bought a single-family house on 5 acres for under $400,000. With the 24 proposed units, this site cost them $16,000 per household. But if the group had bought a 24-unit site that was already zoned as multi-family, the cost would have been about $960,000, since this land is usually appraised for about $40,0000 per unit. By purchasing the single-family lot and rezoning it themselves, the group saved about $24,000 per household, or $69,000 per household once financed. That's a big savings. Cohousing groups and nonprofits are the only ones that I know that predictably can accomplish this. In Stillwater's case we had six brand new state-of-the-art houses that had to be built for $150,000. That's tantamount to magic—that's pulling a rabbit out of the hat in 2010. But for the key people in the group who had less money than the rest—people who everyone loved—it had to be done. We would have not gotten it rezoned without a compelling design and the compelling story of the people who organized the project and clearly needed reduced prices.

Since zoning practices began in the U.S. in 1916, they have been used to keep classes and races separate (see Chapter 7), and redlining continued to reinforce that in the 1930s. Cohousing can uniquely challenge these racist legacies more effectively than other means, because it brings the people to the planning table.

STILLWATER, OK

"So let's just do it ourselves." Not always the most efficient, but always the most fun, and if you count the time to find help—often the most efficient.

Design Closure Workshop: This workshop helps the group approve of what goes to the city and then helps the city approve the design.

VANCOUVER, B.C

The only real questions from banks and city bureaucrats should be "How can we help?" That happened here in the way of a key city councilor, Kerry Chang, when he saw the energy that the group brought to the table.

EYE-LEVEL VIEW: "What will it feel like walking through this village?"

YARROW, B.C.

An onsite sewage system of a septic tank and a marsh pond made this 25-acre project affordable and ecological.

Vancouver, B.C.

Rezone

Another major rezone, Vancouver, B.C. Cohousing changed two single-family house lots to one multi-family lot to allow for 31 dwellings. The two homes that the group purchased were old and run down. In the context of two separate planning applications in series—one to rezone and one to build the 31-unit project—it would have been delayed, cost more, and probably not gone through. Presenting a series of applications is theoretically less risky if the rezone is approved, and then you design it. But apparently that's not the case in high-functioning neighborhoods—you have to show them how great it will be for them to rezone it in the same application. Also they must see the faces of all of the future residents that care so much. They have to see the blood, sweat, and tears of the people that planned it and plan to live there. One of the future residents of the project, an Asian immigrant mother, made her case to the city council. "This is the only project that I can afford, please approve it." "I can't buy one of those houses, no matter how run down they are, and I couldn't afford to fix it up." "Why wouldn't you approve of an environment that we worked so hard to make exceptionally responsive to the real needs of real people?" Sue asked.

Yarrow Ecovillage, B.C.

Rezoned, Refined

The Yarrow Cohousing group bought 25 acres of fallow agricultural land (an old dairy farm that really needed to be rotated to vegetable to save the soil) quite economically in the Frazer Valley, just outside of Chilliwack, B.C. (population 250,000). They asked to rezone the site from farm to ecovillage—then they wrote the land use planning code for ecovillage and it was approved. We requested a 33-unit

VANCOUVER, B.C.

"Let's just do it ourselves," "This building goes over here."

Mission impossible: To make new affordable housing in downtown Vancouver—absolutely requires buy-in first and foremost by the people who plan to live there; others will follow, individuals and city officials.

VANCOUVER, B.C.

. . .and then you get an environment like this.

intergenerational cohousing project, and it was approved and built in 2015. We went back to them to request an additional 17-unit senior cohousing and a 30,000-square-foot commercial area. The City of Chilliwack said to us, "Well, if that is what an ecovillage is, then that's what it's zoned for. Your code and now our code does not preclude these additions, so, fine." All three of these uses are on 5 acres, and the 20-acre organic farm, farmed largely by people who live there in the cohousing next door. They have so many uses on that site, ranging from housing, farming, greenhouses, workshops, to a farmers' market. And in the 30,000 square feet of commercial there are educational services: yoga, music lessons, massage school, language school, and much more. The retail uses include recreation, food, hardware, a café, a deli, and crafts—making this site an authentic ecovillage. Almost anyone could spend a day in the village and have most of their needs met when completed.

Mountain View, CA

Making the Ask

For many projects we have been asked to write 25–35 reasons why a project will help the city. The list is a great way to show how community-enhanced projects defray consequential city costs. One place to start is the services that the neighbors will provide the elderly, which include meals, rides to the doctors and the grocery store, and neighbors checking in with them. The neighborhood will add

MOUNTAIN VIEW, CA

The stairs and gangways that connect the two buildings meant that the project saved hundreds of thousands of dollars in fire suppression costs, and saved about 9,000 square feet of open space that would otherwise have been asphalt.

VANCOUVER COHOUSING, B.C.

As an architect, I always feel like when we spend $2,500 to make a model, we save $100,000 construction costs, and delayed approvals.

I'm pleasantly surprised by how many projects are allowing workers to sleep in the structures once the roofs are on. This can save them up to $20K–$30K for hotel rooms, as construction workers these days often travel large distances to work. In Port Townsend, the workers were traveling 100 miles each way. This is not only unfortunate for the climate, but risky to the project (traffic jams and traffic accidents). This approach to saving money is not new, but these days we have to be creative and embrace old, efficient ideas; even if unorthodox. Moreover, the workers even get to experience some village life along the way.

children to the school district, and volunteers to the nonprofits in the area. The construction models energy efficiency. The residents will drive less as they can share rides, typically a fourth less than people in other neighborhoods. There are also fewer calls to the police, fire department, and emergency calls.

Sometimes you have to help the City Council realize how their shifting or mishandled rule book costs the project a lot of money. In the case of Mountain View, the City told them that they could remove the old houses on the site, then that they couldn't, and then a litany of other shifts that cost them time and money. After the group made their case to the Mountain View City Council, the city dropped $650,000 in

MOUNTAIN VIEW, CA

A three-story single bulky monolith was first proposed on the site. Neighbors stopped it. The seller became much more flexible.

AUBURN, CA

In an offering from Placer County, this 4.6-acre will turn into a new community-enhanced neighborhood.

fees owing to their accidental misrepresentations and other missteps. That can be consequential. In this case, it would have cost about $35,000 more per house, and once financed over 30 years that is about $100,000 per house in savings. You won't get the credits that you deserve unless you make the ask.

Auburn, CA

Proactive Municipal Involvement

The future is that people can help governments accomplish great neighborhoods that are in turn very beneficial to the city. If we can get municipalities to play along, they will increasingly model great neighborhoods, and lower their costs in every line item of running a less than optimum society. From

COMPASS COHOUSING: Langley, B.C.

An advantage of cohousing is flexibility when finding a site. We were looking to purchase a site from the city at a discount as well as other significant variances. We were asked to meet with the city officials before the application and we were able to delineate the advantages of cohousing—but we made no specific asks before we had the entire proposal together.

police calls, to jails, and hospitals, and other costly services, cities stand to save massively. Nevada County (with a population of 100,000) pays over $1 million a year to get seniors to their doctors, pharmacies, physical therapy appointments, friends, groceries, and more. For 15 years the 21 seniors in the Nevada City Cohousing just asked their neighbors for these same services. Cities supplying properties to become high-functioning neighborhoods is the future because it is mutually beneficial (see Chapter 7 for the rest of the Auburn story). In Denmark, the community planning departments seek out cohousing professionals to let them know about sites that they chose to surplus for little or no remuneration to build a cohousing neighborhood. They also let the cohousing professionals know about distressed sites that would be better as high-functioning neighborhoods. Where the entire area would benefit, where a neighborhood center would rejuvenate, where property tax revenue would increase, where schools would do better, and the line investments would be better utilized. They have seen and understand what cohousing brings to the neighborhood: volunteers, eyes on the street, local grocery stores, bakeries, and other local services that do better. This has started in the United States with Placer County, CA, whose county government has signed an agreement with The Cohousing Company to establish a cohousing project for a 4.6-acre site.

Langley, B.C., Cohousing

Negotiating City-Owned Property and the Politics of Improving Neighborhoods

New cohousing groups periodically find city-owned property that could work well for their needs. Sometimes they are old public works sites no longer utilized or even residual sites, as in the case of

Getting nouveau projects through the city requires a clear presentation to the city councils, but mostly it requires the audience: the future residents and their friends and family who know the value of cohousing.

This is what making a new affordable community looks like. It looks like this group in Portland reaching their collective optimum (and far exceeding any individual optimum). Brainstorming, discussing, and deciding in rapid fire succession.

Saving and building community through frequent neighborhood dinners.

Langley. Cohousing groups are a known means of improving larger neighborhoods, and some cities are motivated to see them happen. Some cities finance the purchase of the site, and in Denmark they often gift the site to the group with the provision of building new economical high-functioning neighborhoods. Some towns have financed all or part of the down payments for the first-time home buyers. Down payments can easily be $40,000 or $60,000. The future is that people can help governments accomplish services and most importantly provide affordable housing. This helps stitch together a healthy neighborhood and plays a role in creating a healthy society. If you make your case adequately, municipalities will agree to your development. Cities often want to play a greater role in the process to improve residential development, but they don't know how. This is how it happened in Langley.

The City of Langley gave a new cohousing group a 33 percent discount (equivalent to $1,000,000) off of the appraised value of a one-acre property. This reached a savings of about $3,000,000 once financed, and even better, it gave them 1.5 years to pay it back to the city that usually demands all cash within three months. But the most significant part of the offer was that they will not double charge fees and savings. In other words, whatever service that the city can save by having a cohousing community there, they will not charge the residents.

Counties raise about $2,500 on average from property taxes per house. Cities and towns have to raise another $1,500 per resident in sales taxes, parking meters, and the rest in addition to state and federal money that comes in. The Cohousing Company believes that cities and counties could save from $2,000–$3,000 per citizen each year by having residents living in a high-functioning neighborhood. Is it a coincidence that a town of 20,000 people in Denmark that used to have a dozen police officers no longer had a police department in 2000 after eight cohousing communities were built in the town? They contracted all police services out to the county for much less. It is and isn't a coincidence. Lots of community measures made that difference, but lots of forethinking about high-functioning neighborhoods was definitely one.

Langley Cohousing also has a social response component. That is, they received extra dispensations and subsidies by welcoming some neurodiverse adults into their community, some of whom had

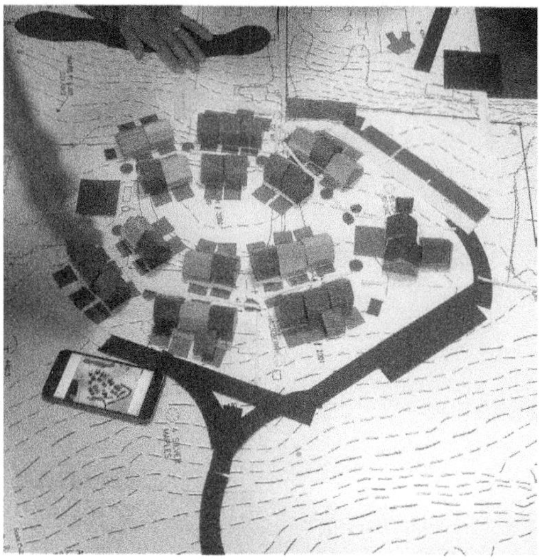

Site: A new world village with no cars in the middle

A site design process that makes the place work, socially, ecologically, and financially.

been diagnosed with autism. The Inclusionary Langley Society (ILS) has bought a couple of units, which they will use to accommodate four or five neurodiverse folks.

Eugene, OR

Good Engineering and Cohousing

As I was sitting in the civil engineer's conference room one day with five future residents of Eugene Cohousing, the engineer handed me the cost estimate to hook up to the City of Eugene's water supply. The number was $465,000 for the new 28-unit community. I looked at it, slowly set it back on the table, and the group passed it around. All their faces were long. Everyone knew that while they could survive, a budget hike like this would make things a lot more difficult to manage; "we'd lose four of five households" someone said. I picked the estimate up again and asked the two civil engineers sitting there, "how do we get out of this?," and they both said, "you don't—it's the code." Then I announced that "of course, this can't happen." We excused ourselves post haste and huddled at the local café. I asked the group if I could find another civil engineer that could help us fix this matter—costing roughly $3,000–$4,000 for that consultation. I interviewed a second, third, fourth, and finally a fifth engineer. The city wanted the water looped, which means that the water would not stop with us, and that we would not and could not be the end of the line.

After a meeting at the water headquarters (a place that looks and feels like Darth Vader's headquarters) and a meeting with a half-a-dozen of the people there (Stormtroopers), they explained that "If the water stopped with you and if someone in the community at the end of the line was gone for a month, they would come back to stagnant water and accidentally get a bacterial overdose." We left and came back with a report from our fifth and most capable civil engineer. In the hybrid of a community and the right engineer, we were able to prove that in a high-functioning community, if someone leaves for a month, we would just go into their house and periodically flush the lines before they come home and use that water for landscaping. We also figured how to loop the lines internally, and to proactively plan to be good neighbors. We got rid of that $465,000

RIVER SONG COHOUSING, EUGENE, OR

Prioritize, prioritize, prioritize. Take a couple of hours to workshop and understand exactly what you need in a highly functional community—and build that.

bill. We paid $42,000 to connect to the city water, not $465,000. I think everyone knows the lesson: don't stop when you smell "illogical" and always consider how this problem can be solved in the context of a functioning neighborhood. One of the things that I like most about cohousing is that reason can prevail. You just have to think it through and make the ask.

Pleasant Hill, CA

Passive Cooling

On one hot July day, elderly Ted Lynch walked into my office's front door unexpectedly. He appeared with a newspaper under his arm, which I thought was odd. He marched to my desk in the far back, and threw the front page of the paper in front of me. Above the fold in bold three-inch high type read: "113°F in Pleasant Hill California Yesterday." He then turned to the door and exclaimed, "It better work" and left the paper.

PLEASANT HILL, CA

Common House: Inspired by historic California Central Valley architecture.

No threat of cars, and a $200,000 savings in not overly accommodating them.

SACRAMENTO, CA: Young people making a new neighborhood that they can afford.

To my surprise, the weekend before the Pleasant Hill group came to a consensus that there would be no air conditioning in their houses, "how can we justify warming the earth to cool our house?," "have you seen the reports of flooding in Bangladesh?," "school kids wade through two and a half feet of water to get to school and it's our fault!" I thought this was a very brave move on their part. By that time, The Cohousing Company had become proficient at designing houses for passive cooling. Extra thick and dense sheetrock to capture the night's diurnal shifts, cooling towers, a mighty sombrero for shading (overhangs/eaves), radiant barrier roof sheathing to reflect the U.V., aggressive venting, window shades, window operations, and even reflective paint. People were given the option to have exterior vents for the interior stand-up A.C. units. Four people bought the stand-up units and only two have ever been used. Start with intention, then refine it to make it work. Ted's warning did not go unheeded. The house interiors have been cool enough for the last 20 years.

Sacramento, CA

Mutually Beneficial and Saving Money

Residents of a future cohousing project in Sacramento purchased a small, 1.25 acres site from the city that seemed affordable. A bigger site would have cost twice as much. But early in the development they thought the site was too small. After they visited a dozen other small sites, they decided. It would work. Then, after more planning, the residents realized too many people couldn't afford to live there. So they went back to the city and renegotiated the price. It took a dedicated committee to show the city officials how the project would benefit the city as well as the residents. The city appreciates the benefits, and reduced the price of the land by 33 percent. Also, the group initially thought that this site was too small for 25 houses. After a trip to Berkeley, CA, to see quality multi-family project at 30 units to the acre, they went with it.

Doyle Street Cohousing: Emeryville, CA: A rehabilitated factory building.

I don't know if we can repeat this enough because it is so consistently missed, but nothing saves money like having a constituency. It saves at city hall because we will do these services ourselves. Common dining saves more money in high-functioning communities. Not only is it reasonable prices ($3–$6 per night), it is also high quality.

Keeping the kids entertained at home is always cheaper, and safer.

Emeryville Cohousing, CA

Zoning and Variances

The implementation process at City Hall needs to be a sizable part of the affordability conversation. You are making a new neighborhood with people rather than for people, so take the high ground. Housing businesses can never get it right compared to the moms that focus on raising their child in a safe and healthy environment. They get it right and they get it approved. Many get intimidated when a planner or another government official says, "Oh, that is not possible" and "You can't do that," and all the rest. It would all work so much better if the planner would just ask "How can we help you reach your goals?"

Regular developers aren't intimidated because they are used to this process. But oftentimes zoning does not support the residents' needs. For example, in Emeryville, CA, the site was zoned for six units, but we needed a minimum of 12. The site was zoned for 15-foot setbacks, and we wanted zero

A clear criterion maintains and saves money, and nothing is more likely to get you what you want.

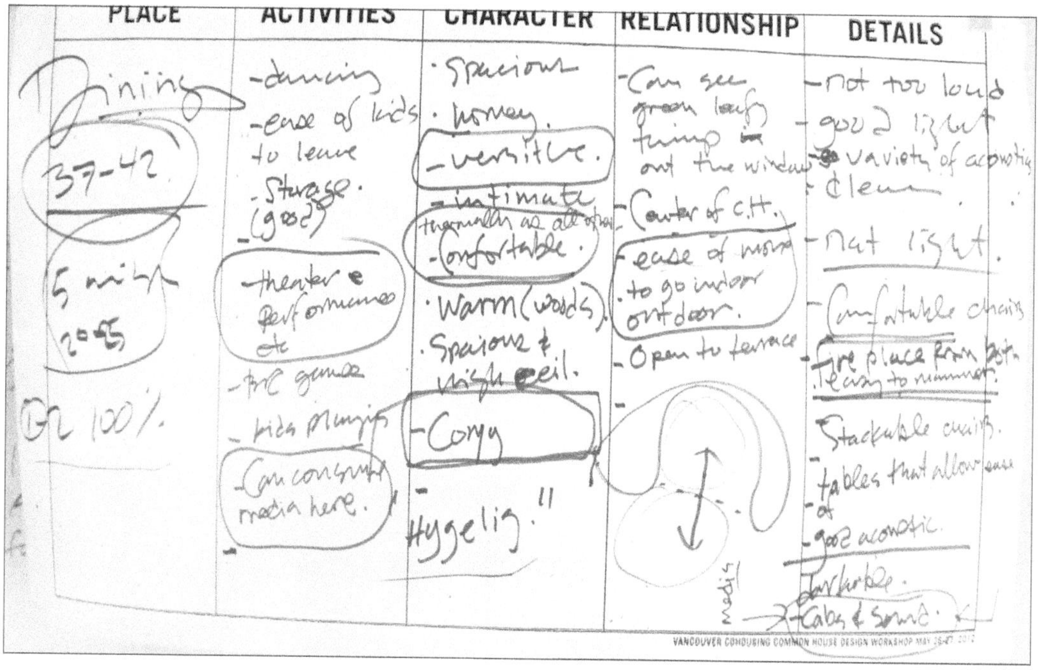

setback; 30-foot height limits, but we needed 33-foot height limits; 24 parking places, but we needed 12. After four hearings, we received all four variances. I do believe that a regular developer would not have been able to do any of that in this case. Often we will have 20–30 people at the podium, including the single mom. She told the city council with grave urgency that she needed a house here, and asked the city to approve the project as proposed so that she could afford it, "and, please, as soon as possible because school starts in the fall." Then she even asked, "Why wouldn't you?" You have to care about the individuals standing in front of you that are planning on living in the community, and work with the zoning regulators to help construct the cohousing that they need. You need to grow the group when you need more money or more energy. To get variances—you need energy.

You can drive down any street in the U.S. and see projects that comply with the zoning code and projects that do not. Today it comes down to who can make the compelling case for variances. Whether you have the "high ground" or not, you have real citizens who can make a tangible case and

Hundreds of pages like this lead to designs that everyone can agree on.

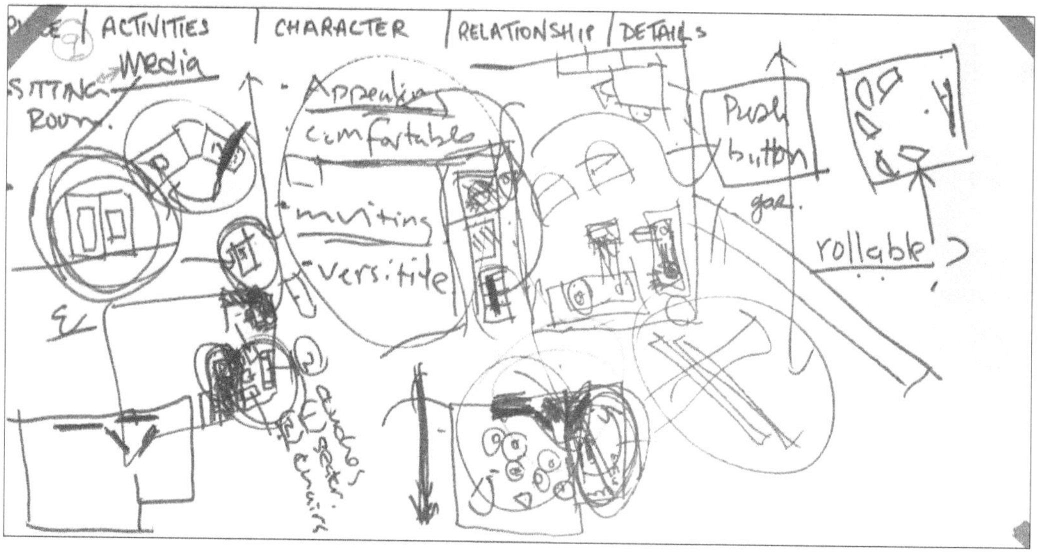

ANCHORAGE, AK

There is considerable single-family development right up to the site. For years developers tried hard to get a hold of this site as well, but the seller held out and then sold it to a cohousing group because they could work around the old farm house that he wanted to live out his life in.

it turns out to be a better design—so it pays to work with someone that can help you make that case. Without this group, this project would have been just another six-unit high-end project starting at \$450,000 (in 1992). Emeryville cohousing units started at \$130,000.

Anchorage Cohousing, AK

Site Selection and Open-mindedness

The site purchase looms large in terms of the success of a project, especially in the context of affordability and lifestyle. Often you will find that the site you want is not zoned correctly, or that it is not for sale. It's beneficial to you if it's not for sale because there is no competition with other developers. In Anchorage, AK, a group of people motivated to create a new cohousing project and myself looked at seven snow-covered sites. It was the coldest day in 20 years. The group gave me the right coat with a tunneled hood and elbow-high gloves. I felt like a periscope as I looked at each of the seven sites. I realized they had their hearts set on one next to a park. Lots of other developers had approached the

A neighborhood gathering node in a functioning community is where neighbors meet in neutral territory to talk about the issues of the day; whether personal, neighborhood wide, nationally, or worldwide. Why not explore the universe while we are at it?

83-year-old gentleman who lived on and owned that site. He was clear with everyone that he would never move or sell the site because he "planned to be on that site to the bitter end." We mentioned that cohousing is unique—we can be more flexible on how your site is utilized, and we can work around your house, and you can live there "'til the bitter end." He agreed to the proposal and now the 35 new homes have been there for a few years, with the now 90-year-old gentleman. The site was discounted because he was going to live there too, and because we were willing to work around his desires and house. All in all, negotiations often need to be much broader than first thought.

Berkeley Cohousing, CA

Affordability by Necessity

If you want an affordable neighborhood, start with the people that need it the most. Many people say that cohousing is not affordable enough in the U.S., and while that's true, the people who say that usually haven't looked very hard. The only prices that you hear about passively are those that

BERKELEY COHOUSING:

A remodeled house, all part of two original construction contracts. In other words, to keep the costs down, most of the remodeling of the dilapidated units were done in one contract.

are being advertised. But when I ask those people if they have heard of Berkeley, Sacramento, Emeryville, Davis, or Bellingham Cohousing and what their original prices were, they always say no. Sometimes the resale is not low because there is not enough supply. When it comes to real estate, everyone does better if they are in first. You never hear about the inexpensive ones because they are rarely for sale and if they are, the sale is an inside deal. For example, Berkeley Cohousing had three single mothers and two elderly women who couldn't afford anything when the average 1995 house price in Berkeley was $500,000. But then they made four houses at $130,000 each and another apartment above the common house for even less. The individuals' needs are what drive the ability to accomplish these projects. The best way to keep the prices down is to have four to five households that are barely squeaking in. In affordable Sacramento, the first house to sell was 12 years after moving in, 1/43 of the average American moving rate.

Many of these buyers bought for less than they were previously renting for. In Berkeley, the majority of people who moved into the cohousing were renters, and that was one of the compelling cases that brought it through the Berkeley City Hall approval process. That was the first project in 30 years to change from rent control to ownership. It was an abandoned and dilapidated housing stock, but it was soon on the books as an ownership housing.

Berkeley Cohousing limits appreciation at resale to 4 percent per year. This is something that should begin to happen more and more at new cohousing communities. Over and over again the original group buys low and sells high—and that can be deleterious to the long-term success of the community. ElderSpirit Community Cohousing in Abingdon, VA, gives 50 percent of the appreciation of the houses at resale back to the community's general fund. It was actually the palpable life between the buildings which facilitated the appreciation in the first place. "After all, they are seniors," "we earned it, we made it beautiful and we fostered the love that everyone appreciates and why they are buying here in the first place. And we don't want it to be an investment property," said Dene Petersen, the key organizer of that project.

Davis Cohousing, CA

Affordability by Lifestyle, Camaraderie, and Social Cohesion

Oftentimes affordability can be achieved through small lifestyle modifications. At Davis Cohousing, 23 out of 28 households were first-time home buyers. Everybody was worried about how they were

DAVIS COHOUSING, CA

In Davis Cohousing, 23 out of 26 people were first-time home buyers. Silent second mortgages were available from the City of Davis, and other internal creative financial provisions also played a role in making this community affordable and even doable.

FRESNO, CA

On-site childcare saves a lot of time and money, is great for the kids, the parents, and the provider (who is a member of the community).

Solar panels have been going into cohousing projects long before the available discounts. Now they are even more attractive.

going to afford it. Gail Work, a mortgage broker, played a huge role in addressing those concerns. She taught the group members both collectively and individually how to sell that new car and buy a used car, go to the movies once a month instead of twice, and send your aunt in Florida a card for every holiday, because you're going to need to borrow part of your down payment from her. The main point is to expand what we think we can do from what we think we can't.

When ready to move in, there were two households that still were $10,000 short in making their down payment. At the last meeting, one of the households noted he was committed to the project, but still needed more funding. Both of those households were approached later with numerous $500 to $2,000 loans, allowing both of them to move forward. Some of them bought a house in a cohousing community as a shared house with two or three others, pooling saved money to buy a single unit. You can always accomplish more with shared resources. Also, this project was part of a 235-unit development. So large, other costs like lumber amortized over a much bigger scale.

Bellingham Cohousing, WA

Hiring Consultants and Constructability

One of the biggest challenges for cohousing groups when trying to save money is figuring out when and how to hire consultants. There are many well-intentioned people who want to get involved with cohousing and other high-functioning neighborhoods, and want to gain the skills in the context of a new community. Sometimes they are paid too little for their project management skills and for learning on the job, and sometimes they are paid too much. And they often don't realize that they cost the new project considerable capital if there are hiccups, and there always will be. The group needs to find people with as much professional experience with housing as possible—an experienced project manager. I often see places where the civil engineer had designed things too expensively, and they needed the architect and the project manager to help them stay on budget. Civil

These 25 houses sit on 1.25 acres. If done right, this density is no problem for folks who are used to single-family houses.

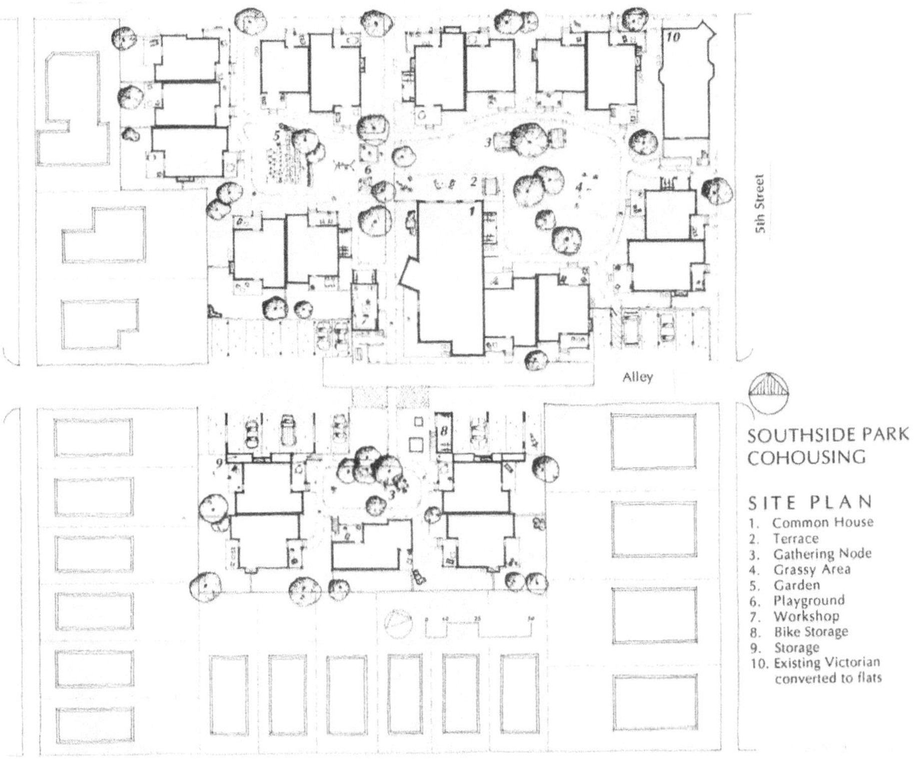

engineering is costly: retaining walls, underground drainage, utility trenches, and other details can be expensive, but making a mistake here is even more expensive.

Bellingham Cohousing hired experienced consultants and got their project built at $67 per square foot (in 2000). A preschool teacher, an elderly woman on social security, and a man on disability needed affordable housing. Their homes started at $120,000—payments were less than previous rent. Although the group brings much to the table, you need to counsel them to avoid unnecessary expenses.

BELLINGHAM, WA.

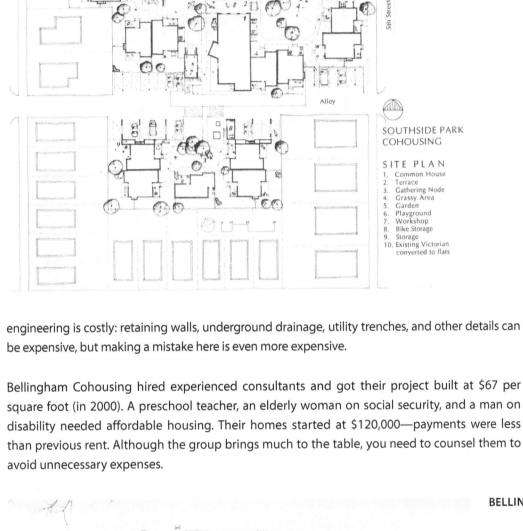

PORT TOWNSEND, WA.

Envision what it can be, outline the steps, then make it so.

Construction methodologies also played a big role in Bellingham's affordability. The professionals took conventional construction, but then caught every detail possible to save money. For example, they saved with single-layer siding, no plywood behind the plywood, studs at 24 inches, no headers above windows, and no headers at interior doors—every stick of wood was engineered to be the minimum. This cut out 25 percent of the lumber and added to 10 percent more insulation. They had gravel driveways and parking (at least to get the project started) and gravel walkways until years after move-in. Although the gravel driveways, parking, and walkways took a couple of awkward negotiations with the fire department, it was worth it and saved the group about $150,000 total, and the road that the fire department wanted all around the project saved another $150,000. Like a lot of projects other local resources are considered. Kate Nichole, a single mom with a young daughter, Emily, organized the five-households that needed help with their down payments to apply for a $125,000 grant with the Seattle-based Low Income Housing Institute (LIHI). The grants helped the five households to get $25,000 each to aid with their down payment. All five were on the edge of being priced out, but once they were awarded the grant, all five were able to move in and proceeded in helping to organize the project.

Port Townsend, WA

Study Group One

Study Group One (SG1) is an important step for the preparation process and for controlling costs in senior cohousing developments. I recently finished three senior cohousing projects. Project A took SG1 twice, Project B took it once, and Project C not at all. Project A was done in three years, Project B in four years, and Project C in six. Coincidence? I don't think so, and time costs money. When working with Project A, the members of the group were proactive about embracing the future and the aging process, "Let's make one-story houses rather than two stories." Group A was easy to work with throughout—they had both feet in the future at all times. Group B went fine, but Group C was constantly confused, with one foot in the future and one foot in the past, and tripping over the easiest questions. SG1 is important in shortening the length of the design time. Group C wasted time and money.

It's equally a social question as much as it is a financial question when it comes to affordability and moving forward in an efficient way. No workshop can address the social side of senior cohousing like Study Group 1. When discussing affordability almost nothing matters as much as process. Moreover, previously proposed developments on Project A's site had been stopped by the neighbors. The cohousing group was able to step into favorable finances by the land seller. In other words, it can be worth it to seek out distressed properties in a timely fashion. That is more likely if you are efficient.

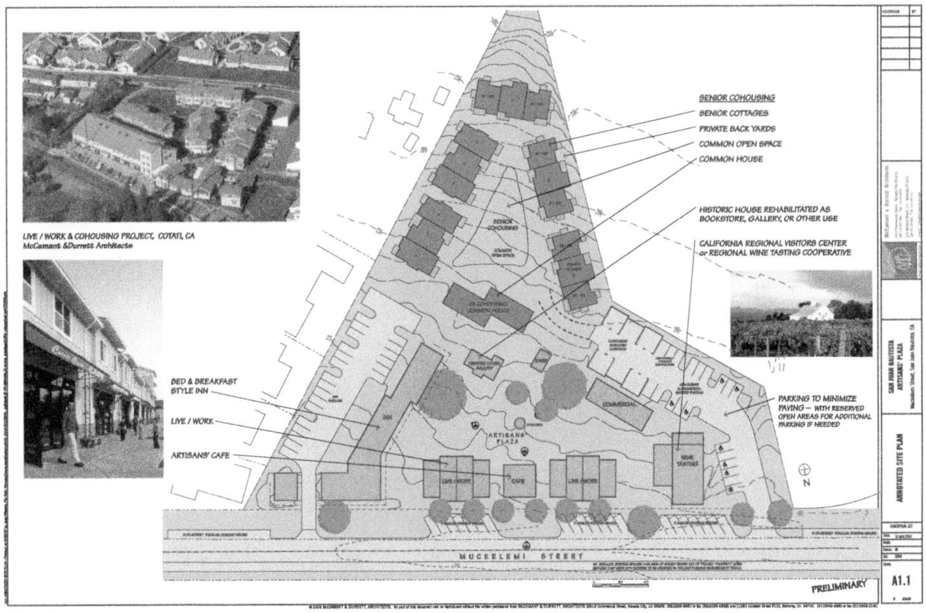

SENIOR COHOUSING: Commercial development complete with a boutique hotel, farmers' market, town orientation center (a historic house), café, plaza, lofts and live/work studios for local artists above the commercial, and a 14-unit senior cohousing community in the rear of the site.

Fort Collins Cohousing, CO, and Others

Grants

In Fort Collins Cohousing the future residents applied for an energy design grant from a local brewery and got it. Many other neighborhoods in the U.S. have asked for grants, ranging from $50,000 to $150,00, from the power company, the utility district, Home Depot, and many others. Fifty thousand dollars is not much in the context of a $10 million project. However, what that capital investment can save you in ongoing energy bills can easily be over $2,000 to $3,000 per house per year. This, over the

FORT COLLINS, CO.

SILVER SAGE COHOUSING, CO

Of these, one resident looked for a house for her mom, but her mom didn't want senior cohousing. So she bought it for herself in her mid-50s at $125,000.

next 30 years in after taxes expenditure (i.e., "disposable income") could save a household $60,000. Moreover, institutions like to donate to organizations who have already received funding, so these grant funds might even compound further.

Boulder, CO

Very Mixed Incomes

In Boulder, CO, the house values are high (approximately $800,000)—well over the national average. As part of a new cohousing development, we had to make six houses for $125,000 to satisfy the city's requirements and the group's desires. And the other ten houses cost $450,000 to $750,000 when built, but now those sell for much more. There comes a point where you're not looking for people only in your own socio-economic class, but for people that want to go on bike trips, walks, and to have interesting conversations with—you want companions. And by having people from different classes involved, the costs are kept down overall.

Nevada City Cohousing, CA

Politics, Sharing, and Cost Efficiency

When designing high-functioning neighborhoods, you often have to navigate difficult local politics to see your project through. In California especially, towns often feel the right to stop whatever they don't like, no matter who that might put on the street. People fear change, but real leaders know that change has to happen if we are to correct some housing injustices. On the other hand, all you have to do is look around to see why the anti-development sentiment has developed—there is too little pride and developers too often deprive every tenant and the town of decent environmental design. Power has gone to the regulators—power that they are happy to abuse. Upon first showing the Mayor of Nevada City a sketch of the proposed 48-unit downtown project incorporating 34 units of cohousing and 14 units of housing for sale to subsidize the cohousing, he became visibly upset,

Production projects can be rich in texture, but not in cost. These houses were built for $85 per square foot in 2003 (up 5 percent per year since then).

SILVER SAGE COHOUSING, CO

New house in Boulder for $125,000 (in 2005).

NEVADA CITY, CA

Dinners for only $2 to $6 per person per night. 200 residents surveys noted having between $200–$2,430 savings per month after moving into cohousing. Common dinner is a lean move for 34 households, but just one of hundreds of items and services that have everything to do with long-term savings.

claiming that the city only approves four to five homes per year "and that's the way we like it" while literally pounding the table and raising his voice. Tom, a future resident who was with me, was shaken by the encounter. We had 13 school teachers in the future resident group who teach in and around town, but couldn't afford to live in town because the average housing price was $500,000 (in 2002). Cohousing would give them the opportunity to live in the area within their financial means. The homes needed to be between $255,000 and $425,000. If the project had been phased due to what was originally suggested by the mayor, the accruement of additional costs would have exceeded those teachers' price ranges. In fact those prices could have easily been $500,000 per house.

Many other savings were necessary. To move in, the development fees were announced to us by the City Clerk at $625,000. After considerable negotiation, it was lowered to $475,000. After financing, that $150,000 would cost $450,000 more to the residents. People often believe that development is only a business act, but it is equally as much a political act. The politics have to be engineered carefully, just like the water flow, posts and beams, and heating systems. There are usually aspects of the politics that are straightforward. But if you take the politics too casually, the project could cost twice as much to build. Don't ever take the politics for granted until the city has proven to you that they are following their own general plan. This project saved well over $2 million because we pushed back on state, federal, and mostly city requirements on hundreds of line items. If you need to keep the project affordable and you have the hutzpah, I cannot recommend enough to simply push back when the request is not logical. It was no accident that we were able to meet our original $255,000–$425,000 dwelling costs published a full three years earlier. Every time the city made another request, such as overflow and guest parking, we compared that request to the budget and then negotiated. The project is absolutely state of the art in North America, but it would have been highly compromised and much more expensive if we had done what the officials "required." The officials (and neighbors)

NEVADA CITY, CA

If you're going to spend $500,000 for a common house, make sure that it is popular, supplements the houses, and that people have lots of practical reasons to use it, like a newly brewed keg of beer.

NEVADA CITY, CA

These $9 simple warehouse light fixtures shown here work great. After designing 55 cohousing projects, you can imagine that we figured out how to get things done as economically as possible because affordability comes up at every project.

NEVADA CITY, CA

A large enough kid's room in the common house will often mean that you can host childcare on site. Besides the convenience, it usually means lower costs and higher quality childcare. And it also means that bedrooms in the private houses can be as small as 10 x 10.

had successfully stopped three previous proposals on the site: a 34-unit single-family house development (sprawl—the holy grail of American development), a 62-unit assisted-care, and an apartment building. Politics play a big role in keeping things affordable. Sometimes you have very convivial negotiations and sometimes you just have to push back. The project absolutely would have been just another victim of the rabid social injustice like the three previous proposals. But the participation of the future residents made sure that it wasn't.

Construction

To Be Affordable Keep It Straightforward, but Elegant

People often believe that affordability is embedded in the materials that we use. Certainly sustainability is, but we cannot assume that materials are the only way to get the affordability job done. The last thing you want is cheap plywood siding. In fact, we suggest that you invest in quality materials upfront, to avoid recurring repair charges down the line. Over time, the ultimate value of the houses ends up dictating what the land costs, which in turn determines what land appraises for in the area. In other words, if you lower the cost of sticks and bricks, theoretically the cost of the land goes up to compensate for that decrease since the value is still the same. Start by trying to get the land price and the cost of land improvements down, because that will make a much larger difference than cheap materials.

Being an engineering major before architecture, it's easy for me to know whether 2x4 hangers (at $0.49 each) will work just as well as 2 x 6 hangers (at $2.50 each) and there are thousands of them on the job. And there are about 100 other small moves in the context of production construction that will get the job done in a wholesale cost structure, rather than a retail one. Architects who care about the social side of architecture want to get everyone on board. This is how you do it—know what everything costs so that the "optimum" solution can be accomplished on every line item.

The line item that has the most malleability is what is called the civil work. Moving the dirt, building retaining walls, underground drainage, piping underground utilities, and more. When the clients realize that spreading the houses far apart can readily increase this cost from $1 million to $3 million, things contracted again. When a sloped site will cost you another $300,000, or when a street turnout because of a bad traffic study cost another $150,000. That tends to be a large part of the feasibility conversion (see Chapter 14).

The right source of power can also positively affect the costs in the community. For example, my electric bill was minus $86 in 2020 and minus $88 the year before. In addition to the 1.2 kW of solar power, savings occur because the house is efficiently designed, and has walls that are shared between

NEVADA CITY, CA

1. Four buildings next to each other that are all the same, but no one ever notices. 2. The colors, the articulation, the texture, and the landscaping bring plenty of variety. What the residents do notice is that they can afford to move in.

NEVADA CITY, CA:

Some people, like Kathryn McCamant and I, were motivated to move into cohousing because we could have only one child. Our daughter, Jessie, is extremely social, so that would be unfair without the 36 cousins who live there.

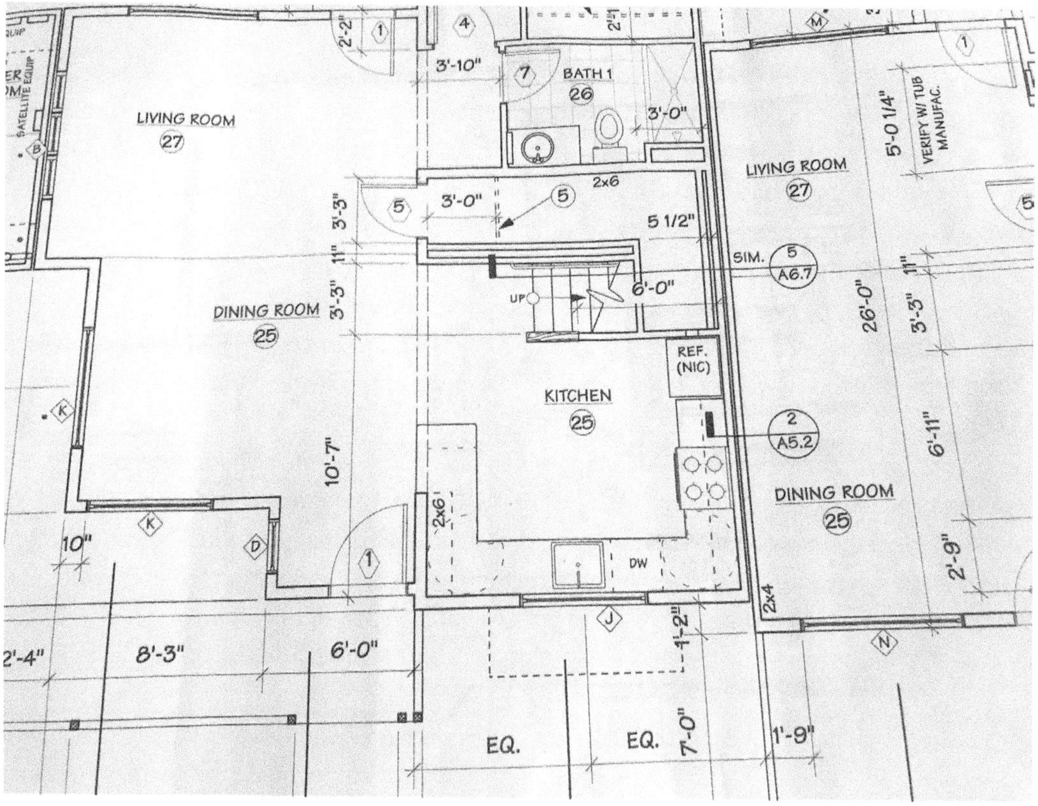

Affordability through very straightforward construction.

NEVADA CITY, CA

Parents learning to be smarter parents is always a great part of intergenerational neighborhoods. You can't really put a price on it—but you can. The likelihood of children being bored, restless, and agitated in general is higher if they don't have peers right outside the front door.

homes. Energy efficiency does take more investment around insulation, energy storage, radiant barriers, and quality roofing; but it's easily offset. We utilize advanced framing, meaning that we can have framing packages that cost about 20 percent less than normal framing packages, and that allows for about 15 percent more insulation and less flanking. The framing packages for one of our larger projects is about $2 million. If designed right, we can save $400,000. Investing in energy-efficient power sources and construction saves considerably in the long run. Production construction is designed to be efficient rather than reiterative. The magic bullet rarely saves enough to mitigate the risks associated with shipping container or straw bale construction, or other new solutions. Our mantra is that no one wins unless everyone wins.

Thirty new houses in one building. A very efficient and ecological way to build neighborhoods, and in this case an archaeology (sun-embracing buildings).

Vigilant construction administration is crucial to controlling costs. Going in later to fix sound mitigation concerns like this could easily cost ten-fold, as opposed to getting it right during construction.

In so many ways the front porch is the most important and least costly "room" in the house.

Building Code

Question It When It Adds Unnecessary Expense

Don't always go along with the building code. There is no provision in the code for cohousing, nor high-functioning neighborhoods, and we will all be better if it stays that way. Sections 105 and 106, however, clearly allow for exceptions for materials and/or methods and allow for provisional requirements. For example, in the 55 projects I have designed, I have never put in more than two bathrooms in the common house, nor does the group ever need or want more than two. If there are 30 dwellings, there are probably 60 bathrooms that people can use on the way up or run home to. It doesn't happen, but we have to tell the building department that so that we can make logical choices. Nor in 30 years has a resident ever complained. On the contrary, they appreciate saving the group $25,000 by working through the logic with the officials. Of these hundreds of line items that can be argued, we usually pick four to five per project to mitigate unnecessary costs that would compromise something more important to the group such as four or five charging stations for electric cars, and in one case, an infant-toddler room. The building code is set up for a one size fits all. Cohousing and high-functioning neighborhoods are not one size fits all and need the opportunity to be molded to work for your residents.

LIFESTYLE: Shared houses will be a key element of neighborhoods in the future. When combined with a common house, all of the pressure of living in a shared home goes away.

Lifestyle

Sharing to Save Money

Sharing is an integral part of cohousing and high-functioning neighborhoods and it greatly helps to lower costs. In a personal survey I asked 200 people how much they thought they saved per month by living in cohousing. The estimated savings ranged from $200 per month to $2,430 per month. One woman's 30 line-item questionnaire included energy, driving, telephone bills, air travel costs, and more that she was saving by moving into cohousing. Apart from overall costs, there are many personal costs that are alleviated because of cohousing. Ridesharing and vehicle sharing are common practices.

One time a single mom and her son moved into a house with a senior resident. They lived in one room and then later rented two rooms for a few hundred dollars a month. Once the older woman passed, people brainstormed how to keep the mom and son in the community, and they ultimately decided to co-purchase her home. Now she rents out rooms so that she can be financially stable.

Another simple solution to combat costs is by having smaller homes. By having shared spaces like the common house, larger homes are not needed. In the common house there are state-of-the-art washers and dryers, biodegradable laundry soap, recycled grey water, shared internet, one lawnmower for 34 homes, and about a hundred other shared costs. These are just a few examples that are hard to accomplish in a standard home without exceeding budgets. The houses are obviously inherently less costly because of their small size, and are usually somewhere between 800 and 1,200 square feet. We just finished a very affordable project using 450-square-foot cottages that provide all the necessities. Minimizing the material things and relying on the social capital results in functional and affordable housing. A 4,000-square-foot common building makes your house about a 5,000-square-foot home.

Co-living, Shared Housing, and Ecovillages

Less Personal Stuff

Cohousing makes shared houses easier. The shared houses of Vancouver Cohousing have a 6,100-square-foot common house to take the pressure off of the more confined living quarters of a

A great clubhouse at a subsidized affordable community. It really helps to have a place to meet together, "To help manage this place."

LIFESTYLE: On-site friends.

LIFESTYLE: The common house: A place for us to be together and a place for me to do my laundry (without the sound of a washing machine in my house). A place for the kids to roam before and after dinner. A place to recycle grey water for plants in a dry climate. A place to help us manage the few things that we have together.

shared home with four bedrooms. A lot of young people have to figure out how to get their foot in the real estate door—but this is true for everyone. The shared house is a typical point of entry.

When ecovillages have used the cohousing design process as a building block, they fire on all cylinders. Cohousing disciplines a group toward efficient and fair information processing, and productive and optimum decision making. If you can build a cohousing community, you can build an ecovillage. These days, there's rarely a cohousing community built without a shared house, and there's rarely an ecovillage built without cohousing. Co-living is largely when you have a suite (bedroom and bath) and a small shared kitchen, dining, and living space; and access to a larger shared kitchen, dining, living, and scores of other shared amenities in the common house.

FEASIBILITY: Is this site a good site?

Stacked rocks make for less costly grade mitigation.

Feasibility

Critical Thinking

The site remedy costs play a large role in the overall feasibility of the project. After we had bought our acreage in Nevada City, we found that there were toxicity problems. The area was once home to an old dump site, so we dug down with consultants and estimated that we needed about $100,000 to remediate the site. In the end, it came to $97,000, so we were fine. The key to good feasibility is to have your estimates of all of the known costs and the contingent costs as accurate as possible, and then account for them in the budget. It's important to factor all these variables and views, otherwise the project can die from a thousand cuts. In other words, it's always cheaper not to cut corners at feasibility. Another project that got a $300,000 toxic remediation estimate then dug no further. In

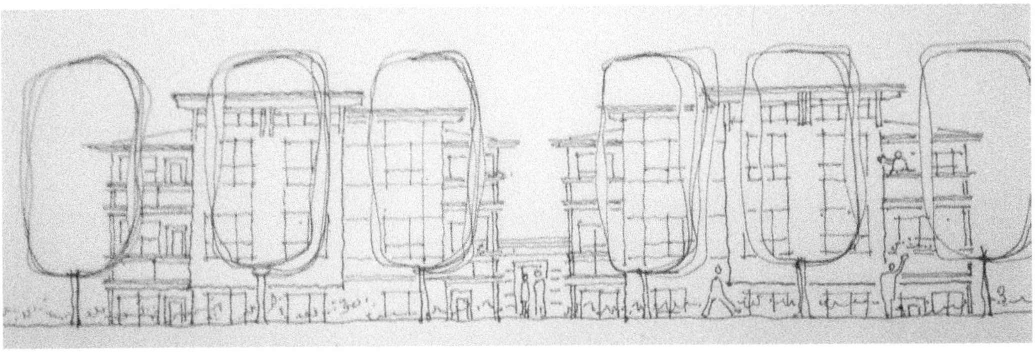

EARLY FEASIBILITY: Geometrically, how many houses can we fit on this 0.63 acre site? Maybe 19, 25, or, in this case, 31 houses—it depends largely on the slope and vehicle access. The more houses, the more economical.

the end that cost came to $900,000 to remove the toxins while under construction. Projects cannot endure this kind of surprise, at least not without losing half of the group. Feasibility plays a big role.

When determining the feasibility (sometimes known as the due diligence or building a budget for the project), the site is critical. This is truly value-added work by the architect. We try to play a role, because it keeps the backtracking to a minimum. Often if we don't, there is a loss of value because there is not enough time to design it right. In other words, don't start programming workshops until you know that you can accomplish your project on budget. There are normally about 30–50 big issues to consider when assessing a new site. The $600,000 for the extra toxic remediation might have been accommodated in the budget if understood early. Maybe all of the houses would be 10 square feet smaller to make the budget work—but you have to know the remedies before you start designing.

Some Feasibility Points

When it comes to feasibility, here are the top 24 of the possible 300 line items, but in reality every time I walk onto a new site I unfocus my eyes and start anew.

1. Group Interest: future residents of the project.
2. Attainability: Can you negotiate to get this site on terms that you can live with? All cash rarely works for cohousing. Have a critical eye, be realistic, but don't negotiate against yourself, and if you like it, make the offer at the terms you need.

3. Neighborhood Politics?
4. Historical and archeological significance.
5. Feasibility Studies (sketches, etc.): Can we get the units on this site that we need? Slope, parking, and access are key.
6. Access to Public Transportation?
7. Funding—all private?, a combination of grants?, etc.
8. Access to Services? (such as groceries, etc.)
9. Fire Department?
10. Noise?
11. Utilities in Place?
12. Soils?
13. Water/Wetlands?
14. Sewer?
15. Toxins?
16. Site Analysis (existing buildings, landscape, terrain, flora, fauna, slope, sun, wind, smells, and turn-out lanes). Logical setbacks/adjacencies to other buildings.
17. Easement/Deed Restrictions
18. Master Planning: If part of a bigger project?
19. Logical Land Use/Zoning/Zoning Codes?
20. Rezoning costs/delays/risks?
21. Planned Unit development?
22. ADA analysis
23. Budget and scope of the project
24. And everything relevant to the specific site (tree ordinances, etc.)

Then come the next steps:

1. Schematic Programming/Design Criteria/Schematics (community involvement in every step)
    a) Site
    b) Common House
    c) Private House
    d) Submittal
2. City Approvals
3. Design Development and with Energy-Efficient Design (integration at every step). Interior design
4. Construction Documents
5. Construction Budgeting/Cost Estimating (on going)
6. Construction Contracts
7. Construction/Construction Administration
8. Physical Maintenance Workshop
9. Post-Occupation Evaluation

LEGACY: More and more condo projects, rental projects, and neighborhoods are building gathering areas in the neighborhood amongst 20–30 houses. These 11 chairs and 20 benches accommodate "thank goodness it's Friday" evening neighborhood get-togethers. They can easily accommodate people playing instruments on a Friday evening, smores, and a potluck—building meaningful connections.

LEGACY: A five-story project for previously homeless people in San Francisco. They make dinner for each other six nights a week.

LEGACY: Depot Commons in Morgan Hill, California. A shared kitchen for 13 single moms in school within this co-living situation is the epitome of saving money.

Legacy

More and More Neighborhoods

Write a clear intent to help make it clear how these neighbors plan to be more neighborly. Often inspired by cohousing or as is sometimes called cohousing like, or cohousing lite. It is a pro-social neighborhood. But those lines will blur in the future as high-functioning neighborhoods become more in demand and as people increasingly see how important functioning neighborhoods are to

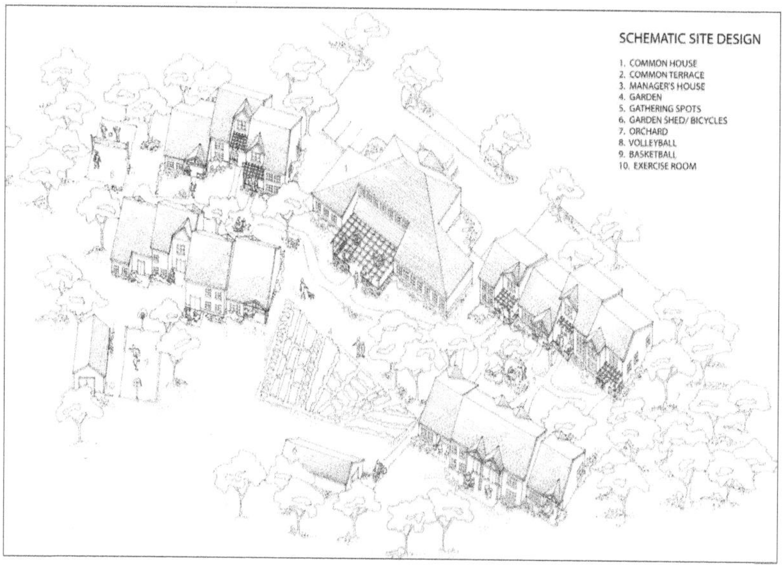

LEGACY: The future of cohousing will make community available for everyone. This community was designed for adults with neurological challenges. The thought process behind this neighborhood was that if someone can use the bus, and someone can shop, someone can cook, and a few people can clean up for each other, that they can meet their individual and collective needs.

COLUMBIA ECOVILLAGE, PORTLAND, OR

This community bought a 24-unit dilapidated motel in need of a major rehab. They then turned the units into new and modern condominiums on a total of six acres. They used the house for guest rooms and the teenage room. They also have gardens and chickens, a workshop, and a common house.

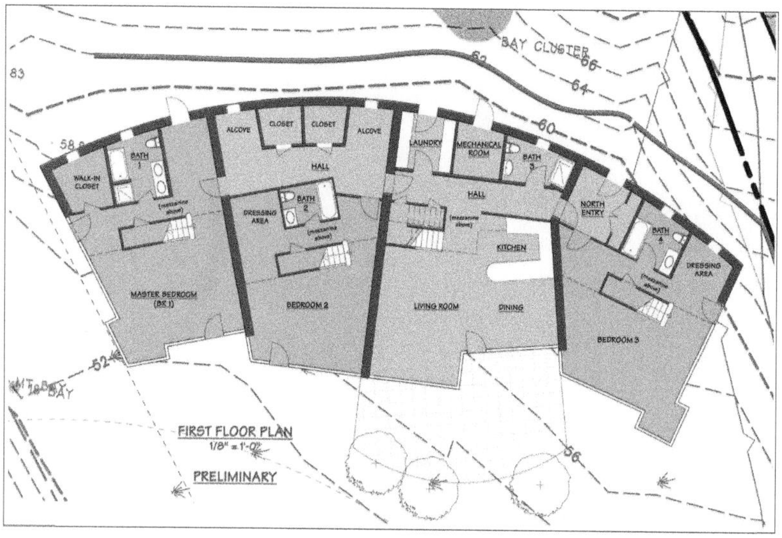

A shared house with rammed earth for three households. One for a professional mom and her child, another for a retired couple. The two couples are helping with the child so the mom with an important job can work a half hour late on occasion. A shared house is a great place to start with affordability.

Columbia Ecovillage Common House by The Cohousing Company.

the city and the family. Hopefully cohousing will be clear, but the other ways to accomplish high-functioning neighborhoods will become many. No skill has led to making affordable housing more available like the skills built up with cohousing. There are so many neighborhoods that have been built in recent years that yearn to make the opportunity real. Although I do have to say that every

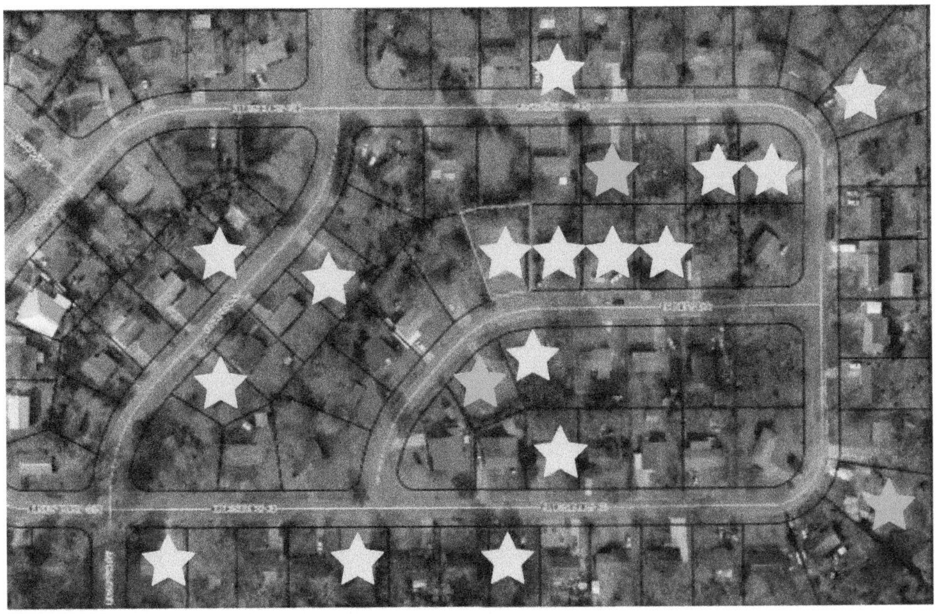

Purchasing individual houses (the yellow stars) and making offers on others (the blue stars) in this very rundown housing stock is an attempt to stitch a new community together.

LEGACY: New Commercial

At the street—a new 30,000 square foot development with low cost housing behind a commercial 30-unit community-enhanced neighborhood and a second 34-dwelling-unit neighborhood. The mixed-use development will accommodate the wider area as a "neighborhood center."

time I sit in on a college critique and someone says—"I put in this picnic table here to facilitate community" or "there's this bench to accommodate that opportunity," I pretty much know that is mostly wishful thinking because it is awkward for people to walk up and say "Can I have a seat?" "What brings you here?" People must have an excuse, a mutual interest that brings them together. Picnic tables do not facilitate community, but relationships do. A picnic table accommodates that desire. Start with the relationships, and then accommodate them. More like, "Hey, there's going to be a garden planning meeting on Saturday morning at 9 a.m., are you going?" Co-building and co-planting the raised beds, whether we should put up a mutual clothesline. There's about a hundred different activities that a neighborhood can plan and work through together to save money, to make life easier, more fun, and to build community.

Heaven for kids.

VANCOUVER, B.C.

Emotional ownership is the easiest way to keep the prices down. People bring the most important equity to the table. And leverage that "social capital" toward city approvals, bank financing, and ongoing working capital. "I'm serious about this neighborhood," "Great, let's get busy!"

Want a great neighborhood? Do it yourself!

The kids are always rearranging the landscape.

14

The Details of Cohousing

What Components Lead to High-Functioning Neighborhoods?

"Healthier behavior in architecture which cannot be measured, should not be touted."
Charles Durrett

To not have a hole in your boat, to not fall through the cracks, to sail smoothly to the other side, to prepare to launch, to journey smoothly, to land, and to settle comfortably. In the practice of smooth sailing, or in this case lifemanship, a few details do matter. Load them to your hold, keep them dry, keep them at bay as necessary, then deploy when needed. Cohousing is a skill set—planning it requires many of the same skills that living there does: diplomacy, respect, listening, and flexibility. But planning it requires a sense of urgency as well, "Don't let there be slack in the chain." The boom-and-bust economy in combination with our own personal impatience make it necessary to stay deliberate, with all of your tools in your satchel.

Sitting around after dinner is the point.

KEY COHOUSING METRICS: A KEY COMPONENT FOR HIGH-FUNCTIONING NEIGHBORHOODS

1. **People-hours in the common house per week.**
   How is this calculated? People often say, "it must be difficult." In fact, it can be extremely fun and it's critical for improving discussions and designs over time. This is how it was done in Nevada City, CA, Port Townsend, WA, and Trudeslund, Denmark. Nevada City receives about 450 people-hours per week and Trudeslund gets about 750. And these metrics are key to post-occupancy evaluation—"Does it work or does it not work?" should be an objectively answerable question.

   Usually this question is best measured just after a Saturday or Sunday morning brunch, when people are more relaxed and have a few minutes. After brunch, I ask six or seven people at random to join me at a table for coffee and number crunching. I would begin the conversation by asking, "How often did you use the common house last week?" and then the specifics, "How many common meals did you have last week?" After some discussion and consulting phone calls, we determined that five was the answer. "What was the average attendance?" The same process happened here, "Well, I had 25 signed up, but ended up getting four extras at the last minute," and so on. Eventually, the number 29 was calculated as the average. Five times 29 is equal to 145 diners for about 1.25 people hours on average, including time hanging around came to a total of 181.25 people-hours.

   There are many other activities that happen in the common house during the prior week that need to be accounted for as well. For example, "Last week we had 12 people at yoga on Saturday morning, and between taking your shoes off, doing yoga, and chatting afterwards, we averaged about 1.25 hours per person." Thus, 12 multiplied by 1.25 equals 15 people-hours. We then repeated the process for the workshop, the art room, and the sitting room (including puzzles), the news cast, a movie, as well as for activities like folks just running into each other, Friday Morning Forum (a conversation, about not cohousing business but personal and local topics), laundry, setting up guests, and meetings, art in the dining room, card making, putting up art, fixing things,

To lighten the load, sometimes four people will cook (two people cook while two others clean) on any given night. So it's best to make a "four-butt kitchen" every time, even when the group says it only has two or three cooks.

Kids bring a lot of people-hours to the common facilities.

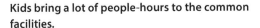

Having a couple of guests is the only excuse you need to drag out the fiddle.

quilting in the dining area during the day or after dinner, and the occasional potluck. "What did you observe or participate in?" Soon you hear the same thing over and over again, and you know that you are honing in on the hours.

Usually about here someone would say, "Chuck, but the week before we had our common meeting and that generated tons of people-hours." To which I reply, "Well, we don't need the exceptions right now. We're just looking for a regular week—specifically last week."

Then there were the guests using the guest room: friends, families, visitors, etc. "But what else was there?" I asked over and over again. "Well, we did have the book club for a couple of hours, and there were approximately 50 lingering conversations lasting on average about half an hour each."

They could be home or elsewhere. But done right—they want to be here.

Connecting with each other over a game of pool. Adults communicating with teens is a goal.

Then someone would walk over to Ingrid, the yoga teacher, to confirm her yoga numbers, and we arrived at a total of 366.5 people-hours last week. That's a high-functioning common house for just 45 residents. That's 8.14 people-hours per person on average. If you take away guests, that's about 6.2 people-hours per resident, per week. That probably ranges from 2 to 12 hours per week per person. Some people take five hours to cook community dinner, some people take two. Some people spend hours on puzzles, some people spend none. All of it matters.

There are other key metrics like togetherness on the common paths, whether management happens on the paths, or health and exercise at the common garden—they all portray the community's supportive interactions. The success of spaces like the common garden, the common terrace, and the neighborhood gathering nodes also serve as metrics for how the design of the cohousing contributes to the community.

Centripetal activities are great excuses to get together, like folding napkins.

A cozy evening with the neighbors. Not the exception—the normal.

2. **Smiles per half hour.**

   Smiles per half hour takes vigilance to record. You need one person observing one person at a time for an entire half hour. It's exhausting. Unlike people-hours in the common house, the smiles per half hour is relative rather than an absolute measurement. With the people-hours in the common house, they are either in the common house or they are not. Presumably people smiled before, but I've looked forever to find out what that average might be. However, I believe that people smile more in the common house than they do at home. There are so many jokes flying around, so much levity, so much camaraderie and history. I have counted over 50 smiles in a half hour by one person, including 17 audible laughs. It depends a great deal on who the person is of course—it's often difficult to tell when a smile begins and ends because some people are smiling all the time. Sometimes there are serious conversations, and of course that is a different measurement of consequence.

   Anything that you can do to improve the measurements will ultimately improve the design. If you don't measure, you will just make the same mistakes over and over again.

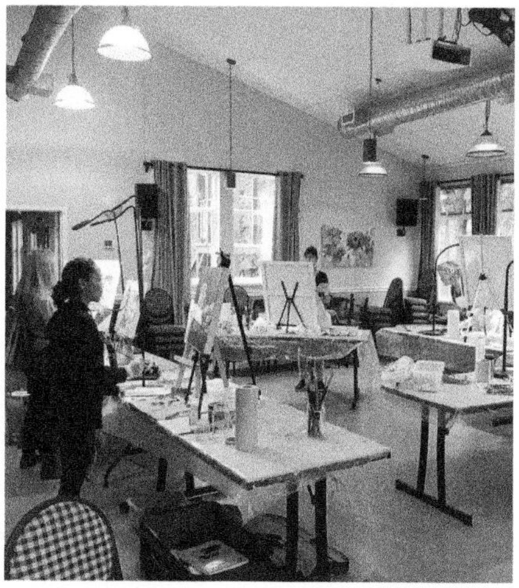

Painting on Tuesday morning in the common house.

25 people gather in this neighborhood common space to play music together on a Thursday evening.

Counting the people-hours in the common house last week—a couple of folks are off interviewing the yoga teacher and the puzzle doers.

Committees at work in a high-functioning neighborhood.

COMMUNITY SIZE

Figuring out the optimal size and number of households seems to be one of the biggest challenges facing cohousing in America. Cohousing communities in Europe have already demonstrated that there is an optimum size range for a cohousing community. There are lots of theories, but after interviewing hundreds and hundreds of residents in cohousing, the answer seems to be somewhere in the range of 15 to 30 houses, but with no more than 50 adults. The Danes come up with the same numbers, not from interviewing, but from social behavior observation. The two extremes of the spectrum pose different challenges and benefits, but still no more than 50 adults.

Larger Cohousing Communities

If the cohousing community is too big, the group's discussions begin to sound more like politics than consensus building. It can have an overly institutional feel and may lack the intimacy required to make its residents feel as if they have a stake in its success. However, the advantage of larger-sized communities is that they increase the probability that each person will have a lot in common with 4–5 people, and they are therefore more likely to make close friends. Not too big (50 adults

Two hours per month is not too much to help manage a high-functioning neighborhood.

Managing the farm—literally in this case. This is the farm committee managing that lovely 1/2 acre.

COVID meeting. Socially separated, but not socially isolated. Socially separated, but getting the job done.

maximum) means that you have time to talk to all of the stakeholders before a meeting, such as key trees that have to be removed—and this is vital. A larger group also helps amortize the costs of a larger common house and other fixed costs such as project management will be buffered across more households. Further, there are more people to help get all of the jobs done both before and after move-in. Also we find that the large communities are easier to organize. They warrant organization and good facilitation. Smaller projects tend to be more conversational and casual, and meetings last longer and are less focused as a result.

Smaller Cohousing Communities

The smaller the community is, the more communal, social, and financial responsibilities each household bears. Even so, small cohousing developments are often simpler and require less land, making them easier to find suitable sites. Small projects are also less likely to attract neighborhood opposition, and the development budget is generally within the financing capacity of small developers or even the residents themselves. However, managing a small cohousing development is no less complicated or less formal because when fewer people are involved, personalities play a larger role in the social dynamic of the community. For better or worse, a community that is built too small will resemble a large family rather than a neighborhood of actively engaged households, and it's possible that some individuals may not resonate with anyone in the community.

A COVID cohousing meeting.

Easier to facilitate, easier to get consensus.

Cohousing and other high-functioning neighborhoods are easier to manage with a maximum of 50 adults.

A monthly two-hour meeting at a typical high-functioning neighborhood. Much community building happens at the meeting, where it is possible to build community as they figure out managing the community together.

Community-Enhanced Neighborhoods

No western country that I know of has considered the social math of housing as thoroughly as the Danes. The Danes are very clear: "Do not have a community with more than 50 adults." They try hard to keep community-enhanced neighborhoods to 30 houses or less. If you have 150 households, make five neighborhoods. At a maximum of 50 adults, coming to an agreement is much easier. Consensus is much more doable with 30 to 40 adults attending meetings. With more than 50 adults there are more difficult decisions, more politics, and less time spent with the individuals that really care about whether a tree is cut down or not. However, with 50 adults or less, it's easier to talk to the three or four people who really care about that tree that you propose to cut down before it comes to the common meeting and surprises people. If there are six or seven people who care about the tree, you might just take it to the neighborhood meeting, but why bother talking with that many? Making proposals at neighborhood meetings without discussing it with the stakeholders beforehand never goes well. You know you need others to say that it's probably a good idea.

50 adults maximum make high-functioning neighborhoods easy to manage.

Management of cohousing is simpler to manage at 50 adults maximum.

Committee work in a high-functioning neighborhood.

Common dinner at Greyrock Commons in Fort Collins, CO.

PROJECT DENSITY

Dense neighborhoods do not need to be overwhelming in scale, or feel tall and enclosed. In fact, some of the densest residential neighborhoods in North America include modestly sized housing with limited parking. In cohousing, a certain density—usually 10 to 30 units per acre—creates enough density so that people feel like they are part of a neighborhood, while enough land remains for shared open space and common facilities. In urban areas, the density could easily be 80 units per acre or more—assuming that a high-rise could have a cohousing community per floor, or one per couple of floors.

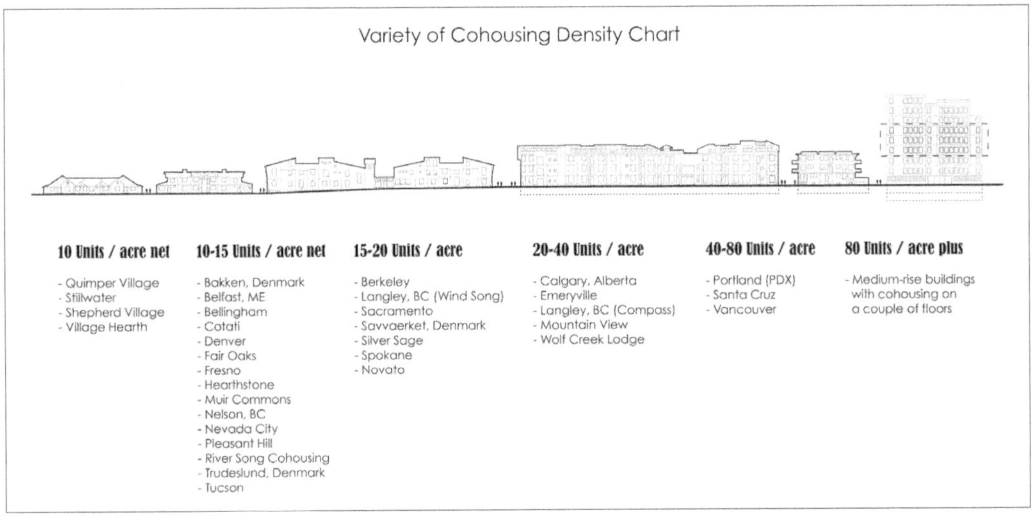
Variety of Cohousing Density Chart
10 Units / acre net
- Quimper Village
- Stillwater
- Shepherd Village
- Village Hearth
10-15 Units / acre net
- Bakken, Denmark
- Belfast, ME
- Bellingham
- Cotati
- Denver
- Fair Oaks
- Fresno
- Hearthstone
- Muir Commons
- Nelson, BC
- Nevada City
- Pleasant Hill
- River Song Cohousing
- Trudeslund, Denmark
- Tucson
15-20 Units / acre
- Berkeley
- Langley, BC (Wind Song)
- Sacramento
- Savvaerket, Denmark
- Silver Sage
- Spokane
- Novato
20-40 Units / acre
- Calgary, Alberta
- Emeryville
- Langley, BC (Compass)
- Mountain View
- Wolf Creek Lodge
40-80 Units / acre
- Portland (PDX)
- Santa Cruz
- Vancouver
80 Units / acre plus
- Medium-rise buildings with cohousing on a couple of floors

In a rural setting, community works much better if it is designed to be more like a village. High-density works fine, but the design of those floors, say in a high-rise, have to be quite different. Corridors have to be 8–12 feet wide (not 5–6 feet), there has to be windows from the kitchens to the corridors, and there has to be full-light front doors to the corridor as well. The design of every detail matters, whether it is how mail delivery happens, where common areas are per floor, and the various progressions from parking to the front door, for example.

There are many benefits to higher density: it makes cohousing more affordable with less infrastructure, saves energy especially with common walls, helps to conserve open space or agricultural land, and reduces the space between front doors creating larger backyards and more privacy. Moreover, it makes it easier to live in a walkable and proximate downtown.

Because most community-enhanced multi-family developments get built anywhere from one to three stories high, I'm often requested to explain if other archetypes or forms will also work for these developments, because in many settings, especially urban, it's not prudent to build that low because the land is too expensive. Why is cohousing generally built at grade anyway? First, we grew up on the

For some reason, high-functioning neighborhoods get more architecture because a cooperation effort comes to the table that knows how to achieve it. And Americans are more likely to accept this density (30 units on 0.9 acre) when it can function like a community.

A new little village in a clearing, with remote parking where no one lives and a common building where everyone lives. Clearly a cohousing community.

An old factory transformed into a tight-knit community.

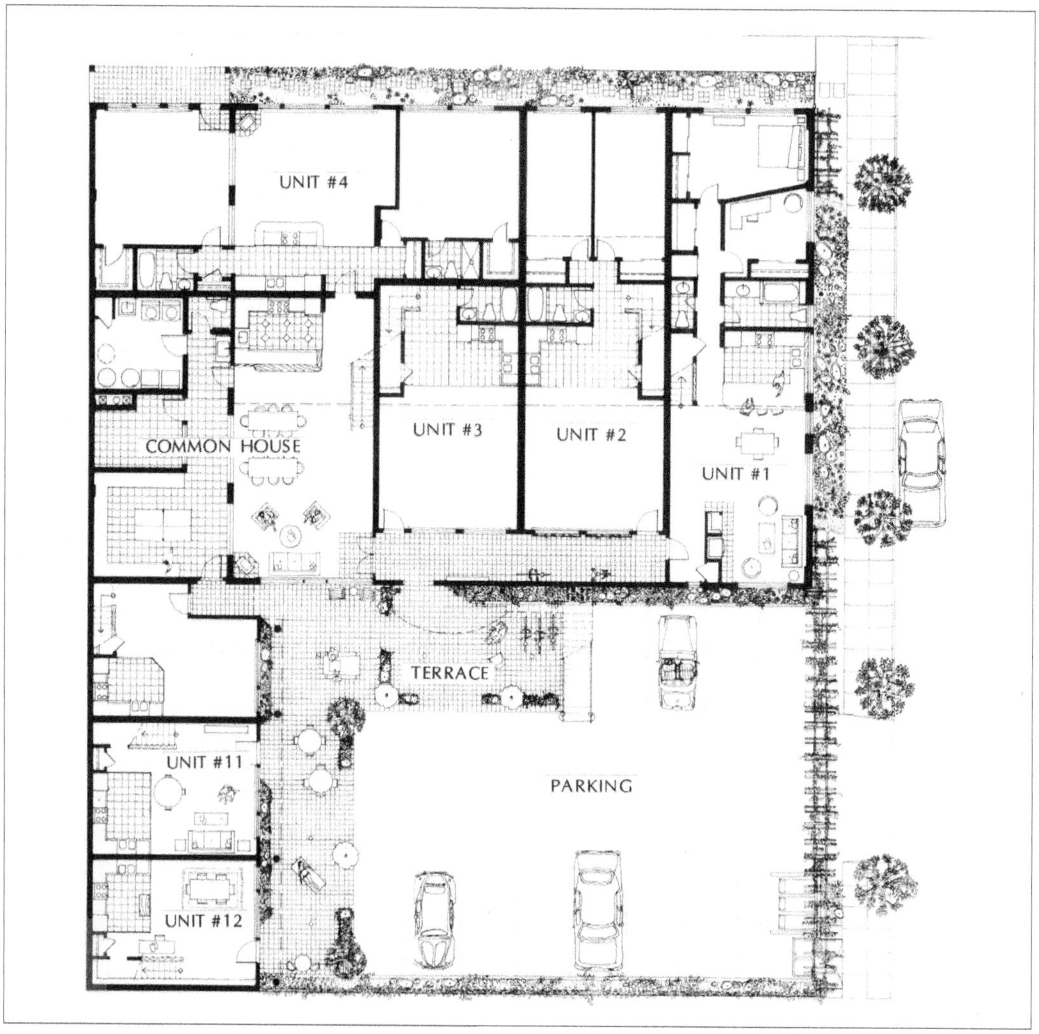

Serengeti Plains—that is, we, as a species, relate to each other most comfortably when communicating horizontally. Exhaustive studies by Jan Gehl et al. have shown that, above four stories, there is very little relation to someone on the ground, and parents tend to let their young children run around outside much less, even in Europe. You can't talk easily at that height, and it's much harder socially. For example, it's strange if you're having a conversation with someone and then one of you stands up on a chair and talks down to the other—it's awkward at best, and normally doesn't last very long.

In Sweden, entire floors of a high-rise building can include 15–20 units of cohousing, with well-designed common areas to gather and solve each other's problems.

At Berkeley Cohousing, the group bought seven of the houses with the site, and rehabilitated them. The other half of the square footage was built new.

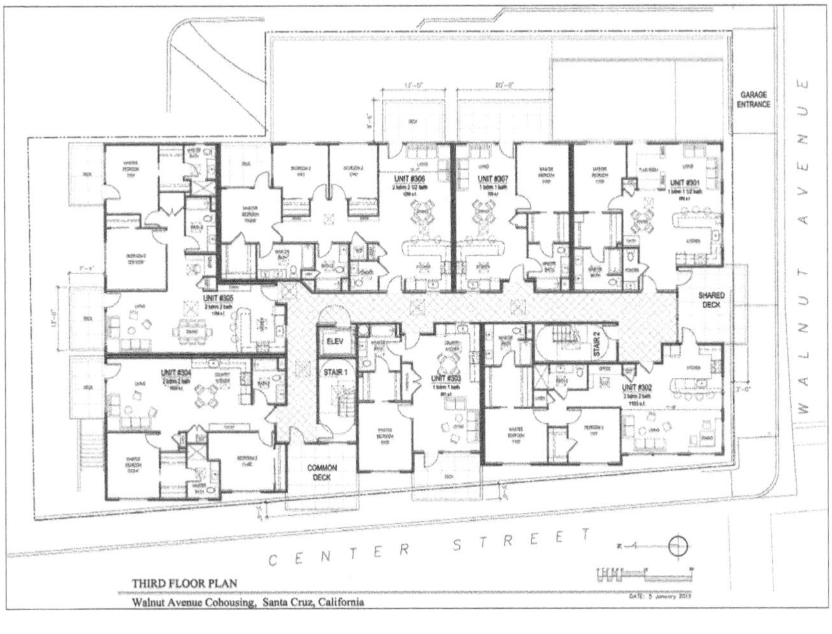

Wide corridors, windows from kitchen to corridor, generous private decks, common facilities on each level. This is how you design at higher densities.

But you can definitely build up when you have to or want to be in that special downtown location. When done right, like downtown Santa Cruz, for example, where the neighborhood is so bustling like Greenwich Village, New York; Noe Valley, San Francisco; Alexandria, VA; Rittenhouse, PA. In these scenarios, up is often the way to go.

In Sweden, there are many high-rise cohousing projects where the cohousing occupies three stories of a brand new 10-story building, or three floors of an old building that have been repurposed or rehabilitated. Most cohousing is more horizontal and village-like, so people may assume that it is the archetype, but there is no single archetype. All archetypes can work, except single-family houses. They are too disparate, too spread out, too energy-inefficient, too atomized, and too expensive by nature. However, single-family neighborhoods, like in Temescal, California, can be converted by not only adding a common building, but also doubling the density from four houses per acre to eight houses per acre. There is no density limit for a high-functioning community. The lower the density, the more difficult it is to facilitate the proximity that helps stitch a well-functioning community together.

Good acoustics make listening to guest musicians easier and more fun.

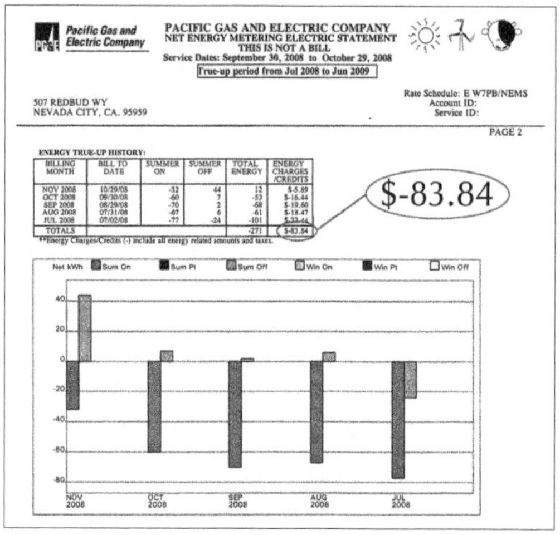

Pacific Gas and Electric Company

PACIFIC GAS AND ELECTRIC COMPANY
NET ENERGY METERING ELECTRIC STATEMENT
THIS IS NOT A BILL
Service Dates: September 30, 2008 to October 29, 2008
True-up period from Jul 2008 to Jun 2009

507 REDBUD WY
NEVADA CITY, CA. 95959

Rate Schedule: E W7PB/NEMS
Account ID:
Service ID:

PAGE 2

ENERGY TRUE-UP HISTORY:

BILLING MONTH	BILL TO DATE	SUMMER ON	SUMMER OFF	TOTAL ENERGY	ENERGY CHARGES /CREDITS
NOV 2008	10/29/08	-32	44	12	$-5.89
OCT 2008	09/30/08	-60	7	-53	$-16.44
SEP 2008	08/29/08	-70	2	-68	$-19.60
AUG 2008	07/31/08	-67	6	-61	$-18.47
JUL 2008	07/02/08	-77	-24	-101	[illegible]
TOTALS				-271	$-83.84

**Energy Charges/Credits (-) include all energy related amounts and taxes.

$-83.84

About an average year's electric bill with 1.2 kW of solar power in Nevada City Cohousing.

Kate, a key early organizer in Mountain View cohousing, appreciates her back porch dining area and workstation. She also appreciates the community that she enjoys just out the front door on the other side of the house.

ECOLOGICALLY ENHANCED PRODUCTION CONSTRUCTION (E.E.P.C.)

There are thousands of books on how to make buildings more energy-efficient, so I will only elaborate on where The Cohousing Company uniquely makes production construction more efficient. (But there are too few books that depend largely on cooperation as a means of saving the Earth's resources and not putting them into the atmosphere. This is that book.)

1. **Shared walls.**

   Because The Cohousing Company has designed numerous straw-bale buildings, we have attended many conferences where we listened to designers debate whether those walls were R-25, or in effect R-35, or perhaps R-45 walls (the R-value being the resistance to heat transfer). I always ask, "What do you think about R-infinity walls?" That's what you get when you have a

Blown-in cellulose insulation, with recycled newspapers in the best.

Cellulose insulation. Effective carbon sequestering keeping CO2 out of the atmosphere.

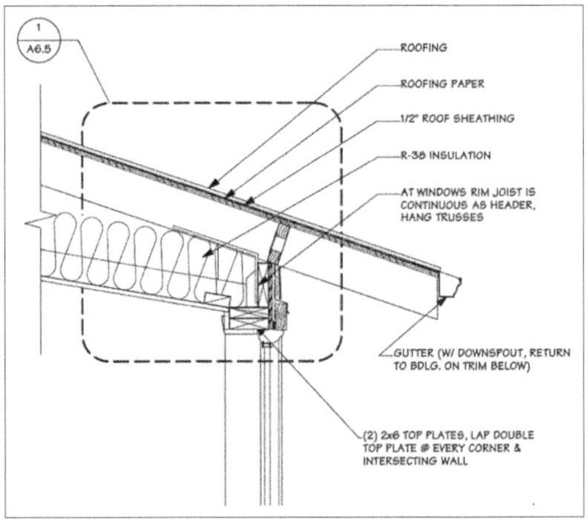

It's easier to put the header into the above framing than it is to build a header. And the removed header helps bring in more light.

Reflective roof sheeting bounces back about 80 percent of the sun's radiation back into the sky to keep the house cool in the summer.

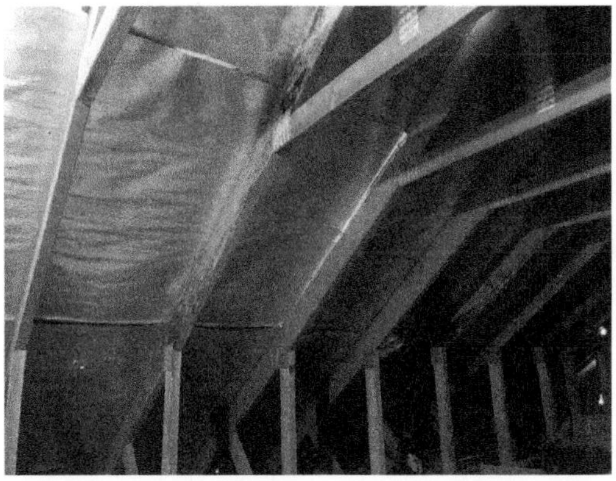

Reflective roof sheeting also bounces considerable heat back into the interior space in the winter.

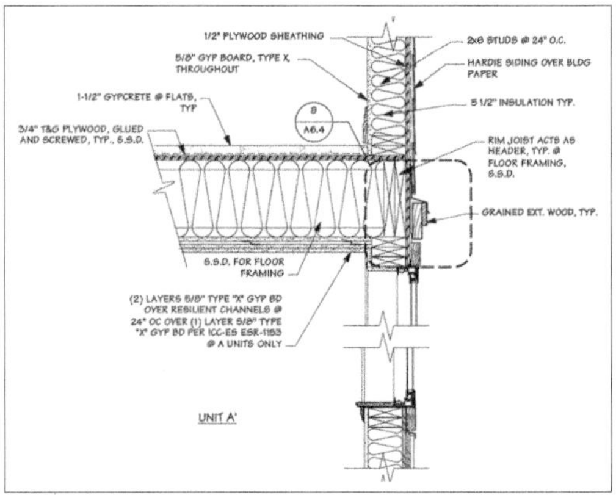

No header above the windows brings a lot more light to the house, and you can see the sky when you look out the window.

The front porch is often a second living room.

In hot climates, shade windows in the summer.

The private back porch, even in a project with 19 units on 0.9 acres.

Overhangs, trellises, ceiling fans on the front porches, canopies, and light colors. In a place like Fresno you need every trick in the book to avoid using the A.C.

Covered streets in far north climates work well.

neighbor's wall next to another—there is virtually no heat transfer to the outside. In the cold climate of Nevada City Cohousing, we have households that have yet to turn on the heat 15 years after move-in. When the residents have a thorough discussion about energy conservation, it can become a game, or even a friendly competition among neighbors.

2. **Effective, non-toxic, repurposed insulation.**
   We often use wet-blown cellulose insulation. It completely seals the void and traps the maximum amount of air surrounded by insulation.

3. **Natural light.**
   Don't put headers above windows, instead use the rim joist (at second floor framing and a rim board at the roof eave). Use the gable truss at the gable end. Use large, but good windows.

Aggressive fire suppression strategies in Northern California over the last century have made fires more devastating than they ever were previously. These forests were regularly thinned by Native Americans (who used fire to make hunting easier) and by random lightning strikes. Both types of fire would reach about 1000° F, which the tree bark had evolved to survive, but they did not evolve to survive temperatures of up to 2000° F which they now experience. To reduce fire risk and to sequester carbon, the reality is that the forests of Northern California and elsewhere must be thinned. For people invested in the environment, the most environmentally sustainable way to do that right now is to use Forest Stewardship Council (FSC) lumber.

Conversations about clear cutting and sustainably cutting wood come up in the context of designing custom-made communities and other high-functioning neighborhoods that desire to use our resources wisely. By participating in cohousing, you're already having a much lower impact on the environment than most people, but there are many material questions that arise. The design phase is perhaps the only chance they might have to contribute to mitigating these problems from a material point of view. If we need train loads of wood, why not make it sustainably grown? The maturity of the smart remedies compound among the group and all of a sudden, they are designing from an ultra-responsible, low carbon footprint point of view. They are thinking about it in holistic terms and the bang for their buck—and where they can make the most difference. Using FSC lumber and countless other sustainability approaches stem from real groups of middle-class or lower middle-class residents—so we know that they are feasible with real projects with tight budgets.

I'll never forget when a woman, who worked for a non-profit (making probably $30k/year) asked rhetorically, "Has anyone here walked through a clear-cut forest lately, seen what it does to a water shed, to the animal habitat or imagined what it does to air quality?" That group who were building new houses for one half of the cost of the other houses in the larger neighborhood choose to have FSC lumber at an additional cost of about $2,000 per house.

We used to use as little wood as possible to save the trees. Now it seems that carbon sequestering works even better to stem the tide of carbon dioxide lofting to the stratosphere and helping to "hold-in" earth-warming gases.

We usually run 21–25 percent of the floor area in window area including glass doors and skylights. Consequently, the lights are never on during the day. If they are, something is wrong. Not long ago, energy-efficient houses were limited to 15 percent and many of the early houses designed by The Cohousing Company come in at that number. Electric bills can average $0 a month (with only an average of 1 kW of PV Power per house) if the natural lighting is done right.

Sometimes spending a little more money on things like window canopies can save a considerable amount in the long term. Items like these can be the difference between needing air conditioning or not. Potentially saving the $10,000 cost of the A.C. per house, smart passive cooling in 10 small homes. Moreover, if you finance the $10,000, it can become $35,000 over time.

STILLWATER, OK

Rainwater catchment.

Use standing A.C. on those rare days that they are essential in a hot climate in a well-designed passive cooling house. This way all of the white noise is in your house instead of disturbing your neighbors with outdoor noise.

What used to cost $10,000 per house is now $3,000 per house.

4. **Sustainably grown (Forest Stewardship Council [FSC] Certified) lumber framed at 24 inches on center (O.C.).**
   Frame at 24 inches O.C. on buildings up to three stories high. By framing at 24 inches O.C., it uses 25 percent less lumber for wall framing and leaves more room for insulation.
5. **Heating, Ventilation, Air Conditioning (HVAC).**
   Have one boiler per building for heat and domestic hot water showers and faucets. Use in-floor heating or radiant baseboards. HVAC costs can run $20–$30 per house per month using either electric or gas. Houses can generally avoid using air conditioning by applying passive cooling techniques. Always use radiant barriers at roof sheathing.

Careful construction oversight is crucial, otherwise you can hear the next-door neighbor snoring. Get it right in the beginning. Don't let gaps like this go unremedied.

6. **Use low to non-toxic materials in paint, glues, cabinets, carpets, linoleum flooring, etc.**
   Limit or avoid the use of volatile organic compounds and formaldehyde which can have adverse health effects on residents in the long term, although the couches that people bring into their houses and the interior repaints often compromise that goal. So residents need to be aware of what they are bringing into the house as well.

7. **Acoustics.**
   The environmentalists of the future will be acoustic engineers who make it easier for the land-gobbling North Americans to live closer together by keeping the building quieter.

   The Cohousing Company uses double 5/8-inch gypsum board on both sides of two separated 2x4 at 24-inches O.C. party walls filled with 8.5 inches of blown-in cellulose insulation, as well as a sheet of plywood under one of those double layers. If there is a flat above, we use two or three layers of 5/8-inch gypsum board as well as acoustic channels on the ceiling. We recommend that you use double 5/8-inch gypsum board on any interior sound-sensitive walls like between the living room and a bedroom. This also saves energy by reinforcing the building's other passive heating and cooling strategies, especially passive cooling. There is a co-living dwelling project with 61 suites (bedroom and bathroom) that did not build adequate sound walls, and the residents' average timeframe between moving in and moving out is less than one year. That isn't conducive to community, nor is it sustainable from a business point of view. Land-gobbling scenarios are also not conducive to community—everyone ends up driving to their own house, becoming increasingly disconnected from one another. And that shouldn't be how we address the acoustic problem nor global warming. We consume more resources than necessary in order to get away from each other's noise. But in regular subdivisions there is a lot of noise heard from window to window. We want none of that in a functioning community.

   Today, acoustics is a bigger issue than ever and is ever changing in importance. During the pandemic, people got used to quieter times. We used to use 0.75-second reverberation in the common house as the standard. Today, 0.70 second is better because people are more sensitive than ever, and will be for at least for the next couple of years. The effects of bad acoustics in subconscious "auditory fatigue" can tire you out when you're not even aware that it's happening. Echoes and reverberation lead to fatigue, unintelligibility, and both lead to overall experiential frustration.

INTRODUCTION TO THE PHYSICAL MAINTENANCE OF THE VILLAGE

Communities often talk about how they want to live lighter on the planet and be good stewards of the physical world that they helped create. Living lighter on the planet means taking care of what you have created. Whether cohousing or community-enhanced architecture, a functional neighborhood absolutely depends on some practical common tasks to be done together to function. That's true of any village, whether in Southeast Africa or North America. There are few things that build community like a practical excuse to get together.

Maintain the Common Spaces, Build the Community

While no one moves into cohousing or a functioning neighborhood with the intent to take advantage of their neighbors, imbalances do happen. Unchecked, this imbalance could grow to have deleterious effects like resentment and acrimony, even to the healthiest communities.

Maintenance Not-at-Work

Imagine this maintenance system: the cohousing community designates four hours on a Saturday each month as a voluntary workday. Two people act as coaches/coordinators and resident volunteers can come and go, fixing whatever the maintenance committee agrees needs to be fixed. It is a completely voluntary system. The community is composed of good cohousers who come when they can. Great plan, right? Nope.

What happens is that several people show up to help out and, over the four hours, other residents naturally pass by the volunteers while shyly stating that they are busy. Of course, they may have legitimate reasons, but those left behind doing the work feel righteous, used, and bitter. A voluntary system does not work.

The only antidote to this type of scenario is to establish a clear and obvious means of preventing apparent imbalances. That is if there is at least a minimum participation—you are almost there.

Maintenance That Works

One might imagine that committing four hours each month to maintenance is a lot to ask. So, let's dig deeper and ask, "Before moving into cohousing, how many hours did you spend working to maintain the exterior of your house?" For Emeryville Cohousing, the average answer was 12 hours per month.

MENDING WALL.

Poet Robert Frost had a community, of course, including the likes of John Fitzgerald Kennedy. But his community was spread all over the world. He only knew his next door neighbor in Ireland (living in a house that his wife inherited) one day a year. That was when they repaired their common rock wall together. Imagine the lithe tall and skinny Robert Frost on one side of the wall and the short stout neighbor farmer on the other side. Together they spent one day per year rebuilding the wall dismantled by the winter's earth heaving, gales, and on occasion stray cows hitting here or there. The farmer says, "Good, fences make good neighbors"—but it was the meaningful togetherness that he was referring to. It means the opposite of what is normally misquoted.

Contextualizing and applying the information, if it took residents 12 hours per month to do exterior maintenance on their previous houses, then every adult can engage in 12 hours per year of exterior maintenance and some interior maintenance on the new community—all the time that should be needed on new and tight cohousing houses, which are designed to be low maintenance and use cooperation to bring forth everyone's highest potential to contribute. The goals are simple and clear: preserve the structures, protect the real estate, and keep the property looking handsome.

In Emeryville, the workdays last three hours, one Saturday each month from 9 a.m. to noon. The coaches have the tools and materials ready to go, along with bagels, lox, cream cheese, and good, hot coffee. The first 15 minutes are spent on project orientation. If you come on time, you get breakfast and you get to do the fun stuff. If you come late, you mostly clean up after others. This plan works because the coaches are organized. The coaches make sure that all of the materials are ready before the workers show up, making it easy. They give clear instructions, orientations, and demonstrations. Furthermore, the role of maintenance coach is occasionally rotated, so that each individual recognizes how difficult the job is, but everybody gets the support they need. Being a coach is a rewarding experience, as you enable the workers to get down to it, get the work done, have a good time doing it, grow tighter as neighbors, and feel great when they're done.

In our culture, we seem to be much clearer about money than effort. For example, would you expect your neighbor to pay your HOA dues? Obviously not. When it's about effort though, it's more challenging. Even so, if the work minimums are well defined, the consequences clear, and people can choose to do whatever they want above the minimum (and they will), then no one will be resentful. When you know that everyone else is doing their formal share, which is usually pretty minimum, then others want to step up and set the community up for success. In Emeryville Cohousing, if you don't log 12 hours of maintenance a year it costs you $40/hour, which goes to maintenance supply costs and hiring others to do the work. However, once a good system is implemented, the residents quickly discover that the official workdays are fun and they find a way to be there on Saturday morning a few times per year.

MUIR COMMONS

Maintenance. Make room for lots of practical activities—they bring people together, forge bonds that last forever, and keep the costs of cohousing down by in-housing the work that would otherwise require hiring professionals.

So, how did it all work out? Today, 29 years later, Emeryville Cohousing still uses this state-of-the-art maintenance plan, and the buildings still look brand new, which will significantly cut long-term costs down. And by all reports, they are still having fun.

Getting Everyone Involved

Like most homeowners, cohousing folks have little or no maintenance background. Groups are comprised of old, young, married, and single people; first-time homebuyers, and long-time homeowners. Of course, there are always a few folks who can't perform certain physical tasks, but these people can sit at the common house phone and call paint suppliers, run errands, make lunch, watch the kids, do paperwork, handle the sound system, or pass out water and cheerlead. Everyone can be included, and no one should feel guilty for what they are able to contribute. Conversely, no one should feel used.

A successful maintenance program works well because everyone is involved. There are no excuses, secret shortcuts, or special skills. People simply decide to get involved and stay involved. In addition, when everyone knows that you will get your share done, then there is no guilt for missing an official workday, or even several. The fastest solution to a problem starts with inclusion. If you are unconvinced, start by giving inclusion a try. Getting the work done together is effective, fair, fun, and guilt-free. In short, include everyone—that's community at work!

Hiring Out Maintenance Work

It almost always takes more time to hire someone else to do the job than for a cohousing community to do it by themselves. By the time you line out the work, check references, sort out the insurance, negotiate an agreement, show them how you want the work done, inspect and correct their work (and also allow for disputes and in some cases redoing the work), you find that it takes less time to just do the work yourselves.

MUIR COMMONS

Maintenance. Work projects give kids a sense of ownership. The kids, with help, built this bridge across the swale. Sure, he could have done it by himself, but that would have missed the main point.

I served as one of the two maintenance coaches at Emeryville Cohousing for about 12.5 years. During this time, a couple of other people and I analyzed the yield of the marketplace compared to the yield of the resident group. In almost every category, we determined that the group yielded more. If the group painted a fence, they did the preparation several times better, primed several times better, and had about twofold better coverage. Consequently, the final product of their labors lasted longer. The quality of labor can be considered in other ways as well. If the weather was too wet, the group didn't paint. By contrast, the professionals typically want to keep working even if it's too damp to paint. For professionals, it can sometimes just be about getting paid, getting the job done, and getting out of there.

If you don't believe that a resident group can do a job more efficiently than the professionals, both in terms of money and aggravation, then try doing the math. Take a simple task. Count the people-hours to bid it out. Count the people-hours to do it yourself. Compare the cost and the results. I have found that an honest assessment will reveal that, for simple maintenance projects, the group provides the best value most of the time. Furthermore, many contractors don't really want to work with homeowners' associations.

The only maintenance works that you want to hire out are works that are too dangerous, too technical, or too large of a scale that others can obviously do them cheaper. For example, after cleaning out the gutters in Emeryville ourselves for many years, we finally started hiring that out, which helped cut down cost, prevent potential accidents, and made us become more efficient.

Remember though, you can often do it better yourself. Doing it yourself costs less and benefits the community more. What's more, you will earn the satisfaction of working with your own hands while strengthening your community physically and socially, which always exceeds expectations. For example, every year at Emeryville Cohousing, we would refinish the woodwork in the common house. We would give the wood a light sanding, rag the finish on, and rag it off. The results were always terrific, and the effort we put into this refinishing work was reflected in how everyone treated the woodwork in the common house—that is, with great pride and care.

MUIR COMMONS

"O.K. everyone, we need this rock to move from here to over there. How are we going to do it?"

MUIR COMMONS

While the moms are gardening.

The Physical Plant Maintenance Workshop and Staying on Top of Maintenance

Before moving in, the cohousing community attends a Physical Plant Maintenance Workshop. It involves all of the trades that engaged the construction of the project and serves as a transfer of information. While some tasks are done as a larger community or by hired professionals, each individual cohouser has many items that are entirely their responsibility; for instance, internal plumbing fixtures, internal electrical, internal paint, and flooring—which last forever if properly cared for. In addition to maintaining the interior of their own home, each resident also has a responsibility to help the maintenance committee succeed. For instance, there are things that will occur in one house or elsewhere on the site that will pertain to the whole building. Every individual needs to know what those things are so that they can report anomalies/problems to others if necessary, or better yet, so they can readily repair them themselves. Think of doing it yourself as an act of independence and privacy: others won't need to tromp through your house to inspect things if you can report them

FAIR OAKS, CA

Learning how to take care of the house's exterior.

yourself. Inspecting is intrusive, fixing is not. You can let the maintenance committee know about that little black spot, the size of a quarter, before it becomes a black spot the size of my black beret and just as furry—possibly a leak in the exterior wall or an internal plumbing leak. Considering that cohousing houses are very tight and energy-efficient, they require a little more vigilance. This workshop teaches the soon-to-be residents everything they need to know and if they have questions, it's the perfect time to get them answered.

FAIR OAKS, CA

Communities know how to take care of most of their own buildings, as I'm reminded every time I go to Greece or a high-functioning community.

FAIR OAKS, CA

Just as critical as good design and construction is successfully passing off the baton. Now, at construction's completion, the buildings are no longer in the hands of the builders. Now, they are in the hands of the residents who need to be oriented on every component—inside and outside. These landscape drains need to be kept open to the free flow of water, and the debris must be removed at least yearly on the interior. This is how you remove the toxins from your kitchen sink's cold water supply.

Although many neighbors have successfully maintained their own houses for years, it is different in a cohousing community, and requires additional skills. Maintenance can be a positive and community-building experience, even spiritual. Deferred maintenance is a source of wasted meetings, acrimony, overdependence on a few, and costs. We propose the former.

A neighborhood-wide meeting during the pandemic.

CULTURE WORKERS

When it comes to programming, the Danes have a huge advantage. They have a profession that often participates in the creation of new community-enhanced architecture, and they're called culture workers. Similar to social workers in the U.S. who usually work with individuals and families, culture workers look at the big picture when it comes to a fledgling town and all of its components. If a grocery store and a post office in a town are failing, then the culture worker might, for example, give them incentives to combine into one entity to survive, therefore saving both of them and helping the people in the town. "If we put the post boxes into the store and a café in the store, then when Ms. Johnsen comes to get her mail, and Ms. Svenssen goes to grab her groceries, they can meet up, sit down, and enjoy a pot of tea together and stay connected over time."

Also, in Denmark, to accomplish a deliberate future, culture workers are involved in highway projects. Progress does not have to include damaging cultures. So, for example, if a new road is proposed through a town, numerous scenarios are considered around town. There is an aggregate sum of considerations. If, for one, the road goes through town, to what extent does it adversely affect a granddaughter biking to her grandma's house after school? What happens if the road is

If we only built cohousing for the kids, it's worth it. The biggest critique I get from parents these days is, "Why didn't we have this in our youth?"

STILLWATER COHOUSING, OK

The Oakcreek Community Well Being Team and Social Team used their creativity to provide opportunities during the pandemic. There have been Zoom Conferences of Gratitude, distanced Bring-Your-Own Dinners in the meadow, and three outdoor concerts.

Staying connected in the neighborhood, even during the COVID-19 pandemic.

here, here, or here? And in this manner, the road that best serves the granddaughter, grandma, and thousands of other kinships are measured. That way, they maintain a culture that they want, while goods and services can also move more efficiently. Based on their findings, they would often propose a different location. Using Σ (sigma), they would sum up the social affordances of each possible solution, grading (based on importance) each variable from -10 to 10 and asking, "How does this design add up in regards to a solution that positively affects the most people?"

$$\sum_{1} = n_1 + n_2 + n_3 + n_4 \ldots n_{100} = ?$$

$$\sum_{2} = n_1 + n_2 + n_3 + n_4 \ldots n_{100} = ?$$

$$\sum_{3} = n_1 + n_2 + n_3 + n_4 \ldots n_{100} = ?$$

In this case, Person A is a 13-year-old girl that bicycles to visit Person B, her grandma, after school each day. That was given a 10 (out of 10) in terms of benefiting the culture. This process would be repeated for all other relationships severed or damaged or benefitted.

$$\sum_{1} = -9 + n_2 + n_3 + n_4 \ldots n_{100} = ?$$

$$\sum_{2} = +10 + 8 + 6 + 5 \ldots n_{100} = ?$$

$$\sum_{3} = +10 + 8 + 6 + 5 \ldots n_{100} = ?$$

People love company when working. We are all Tom Sawyer and Huck Finn. Working together is not really work—at least you don't notice it until you lie down later that afternoon.

Bocce ball amongst neighbors.

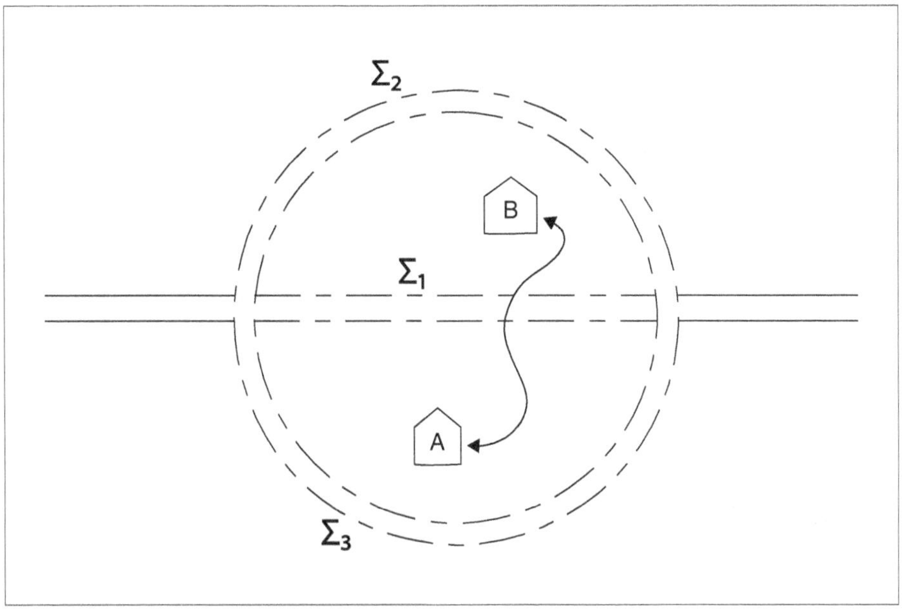

Culture workers make a huge difference in the trajectories of towns, especially small towns: towns that have their attention thrive.

In this scenario, Σ_2 won as the location of the new road because the benefits outweighed the detriments.

Conversely, I was driving through Berkeley, California, and there was a 20-foot wide, 10-foot long billboard on its own plot of land that announced in 1-foot-high letters, "The teenage girl that gets pregnant, gets pregnant on average between 3 p.m. and 6 p.m. in the afternoon." One society applies land use to best encourage a viable society that they want and deliberately plans in that direction. Another society uses guilt, shame, and influence after the fact. One was proactively planning to avert the deleteriously ill effects of random, non-people-specific planning. And that's what good design criteria does for cohousing. It intentionally takes you to where you want to be. Serendipity, yes. But random? No.

This rarely happens by accident these days in spread-out American neighborhoods. But in community-enhanced neighborhoods, this is a common occurrence.

TAKING COHOUSING TO THE AMERICAN CULTURE

During our public presentation at Paul Cézanne University in Aix-en-Provence a couple years ago, numerous folks questioned whether French culture is too "independent-minded" for cohousing. America has some of that as well. But here like there, society is growing wiser. Now there are well over 150 cohousing communities in North America and at least 1,000 legacy projects—projects that have looked to cohousing for inspiration. And if we do it right, there will probably be another 150 cohousing communities and 1,000 legacy projects in the next 10 years. However, you have to make sure that the early cohousing projects are very high functioning to set the standard in your town. Otherwise all subsequent communities will be stalled—nobody wants to go through the process if it doesn't produce positive results.

Before the first book came out in July 1988, Katie and I had done public presentations from Anchorage and Kodak Island, AK, to Miami, FL, to Northfield, MN (pictured here) to Los Angeles, CA. Today there are many more advocates working to get high-functioning neighborhoods a mainstay of new neighborhood making or neighborhood repairing.

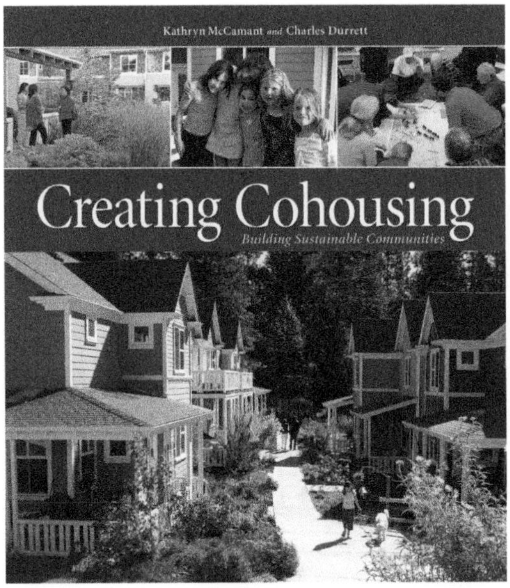

When folks ask, "Why are there 10 cohousing communities in the Seattle area?" I argue that it's because the bookstores in the Seattle area have sold over 1,000 copies of these two books. "Why are there 20 cohousing communities in the Bay Area?" Because bookstores in the Bay Area have sold 2,000 copies. Bookstores and libraries play a big role in growing cohousing, and culture change in general. Cohousing is so much more than a sound bite. We wrote these two books to help groups build high-functioning cohousing community, and they have helped over ten communities in Seattle.

When studying cohousing in Denmark, I was extremely surprised at how many Danes did not support us introducing cohousing to America. They were certain that it would get adulterated, watered down, and eventually abused by a business culture that does not put people first despite what they advertise. They would always invoke examples like McDonald's as to what America has done to food and dining. The best of the Danish cohousing communities were designed to be high-functioning socially, even when they were designed and built to be inexpensive. The same can be achieved in North America by sharing everything we have learned here, and in Denmark. By putting it on the table and learning from successful firms and communities, we can look forward to creating very high-functioning cohousing communities and neighborhoods in the future.

When I committed to bring cohousing to the U.S., I feel like I gave the Danes my word that we would not dilute, corrupt, or otherwise soil cohousing just to amp up the numbers—because amping up the numbers without quality is not sustainable.

The basics learned from the Danes.

- The ideal size of the community is no more than 50 adults
- Conducive to community site design
- Common house design that is giving and welcoming
- Private house design that serves us
- Address acoustics in common house and between units
- Keep the costs down
- Durability: don't burden a group with excessive maintenance down the line
- The architecture: craft the architecture to fit the culture
- . . . and many more factors.

What a wonderfully diverse world we have. This LGBTQ and allies community is determined to learn to live peacefully with everyone.

A dance party in the long winter nights of 2020.

In other words, we strongly feel that if you can achieve cohousing in the U.S., you can achieve it anywhere. John Wayne doesn't get to have his way or the last word with our culture. There is communitarianism in all of us—a harkening back to civitas—the social body of the citizens. We are proud to say that cohousing plays a role along with 100 other important current trends—social justice, environmental justice, accurate news, energy conservation, non-violent communication, antiwar, Doctors without Borders, Black Lives Matter, LGBTQ rights, and so on.

What a wonderfully diverse population we have in America. Bringing us together to care about each other is going to take making a place for people.

Evening time drumming in Covid.

An existing senior cohousing in Northern California hosting aspiring new neighborhood makers from around the country.

Having all or almost all of the future residents at the ground breaking for a new neighborhood means a lot.

When I asked Philip Arctander, one of the most philosophical minds on cohousing in Denmark, "Why did cohousing start in Denmark?" he replied, "That's like asking who stopped the Vietnam War? Was it the Viet Cong, the North Vietnam regular army? Was it the protesting American people? Was it the Paris Peace Accords? Was it world pressure? Was it just time, or what? It was those things and it was the aggregate sum of all of those things."

"Whatever started cohousing in Denmark, it has clearly had a big influence on our (Danish) culture." He continued, "We are looking for the same thing in the U.S." As the former head of the Housing Ministry, Mr. Arctander took cohousing to the affordable non-profit world in Denmark, he always had the big picture in mind. Other leaders will emerge in the U.S. who view high-functioning neighborhoods as key to building high-functioning towns that thrive, and who want to bring positive and real neighborhood experiences into the hearts and minds of happier children and adults alike.

BERKELEY COHOUSING, CA

Afterword

With recent concerns revolving around inequity and social injustice, one might ask, "How will increasing ethnic diversity affect the design of cohousing?" All for the better—both the product and the process are important. The process is one of figuring out what housing best serves the culture sitting in front of us on the initial design workshop day, and refining that understanding in the twelve workshop design days that follow; this is true no matter who. It might be surprising how well designs perform socially with such rich diversity when implementing this intensive process. Cohousing is not something that you can create for people. It is a participatory process, developed with the future residents. Although groups have in the past done their best to recruit diversity by going to churches, for example, it must be accomplished carefully. Assuming how others should live does not work. That said, our culture is becoming increasingly integrated. And The Cohousing Company is motivated to help in any way we can to assist diverse cultures, see a way to in fact best reflect an essence of their own culture. I went to a foreign country (Denmark), learned a foreign language and a foreign culture to figure out the methodologies that they used to understand and to modify their own culture—we used similar processes but came up with unique product—one that reflects our cultures. I was introduced in Cleveland as the guy who's here to talk about putting the "neighbor" back into "the hood." I was the only Caucasian in the large gathering. This encourages us all in the nationwide cohousing movement.

To everyone who doesn't live in cohousing yet, let us suggest that you get to know your current neighbors. Talk to them, invite them to your front porch for coffee, then to the neighborhood BBQ that you help organize, then over for dinner. Get to know their kids and when their birthdays are. Get to know their pets and what treats that the owners would support. Instead of traveling somewhere like Greece where they do all of the above and community is palpable and just being another voyeur there—be the Shakespearean actor in your own play. Katie and I, before we got our own high-functioning community under construction, started a neighborhood dining club. Six or seven households would meet most Sunday evenings (about eight or ten attending). Take down the back fences to get the ball rolling—and start planning your new community-enhanced neighborhood.

Charles Durrett, Architect, AIA

Getting-It-Built!

Do you want to live in cohousing? We'll help you make it happen!
This workshop saves money and *years* of delays.

Host a Getting-It-Built Workshop to organize a local cohousing community.

Members

Learn how to:

- Organize a strong group
- Work together efficiently
- Make decisions effectively
- Build and grow your community
- Define your role, the Group's role and the role of Professionals
- Seniors (SG1)

Development

Get vital guidance for:

- Overview of the development process from first meetings to move-in
- Finding a site (if appropriate)
- Planning and designing a community
- Working through city approvals
- Hiring and managing construction professionals

Technical

Take control of:

- Getting money in, getting money out
- Financial realities (costs)
- Cash flow
- Investment structures (raising the money)
- Financing options
- Ownership structures
- Keep *on track* and *on budget*
- Hiring a developer
- 500 Communities

Workshop led by: Chuck Durrett

The Cohousing Company | www.cohousingco.com

We design it. We live it!

Chuck is a leading expert on cohousing and has either designed over fifty cohousing communities and consulted on many more. They introduced cohousing to North America with the book (in its second edition), **"Creating Cohousing: Building Sustainable Communities."** Chuck also authored ***"The Senior Cohousing Handbook: A Community Approach to Independent Living,"*** an invaluable resource for aging-in-community.

This workshop shares best practices and lessons learned throughout 30 years of experience, while also recognizing each community is unique and each group needs to decide what approach makes the most sense for its specific location and situation. More cohousing communities have been started by the **Getting-It-Built Workshop** than by any other method in North America. With this workshop, ***you will get it built!***

GETTING-IT-BUILT WORKSHOP

Anything can be accomplished with a smart process. What is the Getting-It-Built workshop? It gives a delineated plan and a deliberate process on how the project will proceed month to month over the next year, including priorities like finding a site, working as a group, understanding city approvals, understanding an organized design process, understanding how to get your money in and out, and much more. The public presentation helps determine the project's feasibility. In Nevada City, we had 21 households that proceeded just a couple weekends after the Getting-It-Built workshop which had 25 households, after a public presentation with 150 people in attendance. Do we have enough people? Part and parcel to a project being feasible is that there must be a "market", once you have a large group to choose from, a smaller portion of them will be ready to proceed. And we like you to view the Getting-It-Built Workshop from a feasibility standpoint: are these people comfortable with the probable prices and the investments along the way? Are there enough people on the various committees? In other words, if you want to save money—stay organized.

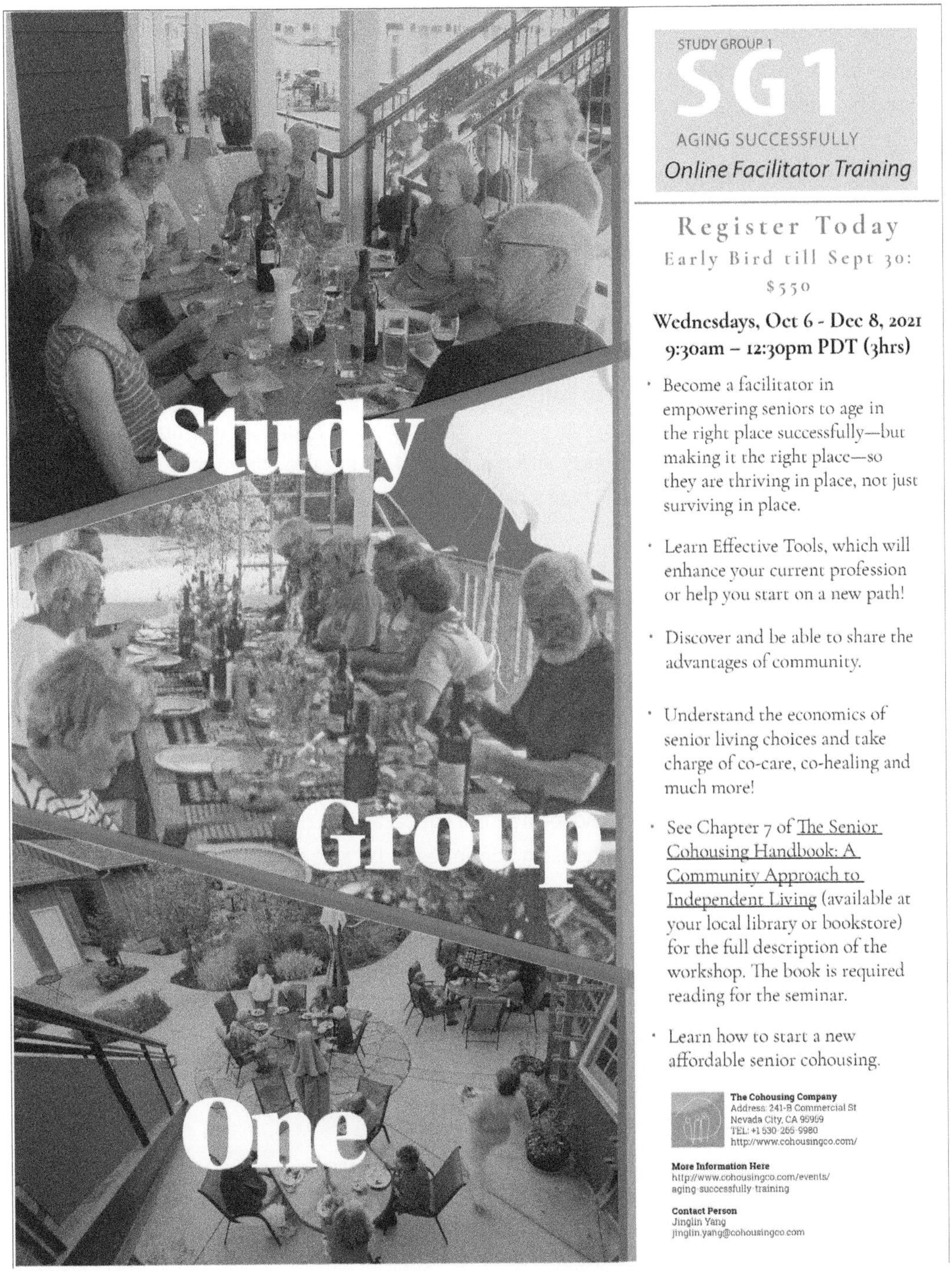

STUDY GROUP ONE

The Danes would say that if you ask 100 seniors, "Would you like to live in senior cohousing?" Maybe one would say yes. If you asked a hundred who had taken Study Group One, Aging Successfully, probably about 40 would say yes. And that has been our exact same experience here in North America. Becoming conscious of the issues, out of denial (you're lucky if you're growing older), and becoming proactive in the pedagogy here. And addressing the curiosity of growing older in a community versus not.

SENIOR COHOUSING CERTIFICATION

Americans are fast and furious with the English language—especially when it comes to real estate. The business plaza without the plaza, the industrial park without the park, and there are many other examples. There are communities that inadvertently call themselves cohousing that are in fact very cohousing inspired, cohousing-like, and are lovely places for sure, but are not cohousing. I firmly believe cohousing needs to be certified for its continuing success, just as organic farming needed certification before it really took off in the U.S.

I get too many emails from folks saying how their cohousing community failed or never worked in the first place. This is invariably because some of the six criteria that are involved in cohousing were not employed. When cohousing is firing on all cylinders, there is not a more beautiful habitat to see—people know each other, care about each other, and support one another as if they were family. Where cooperation is easy and natural and where the community is obvious, and you can measure it. This is especially true when it comes to senior cohousing.

This raises the question: What is cohousing (hence, validating its certification)?

The senior cohousing communities of Oakcreek Cohousing in Stillwater, Oklahoma; Quimper Village in Port Townsend, Washington; Mountain View Cohousing in Mountain View, California; Wolf Creek Lodge in Grass Valley, California; and Silver Sage in Boulder, Colorado, are great examples and models. Being clear what cohousing is, and by contrast what it isn't, preserves the integrity and credibility of cohousing over time. It is a form of consumer protection. The certification of a cohousing project, provided by Sage Senior Cohousing Advocates, is a critical aspect of this consumer protection for seniors. Certification ensures that cohousing continues to be a concept that people can rely on.

Having an actual certification could prove to be beneficial in helping city officials see that cohousing is not just a marketing ploy; it's a certain kind of neighborhood.

For example, in the fall of 2017, the City of Durham, North Carolina, asked the residents of Village Hearth Senior Cohousing to provide proof that they were in fact a cohousing community. That was critical because residents were asking for numerous favors, like less parking and less road (by about 1,000 feet, which would have cost a fortune) and numerous other things from the city in order to get the project done on budget, and in return the city wanted to see a certification. The city wanted to cooperate, but they did not want to be hoodwinked. The certification provided the reassurances that the city needed, and our requests were ultimately approved.

By contrast, a developer in Petaluma, California, called his project cohousing, even though it featured no resident participation and the design did nothing to promote community interaction. He told the

city council it was cohousing, because he wanted to ride the coattails of a very successful but legitimate cohousing community in a neighboring town. The project was approved. The developer hoodwinked the city council and they were angry. How was the city council to know? They did not have a certification that said, "This is the genuine article." The upshot is that when real cohousing communities came to the table down the line, the head planner said, "Whatever you do, do not call it cohousing." They had been fooled once but would not be fooled twice. No other cohousing has been built in that town despite considerable interest.

Another example is in the city of Bellingham, Washington. Bellingham is home to a sweet, 33-unit cohousing community, a village really, that is reminiscent of a traditional settlement, where people know, care about, and support each other. The city council admired this project so much that they passed some code variances for the next developer who proposed a new cohousing project, allowing for a number of breaks. The developer took advantage of the breaks (less parking, more units) but did not build cohousing. The developer gamed the system, and gamed the city council, the proximate neighbors, and the consumers. As a result, building another new "cohousing" community in Bellingham will prove very difficult if not impossible. One feels like a conventional suburb, the other one feels like a village, bustling with life.

To ensure that cohousing remains genuine and is not conflated with other housing models that are not as credible, please adhere to the following principles when creating your cohousing community or please do not call it cohousing.

CRITERIA THAT DEFINE COHOUSING

1. Participation. Co-developed, co-designed, and co-organized with the future resident group. First and foremost, the future residents are an integral part of creating the future community.
2. A private home but also extensive common facilities that supplement and facilitate daily living. Common facilities are perceived as an extension of each resident's house and supplement each home. There must be practical reasons to bring people together. Common meals must be held

at least once a week. There is no more timeless means of sustaining community than breaking bread together.

3. Designed to facilitate naturally oriented community interaction over time. Not auto oriented.
4. Almost entirely resident managed. The residents, who are the owners of their own homes, in a cohousing community have the privilege and responsibility of determining how they will organize themselves and the work (and play) of managing their own lives and homes. Every household is on the board.
5. No hierarchy in decision making. Cohousing is about cooperation rather than type of ownership. And, as it turns out, cooperation transcends ownership type. Cohousing relies on consensus.
6. No shared economy. Unlike that of the commune or sometimes a co-op structure, cohousing community members do not share personal income.

Being clear about nomenclature and certifying cohousing is about consumer protection. Selling "lakefront" property without a lake is wrong. Selling housing without participation is not cohousing. Selling cohousing without the co (co-designed, for example) means just selling real estate, without the value added by the co.

Unfortunately, the temptation to build senior cohousing without the co is based on the misconception that co-designing will slow the process down, but it actually speeds it up. When we co-developed/co-designed Cotati Cohousing in less than three years, Cotati outpaced the other two brand new projects surrounding it. Those two neighboring projects took five and seven years (respectively) to develop. They took longer to get through city approvals because they hadn't involved the future residents. For senior cohousing to continue to be faster to build and higher functioning than other senior housing alternatives, what is and isn't cohousing must be clearly defined and actively defended. Marketers are cavalier when it comes to real estate nomenclature, but our firm will continue to work hard to preserve the integrity of cohousing.

Our ultimate goal with this certification is consumer protection and ensuring that cohousing continues to be a concept that people can rely on. Having an actual document (this certification) proved to be beneficial in helping the city see that cohousing is not just hyperbolic marketing.

Thanks to Pat Darlington, of Oakcreek Cohousing, and David and Pat Hundhausen, of Quimper Village Senior Cohousing, who co-authored this certification program. It is through individuals like these cohousers and the dedication of organizations like SAGE: Senior Cohousing Advocates (sagecohoadvocates.org) that cohousing will become readily accepted as a successful model for cohousing in the U.S. and around the globe.

Thank you for adhering to these criteria when naming your project Cohousing.

Nashville Cohousing, site design by The Cohousing Company, project finished by Caddis Collaborative.

HOW TO HIRE A LOCAL ARCHITECT

Historically, architects have played a bigger cohousing advocacy role than any other professions. This framework is used by local architect collaborations including The Cohousing Company, Caddis Collaborative, and Schemata Workshop. These firms are very motivated to see more cohousing built via more cohousing skilled local practitioners.

The abbreviated framework that we use for working with a local architect is summarized as follows:

> The Cohousing Company seeks for local architects who want to join the growing skill base of "cohousing architects," meaning that they want to make it a part of their business model to work on future cohousing projects and to help advocate for the broader movement in North America and beyond.
>
> To supporting others with our expertise through those additional future projects in whatever way they need and that we believe to be a minimum, as a longer-term mentorship.

We bring them into the integrated design process early, involving them with workshop planning and in the workshops themselves, to be sure they gain a full understanding of the process we use.

We share the architectural fee proportionally by phase and usually rely on the local architect to be the architect of record since they are present, familiar with local codes, climate, and have

Daybreak Cohousing, Portland OR: Site design by The Cohousing Company, project finished by Schemata Workshop.

Tokyo, Japan, 25,000-square-foot learning community (school) and 28 new apartments by The Cohousing Company.

Working drawings by Design Works.

relevant relationships with consultants, developers, and builders. This allows us to work on more communities and gives the local architect enough scope to make it worth their while.

We collaborate on design with the architect—but the project is bettered by every good idea and experience, no matter where it comes from. But in the end it must meet the needs of the group—not the architect—and you'll be more proud if it does.

We connect our local partners with the network of other cohousing professionals (500 Communities Program Graduates, Process Consultants, Architects, and Outreach Experts) as well as CohoUS and the FIC to create long-term relationships, engagement, and to advance the movement.

We look forward to working with you!

About the Authors

Charles Durrett

Charles Durrett is an architect, author, and advocate of affordable, socially responsible and sustainable design. He has made major contributions to community-based architecture and cohousing. Charles has designed over 50 cohousing communities in North America and has consulted on many more around the world. He also designed an equal number of affordable housing projects. He is the principal architect at The Cohousing Company, based in Nevada City, California. His work has been featured in *Time Magazine, The New York Times, LA Times, San Francisco Chronicle, The Boston Globe, The Washington Post, The Guardian, Architecture, Architectural Record, Wall Street Journal, The Economist*, and a wide variety of other publications.

In addition to numerous awards for his contributions to cohousing and community-based architecture, he has given many public presentations, including two to the U.S. Congress and The Commonwealth Club of California. He continues to devote his time to new cohousing groups and affordable housing developments start-ups.

His other books include *Creating Cohousing: Building Sustainable Communities*, coauthored with Kathryn McCamant, the book that introduced cohousing to the United States. *The Senior Cohousing Handbook: A Community Approach to Independent Living*, as well as a dozen other books about housing. He lives in a 34-unit community, Nevada City Cohousing, in Northern California, which he designed. He previously lived in Doyle Street Cohousing in Emeryville, California, with his family for 12 years. The *Oxford English Dictionary* credits him with coining the word cohousing.

He realized long ago that developing healthy environments requires starting with the culture—and seeing a much wider array of issues than just the sticks and bricks.

Jinglin Yang

Jinglin Yang, LEED BD+C, is a designer who grew up in Hunan, China, and currently lives in Nevada City Cohousing in Northern California. She graduated from the University of Oregon with a Bachelor of Architecture, and Georgia Institute of Technology with a master's degree in High Performance Building. She works for The Cohousing Company in Nevada City, California. Her focus is sustainable design, building performance, community-based architecture, and communicating these efforts so that they can be replicated.

There's a saying in China, "A near neighbor is more helpful than a distant relative." It is common for Chinese children to have dinner at a neighbor's place if their parents are busy that night, and kids always have car-free areas in their neighborhoods to play with other kids who live in the same neighborhood. However, she realizes that this type of community is fading away, and it is time to start prosocial neighborhoods.

Alex Lin

Alex Lin, LEED GA, Ecodistricts AP, is a designer who grew up in Avon, Connecticut. He graduated from Carnegie Mellon University's School of Architecture with an additional minor in Intelligent Environments. He has worked for The Cohousing Company in Nevada City, California, and Schemata Workshop in Seattle, Washington.

Since his experience with Urban Design Build Studio, Carnegie Mellon University's Freedom by Design chapter, and co-authoring a thesis with his colleague Alison Katz entitled "RE_VISION: A Resource for Community Organizers and Housing Advocates," his focus has been on public interest design, urban design, and affordable housing. Through his work he seeks to apply design and research as tools for advocating and engaging with the communities that he serves.

Spencer Nash

Spencer Nash, is an aspiring urban planner from Naarm, Melbourne, Australia, currently based in Italy. He graduated from the University of Melbourne in 2020 with a Bachelor of Design, majoring in Urban Planning and specializing in Environmental Design. He is currently working for The Cohousing Company in Nevada City, California, and collaborating with Studio Corinna Del Bianco in Florence, Italy.

He grew up in a single-family house in the suburbs of Melbourne, but he later became interested in cohousing and community-enhanced design after a visit to Nevada City Cohousing at the age of 14. Ever since, Nash has had a keen interest in self-organized communities, which has brought him to work in the informal settlements of Cairo, Egypt, and now to cohousing and other community-enhanced neighborhoods in the United States and in other countries.

Nadthachai Kongkhajornkidsuk

Nadthachai Kongkhajornkidsuk is a designer who grew up in Bangkok, Thailand. He recently graduated from California Polytechnic State University, San Luis Obispo, with a Bachelor of Architecture, and is currently interning for The Cohousing Company, in Nevada City, California.

His interest in architecture, especially in community design, is long-standing and truly started to flourish when he began pursuing his senior design thesis, which focused on housing as an everyday space and its social ability to create collectivity within a community. He truly believes that consciously designed housing not only can provide shelter for its dweller, but also can foster growth in their connections with others and community as a whole. Through his work, he strives to grow as a prosocial architectural designer, who uses his knowledge and experience to provide architecture that advocates social equity and human connections.

Acknowledgments

This book was written with the participation of the many residents—either knowingly or unknowingly. Residents from cohousing communities, residents from non-profit low-income projects, people from the five-story homeless project in San Francisco who cook dinner for each other six nights a week, which I've gone to when I'm in the neighborhood. Residents like Victoria, a tall, proud African American woman in Napa County, and Matt, a previously homeless Vietnam veteran. To the many lower-middle-class, middle-class, and upper-middle-class folks who are all trying to figure out a good way to live and have volunteered their time to share their experiences in great detail. The emotional advantages of living around people who care about you as well as the economic advantages of sharing, the convenience, the safety, the health and intellectual benefits, and the cost savings.

I believe in design with others, and not for others. This book was designed primarily to help architects new to cohousing and community-enhanced neighborhoods. Primarily millennial architects, I suspect. Four very dedicated millennials were very involved in the production of this book, and therefore they are on the cover as well. Another millenial intern who helped this project immensely is Ava Wessels.

And of course, I will never overlook Katie McCamant. She helped me import high-functioning neighborhoods to North America from Denmark, she accepted my proposed English name of "cohousing," and she is a key implementer in North America today—in fact we couldn't have done it without each other. All we need now is more places where children grow up and seniors grow old—in a place and among people they love.

And to Wiley, who with foresight and forethought, sees the benefits of publishing a book about high-functioning neighborhoods.

High-functioning neighborhood is not a nebulous term—and it takes a team. No single party can do it—it takes a party of lots. Build on the success of others and jump up and just do it.

Other Books by Charles Durrett and Company

(in reverse chronological order)

A Solution to Homelessness in Your Town. ORO Editions.

State-Of-The-Art Cohousing: Lessons Learned from Quimper Village. Kindle Direct Publishing. With Alexandria Levitt.

Senior Cohousing Primer: Recent Examples & New Projects. Habitat Press Publishing.

Senior Cohousing Study Group 1, Aging Successfully: Workshop Facilitator Guide. Habitat Press Publishing.

Senior Cohousing Study Group 1, Aging Successfully: Workshop Participant Guide. Habitat Press Publishing.

Revitalizing Our Small Towns: Recent Examples from Southern France. Habitat Press Publishing.

Happily Every Aftering In Cohousing. Habitat Press Publishing.

Growing Community: How to Find New Cohousing Members. Habitat Press Publishing.

Finding A Site: Cohousing From the Ground Up. Habitat Press Publishing.

The Senior Cohousing Handbook: A Community Approach to Independent Living, 2nd ed. New Society Publishers.

Creating Cohousing: Building Sustainable Communities. New Society Publishers. With Kathryn McCamant.

The Senior Cohousing Handbook: A Community Approach to Independent Living. New Society Publishers.

Cohousing: A Contemporary Approach to Housing Ourselves, 2nd ed. Ten Speed Press. With Kathryn McCamant. (Out of print)

Cohousing: A Contemporary Approach to Housing Ourselves. Ten Speed Press. With Kathryn McCamant. (Out of print)

The Danish Ministry of Housing called me (Charles Durrett) one afternoon in 1985, and requested that I come up with an English translation for the Danish word bofællesskaber by the next day. They planned to submit a bilingual manuscript about the Danish community phenomena of which there are over 600 communities in a country of 6 million called Bofællesskaber within the week to the publisher. I stayed up all night and came up with 35 options. I called the Ministry in the morning and told them that I settled on "cohousing." I informed Kathryn later that morning and she exclaimed, "You can't make up a new word." To which I replied, "well I just did."

And even though my daughter often acts like that is such an important thing to do, I want to note than when it comes to designing cohousing and getting bofællesskaber imported to the English speaking countries, you just have to do whatever creative things that you have to do to move things forward. Read a book, do your research, take your physics book into the building department, talk to the mayor, pass a law—just do it—it's worth it.

Index